WORK IN PROGRESS

MICHAEL D. EISNER

with **Tony Schwartz**

HYPERION

NEW YORK

Library of Congress Cataloging-in-Publication Data

Eisner, Michael D.

Work in progress / Michael D. Eisner with
Tony Schwartz. — 1st ed.

p.   cm.

Includes index.

ISBN 0-7868-8507-6

1. Eisner, Micheal.   2. Walt Disney Company—History.
3. Chief executive Officers—United States Biography.
I. Schwartz, Tony.   II. Title.

PN1998.3.E36A3 1999

384'.8'092—dc21

[B]   99-15803

CIP

Book design by Holly McNeely

FIRST PAPERBACK EDITION

2 4 6 8 9 7 5 3 1

To Jane and our sons,
Breck, Eric, Anders

What hope there is for us lies in our nascent arts, for if we are to be remembered as more than a mass of people who lived and fought wars and died, it is for our arts that we will be remembered. The captains and the kings depart; the great fortunes wither, leaving no trace; inherited morals dissipate as rapidly as inherited wealth; the multitudes blow away like locusts; the records and barriers go down. The rulers, too, are forgotten unless they have had the forethought to surround themselves with singers and makers, poets and artificers in things of the mind.

—Maxwell Anderson,
  "Whatever Hope We Have"

Preface

When I set out to write *Work in Progress,* I envisioned it less as a way to communicate specific business maxims than as an opportunity to re-think Disney's future, in part by re-examining its past—both our successes and our failures. In the months since hardcover publication, what's been striking about the thousands (well, maybe eight hundred) of letters I've received from readers is how many of them focused on the business lessons they've found embedded in the stories I told.

Although re-inventing and re-igniting a company is not exactly like creating a controlled forest fire, there are some similarities. A company, like the forest, must be fertilized and prepared for new growth in each new season. This simple thesis I saw borne out over and over again during thirty years of working in public companies (ABC, Paramount, Disney). Attending business school surely would have prepared me for those jobs, but instead of the classroom it was the movie set, the television studio, the sports field, the theme park, the boardroom, and my kids who became the source of my lessons. One of those lessons is that while change is invariably unsettling, it is also critical in a world in which rapidly evolving technology can render entire industries obsolete virtually overnight. If this book does indeed contain lessons about business, they are ones that emerged intuitively, in the course of building and managing a series of creative companies.

Today, the Walt Disney Company has a new generation of young leaders, nearly all of whom have assumed their current positions by moving from other roles within the company. This itself is a reflection of our commitment to providing the talented members of our team with new challenges, while offsetting the dangers of restlessness and complacency that so often undermine great corporations. In turn, we continue to rethink our existing businesses and to initiate new ones. During the past year, for example, we launched the Go Network on line; a cruise business with the first of two ships, the *Disney Magic;* and the first two of our ESPN Zone sports restaurants in Baltimore and Chicago.

Whatever new directions we take, I see more clearly than ever that they are guided by an unchanging set of simple core values and beliefs. Several of them—the commitment to excellence, the importance of teamwork, the discipline to behave gracefully under difficult circumstances—I learned first at Keewaydin, the wilderness camp I attended all through my youth. Pitching tents, canoeing down rivers avoiding waterfalls and rocks, learning to help the other fellow, and cooking in the wilderness do teach broader life lessons. Many of the others I learned growing up in the workplace environment, and they are surprisingly simple. Much as I did when I was a kid, I still ask people dozens of obvious questions because I find that the result is often fresh and unexpected answers. I still share ideas that seem outlandish because suggesting the impossible often extends the limits of the possible. I still believe that if an idea can't be communicated simply, crisply, and accessibly, it probably isn't a great idea.

For better and sometimes for worse, I accept the verdict of readers that the stories in this book may be viewed as case studies—personal case studies at that. If I have any ultimate hope for the value of *Work in Progress,* it is that readers who work in companies large and small may be inspired to look for solutions that defy the conventional wisdom, to avoid the mistakes we made, and to truly value the power of ideas.

Foreword

By the time we gathered for our annual executives' retreat in the summer of 1993, Frank Wells and I had been at Disney for nearly a decade. We were enjoying success on a variety of fronts—movies, television, theme parks, and consumer products. It was tempting to keep doing things exactly the way we had. But rather than a sense of confidence, we felt a growing apprehension. The problem, we sensed, was that some of our executives were feeling not just complacent and self-satisfied but bored and restless. The business equivalent of the seven-year itch was setting in. I had been in this situation twice before—first as an executive at ABC, and then at Paramount. In both instances, I was part of the group who helped turn the companies around, but in neither case were the successes sustained. Now I was running a company that was prospering much as ABC and Paramount once had. It was our responsibility at Disney to prevent a slide—to survive success in part by continuing to risk failure.

Writing a book, I suggested to Frank, my partner and Disney's president, might be one more way to keep our focus on the challenge at hand. If we committed our intentions to paper—and faced a deadline—we'd feel more compelled to implement significant changes, even if they proved unsettling to the company in the short term. A book was also a way of sharing with our employees (whom we call our cast members), and anyone else who might be interested, why we do what we do at Disney and what we stand for. Above all, writing a book simply seemed like something fun to do—a new adventure.

The book took nearly five years. In that time, Disney weathered a series of storms. Difficult as some of these were—most of all Frank's tragic and unexpected death—the opportunity to reflect on them in writing was invaluable. I even learned to enjoy the agony of rewriting. As Disney evolved and expanded, so did the scope of the book. In 1984, the company's revenues were $1.65 billion and $98 million in net income. Last year, revenues reached nearly $23 billion, and net earnings were nearly $2 billion. During that same period, the size of our cast grew from 29,000 to 117,000. The company's market value jumped from $2 billion to $52 billion and our stock price increased twenty-five-fold.

These numbers are dramatic, but they offer only a small window into a much richer and more multidimensional story. Walt and his brother Roy built one of the great American institutions in The Walt Disney Company by producing unique family entertainment for several decades. Our job during the past fourteen years has been to revive, nurture, and broaden the reach of the Disney name around the world. Companies such as Coca-Cola, McDonald's, and Federal Express are largely built around a single product. At Disney, we must invent new products every day. Our success depends on the ability of our cast to come up with a constant flow of original ideas for our motion-picture studio, television and cable networks, theme parks, hotels and restaurants, book and magazine divisions, stores, and Web sites. More than 60 percent of Disney's revenues today come from businesses that we've started or acquired since 1985. In the past three years alone, we've started more than 100 new businesses.

My job involves juggling multiple roles and finding common ground between conflicting impulses. I serve not just as chief executive officer but as chief creative officer, overseeing a team that is far more creative than I will ever be. I'm a cheerleader but also an editor; an advocate for change but also a fierce protector of our brand. No tension is as great as the one between quality and commerce, balancing a passion for excellence with a commitment to containing costs and reaching a broad audience. There is a constant push-and-pull between tradition and innovation; the company's good and the greater good; teamwork and individual accomplishment; logic and instinct; leading and letting go. When crises arise, it's almost invariably because an imbalance has occurred somewhere in this complex equation.

At a certain level, what we do at Disney is very simple. We set our goals, aim for perfection, inevitably fall short, try to learn from our mistakes, and hope that our successes will continue to outnumber our failures. Above all, we tell stories, in the hope that they will entertain, inform, and engage. These are mine.

Contents

WORK IN PROGRESS

CHAPTER

I

Emergency—July 1994

FRANK WELLS WAS FIFTY YEARS OLD WHEN OUR PATHS CROSSED ON the ski slopes of Vail, Colorado, in the spring of 1982. We agreed to have dinner together that evening, with our wives. Until then, I had never really known Frank, except by reputation. On one level, he was just another Hollywood entertainment executive like me. But Frank had also been a Rhodes scholar, an editor of the law review at Stanford, and a top entertainment lawyer handsome enough to be mistaken for his good friend Clint Eastwood. His outside interests especially intrigued me. He was an environmentalist, a liberal political activist, and a true adventurer. Weeks before we met, he had quit his job as vice chairman of Warner Bros. in order to spend a year trying to climb the highest mountains on each of the seven continents. What sort of man, I wondered, would give up a secure and prestigious position to pursue a lifelong fantasy?

Over dinner, I grilled Frank about his upcoming expedition. I've always been an insatiable interrogator, and there were dozens of times in my childhood when my father begged for relief from my incessant questions. Now I felt compelled to find out exactly what food, ropes, maps, and other equipment Frank intended to bring on his trip; how he would deal with altitude sickness and possible injuries; what sorts of socks, gloves, and underwear he would wear; where he would re-

lieve himself when it was 30 degrees below zero; and how he had chosen his guides and fellow climbers. I was amazed to learn that he didn't
have much experience climbing mountains and that he wasn't intending
to do any intensive training for his quixotic expedition. His enthusiasm,
he freely acknowledged, far exceeded his expertise. As we talked, I felt an
odd blend of admiration, envy, and concern that this unusual man sitting
across the table from me might be too reckless for his own good.

By the time we parted that evening, we each sensed that our
paths would cross again. Sure enough, two years later circumstances
pulled us together as partners in running The Walt Disney Company—
I as chairman, he as president. From that point on, we began to sail
around the world on the Disney adventure. If I was the rudder, he was
the keel. For ten years, we never had a fight or a disagreement, or even a
misunderstanding. I never once felt angry at him—not until the Easter
Sunday afternoon in April 1994 when the ski helicopter carrying him
out of the backcountry in northern Nevada crashed and he died instantly. Even then, I felt angry only because Frank was not around to
help me deal with a very difficult situation, as he had so many times before. But mostly what I felt was an overwhelming sense of sadness and
loss.

For weeks after his death, I still found myself wishing I could
pick up the phone to call and get Frank's opinion on one issue or another. During our years together, we must have spoken a dozen times
nearly every day. Even today, Frank still appears in flashes of thoughts,
streaks of images, wishful fantasies. The loss was bigger than I could have
anticipated because Frank occupied so much space in my life, and in
Disney's. Three months later, in July 1994, as I prepared to leave for a
conference in Sun Valley, Idaho, I was still trying to fill the void.

In a way, I was paying homage to Frank by taking this trip. For
years, he had urged me to join him at the annual conference that the investment banker Herb Allen throws every July for executives, including
several dozen key people in the media and entertainment industries.
Frank loved it. He loved the interplay between all the big players in these
companies—the purposeful posturing, the subtle gamesmanship, the camaraderie of shared interests, and the fierce underlying competitiveness.
I mostly avoided these clubby events. They just made me uncomfortable. On a rational level, I had no reason to feel out of place, but I did.

Somehow, it seemed better business to perform well than to talk about how well you were going to perform. But now that Frank couldn't go, I decided I should.

There was one other reason for attending. It would give me a chance to sit down and talk with Michael Ovitz, the head of CAA (Creative Artists Agency), about the possibility of his taking over Frank's job. Immediately after Frank's death, I had decided not to name a new president. One possible choice was Jeffrey Katzenberg, the head of Disney's filmed entertainment division, and, effectively, our third-ranking executive. But our relationship had grown strained during the past couple of years. Then, on April 5, less than thirty-six hours after Frank's death, Jeffrey stunned me with an ultimatum over lunch. "Either I get Frank's job as president," he said, "or I'm going to leave the company."

For many reasons—not least that he would choose a moment like this to force the issue—I wasn't prepared to give Jeffrey what he wanted. In the aftermath of Frank's death, I spent time considering other candidates ranging from Bob Daly, the head of Warner Bros., to George Mitchell, the retiring majority leader of the Senate. As the weeks passed, I felt increasingly vulnerable and unsettled. Frank had always made my life fun. We laughed and commiserated and gossiped together. He handled many financial issues and all the details of negotiations on deals, personnel and labor issues. He also mediated disputes among the different divisions in our company. Frank freed me to devote most of my time to broad company issues and to the creative process, but he also served as a sounding board and a devil's advocate on dozens of other issues. He had only one agenda—the company's best interests—and that gave me a great sense of comfort. Over the years, for example, I had occasionally suggested trying to hire Ovitz in one capacity or another. Frank was always completely supportive and unthreatened.

I believed that Michael Ovitz had a certain magic. We first met in 1972, when I was a young programming executive at ABC and he was an agent at William Morris. From the start, I was impressed by his doggedness in trying to sell me game shows, and later, by his entrepreneurial skills. Michael built CAA from the ground up into the most successful talent agency in Hollywood. While we never did much business together—I was rarely willing to pay the prices he sought for his clients —we did become good friends and our families vacationed together frequently. I liked the fact that he was devoted to his wife, Judy, and to his three children, and that he seemed to genuinely care for my wife, Jane, and our three sons. He was tightly wound, with an edgy sense of humor that sometimes put people off balance, but he could also be charming, solicitous, and self-deprecating.

I had sensed for some time that Michael was feeling restless as an agent. In mid-July, I suggested that we fly together to Herb Allen's conference in Sun Valley, so that we could discuss the possibility of his coming to Disney. He agreed, with more enthusiasm than I had expected. On the afternoon of Wednesday, July 13, we took off from Burbank on the Disney plane, along with our wives. Jane had urged me to hire Michael, and while he and I sat talking in the front cabin, she and Judy Ovitz sat talking in the back. For the first time, Michael began to open up further about his ambitions. "I'm ready for a change," he told me. "I think the idea of working together is great. We would make an unbeatable team." For a moment, I felt encouraged, but almost in the next breath, he drew a line in the sand. "We should be co-CEOs," he said. That wasn't what I had in mind. Instead, I tried to find a way to excite him about assuming Frank's role. I talked about what a huge challenge Disney represented, how much freedom he would have in running the company day to day, and the degree to which Frank and I had operated as partners. But it was obvious that Michael was not buying my pitch, and our discussion took on an unacknowledged awkwardness. We agreed to continue talking, but I was upset by the conversation.

In my heart, I had nurtured the hope that Michael would respond to my offer with excitement and support and selflessness. Instead, what I came up against was a man who was accustomed to being described as the most powerful person in Hollywood. He made it very clear that he didn't want to be anyone's number two. From his perspective, and for his ego, he may have been right. From my perspective and my ego—and for Disney's sake—I believed that I was right. One person had to have the final authority. In this view, I had been strongly influenced by Sid Bass, the savvy investor from a legendary Fort Worth, Texas, family, who bought effective control of Disney during a takeover battle in 1984. Sid had also played a decisive role in bringing Frank and me to the company, and over the past decade he had become both an invaluable adviser and a good friend. We discussed everything from arbitrage to architecture, family to finance. On the subject of corporate governance, Sid was unequivocal: one company, one boss.

As we prepared to land, Michael and I were at an impasse, and I was no closer to solving my problem. It was perfectly understandable but nonetheless disappointing. We were headed for separate rental cars when Jane—still not aware how the conversation had gone—said something to Michael about how much I needed his help at Disney. He turned to me. "Yeah," he responded, only half-joking, "I'm the one guy who can save you from having a heart attack."

Moments later, I noticed a little pain in my arms. For years, I had been experiencing this sort of pain during intense exercise. Regular tests showed no abnormalities, and I grew convinced that the pain was caused by stress. The enormous pressures of my job, I concluded, sometimes showed up in psychosomatic symptoms. The pain in the parking lot was a little different, since it had occurred without exercise. Still, I figured it was the altitude, or the tension created by Ovitz's reaction to my offer, or perhaps even an unconscious reaction to his joke about my having a heart attack. In any case, I didn't pay it much heed.

When we arrived at the lodge, the first person I ran into was Barry Diller, with whom I had first worked at ABC, and later at Paramount, where he was chairman and I was president. During the previous several weeks, he had mounted what appeared to be a successful bid to purchase CBS, only to have it fall apart at the last moment. Now Diller took me aside. "John Malone is going to back me in a new bid," he confided, referring to the chairman of TCI, one of the country's largest cable operators, which was later purchased by AT&T. We had recently begun to consider buying NBC, but I didn't have a chance to share this news with Barry. We spoke only briefly before being interrupted by another group of guests, Malone among them. When it came to talking with him, I felt as if I were guarding Michael Jordan one-on-one. Malone is so verbally facile and so knowledgeable on many subjects —among them technology, about which I knew relatively little at the time—that I didn't feel entirely comfortable with him. Self-protectively, I kept my distance.

Before long, I was mingling with other guests, including Bill Gates, the head of Microsoft; Tom Murphy, chairman of Capital Cities/ABC; Warren Buffett, the biggest shareholder in Cap Cities and a legendary investor; Bob Wright of NBC, with whom our acquisition talks had just begun; Jeffrey Katzenberg; and perhaps two dozen others. A photographer hired for the occasion walked around snapping off pictures, and the atmosphere was relaxed. It was as if a group of top college basketball coaches had come together to share a beer and swap stories before the NCAA finals. This was a group of men who were totally driven and fiercely competitive, but in an informal setting they seemed to share an easy connection.

The explanation wasn't suprising. People are always most comfortable in their own clubs—whether that means a bowling league, a church choir, or, in this case, the small group of executives who happen to run media and entertainment companies. Even so, there was an unspoken pecking order. The most favored guests—the Ovitzes among them—stayed in condominiums. The next tier—which included Jane and me—got smaller rooms in the main lodge but were among the group invited for meals at Herb Allen's condominium. I never learned where the rest of the invited guests ate their meals.

Jane and I were walking the two hundred yards to dinner when the pain returned, this time in both my biceps. I had to stop and rest along the way. My mind ran on two tracks when it came to pain that might relate to my heart. One was psychological. I've always been fascinated by the power of the unconscious. We all have unacknowledged desires, hatreds, and fears that cause anxious states of mind and sometimes show up in physical symptoms. But I also felt real fear. My father began experiencing bad angina in his fifties. When he had quadruple bypass surgery, at sixty-five, I felt certain that I, too, was doomed. On one level, I was convinced that any physical pain I experienced was really in my head. On another, I assumed fatalistically that heart disease was my genetic destiny.

The medical experts said otherwise. Each year, and sometimes twice, I went to the hospital and took a stress test, and each time the doctors told me I was fine. Two years earlier, I had flown to Houston to undergo a state-of-the-art PET scan. In this procedure, a chemical is injected into the coronary arteries which makes it possible to measure very precisely even small changes in levels of blockage. My friend Dustin Hoffman, who came along for the adventure, referred to the trip as a

"Jewish *Deliverance*." As my injections were being prepared, the only thing that interested the nurses was getting Dustin's autograph.

Once again, I was given a clean bill of health. Not long afterwards, Disney decided to take out insurance on my life. Doctors from three separate insurance companies examined me and approved a $100 million policy payable to the company in the event of my death. It provided some solace that three large, highly conservative insurance companies were willing to bet on my life.

I spent much of dinner at Herb Allen's talking to Tom Brokaw, the NBC anchorman, who told me a long story about fly-fishing with his friend Robert Redford—evidence of just how intermingled the worlds of news and entertainment had become. It was hard to know who was a bigger celebrity at this point, Redford or Brokaw. As we talked, a photographer continued to click away, memorializing much the same group of people shown on the walls from last year's conference. I felt a wave of sadness when I came across several photographs of Frank. In each one, he had a big, buoyant smile on his face.

About 11:00 p.m., Jane and I finally left with a group of other guests to walk back to our rooms. I noticed the local hospital across the street from Herb's condo and joked that it looked more like a camp infirmary than a big-time medical facility. As we walked, the pain in my arms returned. I didn't want to create a scene, so I announced a sudden craving for frozen yogurt and stopped to buy a cup at a store along the way. It gave me an excuse to rest a moment. I pretended to find the other stores equally compelling, pausing several more times to window-shop.

Jane went to bed shortly after 11:30, while I stayed up reading magazines. Although I was lying down, the pain persisted. I tried to ignore it, but eventually I couldn't. "Jane," I said, "I think I'm having a real problem." She had heard it all before, indulged my minor hypochondria dozens of times.

"Roll over and go to sleep. You'll be fine in the morning," she replied, knowing that I was looking for reassurance. But the pain, the anxiety, and now some nausea kept escalating.

"Jane," I said finally, "I'm going to the hospital. If I drop dead right here, you're going to feel really dumb." Sympathetic but still unconvinced, she got up and we both got dressed. By the time we arrived at the hospital, the pain had gone away. Now I was the one who felt dumb. The doctor did a precautionary electrocardiogram, but as he expected, it showed nothing unusual. "What you felt were probably transitory esophageal spasms," he said, "or maybe it was something you ate. It's certainly nothing serious." He prescribed Xanax to help me sleep.

"Do you really feel confident about letting me go?" I asked.

"Mr. Eisner," he said, "I recognize your name, and I want you to know that my wife and my kids and I all love the Disney Company. We took our spring vacation at Disneyland, and last week we all went to see *The Lion King* together. I promise you that I would never, ever, let you out of this hospital if anything could possibly be wrong."

I felt reassured. There were certainly enough pressures in my life to account for my symptoms. Never before had I dealt with so many difficult events in such a short period. There was Frank's death, above all, and then the ongoing tension with Jeffrey, including the possibility that he might soon exercise his contractual right to leave the company. There were also business problems, led by Euro Disney, the theme park we had opened outside Paris two years earlier. By the summer of 1993—having spent far too much to build it, overestimated demand, and then run into a severe recession—the park was hemorrhaging money. Frank and I had put together a team from Disney to restructure our deal with the international consortium of banks that financed Euro Disney, and months were spent in difficult negotiations. In March 1994, just a month before Frank's death, we had finally come to an agreement that bought us time to turn the park around. Still, the long uncertainty and the relentless bad press had been hard on everyone involved.

Meanwhile, attendance at our domestic theme parks, Walt Disney World in Orlando and Disneyland in Anaheim, had been flat for nearly a year, and none of us was really sure why. Live-action movies were also lagging. Our extraordinary success in animation—*The Lion King* had just opened to gigantic business—deflected public attention from the fact that for more than two years, most of our other movies had been losing money. Finally, there was the growing controversy over Disney's America, the new theme park that we were proposing to build in northern Virginia, just outside Washington, D.C. I had championed the project myself. Despite opposition from wealthy landowners in the surrounding countryside, I believed that we would eventually prevail. But I was also beginning to wonder whether a long, ugly battle now being led by prominent historians was worth the toll it was taking on our company.

For months before his death, Frank and I had been talking about our plans to reinvent and reenergize Disney. We already had significant executive changes in mind, and new businesses we were prepared to launch. I had begun working longer hours than ever, and for the first time in my life I had difficulty sleeping. I also gave up exercising, rationalizing that I had no time, and ate whatever I could catch on the run. Often, it wasn't very healthy. As for the worries about my heart, I dealt with them mostly through a blend of denial and cholesterol-lowering drugs.

By the time Jane and I returned from the hospital, and I fell back asleep, it was 4:00 a.m. I awoke three hours later, in order to hear a presentation about the future of broadcasting by Tom Murphy and his team at Capital Cities/ABC, a company that we had nearly made a deal to buy a year earlier. The presentation took me aback. It was built around a series of large poster boards, showing in different colors exactly which of their prime-time series were licensed from outside producers, which ones they owned in partnership with others, and which they owned outright. "We want to move toward owning every show on the schedule, either wholly or in part," Murphy explained. I certainly understood the value of such a strategy for ABC, but it made me more concerned than ever about Disney's ability to sell its programs to the networks.

My bigger concern was that I still felt a lot of pain when I tried to walk more than a few steps. I made it through two more morning presentations, and then another lunch hosted by Herb Allen. Afterwards, while others went off to hike and play golf in their Allen & Company shirts, I returned to my room, feeling as if I had attended one fraternity party too many. I called Lucille Martin, who was once Walt Disney's secretary and had been mine for the past ten years, to tell her that I wanted to come home the next day, Friday, instead of Saturday, as originally planned.

I also told Lucille about my visit to the hospital the night before. Jane had paid with a Disney insurance card, and I was concerned that when our personnel department received the bill, it could prompt rumors about the state of my health. "Just to be safe," I said, "why don't you call the hospital and have them send the bill directly to the office? I'll pay it myself." Then I asked her when I last had a stress test. After a quick check, she told me that it had been eighteen months, meaning that I was six months overdue. "Could you schedule a new one?" I asked. Several hours later, Lucille called to say that she had set up the test at Cedars-Sinai Hospital for July 28—less than two weeks later—and that I was now scheduled to leave Sun Valley at 3:00 p.m. Friday.

On Thursday evening, I spent most of dinner talking with Warren Buffett, while Jane spoke to his wife, Susie. Warren hardly looked the part of one of the wealthiest men in the world. Casually dressed and understated in manner, he exuded a quiet self-assurance but had no interest in drawing attention to himself. At one point, David Geffen, who had made a lot of money selling his record company to MCA, walked into the room and spotted Buffett. He walked over and immediately dropped to his knees, genuflecting. "Oh my lord," he said. "I'm at the feet of the king." Warren seemed amused, but said nothing.

When I returned to my room that evening, I checked in with Lucille again. Among my messages was one from Michael Engelberg. He said it wasn't urgent, but Engelberg is our family doctor. I decided to call him back. "Are you planning to have a stress test?" he asked.

"Why do you ask?" I replied.

"Because Lucille mentioned that you've been having chest pains," Engelberg said. We talked a little more and I considered getting off without mentioning my hospital visit the night before. I was embarrassed that perhaps I'd made too much fuss over nothing. Finally I mumbled something about the pain in my arms. Engelberg perked up. "Tell me about the symptoms you're having," he said. Reluctantly, I took him through the events of the past two days.

"I think you should have the stress test as soon as you come back," he said. I was about to tell Engelberg that he was overreacting when I remembered a story he had told me about one of his close friends, Richard Levinson, a television writer and producer who helped to create hit shows such as *Columbo*. At dinner one evening, Levinson told Engelberg he'd been experiencing chest pains. Engelberg tried to persuade him to go to a hospital immediately for a stress test. Levinson was on his way to New York but promised that he would schedule a test as soon as he returned to Los Angeles. A night or two later, he dictated some notes into a tape recorder about the location of all of his belongings and dropped dead of a heart attack.

"Is this a Richard Levinson situation?" I asked.

"I doubt it," Engelberg assured me. "But I'd still like you to get the test as soon as possible." We agreed that I would go straight to Cedars-Sinai when I arrived back on Friday afternoon. "I'll meet you there," he told me.

I felt better. Somehow, setting up the test solved the problem. Now I could relax, stay through lunch, and enjoy my last day at the conference. On Friday morning, I awoke in time to attend the first presentation of the day, an entertainment industry forum chaired by Jack Valenti, head of the Motion Picture Association of America. The panel included Jeffrey Katzenberg. As always, he was aggressive and outspoken, but he also interrupted the other speakers and cracked bad jokes. I felt that he was representing Disney poorly, especially for somebody who wanted to be president of the company. When I mentioned my reaction to Jane and to Ovitz, who were sitting beside me, they both told me to let it go. "Jeffrey is Jeffrey," Michael said. "He is not doing anything new or different." I decided I was just being too sensitive. After the panel ended, I had a good conversation with Barry Diller. I told him that we had no interest in pursuing CBS, but that we were having some preliminary discussions about acquiring NBC. For a moment, it all seemed a little surreal: two guys who had started together at the age of twenty-four as low-level assistants at ABC casually talking about buying two of the three major television networks.

Later in the morning, Ovitz suggested that we take a bicycle trip into town together and talk some more. Without explaining that I was reluctant to exert myself, I begged off. At lunch, both Jane and Judy pressed for Michael and me to meet again, and so did he. I agreed, but first we had yet another photo session—this one a group shot by Annie Leibovitz, for a special issue that *Vanity Fair* was doing about Hollywood. Memorializing the conference in pictures seemed to be one of its primary agendas. (Months later, when I saw the photograph in the magazine, I would be amazed by how healthy I looked.) After the photo session, Ovitz suggested we take a walk, but I said I'd prefer to talk in his condominium. Our discussion got no further than it had on the plane.

Finally I had to leave to catch a three o'clock flight back. To my relief, I was able to carry my bags and Jane's to the car without any pain. Because we were considering NBC as a possible acquisition, I had brought along several of their fall pilots—the first episodes of new shows —to watch on the plane. One of them was the two-hour premiere of *ER*, the hospital series created by Michael Crichton and co-produced by Steven Spielberg. It was already generating a buzz in Hollywood. It only takes a single show to turn a network's prime-time schedule around— *Cosby* had done just that for NBC ten years earlier—and I wanted to gauge whether *ER* had similar potential. I was also interested in seeing what Spielberg and Crichton had produced. Their last collaboration, after all, had been *Jurassic Park*. It was immediately obvious that *ER* was a very promising show, but the scenes in the emergency room were so graphic that I could hardly watch them. Jane turned away completely.

When we landed in Burbank, I got in my car and drove to the hospital alone. We agreed that Jane would drop off our bags at home, and then meet me. Michael Engelberg was waiting when I arrived at Cedars-Sinai shortly before 5:00 p.m. So were John Friedman and Dan Berman, cardiologists I had known for years who specialize in nuclear imaging. I was very familiar with the stress test procedure. The first thing they do is inject you, at rest, with a radioactive isotope, and measure the flow of blood as it moves through your coronary arteries. This test proved normal, which was good news. A problem at this stage would have indicated that I had already suffered some sort of heart attack. Next, they put me on the treadmill. The last time I'd taken this test, I walked up a fairly steep incline without a problem for the entire test. This time, both of my arms began to ache almost immediately. The electrocardiogram showed indications that were not normal, and the doctors stopped the test after just four minutes. It was a precautionary move. The last thing they wanted to risk was precipitating a heart attack from overexertion during a medical procedure.

By this time, both Jane and another cardiologist, Neil Buchbinder, had showed up. I remember feeling surprised to see Buchbinder late on a Friday afternoon in July. I didn't even know he'd been called. He took one look at the test results, listened to the description of my symptoms, and concluded that he wanted an immediate angiogram. This is a more precise way to examine the arteries themselves. A needle is inserted into the upper thigh, and then a thin plastic tube is fed through the needle up into the aorta so that a dye can be injected directly into the coronary arteries and the details of the blockages read on an X ray. Alarmed by how rapidly things were moving, Jane tried to slow everyone down. She began asking all the right questions, pointing out that they had never even finished the stress test. To my surprise, I found myself getting angry with her.

"Climb on the bandwagon, Jane," I said. "We've been waiting ten years for this. It's really happening this time. Let's get serious and stop denying." I had moved into my executive mode. Next, I insisted on being checked into the hospital under a false name. Then I called Lucille and asked her to come over and help coordinate our stories to avoid any leaks to the media. I was sure that I would be released that evening, or the next morning at the latest. There was no point in creating unnecessary concerns about my health.

"What are the risks involved in an angiogram?" I asked Buchbinder.

He described the risks in some detail, but all I heard was the last phrase he said: "Ninety-eight percent safe."

I felt as if I had just hit the soft shoulder of a highway at 80 miles an hour. Alarm bells sounded in my head. "You mean the other two percent have a problem or die?" I asked, hoping for a quick no.

"Yes," he said.

My inquisitiveness had backfired on me. Suddenly, I felt unsettled, close to panic. Moments later, I experienced intense pain not just in my arms but also in the neck and chest. My anxiety was making the pain worse. Engelberg called for morphine, which helps to lower the heart rate by reducing the pain that fuels anxiety. Unfortunately, no one could find any. It had been stocked in the pharmacy, apparently out of a concern that drug users were stealing it from the shelves of the supply room. Engelberg became angry, and the tension in the room escalated palpably. The next thing I knew, I was being wheeled into the emergency room. People were hovering over me asking questions and handing me consent forms to sign. All I could think of was *ER*, the pilot I'd just watched. Suddenly, I was living it.

I asked Jane to sign the papers. This was not permissible, we were told. I did the best I could without my reading glasses. Buchbinder explained that he expected the angiogram to show considerable block-age. If it did, he said, they would want to do an immediate angioplasty. In this procedure, a small balloon is passed through a tube inside a coro-nary artery. When the balloon is inflated, it creates more room for the blood to flow freely. In all likelihood I would still be able to leave the hospital the next day.

Once they moved me to the emergency room, they found some morphine. All my cares melted away. Even the screaming of the man in the bed next to me was nothing more than a mild distraction. I doubt that the drug fully accounted for the relief that I felt. I thrive on action, and I was finally getting some. For the first time, I knew that the prob-lem with my heart was real, and it was going to be taken care of, at long last. I felt comfortable consigning my body to these good doctors. It also occurred to me—in my morphine haze—that I had a good excuse to get out of two weekend commitments I had made months earlier. Back then, the prospect of listening to the Three Tenors sing opera at Dodger Stadium and of attending the World Cup soccer finals had both sounded like fun. As the dates grew closer, it dawned on me that I had no desire to fight the traffic and the crowds. I was mulling all this over when Lu-cille arrived. She was carrying a huge pile of mail that had accumulated at the office in my absence. I couldn't resist trying to be cool and dead-pan in the face of adversity. "I don't think I'm going to be able to deal with that just now," I told her, flat on my back.

When the pictures from the angiogram began to come up on the screen, I could see the blockage myself. It was one of the few times that a design image on a computer screen didn't excite me. Well over 95 percent of the anterior descending branch of my left coronary artery—a part of my anatomy to which I'd never before given much considera-tion—was blocked. By this point, another doctor had arrived on the scene. Alfredo Trento was the Italian-born head of cardiac surgery at Cedars-Sinai, and he was blunt in his assessment. "I recommend an im-mediate coronary bypass," he said. This was a double shock. I didn't know anything about Trento, and I had never imagined that I might need a bypass.

I called Jane over. "Where was this guy trained?" She knew I was hoping to hear Harvard or Yale. "Tijuana," she replied, with a straight face. I felt relieved that she could joke at all. Even so, I worried that on a Friday evening, the chances of finding a sharp, well-rested, top-level surgeon were slim. A decade earlier, when my father had his bypass, I had insisted that they perform it on a Monday morning.

"Couldn't we wait and get a second opinion?" I asked Trento.

"Waiting wouldn't be a good idea," he replied. Suddenly, I realized that surgery was fine with me. This was an emergency. The train was already rolling down the tracks. Why stop now and have to spend the whole weekend worrying? Only much later did I learn that Trento is a superb heart surgeon. What I can't remember is how I discovered, while awaiting surgery, that he is also a rabid soccer fan. Apparently I was lucid enough to make a deal with him just before I went under. "You can have my ticket to the finals of the World Cup," I told Trento, "so long as I live to watch the event on television."

It was almost 10:00 p.m. when I was wheeled into the operating room. Jane stood over me with two of our three sons, Breck, then twenty-three, and Eric, twenty. She hadn't yet been able to locate our youngest son, Anders, sixteen. I felt relaxed enough—or melodramatic enough—to spend a few moments making last-minute requests. Perhaps I'd watched too many movies in my day, or maybe I was just trying to stay in control.

"I want to be buried above ground, not below," I told Jane. (Being above ground just sounded more comfortable to me.) "Also," I went on, "I really don't want you to build the new house we've been considering, because ours is fine, and we don't need a bigger one." In both cases, I was using the leverage of my imminent surgery to win deathbed agreements from my wife. My final request was made to Jane, Breck, and Eric together. "If it becomes an issue," I said, "I think that either Ovitz or Diller would be good choices to succeed me." Jane couldn't believe I was making all these preoperative deals. "Fine, fine," she said, and then she kissed me, and told me I'd be all right. For my benefit, she kept her emotions in check. As I watched my sons walk out of the room, I could see that they looked sad and worried.

I don't remember feeling any fear as I went under. When I next opened my eyes and looked at a clock near my bed, it said 6:30 a.m. I was alone in the intensive-care unit and I desperately wanted the tube that had been put in my throat to be taken out. Within a few hours, I would be surrounded by my family again. By 11:00 a.m., Ovitz would show up, having cut short the start of his own family's long-planned vacation cruise to take over my convalescence. My sister and mother were already on their way from New York. Patty and Roy Disney were racing to get a flight back to Los Angeles from their vacation home in Ireland. The tube in my throat was taken out shortly after 9:00 a.m., and as soon as I could speak, I insisted that the press release about my condition include a quote from the surgeon. I had seen too many companies release misleading information about the medical conditions of their executives. If I was truly out of danger, I wanted Alfredo Trento to be the one to say so. Of course, what I really wanted was to be reassured myself.

But none of this was what came into my mind when I first awoke from the anesthesia. Instead, I had a single happy thought: "That's the best night's sleep I've had in a year."

CHAPTER

2

Coming of Age

FOR THE FIRST THREE YEARS OF MY LIFE, MY FATHER WAS AWAY IN THE war, flying transport planes in the air force. I grew up with my mother, my older sister, Margot, and female housekeepers and baby-sitters—the only young male in an otherwise all-female environment. That gave me a special status, and I learned very early that by being clever and playful and likable, I could almost always get what I wanted. It wasn't until my father returned home that my situation changed dramatically. Suddenly, there was a new competitive force in the house—a tall, explosive, charismatic center of attention whom my mother was eager to please. My priorities didn't always prevail, and I learned that I had to adjust. In a sense, the rest of my life has been about finding a balance between the disparate examples set by my parents. From my mother, I discovered how to establish goals, set my own rules, and then cajole and charm people into going along with me. From my father, I learned the ethically straight and narrow path: no shortcuts and no playing the angles.

I grew up in an affluent family, but as a child I never thought much about it. I just assumed that everyone lived the way we did. We had a large, comfortable Park Avenue apartment on the Upper East Side of Manhattan, but so did most of the boys at Allen-Stevenson, the private school I attended just twelve blocks from our home. Starting in the first grade, I wore a uniform that consisted of a blue blazer, gray pants, a white shirt, and a tie with the Allen-Stevenson insignia. It never seemed strange to me that I was expected to wear my jacket and tie to the dinners we ate by candlelight. While my father believed that we should know what we had, I never had the sense that I could have anything I wanted. Money was not to be treated frivolously or paraded ostentatiously. Instead, it was something to save and to protect for generations to come, or to be generous with—anonymously. Mostly, I didn't think much about it. I lived in a safe, self-contained world, and for many years, it was the only one I knew.

I began each weekday morning practicing in the school orchestra in the percussion section, under the tutelage of Stanley Gauger. I played the drums, the glockenspiel (pounding out "Stars and Stripes" with great gusto), the wood blocks, and the timpani. I was better at juggling my drumsticks—eight spins before catching them was my record —than I was as a musician. Still, I participated in the Allen-Stevenson orchestra enthusiastically for six years. I was a good student, but school itself was secondary to my central interest: sports. At the end of most school days, weather permitting, we were bused out to Randalls Island, one of the few playing fields in the city, to practice soccer, or football, or baseball.

At Allen-Stevenson, I was a big fish in a small pond. There were about twenty kids in our class, and for what turned out to be the only time in my life, I was the best athlete in the school—the quarterback on the football team from the fourth grade on, and very competitive in every sport. Even at that early age, I preferred to be in a leadership role. I was very conscious, I now realize, of not seeking power too aggressively, or of lording it over people. I had a lot of buddies, but John Angelo was my best friend. Stick-thin and very funny, he was my sidekick from the age of six. His father had been killed in the war, his mother was my mother's best friend, and my father helped their family out by balancing her checkbook and playing the role of strict surrogate father to John, who was terrified of him.

Each day, I would pick John up at 86th Street and we would walk to school together. "You have a way of taking charge that makes people want to follow," John once told me, "even though they aren't always sure why." At the age of nine, I took the ten-year-old John with me to the off-season reunion of the camp I attended, since he was planning to go the following summer himself. We walked into the ballroom of a midtown hotel, sat down, and began talking with the other boys. No one looked very familiar to me, but we ate lunch with the other boys and even sang the camp song. I couldn't remember the words, but I faked it. Halfway through the meal the director of my camp walked into the room, spotted me, and came over looking slightly amused. "I'm afraid you've got the wrong reunion, boys," he said. I was totally embarrassed, but it takes a lot to deter me when I think I know where I'm going.

From as far back as I can remember, I've been optimistic and upbeat. When I was seven, I remember being told that my dog, Butch, a boxer, had been hit by a car and killed. I refused to believe it. I just sat in my mother's lap waiting for him to return. I was always convinced that things would turn out well in the end. As I grew up, I discovered that I was more comfortable dealing with crisis than I was with too much success. No obstacle ever seemed too difficult to surmount. I vividly remember attending New York Giants football games as a kid with John. The Giants were a mediocre team in those days, and by the fourth quarter they would often be down by four or five touchdowns. "Let's leave and we'll beat the crowds," John would implore me. "No," I'd respond, "we've gotta stay. The Giants have to score four times and get a field goal, but there are five minutes left, and they're going to do it."

Of course, the Giants would end up losing. A couple of weeks later we would return, and they would fall hopelessly behind again, and I would be just as certain that they were going to come back and win. The same pattern held with the Yankees. They could be down by five runs in the ninth inning, but I wouldn't leave until the last pitch was thrown. I once sat in my seat for twenty minutes after one Yankees game ended, hoping that maybe it wasn't *really* over.

On weekends and during summers, our life centered on my maternal grandfather, Milton Dammann, who was clearly the star of the family. My parents had a house on his estate—Cedar Knoll Farm—in Bedford Hills, New York. It was a large complex, and at one time, before I was born, there were more than fifteen employees, including farmers, gardeners, upstairs and downstairs maids. My grandfather was an entirely self-made man who had shined shoes on the streets of Washington,

D.C., as a child and then worked his way through college and George-town Law School. Much later, he became president of The American Safety Razor Company, which was eventually sold to the Philip Morris Company. Despite his success—and the fact that his wife, Reta Weil, came from a privileged family in Savannah, Georgia—Milton never forgot that his fortune had been hard won. My grandfather had a chauffeur, for example, but he was driven to work in a station wagon rather than a limousine. He also insisted on approaching the city each day by way of the Willis Avenue Bridge, which was slightly off his route but saved the quarter toll on the Triborough. "One way to make money," he would say, "is not to spend it."

Frugality was an ethic in our family. My grandmother Reta often refused to use a driver even in her eighties, and sometimes even resisted taking a taxi. One day I happened to be passing Bloomingdale's in a cab of my own and saw my grandmother fighting her way onto a bus, in the driving snow. I jumped out, pulled her from the crush of boarding passengers, and helped her into my taxi, at which point she began to yell at me.

"Why are you wasting money on a cab?" she demanded.

"Why are you taking a bus?" I replied. "And in a snowstorm, during rush hour!"

"Because your cousin needed sheets," my grandmother said, as if it could scarcely be more obvious.

As the head of a big company, Milton was openly proud of his accomplishments. I was his only grandson, and one day when I was five or so, he invited me to see how his company worked. We were driven to the factory in Brooklyn where razor blades were made. I barely said a word during the car ride. Being with my grandfather made me very nervous. As we waited for the elevator in the lobby, a puddle began forming at my feet, forcing his young secretary to run out and buy me some new underwear. Not until years later did my grandfather mention that I also wet the seat in the company car on the way home. I never visited the factory again.

The self-made man on my father's side of the family was his grandfather, Sigmund Eisner, who was born in Horazdovice, Bohemia, in 1859, and set out for America at the age of twenty-two. He arrived with almost no money in his pocket, but plenty of ambition and a willingness to work hard. He began as a peddler, and eventually earned his fortune making uniforms for the U.S. Army—and later for the Boy Scouts. He married Bertha Weis, whose family had been among the first residents of Red Bank, New Jersey, and eventually became one of the town's most prominent and beloved citizens. His son, my grandfather Jacob Lester Eisner, began his career working in the family uniform business, but soon grew restless. In the years following World War I, J. Lester joined the National Guard and rose to the rank of colonel. During World War II, he became head of the American Red Cross in England.

The seminal event in my father's early life was the death of his mother, Madie, from a burst appendix, when he was just ten years old. After a period of grieving, his father, J. Lester, began spending much of his time in New York City, where he ate dinner nearly every night at the "21" Club. My father and his two younger brothers were brought up mostly by servants back in Red Bank, and they learned to fend for themselves. Much of my father's attention turned to school. He attended Princeton as an undergraduate, and Harvard Law School, and then spent a short time working at a law firm, where he quickly realized he wasn't interested in practicing law. He tried out the family uniform business, but that didn't prove much more satisfying. In 1942, the war put his search for a career on hold. His younger brother Jacques was one of the early casualties in the Pacific, another devastating blow to the family. My father survived his missions as a pilot, but when he returned three years later, many of his contemporaries had already launched their careers.

My father's wartime experience prompted his first business initiative: founding an airline in Ecuador, which he eventually lost to a revolution or a weak economy—I was never sure which. He continued to fly himself, however. As a child, I sometimes flew with him until my mother finally forbade it after he did stunt tricks over our country house in Bedford Hills with me in the co-pilot seat. Next, he went to work for his father-in-law—my grandfather Dammann—as a road salesman for Lightfoot-Schultz soap, which was manufactured by American Safety Razor. My father hated the job. I still remember vividly his coming home after seeing the original Broadway production of Arthur Miller's *Death of a Salesman* in 1949. It was the first time I really experienced the power of drama. I was just seven years old, but it was clear to me that the play had touched my father deeply. Horrified by the prospect of ending up like Willy Loman, he quit his salesman's job the next week.

In a short time, my father came up with the idea of starting a sports and vacation trade show at the Kingsbridge Armory in the Bronx, and later at the New York Coliseum on Columbus Circle. He ran it with a businessman friend from his social circle named Victor Oristano. The show became a highlight of my youth. To me, it was romantic and fun, my first brush with show business. After three years, just as the show was about to become highly profitable, Victor and my father lost their lease with the city. They were victims of Robert Moses, the powerful but bullying head of the Triborough Bridge and Tunnel Authority, which controlled the Coliseum. I never felt comfortable questioning my father about it, but even as a teenager, I remember wondering why he hadn't secured a long-term option on a lease for his show.

Instead, my father's solution was to leave the private sector altogether. He was named the eastern regional head of the Housing and Urban Renewal Authority under President Eisenhower and later became the head of public housing for New York State under Governor Nelson Rockefeller. I had always been exposed to successful businessmen, but it was during this period that I grew accustomed to being around government officials and philanthropic leaders in our apartment, at our home in Bedford Hills, and at the Century Country Club in Purchase, where my father played golf. I went there to swim and to learn how to play tennis and golf, but I also sometimes walked the golf course when my father played with his contemporaries—among them Loebs and Lehmans, Sarnoffs and Bloomingdales. To me, they were simply my father's crowd. I was only vaguely aware that they were somehow important and influential. I never had any reason to feel intimidated or impressed by them. What I mostly observed were their missed golf shots, their everyday problems, and their vulnerabilities.

At home, my father was the center of attention. Everyone was drawn to him—for his charm, his dashing good looks, his sense of humor, and his thirst for adventure. He was all my friends' favorite father, which was ironic in a way, because he was never entirely comfortable in the paternal role. From as early as I can remember, my sister Margot and I both called him Lester, at his request. Calling him by his first name put a certain wall between us—a formality—but I still idolized him. My father always seemed incredibly youthful, charismatic, athletic. He was the one who did double somersaults off a diving board at the country club while most of my friends' fathers were reading the newspaper or playing cards.

My father also loved golf, tennis, fishing, and polo, which he had played at Princeton. For him, playing hard meant coming home bruised and bloodied. Working on the Vermont farm he later purchased meant being up at sunrise replacing walls or planting apple trees. Taking care of the property meant cutting trails through the woods, or pruning, or shoeing horses himself—and driving us with his endless energy. Most teenagers sleep late on weekends and vacations, but God forbid you should ever sleep past eight in our home. My father understood adolescence, but he didn't always respect it. My sister and I were never allowed to pass the days hanging out at the pool during the summers the way most of our friends did. We were required to have jobs, or organized activities.

On weekends in Bedford Hills, my father would take me out horseback riding for two hours early in the morning. He rode hard, galloping and jumping fences until the horses were totally lathered. I was expected to keep up. He also took me riding in Central Park, where there were no logs to jump or hills to climb. When all we had to do was avoid pedestrians, the number of falls and concussions was reduced. My sister became terrified of horses and quit riding completely. Years later, when I brought my fiancée, Jane Breckenridge, to my parents' farm in Vermont, my father insisted that the three of us go riding. Jane had never been on a horse before, but she gamely agreed to try. My father's aggressive style frightened her, just as it had my sister twenty years earlier, and Jane never enjoyed riding again. While I hated and feared riding at times, I refused to complain or give up, and my father's pace never slowed. We galloped through the woods until the horses were soaking wet. Then my father would move on to another activity. If he was stuck in our apartment in New York City for a weekend, by Sunday he would be like a caged lion, full of unspent energy.

My sister's passion—relentlessly encouraged by my father—was figure skating. Indefatigable, he would wake her up by five o'clock many mornings to take her to practice at a skating rink in Westchester. For years, I wondered why Margot didn't skate at the New York Skating

Club, above Madison Square Garden. No one had a satisfactory answer. Eventually I learned that Jews were not allowed membership. Still, my sister's dream was to compete in the 1960 Olympics. She was a great athlete and an excellent competitor, but while she was gracious and charming off the ice, she wasn't a charismatic personality in competition. The other girls cooed and bowed, winked and smiled at the judges during their free skating. Margot simply focused on her technique, which frustrated me. I tried to convince her that she needed to sell herself, to play the game, but as the younger brother my advice wasn't taken seriously. She skated hard and well but ended up second and third in competitions and never did make the Olympics. Fortunately, she had many other interests. She went on to Smith College, married a few years later, raised two terrific children, and enjoys a productive life with few regrets. My father's competitive genes went mostly to me.

The other quality that set my father apart from everyone else I knew was his fierce ethical standards. He maintained a strict code of conduct even when doing so meant hurting his own interests. At one point, in the wake of the Watergate scandal, a ruling came down that all state officials had to provide a list of their personal assets. "There's no way I'm going to do that," my father told me. "It's an invasion of my privacy."

I was aghast. "You don't have any assets that could embarrass you," I argued. "The only stock you own is in public companies, and the government is asking for the names of the assets, not the amounts." I wouldn't have blinked at the request—disclosure seemed reasonable and practical—but to my father it was a matter of principle. He wasn't going to continue in public service if it required sacrificing his privacy, and he quit rather than comply.

He was similarly uncompromising in dealing with the Eisner family uniform business when it ran into hard times. After my great-grandfather Sigmund died, in 1925, his sons took over, with my uncle Monroe assuming the most aggressive role. Monroe behaved as if wealth and success could simply be taken for granted. At one point, he concluded that men would always insist on buttons for the flies of their pants. As a result, the company turned down an opportunity to buy the patent on zippers. They also decided that there was no need to spend extra money putting Boy Scout shirts in plastic wrapping, or to label uniform sizes correctly or to concentrate on finding new customers. Sigmund had helped to found the Boy Scouts of America, along with Teddy Roosevelt, and Sigmund's sons simply assumed they would always have the account. But eventually, their hungrier competitors took it away. Later, they got into trouble with the government after some of the parachutes that they manufactured to carry equipment failed to open properly.

At that point, my father stepped in. He simply couldn't bear the embarrassment to the family name. Rather than trying to make excuses, or even amends, he forced the company out of business in 1955. The stories that my father told me about his uncles were among my earliest and most vivid lessons about the danger of overconfidence, the importance of maintaining the highest possible standards in whatever you do, and the need to keep reinventing a business to keep it fresh. In college, when I read another Arthur Miller play, *All My Sons,* it reminded me of our family's story: arrogant, incompetent offspring who lack any moral compass or sense of pride and who ultimately destroy what their father has worked so hard to build.

After my father gave up government service because of the disclosure rule, he bought an apple orchard and farm in Vermont, which prospered. At one point, he needed to buy a 200-acre orchard in the southwestern part of the state in order to produce enough apples to fill up the temperature-controlled storage rooms on his property. My father made a deal to buy a local farmer's land for $16,000, which was exactly what the farmer was asking, even though the property was probably worth three times that amount. When the farmer showed up for the closing, he had one new demand. "I want my tractor paid for, too," he said. It probably would have added $600 to the cost of the deal, but it wasn't in the contract they had signed. My father was so outraged by the last-minute request that he walked out rather than pay up.

Had it been my negotiation, I might have been annoyed but I also would have been pragmatic. I would have thrown in the tractor, resisted complaining, and concluded that I had made a very good deal nonetheless. Today, that land is probably worth between $1 and $2 million. But even if my father had known the land would increase that much in value, he wouldn't have blinked. Several months before he died in 1986, we were driving around the orchards together, and he was musing about his life. "I've done pretty well," he told me, "but what I'm most proud of is that I've never once in my professional life committed an immoral or unethical act." It was a daunting statement.

The biggest area of conflict in my own life was trying to meet my father's expectations, both morally and intellectually. I wanted to please him, and it was nearly impossible. At one point in eighth grade, I was taking a math class, and he gave me some help with a problem that involved the Pythagorean theorem. I had memorized the formula. I didn't feel I needed to understand how Pythagoras had figured out that in a right triangle the square of the hypotenuse is equal to the sum of the squares of the other two legs. I just wanted to get the problem done. "That's not sufficient," my father told me, and he ran off to his study to get his model of Pythagoras drawing his formula in the sand. "When you really understand the formula, I'll give you this statue," he said, and proceeded to explain the formula to me step by step.

Both of my parents were concerned that my sister and I be educated culturally. They took us to museums and concerts, and especially to the theater on Broadway. From the age of five, going to a Broadway show was what we did on birthdays and anniversaries—the way we marked certain milestones in life. I saw everything from *Kiss Me Kate* to *Guys and Dolls*, to *South Pacific* to *Oklahoma!* I can still sing a very poor version of "Once in Love with Amy," from *Where's Charley?* I was also exposed to art and architecture at an early age. My parents had a close friend, Victor Ganz, who was exceptionally knowledgeable in both fields. When I went to Disney and decided that we ought to try to build great, innovative buildings rather than conventional, mediocre ones, Victor became a key adviser in our efforts. At one point in my childhood, Victor needed wall space for his vast art collection and lent my parents a Picasso, *The Bullfight*, which they hung in my bedroom. I stared at that painting for ten years until Victor took it back. To my astonishment, he sold it and bought a big new apartment with the proceeds.

Popular culture didn't interest my parents much. They rarely took us to movies. My father built a television set from an RCA kit before they were widely available commercially, but he and my mother only turned it on when we watched the Milton Berle show together as a family once a week. The rule was that my sister and I could watch an hour of television only after we had read a book for two hours. When my parents went out, I would immediately turn on the TV set, to Margot's horror. As soon as I heard a key in the door or a car in the Bedford Hills driveway, I would scurry to turn it off. Often, my father would walk in and check with his hand to see whether the TV was still warm. If it was, I caught hell, not so much for watching as for trying to deceive him, and for involving my sister in the cover-up. It was my father who taught me to appreciate the famous lines from Sir Walter Scott's *Marmion:* "Oh, what a tangled web we weave, / When first we practice to deceive!"

My father was also demanding when it came to what he considered inappropriate behavior. At the end of the ninth grade, my second year at boarding school at Lawrenceville, my parents received a letter from my housemaster, Bruce McClellan, describing my performance. "Mike has certainly had his difficulties—in self-discipline, in peer relationships, and in his studies," McClellan wrote. He went on to mention an incident in which I'd thrown a cherry bomb out of a third-floor window, and he indicated that I had a tendency to "play the angles." But McClellan also concluded that I had "weathered the storms and emerged a fine and strong young man." I knew that my father would focus on the bad news. McClellan's letter arrived just before spring recess. Usually, my mother picked me up at school, and I still remember the feeling of shock and apprehension when I emerged at the end of the day and saw my father waiting for me, a grim look on his face. It was a long car ride home.

Even then, I didn't quit testing the limits. In tenth grade, lights had to be out at 10:00 p.m. in my dormitory, which was accomplished by turning off a master switch for the whole house. I rigged up a system that allowed me to siphon electricity from an outlet in the bathroom, where the light was left on. Other times, I slipped around the rules to sneak a cigarette, or leave the dorm at night. I was hardly a hellion, but I learned which lines I could afford to cross, and which I couldn't, and found a way to balance basic respect for authority with youthful rebelliousness.

My father's lessons weren't lost on me. One of the reasons I was so powerfully drawn to Frank Wells was that he reminded me of my father, who died of cancer in 1987. They were especially alike in the understated, ethical way that they conducted their business lives. After

Frank's death, his son found a little piece of paper in his wallet which read: "Humility is the essence of life." Later, I discovered that Frank had carried that paper around for thirty years. Like my father, but more gently, Frank served as a governor for me—a source of quiet moral authority to whom I could turn whenever I was tempted to push the boundaries just a little too far.

Those temptations I inherited in part from my mother, Margaret Dammann Eisner. She was fundamentally honest and decent, but she was definitely willing to cajole and rearrange in order to get what she wanted. My mother was also much more ambitious and goal-oriented than my father. "She could have run General Motors if she had grown up in a different time," John Angelo once said to me, and I suspect he was right. A pampered only daughter, my mother was just nineteen when she announced her plans to marry my father. Partly, it was a route to independence from an overprotective father. Shortly before their wedding, my mother and father went out for breakfast at Longchamps, in Manhattan. When my grandfather Milton heard the news, he was mortified. "What if someone had seen you having breakfast with Lester at eight a.m.?" he asked.

"I don't care what other people think," my mother said—or at least I imagine that's what she said.

My mother never had a traditional career, but she was always busy in philanthropic causes, including serving for many years as president of the Irvington Institute, then a hospital for children with rheumatic fever. Irvington was also the place where I got my first real job, if you don't count working for my grandfather cutting grass and raking the driveway when I was eight. The Institute opened my eyes to those less fortunate than I was, and provided my first adult adventure in the workplace.

For my mother, family always came first. She was home when my sister and I returned each afternoon, and she carried on a busy social life with my father in the evenings. Like her mother before her, she made it her business to keep the family ties close, and that included cousins, uncles, and grandparents. She called her own mother every day. "I've never met anyone who didn't like your mother," my father once told me. When it came to my own children, and my sister's, my mother attended every one of their thirteen graduations—the last of them my youngest son Anders's high school graduation, just a month before she suffered a massive stroke in the summer of 1996.

My mother was also my protector. Whenever my father grew impatient or frustrated or irrationally angry at what he perceived as my lapses, my mother was always the mediator and the ameliorator. Whenever my father became tired of my incessant questions, she was there. I knew I could win her over, just as she had learned how to win him over. We had a silent collusion. In grade school, when I left assignments to the last moment, she would help write my papers for me, even forging my handwriting. (Of course, years later she denied this, but it was true.) However angry my father became about one of my transgressions, I knew that my mother would protect me from his wrath and eventually help smooth the waters. If I brought home a stray dog and insisted on keeping him, it was my mother who became my ally against my father's inevitable resistance. If we went out to dinner and I chose the shrimp cocktail—the only appetizer not included in the fixed-price dinner—my father invariably balked. "That's ridiculous and unnecessary," he would announce. At that point, I appealed to my mother and usually got my way, just as she did.

By far the most important formative experience in my life was going to Camp Keewaydin in Salisbury, Vermont. The oldest wilderness-tripping camp in America, Keewaydin taught boys how to cook, pitch tents, portage canoes, "wallop" pans (meaning "clean" in Keewaydinese), and dry them with "elephant bumwad" (paper towels). To this day, it remains spartan, no-frills, and extremely low-tech. Campers live in tents, plumbing is minimal, and the only telephone is in the main office. The summer after my father's mother died, he was sent by his father to Keewaydin. Still grieving, he understandably hated the initial experience. But in time my father grew to love Keewaydin and returned for many years. Eventually, he became a junior staff member, only to be thrown out at seventeen when he was discovered with a girl in a canoe after hours.

I was always amazed that my father found a girl anywhere near camp, or that he cajoled her into a canoe. His ouster, however, didn't dampen his enthusiasm for Keewaydin. When I was seven, he took me there for a weekend and volunteered me for a boxing match against a nine-year-old twice my size. I survived this initiation and went back to

Keewaydin the following year and nearly every summer thereafter until I was twenty-two, the last few times as a staff member. All three of my sons followed in my footsteps. Like me, they sang camp songs in the Indian Circle, acted in the Multi-House, boxed in the outdoor ring, bowed to the Southwest Wind Shawondasee, and walked on the "campus" under the shadow of Mount Moosalamoo.

To a remarkable degree, my core values were shaped in the crucible of those camp summers. In contrast to traditional camps for boys, which emphasize competitive sports, Keewaydin focused on building practical skills and encouraging teamwork, particularly on the long wilderness trips that we took in canoes each summer. Being good at baseball or tennis didn't count for much at Keewaydin, but being a good tripper did. Whether it was on the Allagash River or the Rangeley Lakes or in Algonquin National Park in Canada, the highest virtues were helping the other fellow even as you learned the tools of self-reliance; being a good winner, but an even better loser; and learning to survive, gracefully and without complaint, under challenging conditions. There was something powerful and dramatic about living in such a simple environment, especially during our trips into the wilderness.

Above all, I loved the fact that life at Keewaydin was so different from the much more formal world I inhabited during the rest of the year. I also enjoyed it because the skills of camping came so easily to me. I was the guy on our trips you could count on to complete a task, whether that meant putting up the tent, preparing a meal, or burying the garbage. I was comfortable having authority at the head of a team, but I also learned a lot about teamwork, and the simple congeniality of pulling together for a common goal. It was hokey stuff, but I believed in it.

The next turning point in my childhood came after the eighth grade, when I went off to boarding school at Lawrenceville in New Jersey. I had always breezed through academically at Allen-Stevenson, where I was used to being a leader in a class of twenty kids. Now, suddenly, I found myself in a highly selective, academically rigorous school, with about 180 boys in my grade—a very small fish in a large pond. To this day, Lawrenceville with its academically rigorous curriculum remains the most competitive and challenging environment I've ever encountered, including Hollywood. It didn't help my adjustment that during my first two years, I grew about ten inches. In the process, I lost my coordination, and my athletic arrogance was knocked out of me. The best I could do in football was our house team, and in basketball I only made the junior varsity. I did reasonably well academically, especially in history and English, and even Latin, but I was not among the top students. For the first time, I had to make my peace with being in the middle of the pack rather than at the front. Today, my sons still get a great kick out of looking at my less-than-perfect report cards and housemaster's letters.

Until Lawrenceville, I had never thought much about being Jewish. Allen-Stevenson was mostly Christian, but no one made much of it. Neither my sister nor I attended any religious services growing up. In 1944, before it was clear to most Americans exactly what was happening in Europe, my parents hired a German housekeeper. I was two years old, and Maria stayed with us until I was twelve, long after the war ended. When my parents went out, Maria often took my sister and me to Germantown on 86th Street, and we all ate bratwurst and knockwurst together. Even today, I understand some German, especially terms of endearment. It wasn't for many years that I realized how unusual and even awkward it was for a Jewish family to have a German maid while the United States was at war and Hitler was exterminating Jews throughout Europe. Eventually we would discover that at least sixteen Eisners, many of them my great-grandfather's siblings, had died in the Czechoslovakian concentration camp of Theresienstadt. By then, however, Maria had long since become part of our family.

While my father was proud to be Jewish, the death of his mother had undermined any belief in organized religion. There was slightly more interest on my mother's side of the family, but we were more cultural Jews than religious Jews. At Lawrenceville, I was made aware for the first time of how being Jewish somehow made me different, an outsider. Until one classmate called me a "kike," prompting one of the only fistfights of my life, it had literally never occurred to me that some people didn't like Jews. Now the issue was in the air, and I hated the consequences. I hated being put in a category. I hated the jokes directed at me about Temple and Bar Mitzvahs and Saturday School. Like my father I was proud to be Jewish, but I hated being viewed as different.

Much of the problem was simply the passage of adolescence and the accompanying uncertainty. *Catcher in the Rye* became my favorite book, and I spent a lot of my high school years wondering what Holden Caulfield would do in various boarding school situations. One form that my own rebellion took was to find ways to cut corners academically, which surely would have upset my father if he'd known what I was doing. In my sophomore midterm in Latin, for example, the teacher announced that he was going to ask us to translate one of three dozen Julius Caesar passages from Latin to English. Instead of learning all the vocabulary, I memorized the first three or four Latin words in every passage and the rest of the thirty-six texts in English—a big task, but not as daunting as learning all the Latin. By doing it my way, I could look at the first three words of any passage, and then write the rest out in English from memory, without translating anything. The test took me about twenty minutes instead of two hours and I got a 100. Unfortunately, my technique was not foolproof. The next semester, we weren't told in advance which passages we were going to have to translate, and with my limited Latin vocabulary I ended up failing the final.

Part of it was that I liked doing things my own way. If I had a history final that I knew would be in essay form, I came up in advance with an essay I could adapt to any kind of question. In the process, I memorized twenty important and/or obscure historical facts and somehow worked them into my answer, whatever question we were given. I did have a little guilt about it at the time, but I thought that part of life was learning how to deal with the system, using all the tools at my disposal. I was impatient with the dry, rote way that we were expected to memorize facts and regurgitate them back. What I enjoyed most was using my imagination to create some new way to do things. I probably didn't learn as much as other classmates who spent all their time studying, but I did develop writing skills and imagination, and managed to hold my own.

Even so, I felt suffocated by the rules, the formality, and the constant pressure. I longed for a life that was the opposite of the one I was living. I wanted to attend a co-ed public school. Instead of calling an apartment on Park Avenue home, I dreamed of a modest house with a white picket fence where my mother did all the cooking and all the kids played together on the street until dark. I couldn't have articulated it at the time, but what I yearned for was the quintessential middle-class

1950s suburban life—the one I'd seen in countless Doris Day movies and by watching television shows like *The Adventures of Ozzie and Harriet*, *Father Knows Best*, and *I Love Lucy*. My fantasy was surely shared by millions of far less privileged kids. Different as our starting points may have been, what bound us were the idealized images on the television shows we were all watching.

When I began to think about college, I felt ready for co-education, fraternity life, and unsupervised freedom. My first choice was to attend college somewhere in California, which represented sun, fun, and the good life. My father vetoed that idea immediately. To him, it was too far and the cost of traveling there was too high. In the fall of my senior year, planning for college was derailed when I contracted meningitis and became so sick that I later learned my family feared I might not survive.

Early that winter of 1959, I ran into a guy I knew in my dormitory who was carrying a catalogue from Denison University in Granville, Ohio. The cover was an idyllic campus scene right out of one of the TV shows I'd spent my childhood watching. My father's preference was for me to follow in his path at Princeton, but the prospect of four more years in the same competitive all-male environment was as unappealing to me as California had been to him. I was so determined to try something different that I applied to Denison without even visiting the campus or telling my parents until I was admitted.

From the start, I loved Denison. There were only sixteen hundred students on the scenic campus in rural Ohio. The girls were beautiful and everyone was friendly. It was 1960, John F. Kennedy was about to become the country's young president, the war in Vietnam hadn't yet begun, and there was no such thing as a counterculture or hippies or a psychedelic drug scene. A big weekend meant drinking beer at a fraternity party. Denison was originally a Baptist college, but my being Jewish wasn't an issue. There were perhaps a half-dozen Jews, and we were considered more an oddity than a threatening social minority.

I declared myself premed as a freshman, mostly because I had no better idea and being a doctor seemed romantic. That feeling wore off in a hurry when I took a course in anatomy and had to dissect a cat. I didn't change my major, but mostly I took English and theater courses and tried to avoid the science requirements. At the end of my sophomore year, I finally faced the fact that I had to take organic chemistry and signed up for an intensive summer course at Columbia University. It ran five days a week for eight hours a day, during the brutal summer heat of Manhattan. I lasted about three weeks before dropping the course and taking one in literature instead. That was the end of being pre-med. English became my major. I ended up with a very broad education instead of a more specialized one.

Much later, I appreciated a comment that the filmmaker George Lucas made when my oldest son, Breck, eager to become a director, was thinking about applying to undergraduate film schools. "Making films is like learning to drive. Anyone can do it," George told him. "The real question is, what's your destination? To find that out, you're much better off with a liberal-arts education." Breck took George's advice to heart—far more so than if I had made the same point. He decided to attend Georgetown University, majored in English, and then went on to get his graduate degree in film at USC. George's advice applies equally to the corporate world. Even if the ultimate goal is to enter business, I strongly believe in the value of a broad liberal-arts undergraduate education.

In my case, studying literature was suited to my peculiar kind of creativity. Once, for example, I was taking a course in nineteenth-century literature from a professor named Dominick Consolo, a wonderful teacher who stood on his desk to lecture, loved poetry, and eventually became one of the inspirations for the Robin Williams character in *Dead Poets Society*. In this instance, Professor Consolo was giving a series of lectures about *Moby-Dick*, a novel that I found complicated but fascinating. Finally, after about the third lecture, I raised my hand. "What if," I asked my professor, "this whole thing is a big-fish tale?" I had genuinely begun to wonder whether Melville's aim in *Moby-Dick* was less to craft a giant moral allegory than to write a giant satirical "fish story." When I tried out this theory at more length in a paper, Professor Consolo promptly named me "Mr. What If?" In retrospect, that seems appropriate. "What if?" is something I've been asking all my life. (Breck inherited the trait. "Will dirt go into my eyes when I'm dead and buried?" he asked when he was three. I referred him to his mother.)

I was always looking for ways to be original without going so far as to invite failure. For my history thesis, I wrote a play about

Woodrow Wilson. It was easier than a traditional thesis, more fun, and a little calculating, too. I could easily imagine my professor having to read thirty or forty other long and mostly predictable papers over a weekend. It occurred to me that he would be relieved to have a play to read, and that I would be more likely to get a good grade as a result. Although it wasn't my primary intention, I probably learned more about Woodrow Wilson than I would have by writing a traditional paper. Creating a drama out of his life made it more three-dimensional, and more memorable.

During the summer of my junior year, I landed a job as a page at NBC, mostly because my father knew Bobby Sarnoff, president of NBC and the son of General David Sarnoff, who had founded RCA, NBC's parent company. In the course of those three months, I fell in love with the entertainment business. I spent my time answering phones, running errands, giving studio tours, and standing by the elevators learning how to look into people's eyes in order to recognize who had real business in the building and who didn't. I was at the bottom of the ladder at NBC, but I loved every minute of it.

I also worked on the set of the game shows like *The Price Is Right*, taking audience members to their seats. Once, for the fun of it, I solemnly ushered a group of people into the ladies' room instead of the studio. For a short time, I answered phones for *The Tonight Show*. Jack Paar's reign was coming to an end, and Johnny Carson was scheduled to begin the following fall. When the summer ended, Bobby Sarnoff wrote my father a letter and told him I was one of the best pages NBC had ever had. He may have been trying to be nice, but I *was* good at my job. I was very organized, I showed up on time, and I took what I did seriously. A lot of my fellow pages spent their time moaning and groaning. I was almost always in a good mood.

I went back to college that fall for my senior year and began to write plays. I was reading all the great modern playwrights in my English classes—Miller, Tennessee Williams, Shaw, Pirandello—and I admired their work. I also loved the idea that what you wrote in a play literally came to life and that actors read your lines. The teamwork involved in producing a show also appealed to me, particularly when it was based on something that I had created. I could write a play in three or four days, and dialogue came relatively easily to me. By comparison, writing a novel seemed incredibly difficult, lonely, and isolated. Above all, the reason for writing my first play was the hope of impressing Barbara Eberhardt, a very pretty fellow student in the theater department. I even came up with a pretentious-sounding title, *To Metastasize a River*, which eventually got changed to *To Stop a River* when I discovered that "metastasize" was usually associated with cancer.

Although my relationship with Barbara never went anywhere, the play was produced, and she starred in it. That was more than enough to fuel my fantasy of becoming the next great American playwright. Two weeks after my last summer working at Keewaydin and ten weeks after graduating from Denison, I set off on the ocean liner *Mauritania* for Paris, figuring that I'd find some café to write in, live the bohemian life for several years, and turn out plays that would eventually find their way to Broadway. The voyage was an exciting start. The boat was filled with several hundred other college students who had just graduated and were just as interested as I was in romantic adventure.

I wrote three plays during my first three weeks in Paris, including one about a couple who freeze to death when they get caught on a ski lift in Mont Tremblant, Canada. I also discovered that I wasn't crazy about rewriting, which was clearly going to be necessary if I had any serious ambitions as a playwright. Also, after that initial flurry of productivity, my creative well began to run dry. The romantic life I'd envisioned somehow wasn't panning out. I felt unexpectedly homesick, particularly after I saw Kazan's *America, America* on the Champs-Elysées. The room that I had rented reeked of urine no matter how much I sprayed it with disinfectant. It turned out that until two weeks before my arrival, it had been a men's room. When I made that discovery, I tried unsuccessfully to find another hotel. The most horrifying incident occurred one sunny summer afternoon when an American student took a suicide leap from the top of Notre Dame and landed just across the plaza from where I happened to be standing.

The truth, I realized, was that I had come to Paris on a vacation to celebrate graduating from college, not to live the far harder life of a fledgling artist. After a few weeks, with nothing formal or structured to do in Paris, the main hunger I felt was to get back to New York and find a job. I wasn't sure exactly what I wanted to do, but I was eager to start the search.

3

You Can't Fall off the Floor

I RETURNED TO NEW YORK IN THE FALL OF 1964, PLANNING TO LIVE full time with my parents for the first time in eight years. Within a few weeks, I realized that it made no more sense for me to live at home than it had to be an expatriate in Paris. "I'll help you look for an apartment," my mother said, which was a pretty strong sign that she agreed it was time for me to be on my own. Within a few days, I had found a one-bedroom, fifth-floor walk-up on 64th Street between Madison and Park Avenues for $182.50 a month. No sooner had I moved in than I realized I had no idea how to do anything for myself. I had gone from home to camp to boarding school to a college dormitory to a fraternity but had never truly fended for myself. I'd even learned to like institutional coffee, although I drew the line at chipped beef on toast. But once I finally had an apartment, I found that I liked the independence, and I even enjoyed making simple meals, having learned basic cooking skills at Keewaydin.

The only problem was that I couldn't get a job. The corporate world, I discovered, was not clamoring for my services. Despite the wonderful letter that Bobby Sarnoff had written to my father about my tenure as an NBC page the previous summer, neither my father nor I could ever get him on the phone again. Instead, I wrote a lot of letters and went to several perfunctory interviews my parents managed to set up for jobs in television and advertising. I got plenty of banal, friendly advice with no job offers attached. At one point, my father arranged for me to see the head of what would become WNET, public television's flagship station in New York, who could not have been more discouraging. "The entertainment business is insecure, cutthroat, and mean-spirited," this executive told me. "You are best off steering clear of it altogether. Find an intelligent industry, a decent industry. This one is not for you." My father was infuriated that someone would disparage his own industry to a young person seeking a first job.

I spent most of my time that fall either sitting in my apartment waiting for return calls—answering machines were still a decade away—or going to movies, often by myself. My inability to land a job left me feeling lonely, dislocated, and slightly frantic. I had energy and ambition but nowhere to direct them. I had an education and a college degree but no place to apply them. For a short time, I continued to harbor hopes that my playwriting career might take off. I sent the play that I was most proud of, *Unscrew the Lock*, to every contact I could find. The replies weren't encouraging. "I am sorry to say that I really don't think you have anything to say—at least not in this play," wrote Jack Hutto, an agent at William Morris. Later, when I managed to get the play to the producer Hal Prince—through his accountant—he had an even more curt reaction: "I just don't care for it." After those rejections, I never sent any of my scripts out again.

Finally, one day in late November, the phone rang. It was someone from the personnel department at NBC, offering me a job as a Federal Communications Commission (FCC) logging clerk for $65 a week. I accepted instantly. My responsibility was to keep records of each time a commercial appeared on the air and note whether it appeared in black and white or in color. It was far better than being unemployed but not nearly as much fun as being a page. Very quickly, I became restless. When I heard that WNBC Radio in New York was looking for a weekend traffic researcher, I jumped at the opportunity. Getting in the door at NBC seemed to be paying off. Now I had two jobs. On the weekends, I went in at 4:00 a.m. and did radio traffic reports until noon for the "Big Wilson" show.

This was show business, and it seemed very exciting to me.

Even climbing onto a bus in the darkness at three-thirty in the morning was exhilarating. The few people who were out on the streets shared with me the secret privilege of the early morning: We were the *real* workers! On my first Saturday, my boss sat me down in front of a radio and gave me a form to fill out. "Listen to the traffic reports on the other radio stations and write them down," he said. Every fifteen minutes I was to hand my findings to Big Wilson, the morning deejay. In short, my job was to borrow traffic reports from rival stations. I wasn't in a position to argue the practice, and I rationalized that it was harmless. To break up the monotony, I began writing up imaginary names for streets where alleged accidents had occurred, often using the names of past girlfriends. The cross street I remember best was Jane and Breckenridge, which happened to be the name of the young woman I was dating at the time.

I met Jane at a Christmas party in 1964. It was thrown by Jeff Bijur, a childhood friend, who wanted me to meet "this great girl" he had known at St. Lawrence University. I resisted the invitation because I was still "pinned"—the now ancient-sounding term for giving a college girlfriend your fraternity pin as a kind of pre-engagement statement. I'd been involved with Judy Armstrong since sophomore year. She was bright, attractive, and funny, but, perhaps most important, she was my first steady girlfriend. Although I now lived in New York and she was back home in Hamilton, Ohio, I was convinced that our relationship would endure, and that she would ultimately move to New York.

On the night of Jeff's Christmas party, I called Judy to find out why the Christmas present I'd sent her had been returned unopened. I assumed I had somehow misaddressed it. Her mother answered the phone. "Judy is out," she said, and after some small talk, I asked about the sweater. Mrs. Armstrong sounded uncomfortable. "Well, I guess I should tell you that Judy got married yesterday," she said. I hung up, devastated. I kept my plans for dinner with my parents, but I couldn't eat a thing. At the end of the meal, I decided to go to Jeff's party after all. Perhaps it might help get my mind off Judy.

I soon found myself sitting on a couch surrounded by a group of people I had never met before. Perhaps because I needed to ventilate, I proceeded to tell everyone in the room my sad story. Turning it into high drama, I explained how my girlfriend had gone away to study in Germany her junior year and returned an experienced woman of the world—now wearing eye shadow and dressing more provocatively. I talked about how I pretended that nothing had changed, even though I knew it had. I tried to tell the story in a light-hearted, self-deprecating way, and it seemed as if everyone enjoyed it.

The exception, I soon learned, was Jane Breckenridge, the girl Jeff had mentioned. She was sitting on the floor talking to a friend when I walked in, and I noticed her immediately. As I told my story, I overheard enough of what Jane was saying to her friend to sense that she was lively, clever, and self-possessed. She was also an exceptionally attractive strawberry blonde. (After thirty-four years of debate I've given up trying to convince her she's a redhead.) We never spoke that evening, but with Jeff's encouragement I called Jane the next week for a date, blithely unaware that she had left the party thinking I was indiscreet, overbearing, and boorish. She turned down my invitation on the phone, and then several subsequent ones, but on each occasion with great wit. These stylish rejections only increased my determination. Finally one day, I called to say that I had theater tickets, and Jane relented. It turned out that she loved the theater as much as I did. It wasn't the last time my persistence would pay off, but it was certainly the most important.

From our first evening together, I felt comfortable with Jane. She was open, direct, and completely unimpressed by money, power, or social position. We began seeing each other all the time, going out for dinner or to movies or the theater and spending weekends walking around New York, or skiing in Vermont. We fell in love, but we also became best friends. Jane seemed to appreciate my relentless enthusiasm and energy. I valued her common sense, as well as her looks, her humor, and her intelligence. She had been an English major in college, but she was now part of the elite staff of Metropolitan Life Insurance programmers who turned the "Argus" language of Honeywell Computers into English, so that three hundred other programmers could do their work. These were the days before Apple, Microsoft, and Netscape, when 64K of memory took up nearly an entire floor of the MetLife Building. She earned $12,000 a year—far more than I did.

As Jane and I became more involved, I was eager to introduce her to one of my lifelong passions. "In order for you to understand what's really important to me," I explained, "we have to take a wilderness camping trip together." I was, I assured her, the sort of outdoorsman

Thoreau would have admired. Reluctantly, she agreed. I immediately began loading up with backpacks from Keewaydin; maps from the Adirondack Park Services; pots and pans from Abercrombie & Fitch; bumwad from the A&P; two sleeping bags from Bloomingdale's; and a reflector oven from Sam's Army & Navy Store in Bellows Falls, Vermont. I also packed up the boundless confidence I'd developed during my years of wilderness experience.

We set out early one Saturday morning. I carried eighty pounds or so on my back, Jane perhaps fifty, and on the first day, we hiked up and down twelve miles. Jane was a great sport, but not especially thrilled by all the walking. I had imagined arriving at our site, cooking a big meal, and then relaxing into a romantic evening. Instead, we were both so exhausted that we fell asleep before the water for the spaghetti came to a boil. The next day, we began hiking again. Along the way, we passed two young men in their twenties who were on their own wilderness expedition, and who walked by us again before long. Once we pitched camp, I walked over to their site, a half-mile away, and invited them to join us for dessert. When they arrived, we ate my great silver cake (learned at Keewaydin) and told scary camping stories to one another as the sun went down.

Just as our two new friends were preparing to leave, a bear began circling our campsite. He was very big, the biggest animal I had ever seen. Jane and I decided to leave and spend the night in our new friends' lean-to—but the bear followed. He circled us as we lay four across in our sleeping bags. The larger of the young men solved his problem by falling asleep. The other one, obviously terrified, simply fell silent. At one point, the bear's gigantic head was a foot from my face. I could smell his breath. The little guy jumped up, hatchet in hand. I stopped him from doing something silly and then we watched as the bear wandered around the lean-to, coming and going all night. Jane and I passed the time like dutiful English majors by discussing Faulkner's story "The Bear." Jane calmly stoked the fire and kept knocking pans together in an effort to keep the bear from attacking us. She never panicked, which kept me from panicking. Clearly the bravest of the four of us, she stayed up all night without complaint, until the bear finally wandered off at dawn.

The next morning, exhausted, Jane suggested that we lighten our load by discarding our pots and pans. I just couldn't abide throwing out my new utensils, nor the uneaten food. Instead, I insisted that we walk the eight miles carrying everything we had brought in. We arrived at our car and collapsed. Jane never again went camping with me, but I was unbelievably impressed with her until we went to a Yankees baseball game, my other lifelong passion. As I watched the game, she did the *New York Times* crossword puzzle. You can't have everything!

For all our compatibility, we could scarcely have come from more different backgrounds. Jane's maternal grandparents, Clara and Victor Lindgren, were born in Sundsvall, Sweden. They eventually immigrated with their daughter, Jane's mother, to Jamestown, New York, a tiny town southwest of Buffalo best known for its furniture-making factories. Jane's mother eventually married James Breckenridge, a boy who grew up on the same street in Jamestown where Jane's family lived, and whose parents had come from Scotland. Like so many immigrants who came to America searching for a better life, both the Lindgren and the Breckenridge clans believed in education. While the women mostly went on to raise families, the men became engineers—as Jane's father did —and physicists and accountants. The next generation followed suit. Jane was one of the first women in the family to go on to college. She got a New York State Regents scholarship to St. Lawrence University. After graduation, she realized that if she didn't want to get married and have kids immediately, she would have to leave Jamestown to launch her career. Moving to New York meant giving up the cocoon of her childhood.

Because Jane came from such a small town, I assumed that I wouldn't have much in common with her parents. I was soon proved wrong. Her father was extremely bright and well informed and read the dictionary for pleasure in the evenings, and I could talk with him about nearly anything. By teaching bridge, her mother, brought up a Lutheran, rebelled against a faith that proscribed even card playing. I suspect that neither of her parents had ever really known anyone Jewish before me, but it was never an issue. Jane herself had been brought up a Unitarian, the most liberal of Protestant faiths. We decided on a small, simple wedding in the summer of 1967 because my sister had just had a huge one.

Even before our marriage, I enlisted Jane in helping me to write letters looking for new jobs. After just three months of working at NBC and at WNBC Radio, I received an offer from CBS to serve as a liaison between the programming and sales departments for the Saturday morning children's schedule. Mostly, that meant making sure that the right cereal and toy commercials were inserted into each show. On my first day at work, I met with Lillian Curtis in personnel. I'd never asked about my salary when I interviewed for the job. "You'll be earning $140 a week," she volunteered. "Wow," I said, "you must be kidding. That's terrific. Thank you, thank you." Six months later, when I felt emboldened to ask for a raise, Lillian reminded me how thrilled I had been by the salary. I had learned my first lesson about discretion in negotiations.

Although the CBS job was barely a step up from NBC, it struck me as a giant promotion, since I was now in "programming." I had some contact with the people who made the shows, even if it amounted mostly to seeing them in the halls. After a while, I was "promoted" to do the same commercial coordination job for game shows, and eventually for *The Ed Sullivan Show*. I was still just a clerk, but much as I had as a page at NBC, I loved being close to the action. My boss was Jackie Smith, a kind, supportive woman who later became the head of daytime programming at the network. She worked for Fred Silverman, who would eventually become a legend as the network's head of programming.

It didn't take long before I began to hunger for something bigger and more challenging. I was soon spending much of my spare time writing letters to everyone I could find in the entertainment business, while at the same time renovating a brownstone on 82nd Street and helping my father redesign the 1785 farmhouse near our apple orchards in Vermont. My life as a real estate developer began and ended in West Rutland, Vermont, with a housing development. John Angelo and I lost $12,000 on that project—the only two people in the sixties to lose money in real estate! In my spare moments I wrote up a prime-time drama, *Made in America*. I never sold it, but I do still have copies of the presentation. Mostly, letter writing was my passion. Jane and I would go to the library and look up the names of station managers in other cities. I also wrote to every programming executive at each of the three major television networks, and to the heads of each of the Hollywood movie studios. In return, I received form letter after form letter of rejection—more than seventy-five in all. In the process, I did manage to forge telephone relationships with several of the secretaries of CBS executives.

In Fred Silverman's case, I started by sending him an earnest letter: "I have several presentations that I have been working on," I wrote. "In addition to my serious writing in theater, one of these presentations is a game show entitled *Bet Your Bottom Dollar,* and I look forward to discussing this project with you." When I got no response to my letter or to a follow-up, I started calling Cathy Kihn, who was Silverman's secretary and would later become his wife. Finally, either because she felt sorry for me or couldn't stand my calls any longer, she arranged a meeting with her boss. It wasn't even a formal interview. As instructed, I just showed up one morning at his office at CBS on 52nd Street and the Avenue of the Americas. I had long been awed by the CBS headquarters. I considered the building—designed by Eero Saarinen and known as Black Rock—the epitome of sleek elegance and good taste.

"What can I do for you?" a harried Silverman asked when I walked into his office. He barely looked up.

"Well," I replied, "I've worked at CBS for more than a year, and I'd like to get into a more creative area. I was an English and theater major at college and I was hoping I could do more."

"Listen to these," Silverman said, "and tell me which one you like better." It turned out that he had audiotapes of two new game shows, one called *Hollywood Squares,* the other *The Face Is Familiar.* I considered myself something of an expert on game shows, having been an usher on *Jeopardy*. Still, without being able to actually *watch* the shows, I was completely confused by what I was hearing on the audiotapes.

"Mr. Silverman," I said finally, "I have no idea what these shows are all about." He tried to draw them out for me on a piece of paper, and then literally acted them out, but I was still puzzled. I asked if I could see the pilots. "There isn't time," he said. "I have to make a decision right away." In the end, Silverman decided to pick up *The Face Is Familiar,* which bombed completely, while passing on *Hollywood Squares,* which became one of the most successful game shows in history. It was one of Silverman's rare mistakes while running daytime television. I, of course, had been no help at all. I returned to my office at the old Borden's Milk Factory on 57th Street and Tenth Avenue and never heard from Silverman again during my tenure at CBS. I filled my free hours instead by writing more letters, developing ideas for other game shows, and enrolling in graduate school at night at New York University to take a course in business accounting.

After months of silence, I finally heard back in the fall of 1966 from a man named Ted Fetter, who had the impressive title of national program director at ABC. I later learned that titles are vastly inflated in the entertainment business. Fetter had once been a high-level executive, but now he was simply in charge of specials—not a key job. For me, however, this was a big opportunity. The interview went well, but then weeks went by with no response. Finally, Fetter called me back. "I'd like to bring you here, but first you have to be interviewed by Leonard Goldberg," he explained. Goldberg was the vice president in charge of programming at ABC. I knew about him, not just from what I read in the newspaper—he was a major executive and he was dating the actress Marlo Thomas—but from my brother-in-law-to-be, Norman Freedman, who had grown up with Goldberg in the same Brooklyn apartment building. Their two mothers remained best friends.

The day of the interview arrived, and at midday I went home to change clothes, since I'd forgotten to put on my best suit. I also forgot the keys to my apartment, and a secretary in the office ended up running over with them after I pleaded with her in desperation. The ABC building was a disappointment: a bland, boxy structure that wasn't nearly as elegant as Black Rock. When I arrived at the thirty-seventh-floor reception room, I was greeted by a young man about my age. "Are you here to see Len Goldberg?" he asked. I said I was and he motioned me to follow him back to his office. I was struck immediately by the fact that he was balding prematurely and that he was wearing a stylish, expensive-looking suit.

Without ever actually introducing himself, this young man proceeded to interview me for about twenty minutes. He was polite but perfunctory, and it was clear that he considered this interview a low priority. The most peculiar thing about the experience was that every five minutes or so, a light glowed on his phone and he would pick up an earpiece, listen for a minute or so in silence, and then resume our conversation. He never offered any explanation. Although he wasn't explicitly encouraging, I had the sense that our interview was a formality and that

I was going to get the job. Feeling optimistic, I went off for a dinner that Jane and I had arranged with Margot and Norman.

As we ate, I described my strange interview with Leonard Goldberg. I mentioned that Goldberg was quite short. "No, he's not," Norman said. Then I remarked that Goldberg was going bald. "That's not true either," Norman responded. Finally, I described Goldberg as abrupt and businesslike. "That's possible," said Norman, "but based on everything you've told me, you didn't meet with the Leonard Goldberg I know."

It turned out that I had been interviewed by Barry Diller, Goldberg's assistant. Barry was exactly my age, and he had been hired out of the William Morris mailroom at the suggestion of Marlo Thomas, who was an old friend of Barry's family. Later, I learned that it was standard practice at ABC for secretaries and assistants to listen in on their bosses' calls, partly to learn more about the business but mostly in order to be able to follow up on any business that arose during the call. I never found out why it was that Barry didn't introduce himself to me during our interview, but apparently it had gone well enough. The next day Ted Fetter called, offering me the job as his assistant.

ABC had been formed in 1943 to operate NBC's second, "Blue" network, which the Federal Communications Commission had just ordered split off from its parent company. Ten years later, in 1953, ABC merged with Leonard Goldenson's United Paramount Theatres. Goldenson became president of American Broadcasting–Paramount Theatres. The new company included just fourteen affiliates—compared to more than sixty for both CBS and NBC. That fall, Goldenson expanded to thirty-five hours a week of programming, including future hits such as *The Adventures of Ozzie and Harriet* and *The Lone Ranger*. The following spring, the network debuted its first fifteen-minute nightly newscast. With no daytime program schedule yet, ABC chose to run all 186 hours of the McCarthy hearings in 1954, a decision for which it won well-deserved kudos. Three years later, the young network won a prestigious Peabody Award for its coverage of the 1956 political conventions.

By 1960, ABC had grown to over one hundred affiliates. The following year, a young executive named Roone Arledge helped revolutionize television sports coverage with the debut of *Wide World of Sports*. While ABC continued to run a distant third behind NBC and CBS in prime time, it built other pockets of strength. The debut of *General Hospital* in 1963 helped put the network's daytime schedule on the map. A year later, ABC began a long, mostly exclusive association with the Olympic Games, hosted by Jim McKay. The news division also expanded, and in 1965, twenty-six-year-old Peter Jennings began his first stint as anchorman for the evening news. The following year, the network moved into new headquarters at 1330 Avenue of the Americas, where I went to work early in 1966.

My sudden rise in status was thrilling, and so were the perks that came with it. I was twenty-four years old, and suddenly I had my own small office, next to Warren Lyons, ABC's head of casting and the son of the famous *New York Post* columnist Leonard Lyons. My office had a window—which looked out on Black Rock—and I had my own secretary. The one problem was that I didn't have much to do, and neither did she. Mostly, I kept myself busy reading the various personnel pamphlets I was given. Even so, I felt I was finally in the middle of the action, with an office on the floor where prime-time programming decisions were made. I also began to get to know Barry, although not so much on a personal level. He was intensely private, and in all our years in New York, he only invited me to his apartment on one occasion. At work, however, we spoke all the time, and I quickly discovered that he was smart, ambitious, no-nonsense, and very focused.

Early on, I mentioned something to Barry about how I thought that *Ethan Frome* was the best of Edith Wharton's novels. He nodded but he didn't say much. Several days later, I ran into him at the elevator on a Friday night, and he was carrying several Edith Wharton books, along with a biography. Barry had never attended college, but he was a perpetual student with an enormous thirst for knowledge. Unlike many people I would meet in show business, he never tried to fake it. Where there were gaps in his education, he set out to fill them in.

Because Barry ranked above me in the pecking order, he also treated me with a certain condescension. Eventually, it led to our first showdown. One day, without leaving his desk, he yelled across the floor: "Eisner!" I walked straight over to his office and closed the door behind me. "It just isn't going to work for you to talk to me the way you just did," I said. To my surprise, he accepted the challenge undefensively. "You're right," he said. "I'm sorry."

Almost immediately, Barry's behavior toward me began to change. I soon learned that he only respected strength and directness, and that he enjoyed intellectual confrontation. On another occasion, I grew very angry at him when it became clear that he couldn't remember Jane's name after the third or fourth time he'd met her. Once again, he acknowledged that I had a point and never forgot her name again. He and Jane went on to develop a great relationship. On a third occasion, I was annoyed with Barry when I started to say something in front of a group of people and he literally put his hand over my mouth to keep me from talking. That too only happened once. Because I reacted to these early confrontations quickly and decisively, they didn't create a permanent problem between us. On those occasions when I went overboard in my anger, Barry would often remain silent, and eventually I would realize that it was more my issue than his. We had plenty of arguments and battles over the years, but once we understood each other, I felt that Barry treated me honestly and with respect, and I tried to do the same with him. The result was a bond that has withstood ups and downs for more than thirty years.

ABC was still struggling in the mid-1960s. The joke went that we were fourth among the three major networks. Milton Berle was once quoted as saying that if Lyndon Johnson put the Vietnam War on ABC, it would be over in thirteen weeks. With so much that needed to be fixed, there was plenty of opportunity to make a contribution and very little formal bureaucracy standing in my way. Before long, in between handling Ted Fetter's calls, I was reading scripts, suggesting ideas for shows, and involving myself wherever I could. At one point, for example, I briefly coordinated the pilot screenings for the upcoming fall season. One of the new half-hour comedies was called *And Justice for All*, and it was based on a British series called *Till Death Us Do Part*. It starred Carroll O'Connor and Jean Stapleton and dealt very openly with issues of stereotyping and racism. The executives in the room spent a long time debating whether to put it on the air. "What do you think?" they asked me at one point. I said I thought it was funny and original and that they should go with it. (At least I think I said that. If I didn't, I wish I had.) In the end, they decided to pass, in large part because the reaction from test audiences—"research," as it is known euphemistically—was so negative.

It is easy, I would discover, to take false comfort in audience research, since it seems to provide hard data—impressive-looking graphs and charts and statistics. In fact, you can elicit nearly any answer you want from people you interview, depending on how you ask the questions. What's more, audiences, like most executives, favor the familiar and tend to resist anything new and different. It's almost worthless, for example, to ask people open-ended questions about what they want to see on television, because either they'll tell you that they want more of what they already know, or they'll say what they think you want to hear.

In the case of *And Justice for All*, CBS eventually picked the show up from producers Norman Lear and Alan "Bud" Yorkin, despite the negative research. Sally Struthers and Rob Reiner were added to the cast. The show was renamed *All in the Family*, and after a short time on the air, it became the top-rated series on television. Focus group research is another area in which it's easy to be misled. A group of people are brought together and asked a series of questions about a given program. The problem is that one or two articulate or charismatic members of a group can sway the opinion of everyone else, much the way they can in a jury. Even in focus groups without a dominant voice, people tend to say what they feel will be most acceptable to the group as a whole rather than what they really feel. In time, I learned to use research as just one tool in the decision-making process. (It is especially useful when it agrees with you!)

Trusting one's instincts requires a willingness to take chances, ask seemingly silly questions, share outlandish ideas, and risk failure. From my earliest jobs, I rarely censored myself. At one point, I wrote a four-page proposal for a half-hour situation comedy called *The Funeral*, about a family that owns a funeral home and lives above it. It was a terrible idea—death isn't something that audiences are interested in hearing about on a weekly basis—but it was also an honest attempt to push boundaries in the search for something original. Later, when I was in a position of more authority, I made certain that no one would ever fear being humiliated by saying the "wrong" thing. The more people who contribute, I found, the better the chances of coming up with something compelling and original. If I liked someone's idea, I said so immediately and enthusiastically. If I didn't, I was equally blunt. Many executives in Hollywood agonize over decisions. My experience is that ideas don't get better or worse over time, and success depends not just on having good creative instincts but on the willingness to act on them quickly and decisively. My confidence came from knowing what I liked and discovering, over the years, that I was right often enough that it made up for the many times when I proved to be wrong.

For every idea that a qualified producer submits to a network, he or she has gone through at least ten possibilities first. For every three ideas the network finally hears, one script is put into development. For every three scripts put into development, the network orders one pilot episode. For every three pilots, one goes on the air. For every four series that go on the air, one of them returns the following season. Even then, one out of every four returning shows becomes a true hit. Perhaps two or three times a decade, a cultural phenomenon occurs with shows like *All in the Family* or *Cheers* or *Hill Street Blues* or *Home Improvement* or *Cosby* or *Seinfeld* or *ER*. Putting aside those mega-hits, the odds are approximately 1 in 4,000 of achieving a moderate success, even for a seasoned producer. Nonetheless, one big success offsets a lot of failures. Persistence is as important as inspiration.

The sheer volume of work in my job made it an incredible training ground. Early on, I began making an inventory of all the feature films to which we had broadcast rights. In the process, I discovered that we didn't have a single one from Warner Bros. I went to the Rolodex, looked up the name of the person in charge of selling Warner films to the network, and put in a call. Somehow this executive came to the phone. When he asked what I wanted, I said, "I'm Michael Eisner from ABC and I was just wondering why we don't have any of your movies."

I might as well have accused him of child abuse. "Do you know who I am?" he shouted at me. "I'm the chairman of Warner Bros. If I want to sell movies to ABC, I'll talk directly to Leonard Goldenson." At which point he hung up. I was shaken, but I took this as another step in my education. Even at the highest levels of the entertainment business, the people at the top can be insecure enough to let their vanity get in the way of better judgment. If some young junior executive had the audacity and persistence to reach me on the phone today to say that Disney ought to be selling his company *more* product, I hope I'd not only be polite to him, but that I'd try to hire him away from his employer.

At ABC, I was achievement-conscious more than image-conscious. Competitive as I was, I never became involved in corporate politics in the sense of trying to figure out what the guy in the next office was up to, or showing up at the right restaurants, or attempting to ingratiate myself with my bosses by figuring out what they wanted to hear. Nor did I ever quite look the part of an executive on the rise. Even though I wore a necktie from first grade on, I'd never learned to tie one very well. Long after I left ABC, I visited the Oregon Shakespeare Festival in Ashland and was given a backstage tour. Tacked onto the back of one dressing-room door were instructions on two ways to tie a necktie. I kept walking, but I lusted after that piece of paper. I didn't think about it again for a year, until I was solicited for a contribution to the same theater. I agreed, but on the sole condition that they send me a copy of those instructions I'd seen. The fund-raising office must have thought I was a little odd, but sure enough, the directions arrived in the mail. I sent back a contribution, and I've tied a perfect knot ever since.

At ABC, however, my tie was inevitably askew, my suits never hung quite right, and my hair always had a mind of its own. By contrast, Len Goldberg was impeccable. Smooth and urbane, he wore suits made by Roland Meledandi, the tailor of the moment, and he was always perfectly groomed. One day, Barry approached me and said bluntly, "Len asked me to find out how come your hair is messed up all the time." I thought for a moment. "Tell him," I said, "it's because I drive to work on a motor scooter." That was true enough. It was also true that my hair behaved no better when I took the subway to work.

A year after my arrival at ABC, I was given a new boss, Gary Pudney, and a new title, manager of specials and talent. My first big break came in 1967, when the top management at ABC wanted to do a television special promoting a new business they had just entered: theme parks. Construction was just being completed on Marine World, outside San Francisco, but no one in our programming department wanted anything to do with it. I volunteered, figuring it was a chance to take charge of something. The key, I concluded, was to build the special around recognizable stars. My first discovery was that ABC had a commitment to do a show with Bing Crosby in return for broadcasting rights to his annual golf tournament from Pebble Beach, California.

I flew out to Pebble Beach, and convinced Crosby to serve as the host for a special about Marine World. Next, we signed the Young Rascals, who had a hit single on the charts called "Groovin'," to perform live from the new park. We named the special *Feelin' Groovy at Marine World,* and went to great lengths to fill it with all kinds of acts, including a water-skiing elephant. Because no established director would consider such a silly program, we signed a young commercial director, who saw it as a big break. It was my first experience of turning to someone unknown and unproven but talented and hungry. The special did well in the ratings, and it earned me my first notice from the top ABC corporate executives. I never knew how they felt about the show itself, but they clearly appreciated its immediate impact on ticket sales at Marine World.

My next break came in mid-1968, when the advertising agency Foote Cone & Belding offered me a job. I wasn't interested in advertising, and turned it down, but I mentioned that they might consider one of my colleagues on the thirty-seventh floor. When he jumped at the opportunity, I asked for and was given his job as director of East Coast prime-time development, which broadened my responsibilities. Around the same time, Barry Diller also moved into a bigger role at ABC when Len Goldberg and Martin Starger, Len's number two, decided to launch a new series form: the made-for-television movie. Other than Disney films broadcast on ABC in the 1950s, the networks only began showing theatrical films on the small screen in 1961. They did very well in the ratings, but only a limited number of them were deemed suitable for family viewing.

In 1964, NBC president Robert Kintner made an experimental deal with Universal executives Jennings Lang and Lew Wasserman. The networks had been paying up to $1 million to license theatrical films from the studios. Now Kintner offered to pay Universal $800,000 each for a series of two-hour movies produced specifically for television, using TV stars in the leading roles. In 1966, NBC began occasionally scheduling what they called "World Premiere Movies." The second one —an airplane disaster film called *Doomsday Flight*—attracted nearly a 50 percent share of all viewers. It was clear that even on a relatively low budget, television movies could be very successful. For Universal, there was a double benefit. In addition to being paid to make the movies, they used many of them as pilots for series.

In 1968, Len Goldberg decided to go NBC one better. Armed with his own research showing that viewers preferred movies to any form of series programming—the sort of simple research conclusion that I was inclined to believe—he assigned Barry to create a weekly series of twenty-six movies made specifically for television. Each one was to be ninety minutes in length. The budget for the movies was $375,000, plus a $75,000 contribution from the ABC-owned stations, which meant about half what NBC had spent producing their TV movies.

Finding producers for the films wasn't easy. When Barry approached the major studios, they balked, not just at making original films for such a low price but also about competing against their own feature films. Finally, Len and Barry turned to independent producers, including Aaron Spelling and Lee Rich, who were hungry for work and unencumbered by the overhead of the major studios. When Len announced publicly that ABC was moving into production on its first two movies and was committed to twenty-four more, the phones began to ring off the hook. Suddenly, studio executives scrambled to avoid being left out. Still, the experiment was considered to be highly risky. Even within ABC, the consensus among most of the top corporate executives was that these low-budget movies would fail in the ratings.

In the summer of 1969, I was given yet another new title—director, feature films and program development—and went to work directly under Barry for the first time. By then, he had hired an executive named Jerry Isenberg to help run the operation in Los Angeles. Still, producing twenty-six movies was a huge job, and Barry clearly needed more help. One of my jobs was to function as something of a conduit between Barry, who could be prickly and hard to reach, and those who worked for him. I also got closely involved in story, scripts, and promotion. It became a challenge for Barry and me to resist the seductive pitches and relentless lobbying of agents, producers, and screenwriters. We tried to focus our attention instead on the basic premise for a movie and the script that grew out of it—the substance of the project, stripped of all other considerations. Nothing else, we soon learned, mattered nearly as much.

That fall, ABC's made-for-television movies became a weekly event on Tuesday night. Len Goldberg and Marty Starger found the ideal time slot for them—from 8:30 to 10:00 p.m.—between two of the only hits on our schedule: *The Mod Squad*, from 7:30 to 8:30, and *Marcus Welby, M.D.*, which premiered that fall in the 10:00 p.m. slot and quickly became the first number one–rated show in ABC's history. Our very first movie happened to be another airplane disaster story—a near sure-fire formula, I was learning—but in this case with a novel twist. *Seven in Darkness*, starring Milton Berle, was about an airplane crash in which the only survivors are seven blind passengers who have to find their way down a mountain to safety. (Today that sounds like a parody from *Saturday Night Live*.) It was a big ratings hit, and within a year our made-for-TV movies were regularly finishing among the top ten–rated shows each week. Slowly, we branched out to topical movies on provocative subjects ranging from divorce to teenage drug addiction to Vietnam.

It was during this period that the term "high concept" was born, referring to an idea for a movie or a TV show that could be summarized in a sentence or two. Ultimately, the term would be maligned by critics as a symbol of oversimplification. My experience had shown me that when an idea couldn't be articulated simply, crisply, and accessibly, there was usually something wrong with it. On a practical level, movies based on simple dramatic concepts—particularly those tied to real-life events—were far easier to promote and tended to do very well in the ratings. I learned that when I heard a good idea it had an effect on my mind and my body. Sometimes I felt it in my stomach, other times in my throat, still others on my skin—a kind of instant truth detector test.

Our success allowed us to take chances with more ambitious dramas. *Brian's Song*, for example, was the true story of the friendship between two football players, Gayle Sayers and Brian Piccolo (who, tragically, developed cancer and ultimately died). *That Certain Summer*, starring Hal Holbrook, was the first network drama to openly take on homosexuality, through the story of a father struggling to acknowledge his long-held secret to his son. These movies not only did well in the ratings but earned enthusiastic critical notices, and helped make Barry a fast-rising star at ABC.

Meanwhile, ABC's programming department was in transition

at the highest levels. Shortly before the first *Movie of the Week* aired, Len Goldberg left for Screen Gems Television, a division of Columbia. Marty Starger, with whom I was close, took over from Len as the head of programming. In the summer of 1970, Marty decided to send Barry to Los Angeles, partly because that was where the business of making movies was centered, and partly because Barry was difficult to manage and Marty wanted some breathing room. Barry continued to prosper in L.A. Within a couple of years, his made-for-TV movies commanded the 8:30–10 p.m. slot three nights a week on ABC, giving him control over a substantial percentage of the network's prime-time schedule.

I became Marty's executive assistant, which meant I took part in all of the major decisions about the schedule. My relationship with Barry changed almost immediately, as I moved from his corporate inferior to much more of an equal. Unfortunately, most of ABC's nighttime schedule remained a disaster. Marty simply wasn't much excited by the grind of producing weekly mass audience shows. He understood the commercial television business but it wasn't where he preferred to put his energies. Instead, he wanted to make a statement—to uplift television. If William Paley could put on *Playhouse 90* at CBS and give serious dramas a place on the CBS schedule, then Marty was determined to match Paley with *ABC Theater*. Over time, he also acquired a number of high-minded projects, including a ten-hour BBC production about the life and times of William Shakespeare; a seven-part series about the Strauss family of composers; and a group of dramas based on short stories by literary writers.

Marty's was a noble effort but not a practical one. Whenever we seemed to be gaining a little momentum with our prime-time series, one of these more esoteric and over-long programs would show up on the schedule, causing the whole night to fall apart in the ratings. It wasn't that quality had no place on the ABC schedule but rather that, unlike CBS, we weren't yet successful enough to schedule programs that were likely to have limited audience appeal. I spent much of my time trying to develop new prime-time series. In the summer of 1970, three months after the birth of our first son, Breck, Jane and I were stuck at Newark Airport when our plane to L.A. was canceled. While we sat around in the waiting room, I bumped into Tom Miller, then head of television development for Paramount. With three hours to kill before the next flight, I was looking for some way to use the time productively. "Why don't we try coming up with a new show?" I asked him.

"Great," Tom said, sensing an opportunity. I was the buyer, after all. If he could get me invested in an idea that we conceived together, his odds of selling it to ABC rose significantly. We ran through a dozen concepts. "Do you recall the show *I Remember Mama?*" I asked, finally. This series, about the life of a Scandinavian family at the turn of the century, had been a hit in the 1950s. We had just lived through the tumultuous sixties and I sensed that the audience would respond to a nostalgic show, one that harkened back to simpler times. For the next couple of hours, Tom and I sat together in the airport trading ideas. On the flight to Los Angeles, I wrote them up into a four-page presentation for a series that we eventually named *New Family in Town*. When we arrived back in L.A., we began looking for someone to write it. Garry Marshall, who had just adapted Neil Simon's *The Odd Couple* for television, soon signed on as both writer and producer, and we set the show in Tom Miller's hometown of Milwaukee, circa 1955. Ron Howard agreed to star as a high school student named Richie Cunningham.

Our idea was to build each of the first thirteen episodes around something unique to the fifties—a family buying its first television set, for example, or experiencing Elvis for the first time. The program department loved both the initial script and the pilot. Unfortunately, we were arguing against stacks of research reports indicating that test audiences disliked the concept. Sure enough, ABC's top executives ultimately turned it down.

In the spring of 1971, after I'd spent four years in midlevel executive jobs at ABC, Marty Starger decided to make me head of daytime and children's programming. I had pushed hard for the job, even though daytime was scarcely a high-status place to work in network television. (So much for good tables at restaurants!) Still, I recognized that daytime was a huge profit center for ABC. By moving there, I would finally be able to make some creative decisions of my own. If I were successful, the top executives would certainly notice. Also, ABC was last in daytime. You can't fall off the floor, so the risks were minimal.

The immediate problem was that I knew absolutely nothing about soap operas, which were the core of daytime programming. My crash course came from watching five episodes of each of our soap operas at a sitting for several weeks. It soon became obvious that making soaps is no different from creating any effective drama. I also learned that the mostly female soap opera audiences are fiercely loyal to their shows. Once they become hooked on a set of characters and their stories, it's very hard to lure them away. Our job was to find a way to do just that, by sharpening our story lines, by making our characters more appealing, and by increasing and improving our on-air promotions for the shows.

Along with my erudite, Yale-educated lieutenant, Brandon Stoddard, I focused on developing two new soaps—*All My Children* and *One Life to Live*—and on shoring up our most successful ongoing show, *General Hospital*. The creators and writers of daytime serials remain among the most hard-working and original personalities I have ever met in the entertainment business. At *General Hospital*, for example, the writers Doris and Frank Hursley were unique. Frank began his career as an academic and rose to be chairman of the English department at the University of Wisconsin. When he met his future wife, Doris, she was an attorney, married to another professor. Frank and Doris began an affair, which created a scandal and ended up on the front pages of the local newspaper. It was a real-life soap opera, not least because Doris's mother also happened to be head of the Board of Regents at the university.

Doris and Frank eventually married, and at one point, on a lark, they submitted a jointly written script for a radio serial to a contest sponsored by Wrigley's Chewing Gum. When they won, Doris, who hated being a lawyer, implored her husband to move to L.A. so that they could launch a new career together. Sure enough, they became enormously successful and prolific soap opera writers, beginning with *Search for Tomorrow* on CBS. In 1963, the Hursleys created *General Hospital* for ABC, writing five half-hour scripts week in and week out.

When I met the Hursleys in 1972, they were neither burned out nor fixed in their ways. At Brandon's and my urging, they completely reinvented *General Hospital*. They also passed on their legacy. The Hursleys' daughter, Bridget Dobson, who graduated from Stanford University and Harvard Business School, ended up going to work for her parents on *General Hospital*. Later, with her husband, Bridget took over *Guiding Light* and *As the World Turns* on CBS and then went on to create *Santa Barbara*, another successful soap, for NBC. It still intrigues me that a writer can spend three years to produce the book for a Broadway show and as much as a year for a film script, while people like the Hursleys could turn out surprisingly solid soap opera scripts in a single day, for years on end.

The second area of daytime was game shows. My experience in this case consisted mostly of the summer I had served as an NBC page during college. Now part of my job was to watch the run-throughs for game shows that we might buy. On one trip to California, I took Jane with me. We walked into a studio filled with friends of the producers and a slew of William Morris agents stacked along the back wall. The show, created by Jack Barry of *21* fame, struck me as fairly dull and silly. As I left, a young agent walked up and introduced himself to me. "I'm Mike Ovitz," he said, and we exchanged a few perfunctory words before I left. No sooner did Jane and I get back to the hotel than the phone rang. "Hi, it's Mike Ovitz, and I was just wondering how you liked the show," he said, unself-consciously.

"It was okay, not bad," I said, searching for a way to end the call as quickly as possible. "Well, how did your wife like it?" he persisted. "Oh, she loved it," I said, figuring that would get me off the hook. The next day, when Jane and I flew back to New York, there were two dozen roses waiting for her. "Dear Jane," said the card, "glad you loved our show. Thanks for the help. Mike Ovitz." Infuriated by his brazenness, I called him immediately. "It's completely inappropriate to try to use my wife to sell your show," I said. He apologized, made three funny jokes, and completely disarmed me. It was my first introduction to Ovitz's gifts as a salesman.

The third responsibility of my new job was to oversee Saturday morning children's programming. I knew as little about kids' shows as I did about soaps, but, once again, Brandon and I dove in. In this case, the pressure for change came partly from outside ABC. Both the FCC and public interest groups such as Action for Children's Television were pushing us to do more responsible programming for children. Our mandate was to somehow find a balance between creating popular shows and producing the sort of higher-minded programs that would satisfy our critics.

One of the first ideas came from an unlikely source: David Mc-Call, head of the advertising agency McCaffrey & McCall. McCall's agency handled ABC's advertising, but the first time he came to see me, it was to lament the quality of children's television. "My kids know the lyrics to every rock song," he told me, "but they can't multiply three and three. Is there any way to put music and information together so kids could learn something?" Out of that conversation, we decided to produce a series of three-minute animated segments that delivered different kinds of information in the form of rock lyrics and original music. Spearheaded by a wonderfully imaginative young McCaffrey & McCall executive named Tom Yohe, we pioneered *Schoolhouse Rock*. *Three Is a Magic Number* served as our pilot episode, and it focused on teaching multiplication and division in an entertaining way. Our most interesting meetings concerned which number to pick. We decided that 3 was the most emotional number of all. Later, we turned to grammar, with segments such as *Conjunction Junction*. We inserted these segments between our regular shows, and successive generations of young children, including my own, grew up singing the songs associated with *Schoolhouse Rock*. Thirty years later, the concept remained strong enough to serve as the basis for an off-Broadway show in New York.

We also launched *The ABC Afterschool Specials*—sixty-minute dramas that focused on social issues relevant to kids. Our premiere effort, *Last of the Curlews*, remains one of my favorite television movies ever. An animated hour produced by Hanna-Barbera, it told two parallel stories. One was about the last male bird of the curlew family taking a long flight to hook up with the last remaining female curlew. The second focused on a father and son setting out on a hunting trip in Kansas. The father ends up shooting and killing the female curlew, and the film concludes with her male mate circling sadly overhead. It was a powerful drama about the power of close relationships and the destructive impact of guns, but without ever being preachy. (No water-skiing elephants in my life anymore.)

We went on to produce *Afterschool Specials* on subjects ranging from teen suicide, to the story of an immigrant boy on his way to join his father in America, to a drama about a girl struggling to join an all-male Little League team. The last, called *Rookie of the Year*, starred an unknown young actress named Jodie Foster. Our goal was to attract not just kids but also their parents—most often their mothers—and it proved highly successful, drawing a whole new audience to late-afternoon television. These dramas not only found a large audience but allowed us to stretch creatively.

When it came to programming Saturday morning, I began by watching hundreds of cartoons. One night, on an impulse, Jane and I took nine-month-old Breck to a drive-in in the Bronx to see our first Disney movie, *Pinocchio*. Breck slept through the film, but I was captivated by it. Despite our smudged windshield and the tinny, drive-in sound system, the quality of the animation was obvious, and the overhead shot in which Stromboli's wagon moves down the street was nothing short of miraculous. Although the movie was made in the 1940s, it was vastly more realistic, complex, and inventive than anything we were doing for our Saturday morning shows. It was unrealistic to try to match what Disney did, since their animated features took four or five years to produce, while at ABC we had to churn out new cartoons every week of the year. Most important, we didn't have a Walt Disney. Still, *Pinocchio* provided a whole new standard against which to measure ourselves.

I also began to look for more contemporary ideas for shows. Everything at the time was on the order of *Heckle & Jeckle* and *Mighty Mouse*. When a group of brothers calling themselves the "Jackson Five" suddenly became hugely popular, I decided to fly to Las Vegas to hear them sing, accompanied by two children's TV producers, Jules Bass and Arthur Rankin. The Jackson Five were charming, sweet, and winning— it was an earlier, more innocent time in their lives—and it occurred to us that we could make a terrific animated cartoon show based on the group. When *The Jackson Five Show* proved successful, we decided to do one based on the Osmond Brothers, another group popular with young kids. We also persuaded Warner Bros. to do a series called *Superfriends*. Pulling together Superman, Batman, Aquaman, and Wonder Woman on the same show seemed a sure-fire formula for a hit.

The impact of these changes was nearly instantaneous. In contrast to the soaps, whose audiences grow deeply attached to the characters, young kids are fickle. Building our soaps was a slow process. Saturday morning success depends on anticipating the next wave and reacting to it just before it crests. In less than a year, we had climbed from third place to number one on Saturday morning, while also winning a slew of Emmys for our *Afterschool Specials*.

In July 1973, after two years of running children's and daytime programming, Marty Starger asked me to return to prime-time development, this time as a vice president. His offer raised the issue of moving. With one young child and a second on the way, Jane and I had both grown unhappy in New York City. We sensed that our children would be better off having grass to play on rather than cement. My first experiment was to try commuting to the city from the same Westchester suburb where my sister lived. One evening, at the end of a long workday, I took a cab from ABC to Grand Central Station, caught the train at the last possible minute, and stood in the aisles until it reached 125th Street. At that point, I was able to find an open seat. I pulled out one of my ABC scripts and started to read but soon felt nauseated, perhaps from the smoke in what was supposed to be a nonsmoking car, perhaps from the relentless rocking of the train. I put the script away and spent the rest of my ride fantasizing about the lives of the commuters around me. At the Mamaroneck station, I called for a cab—no hailing in the suburbs. I arrived at my sister's house just as everyone was finishing dinner. By that time, I had long since concluded that I was far too high-strung to endure crowded, moderate-speed rail transportation. The suburban commuter's life wasn't for me.

Los Angeles seemed increasingly attractive. Jane and I had begun to fall in love with the city during my periodic visits there for work. One summer, we had rented Ricky Nelson's house—yes, Ricky Nelson—in the Hollywood Hills. We loved the experience. My sense of L.A. was still admittedly narrow: working breakfasts at the Bel Air Hotel, with its swans and lush landscaping, and the sand and surf that I mostly knew from movies like *Beach Blanket Bingo*. The most compelling reason for moving was that nearly all prime-time program development took place in L.A. I was tired of the three-hour time difference, which meant being on the phone until 11:00 p.m. in New York when it was only 8:00 p.m. on the West Coast. I wanted to be in the center of the action, during waking hours.

For months, Jane had retained some ambivalence about the move. Then one afternoon, she called me at the office, hysterical. Several months pregnant with our second child, she had been resting on a couch when bullets came blasting in through the window and over her head. By the time the police got there, the incident was over, and we never found out what happened. But for Jane it was the final straw. Marty agreed to our move. It also meant a reunion with Barry, who was now in charge not just of movies-for-television but of all prime-time series development.

We rented Ricky Nelson's house for a second time while we searched for something to buy. One day, Barry mentioned to me that Paul Newman was selling his home off Coldwater Canyon. "He wants to get rid of it quickly," Barry said, "and you really ought to take a look." It was a fantastic place, if a bit grand. We certainly didn't need a screening room or thirteen bathrooms, but when we were able to negotiate a reasonable price, the deal seemed irresistible. Then, on the night before we closed the contract, Jane had a dream that there was a foxhunt going on through the Newman property and we weren't invited. We both interpreted this to mean that we were overstepping ourselves and didn't really belong in such a fancy place. Within a year, the house sold for four times what we would have paid for it. I've always been better at entertainment than at real estate.

During our first three months in Los Angeles, Jane and I began Lamaze classes in preparation for the birth of our second child. Once a week, I would dash home from the office at the end of the day, pick up Jane and her pillow, and head to class. Our fellow Lamaze couples were an eclectic crew, and I was invariably the only man wearing a suit. There was a female rock star and her partner who came to class together in a Rolls-Royce; a woman who brought her mother; another who came with a female friend; and two close friends who had become pregnant at the same time and were now sharing the Lamaze experience. Over eight weeks we all became friendly, and I asked enough questions to learn a great deal about everyone's lives. Finally, the couples began to peel off as they had their babies, and the class came to an end.

Jane went into labor in the middle of the night on October 15, 1973. On the drive to the hospital, we ran out of gas. Fortunately, we were driving on Sunset Boulevard, which has plenty of twenty-four-hour gas stations, and I managed to roll downhill into one. In the time it took to fill our tank, the space between Jane's contractions diminished from six minutes to four. When we arrived at the old Cedars-Sinai—now a Scientology Center—I rushed Jane to a room. Through the Lamaze breathing, she was able to reduce the pain of the contractions, and I marveled at the mind's power over the body. I also couldn't help noticing a curious fact about the scene in the hospital. Here we were in the middle of the night, yet all around us workers were mopping the floors, cleaning the windows, and making everything neat and tidy. When a woman came in to empty the trash from our room for a second time in ten minutes, I casually inquired whether the hospital was always kept this clean.

"Oh, no—this is special," she explained. "We're making a television show here in the morning." I looked out, and walking down the corridor toward our room was the producer and *American Bandstand* host Dick Clark. "What are you doing here?" I asked, stepping into the hall.

"I'm making the special you ordered six months ago in New York," he said. "We're going to film a live birth here tonight." Suddenly, I remembered that I'd hired Dick Clark to produce this show as part of a *Wide World of Entertainment* series we had developed for late night at Marty Starger's request.

"What are *you* doing here?" Clark asked me.

"Having a baby," I said, somewhat proudly, only to look up and see another vaguely familiar face coming toward me. This time it was David Hartman, from ABC's *Good Morning America,* whom Dick Clark had hired to host his special. The last person I encountered made the experience truly surreal. It was Phil Brooks, Jane's obstetrician—in full makeup. After some confusing hellos, I deduced that he was going to deliver the baby on the Dick Clark special. Dr. Brooks genially asked if Jane and I wanted to participate. I politely declined. An hour later, he delivered our healthy redheaded baby boy—more evidence of Jane's own redheadedness!—and then hurried off to assume his more prominent role as a television doctor.

Several months later, Jane and I watched *Of Birth and Babies* with the infant Eric beside us. Dr. Brooks delivered a different baby and David Hartman did an excellent job as the narrator. I decided to put into development a TV movie script called *Lamaze,* based on couples like the ones Jane and I had met going through natural childbirth classes, concluding with the birth of each woman's child. To everyone's surprise, it ended up as the highest-rated television movie of the next season and became the basis for a regular series of movies, *Having Babies!,* which we launched the next fall. In a way, all this was nothing new. I've always found that experiences from everyday life make the best drama.

The biggest challenge Barry and I faced was to turn around prime time. Year after year, ABC had continued to finish last in the prime-time ratings. Barry had been given the top job shortly before I arrived in L.A. Although I wasn't yet in a position to make the ultimate programming decisions, I certainly had more influence than ever before. One of my first pushes was to resurrect the show that Tom Miller and I worked on, *New Family in Town.* The movie *American Graffiti,* directed by George Lucas and starring Ron Howard, had just become a giant hit, as had the Broadway musical *Grease.* These successes provided more evidence that there was a broad audience appetite for nostalgic themes and bolstered our research department's faith in the 1950s as a promising setting for a show.

We renamed Garry Marshall's pilot *Happy Days,* and added a secondary character—a greaser named Fonzie designed to give the show a little more edge. To play the role of this Italian American hoodlum with a soft heart, we cast a Jewish, classically trained actor from Yale named Henry Winkler. He was very funny, convincingly Italian, and the obvious choice. Even so, we had no idea how critical he would prove to be to the show's success. After the casting session at Paramount, Barry and I climbed into Barry's yellow Jaguar, which looked like a banana. As we drove out the studio gate, we noticed Henry Winkler trying to hitchhike. Barry and I looked at each other.

"Nah," Barry said. I agreed.

We drove on, both feeling a little guilty. Years later I confessed the story to Henry, but assured him that he was fortunate. Barry was a tormenting driver. He never carried a license or wore shoes, and he drove at terrifying speeds. I was always relieved to escape his car alive.

Happy Days was launched in January 1974, and it took off immediately, beating out the hit series *Maude* on CBS. Our success prompted a derisive response from Fred Silverman: "CBS," he told a reporter, "is interested in programming for adults in prime time, not for kids." In truth, Silverman was acutely aware that our new show had captured precisely the young-adult demographic group that has long been most attractive to advertisers. By the spring, he had ordered up *Good*

Times, his own nostalgic family comedy aimed at kids, this one starring the comedian Jimmie Walker.

Unfortunately, the rest of our prime-time schedule showed little improvement. In October 1974, a year after I arrived in L.A., Barry accepted an offer from Charlie Bluhdorn, the chief executive of the conglomerate Gulf & Western, to become chairman of its studio, Paramount Pictures. Fred Silverman, forever competitive, was quoted in *Variety* as saying that "Barry Diller has failed upward"—a preposterous statement given Barry's many successes at ABC. Still, it was true that Barry's selection to run Paramount stunned the industry. He was just thirty-two, and he had never before worked at a movie studio, much less run one.

For ABC, Barry's departure left a void. Marty Starger remained in New York as the overall head of programming, but he had begun to devote more and more time to producing his own films and plays. A few months after Barry left, Marty decided to become a full-time producer. For the first time, I effectively became the top prime-time development executive, with the mandate to put together our schedule for the fall 1975 season. I worked closely with Fred Pierce, by then the heir apparent as president of ABC Television. Fred and I couldn't have been more different. The son of a New York City cabdriver, he had worked his way through City College, majoring in accounting. He was the first member of his family to earn a college degree. To the outside world, Fred seemed the embodiment of a by-the-numbers corporate executive. As it turned out, he also had strong creative instincts.

What Fred Pierce and I shared above all was a fierce drive to succeed. Every one of ABC's new shows in the fall of 1974 had failed. Even *Happy Days* was struggling, faced now with competition from Silverman's faster-paced *Good Times* on CBS. One of the first decisions we made was to start filming *Happy Days* live, in front of an audience, with no laugh track added. We rehearsed for four days and shot the show on a sound stage on the fifth day, using at least three cameras. Rewriting often takes place until the very last minute, influenced by the live audience response. We also decided that moving Henry Winkler's Fonz into a more prominent role would add excitement. Sure enough, *Happy Days* jumped in the ratings immediately, and "the Fonz" became a national phenomenon.

It still remained difficult to attract first-rank television producers to ABC. CBS had long since locked up top writer-producers such as Jim Brooks and Allan Burns, who were writing *The Mary Tyler Moore Show*; Gene Reynolds and Larry Gelbart, who did *M*A*S*H;* and Norman Lear, who created *All in the Family* and *Maude*. We learned to make a virtue out of necessity. Rather than go after the biggest names, we sought out promising younger writers with more limited track records, or older ones who had fallen out of favor but who clearly had talent.

Danny Arnold was one example. A crusty, intense New Yorker with a highly original mind, Arnold had written and produced the Thurberesque *My World and Welcome to It* for NBC. A quirky, original concept, it was a critical success but a commercial failure. Arnold's next idea was more accessible. A half-hour comedy he titled *Barney Miller*, it was set in a New York police precinct. Unlike most cop shows, it was more talk than action. As with *Happy Days*, our program department loved the pilot, but the top ABC executives decided not to put it on the air after seeing the research. The preview audiences were especially put off by Arnold's novel use of several interwoven story lines in a single show—an approach that Steven Bochco would eventually make the signature of his tremendously successful hour-long dramas, including *Hill Street Blues, L.A. Law,* and *NYPD Blue*. Although we failed to lobby *Barney Miller* onto the fall schedule for 1974, my consolation was permission to order four more scripts, keeping the series alive as a potential midseason replacement.

In January 1975, with ABC still struggling in third place, we convinced Fred Pierce to give *Barney Miller* a shot. It started slowly in the ratings, but the fifth episode centered on the naive Detective Wojohowicz falling for a fast-talking prostitute on his beat. Suddenly we had a controversy. *Barney Miller* ran from 8:00 to 8:30 p.m., in the so-called Family Hour, and ABC's in-house censors—euphemistically called "Standards and Practices"—ruled that a show about a prostitute was inappropriate for that time period. Danny insisted that he would close down production on his series if ABC didn't allow the episode to go forward. The showdown attracted enormous media attention, and ABC's censors finally gave in. When the episode aired a couple of days later, a whole new audience tuned in, and overnight, we had a hit.

By midyear, we had developed a slate of series that seemed promising, led by several new action shows including *S.W.A.T.*, *Baretta*, and *Starsky and Hutch*. We also launched the situation comedy *Welcome Back, Kotter*, with a cast that included a young actor named John Travolta. Within a few episodes it was clear that Travolta had an exceptional presence. He quickly became at least as big a lure for kids as Henry Winkler's Fonzie. In the press, we were given credit for a hip, urban-oriented strategy that targeted a young audience which neither CBS nor NBC seemed to be reaching. Our approach was really much simpler: to make dramas and comedies that we liked ourselves, hoping that the audience shared our taste. By May 1975, a half dozen of these shows were on their way to becoming hits. For years, we had been experts in failure. No one asked for raises, and no executives threatened to leave. Now, for the first time, we had to learn how to manage in success. We had to contend with hot stars and newly temperamental writers, producers, and directors. I myself had to learn how to prioritize my phone calls, returning the important ones promptly.

I also agreed to a long-term contract extension, assuming that I had now earned the right to continue as ABC's top prime-time programmer. But in mid-June, Fred Pierce called me into his thirty-eighth-floor office. "I've decided to hire Fred Silverman away from CBS and make him the head of all programming," he told me. I understood Pierce's impulse. Silverman was clearly the leading programmer in television. Stealing him away immediately weakened CBS, which had been number one in prime time for more than a decade. But none of that was especially comforting to me. For the first time in my career, I felt underestimated and decided to look for a way out. I immediately called the heads of two studios who had periodically offered me jobs over the years. They were slow to get back to me, and when they did, they had forgotten about those earlier offers. It was sobering. As a supplicant, I was no longer such a hot property.

A more practical streak kicked in. Without a better alternative, it made no sense for me to quit my job simply because my feelings were hurt. "I'm just going to have to make my peace with it and do the best I can," I told Jane. Pierce implored me to stay at ABC. "I'll protect your independence and I won't let Silverman run over you," he said. "ABC will be stronger than ever with the two of you working together."

To my surprise, I got along terrifically with Silverman from the start. Contrary to the stories I'd been told about his fierce temper and his need for total control, he was solicitous of me, neither arrogant nor autocratic. We agreed on almost everything creatively, and he seemed relieved to have someone working for him who made things happen and didn't need constant oversight. Fred was also entertaining to be around —street-smart and very direct, with a wry, self-deprecating sense of humor. Passionate and theatrical, he had outsized appetites—for food and tobacco and conversation, but most of all for television itself, which he seemed to live and breathe twenty-four hours a day.

Being anything but loyal to your immediate boss is almost always stupid and self-destructive. Still, having a close relationship with my boss's boss provided an extra level of protection and comfort. Silverman was surely aware that if we had a major disagreement, I could take my case to Fred Pierce. Fortunately, it proved unnecessary. Silverman was in New York, I was in Los Angeles, and he allowed me full license to run our West Coast operation.

Silverman left our entire group intact when he arrived. It included Brandon Stoddard, then in charge of movies and miniseries; Brandon Tartikoff, a young executive who would eventually run NBC; and Marcy Carsey and Tom Werner, who together ran comedy. I hired Marcy as a junior executive when she was three months pregnant, and within a short time she was developing her own shows for the network. One of her first successes was *Soap*—a hip, wry, novel takeoff on traditional soap operas written by Susan Harris. It became an instant hit. Fred himself was especially good at scheduling and tinkering with shows. He had the idea, for example, of convincing Garry Marshall to create a spin-off series based on Laverne De Fazio and Shirley Feeney, two friends of Fonzie who had appeared in one episode of *Happy Days*. *Laverne and Shirley* became an overnight hit.

In addition to focusing on prime-time series, we continued to experiment with more ambitious TV movies. Perhaps my favorite was *Friendly Fire*. A year after Marty Starger left ABC to become an independent producer, I ran into him on Fifth Avenue in New York, and he described a great article that he had just read in *The New Yorker* by C.D.B. Bryan. It was about an Iowa farm mother whose son is killed in Vietnam. Refusing to accept the government's explanation for her son's death, she uncovers deceptions and cover-ups and ultimately learns that he was actually killed by one of his own men. In the process, she launches an unlikely antiwar movement built around other mothers. We commissioned the project immediately and it ultimately won numerous critical awards.

The other new programming form that Barry Diller had helped to pioneer on ABC was the miniseries. In 1973, Barry had commissioned a twelve-hour drama based on Irwin Shaw's novel *Rich Man, Poor Man*. Despite predictions that the audience wouldn't tune in to a program on consecutive nights, the series proved to be a gigantic success when it finally aired, in 1976. Several months later, that success was overshadowed by another project that Barry bought just before leaving ABC: Alex Haley's *Roots*. A powerfully archetypal story of the strength of family ties and of triumph over extraordinary adversity, *Roots* went on to become the television event of the 1970s. Transcending race, it touched people from every conceivable background. More than 100 million people watched the final episode. The decision to schedule *Roots* over eight consecutive nights dramatically intensified its impact. The irony is that this move was made with precisely the opposite motive in mind. The original plan had been to run one episode each week over twelve weeks. At a certain point, the research department started to get cold feet. We hadn't yet seen the finished product and they were nervous about how wide the appeal would be for an all-black epic.

Finally, Silverman decided to view the entire twelve hours of *Roots* over a single weekend. He loved the series, but concluded that it was too risky to schedule the show every Monday evening for nearly three months. If it did poorly in the ratings, as he feared it might, it could undermine the whole first quarter of 1977 for ABC in prime time. By playing it all during one week in January—and avoiding the key February sweeps ratings period, the show's overall effect on ABC wouldn't be so great. As it turned out, *Roots* attracted unprecedented ratings for a dramatic show, as well as enormous kudos to ABC for giving the series such prominence. Silverman, in turn, was recanonized as a scheduling genius.

Meanwhile, I was beginning to feel restless. It wasn't so much that Fred was receiving nearly all the credit for the network's turnaround. I considered that inevitable. The far bigger issue was that I didn't see much upward mobility at ABC and I felt ready for a new challenge. The opportunity first arose in the late spring of 1976. The producer David Geffen was serving what would turn out to be a short-lived stint as vice chairman of Warner Bros. He called me one day and asked if I would consider coming over to head the studio's television division. I wasn't especially interested in another job solely in television, but I did like being courted. I agreed to have a meeting with Geffen and subsequently to sit down with his bosses, Ted Ashley and Frank Wells. Hollywood is a small town, and it happened that Geffen was a close friend of Marlo Thomas, who mentioned to her old pal Barry Diller that Geffen was trying to hire me.

Suddenly, Barry's competitive instincts were stoked. We had barely spoken since he left ABC for Paramount two years earlier. He was hanging out now with Warren Beatty and Robert Evans and other people in the film business, and I was still just a TV executive. He sought me out now only when he wanted something. On one occasion, for example, he called to ask if ABC would agree to let John Travolta out of *Welcome Back, Kotter* long enough to star in a movie called *Days of Heaven*, which Paramount had committed to make with director Terrence Malick.

"Barry, you know I'm not going to do that," I told him. "Go find your own actor." He ended up casting Richard Gere to play the lead role. It was an inspired choice, and *Days of Heaven* remains one of my favorite movies of all time.

Midway during my talks with Geffen and Warner Bros., I received a different sort of call from Barry. "I hear you've really matured as an executive," he said. "You even return your phone calls." Barry was still struggling to turn Paramount around and he wanted to sound me out about being his number two. I would be coming to feature films with the same lack of experience he had been forced to overcome two years earlier. But he trusted my creative instincts, and he knew that he could work with me. I had been a successful conduit between Barry and other executives at ABC, and it occurred to me that he hoped I might play a similar role at Paramount. I also guessed that Barry didn't want me to go to work for his friend Geffen or for Warner Bros., a chief competitor. At the end of our first meeting, Barry offered me a job as president of Paramount. Like him, I was thirty-four years old.

It seemed like the right move. I'd still be working for a strong, difficult boss, but now I'd have much broader responsibilities, which included not only developing TV shows but also overseeing feature films —an entirely new area that intrigued me. I had a contract with ABC, but I made it very clear to both Freds that I wanted to accept the Paramount offer. Silverman immediately expressed a willingness to let me go. Fred Pierce was more reluctant, but in the end he too gave in. Within three months of my departure ABC would reach number one in the prime-time ratings. I never looked back.

CHAPTER

4

The Idea Is Everything

JUST BEFORE I WAS OFFICIALLY HIRED, CHARLIE BLUHDORN, chairman of Gulf & Western, told Barry that he wanted to meet me. Charlie never did anything in an ordinary way, so instead of going to his office, we got together over brunch at Nate & Al's Delicatessen in Beverly Hills. The group included me, Barry, Charlie, his wife, Yvette, and Richard Snyder, then chairman of Simon & Schuster, another G&W subsidiary. I felt drawn to Charlie immediately. He was full of energy, passionate about the movie business, and obviously very smart. He also came to immediate conclusions. At mid-meal, he turned to Barry and me. "You're the future," he told us, in between bites of a corned beef sandwich. "It's a great business, making movies, and you boys are going to save the company."

Paramount was struggling, despite its illustrious past. The company had been founded by a Hungarian immigrant named Adolph Zukor, one of the earliest and most enduring of Hollywood moguls, who headed it for fifty years. Its list of stars and directors ranged from Mae West to Cary Grant; W. C. Fields to Bing Crosby and Bob Hope; Cecil B. deMille to Billy Wilder. In 1964, Zukor finally retired, at the age of ninety-one, and his longtime president Barney Balaban became chairman of the board. Two years later, Bluhdorn bought Paramount in a deal that Martin Davis, then chief financial officer for the studio, secretly brokered behind Balaban's back.

Over the next several years, the studio sometimes struggled financially, even as it produced its share of blockbusters. *Love Story* set a Paramount record by grossing $100 million in 1970 and earning seven Academy Award nominations. The following year, Frank Yablans, having risen through the ranks in sales, was named president of the studio. Bob Evans continued as head of production. During their tenure, Paramount produced Francis Ford Coppola's two great *Godfather* movies—both of which won Oscars for Best Picture—and a raft of other hits, including *Chinatown, Nashville, Paper Moon, Save the Tiger,* and *The Conversation.*

The problem was that neither Yablans nor Evans remained in Bluhdorn's favor. While many of their movies were successful, he believed that they paid insufficient attention to controlling costs and to the lucrative but less fashionable television business. Evans was also spending much of his time producing his own films, while Yablans half jokingly announced that he intended to make his acting debut in an upcoming Paramount film, Elaine May's *Mikey and Nicky.* In the summer of 1974, Andrew Tobias wrote an article for *New York* magazine titled "The Apprenticeship of Frank Yablans," in which Yablans was decidedly less than respectful in his comments about his boss.

A few weeks later, Bluhdorn decided to bring Barry in as chairman of Paramount. Barry couldn't fire Yablans, because Bluhdorn made it clear that he wasn't willing to pay off Yablans's contract. Barry solved the problem by setting up an organizational structure that Yablans was certain to find intolerable. All of the executives who had previously reported to him would now report to Barry instead. It was a technique that Barry called "firing by process"—essentially freezing a person out. Within six weeks, Yablans settled his contract and quit. Bob Evans left a short time later to become a full-time producer, and Barry soon hired David Picker, the former head of production at United Artists (UA), as president of Paramount.

Bringing me to Paramount served a purpose for Barry similar to Bluhdorn's hiring Barry over Yablans. Picker came from a legendary movie family (his uncle had owned United Artists and his father had been president of Loews), and he was very well liked in the Hollywood community. But he and Barry were a poor fit from the start. Picker's style was laid back, passive, and laissez-faire. Barry's was intense, aggressive, and completely hands-on. At UA, the affable Picker had been famous for leaving filmmakers alone, and he brought the same philosophy to Paramount. Barry believed in tight financial discipline and close creative involvement in the moviemaking process. Rather than face his dissatisfaction with Picker directly, Barry did what he had done two years earlier with Yablans. He took away most of his responsibilities, and, in this case, gave them to me.

My way of dealing with the whole messy situation was to ignore it and focus instead on the job at hand, which had its own obstacles. The major players in the film business made no secret of believing that one of their own ought to be running the studio. Now, both top executives at Paramount came from the world of television. Barry had taken easily to the sort of socializing that is central to the way deals get done in the movie business, and in a short time, he achieved a modicum of acceptance. By contrast, I was still a pure television guy. To Barry's chagrin, it took me six months to stop referring to movies as "shows."

I had spent a good deal of time developing made-for-television movies and miniseries at ABC, so the movie form wasn't entirely new to me. I had my first idea for a film on my way to work the week I started at Paramount. The inspiration, indirectly, was the car I was driving—one of the unexpected perks of my new job. Nobody at ABC in New York was given a car, but toward the end of my negotiation with Barry, he asked me what kind I wanted. In New York, a used car had always been preferable to a new one, because whatever kind of car you owned, it was inevitably banged up by drivers maneuvering in and out of parking spaces. When your car was stolen, as mine was three times, you felt a certain relief mixed in with a sense of violation. "Well, that piece of junk is gone," I would say to Jane. "Now we can go back to Queens Boulevard and find one that runs a little better."

After moving to Los Angeles, we upgraded slightly—to a new Audi—but that proved of no value when it came to trying to park at a restaurant. No self-respecting valet put an Audi anywhere near his establishment, which meant that Jane and I were inevitably the last to have our car delivered when we finished dinner. The same was true when it came to being cleared at the gates of movie studios. During my years at

ABC, I would frequently drive over to a studio to see some executive and stop at the guard gate. "Michael Eisner to see Mr. So-and-So," I'd say. "Just a minute," the guard would respond and then walk back inside his outpost to check on me. While I waited, he would wave through countless drivers in Porsches, BMWs, and Mercedes. When Barry told me that he had chosen a Mercedes for himself, I said, "Sounds good to me." Suddenly I had a powerful, highly tuned 1976 Colorado Buff Mercedes convertible 450.

On my first day behind the wheel, I raced down Santa Monica Boulevard with the stereo blasting. Suddenly, I heard a siren. Looking in my rearview mirror, I saw a cop, the lights flashing atop his car, signaling me to pull over. A big, burly, intimidating-looking guy, he literally pulled me out of my car. "Do you have any idea how fast you were going?" he asked. I said I didn't, at which point he threw me against the side of his car while he checked my license and registration. I was both frightened and fascinated. Peering into the window of his car, I saw that it was filled with enough computers, electronic equipment, and racked guns to operate a small CIA outpost.

"I'm really sorry, I apologize, it's my first day in this car," I said. "I've never owned anything like it before, and I just didn't realize how fast I was going." At that point, he relaxed a little, told me he was having a bad day, wrote me a ticket, and off I drove toward Paramount. For the rest of the ride, I found myself thinking about this guy's life as a cop—working in Beverly Hills protecting the rich and famous while almost surely living in a blue-collar community an hour away. The more I thought about it, the more I felt that there was an interesting movie to be made about the life of a Beverly Hills cop.

When I finally arrived at Paramount, it was evident that Barry hadn't prepared anyone for my arrival. I barely even met David Picker. Barry never thought to hold a cocktail party or a meeting of senior staff to welcome me. Finally, after a couple of days, I said to him, "Listen, I'm the new president of the company. You've got to take me around and introduce me to people here." He seemed surprised, but reluctantly agreed. At midmorning, we set off down the corridor in the main Paramount building, knocking on people's mostly closed doors. At one point, we came to the office of a midlevel woman who also happened to be the daughter of the head of another major entertainment company in town. Barry had hired her as a favor to her father. We knocked on her door.

"Just a minute," a female voice said, and then there was a lot of scurrying and rustling around. Finally, the door opened. A young, disheveled-looking man emerged, still pulling on his clothes as he flew by us. The female executive followed, with a slightly flushed look on her face. Barry just turned to me and shrugged his shoulders. Plainly, the culture I was joining was very different from the one I'd left behind at ABC.

This became even clearer several weeks later when I attended an advance preview for one of the movies developed before my arrival, a remake of *King Kong*, starring Jessica Lange. The preview was held in Denver, and it included Charlie Bluhdorn, who loved events like these, and Dino de Laurentiis, the producer of the movie. At ABC, people like Fred Pierce and Leonard Goldenson could easily have passed for bankers or corporate lawyers. They were staid and businesslike. By contrast, people like Charlie and Dino were outsize personalities, funny and flamboyant, expressive and excitable. They hugged and mugged, joked and threw tantrums. They lived in a world of Gulfstream jets and grand gestures. I pretended to be comfortable, and so did Barry, but we really weren't.

The vision that Barry and I shared lay somewhere in between the meticulousness and rigidity of the network television culture and the freedom and looseness of the motion picture culture. At ABC, discipline was imposed on us by the fact that we had to fill twenty-one hours of prime time every week, set budgets based on what advertisers were willing to pay for spots on shows, and respond to the pressure of daily ratings. In addition, the FCC was an ever-vigilant watchdog. By contrast, the movie business was largely unregulated by the government and movies themselves were budgeted far more subjectively. There was room for extraordinary creativity and huge scores, but also for spectacular overreaching and devastating losses. It was both exciting and overwhelming. Our challenge at Paramount was to bring financial discipline and sanity to the movie business without sacrificing creativity and spontaneity—to find a more reasonable balance between art and commerce.

Together, Barry and David Picker had been responsible for several promising movies, including *Marathon Man, Looking for Mr. Goodbar,* and *The Bad News Bears*. The problem when I arrived was that we had only a handful of scripts in development. After my second or third day on the job, I called an early morning meeting of all of our production heads—perhaps a dozen people. "We're going to come up with twenty good ideas today," I told them, "even if we have to stay here till midnight." I began by pitching my cop story, and we agreed to put it into development. Many years and many scripts later it would evolve into the hit comedy *Beverly Hills Cop*. By the end of that first day, we had come up with several other strong ideas.

This was the way I'd always operated. At ABC, the demand for new shows had been relentless, and it was impossible to be successful in television simply by relying on outside suppliers to provide ideas. It never occurred to me to take a different approach when it came to developing movies. Why wait for writers to come to us with ideas or for agents and producers to put us into bidding wars for hot scripts? Only later did I realize that this notion bordered on the revolutionary. Even now, most studios are in the business of financing other people's ideas and scripts, and marketing the movies that result. Few of them regularly develop their own ideas.

By far the most impressive person at our first meeting was a thirty-one-year-old, midlevel executive in the story department named Don Simpson—bearded, barrel-chested, and blunt. It was immediately clear that Don was smarter, better read, and more theatrical than anyone else in the room. He was brash but articulate, exceptionally knowledgeable about movies, and unabashedly in love with Hollywood. Born and raised in Alaska, where his parents were Bible-thumping fundamentalists, Don fancied himself a literary rebel. "Basically I lived in the library and stole cars," he later told a reporter. After graduating from the University of Oregon, Don made his way to Hollywood and joined the marketing department at Warner Bros., where he wrote screenplays in his spare time. He was hired at Paramount just before I arrived.

I appreciated Don partly because he was the only person in our group who seemed to know something about both movies and literature. I also liked him personally. Funny, melodramatic, and larger than life, he loved to regale me with tales of his childhood in Alaska or describe his latest adventures as a single guy. I was fascinated by his endless contradictions. Tough and macho on the outside, Don was sensitive, vulnerable, and even sweet underneath. He had an instinctive feel for commercial movie ideas—what he liked to call a "cheeseburger heart"—but he was also a closet intellectual who read voraciously. He was arrogant and fiercely independent, yet insecure and hungry for conventional success. At moments, I viewed Don with envy: the parties, the freedom, the self-indulgent adventures that had never really been a part of my own more conventional youth. More often though, I saw how lonely he was, and how much he hungered for a more stable life like my own. In time, success became Don's worst enemy. The more power and money he amassed, the more insecure he felt and the more abusively he behaved—to others and ultimately to himself. Eventually, his excesses with drugs and alcohol would cost him his life.

But in the early years, Don was a highly creative executive with great story sense. Within a month of my arrival at Paramount, we sat down together with the writer Paul Brickman and managed to knock out a script in a few days for a sequel to *The Bad News Bears*—the first movie Barry had put into production when he got to Paramount. As he later put it, "Having been at ABC, I was used to quick action and reaction. At Paramount, nothing seemed to happen. Then one day I looked in a drawer and there was a script called *The Bad News Bears*. This I understood. Three acts. A rotten little team gets better, falls apart and then prevails. I said, 'My God, a story.'" The movie was a hit. It was Len Goldberg, our former boss at ABC and now an independent producer, who suggested a sequel. By the spring of 1977 *The Bad News Bears in Breaking Training* was in the theaters. It proved to be nearly as successful as the original. Paul Brickman went on to write and direct *Risky Business,* starring Tom Cruise, while Simpson became our main creative executive.

Saturday Night Fever was the first movie to really put us back on the map. Ironically, it was David Picker who brought the project to the studio. He and Barry made the deal with the producer Robert Stigwood, who owned rights to the *New York* magazine article "Tribal Rites of a Saturday Night," by Nik Cohn, which inspired the movie. Cohn's was an accessible, emotionally appealing, classically "high concept" story about overcoming the odds and having the courage of your convictions. Tony Manero, a working-class kid from Brooklyn, refuses to settle for life as the best dancer and the coolest guy in his local neighborhood. Instead, he reaches for a bigger dream, literally crossing the Brooklyn Bridge at the movie's end to try to launch a new life in Manhattan.

Above all, it was the basic premise that made the movie work—one young man's passionate search for a better life. I bought into it completely and always wanted to meet the *real* Tony Manero—only to learn twenty years later in a *New York* magazine follow-up story by Nik Cohn that there was no Tony Manero. Cohn had created the character out of an amalgam of people he met during his research.

Rather than seeking an expensive movie star for the lead role in *Saturday Night Fever*, we agreed on John Travolta, the appealing young actor Barry and I had first cast in *Welcome Back, Kotter.* With modest costs for both talent and production, we were able to keep our costs very low. We further minimized our downside exposure by selling broadcast rights for a substantial sum to ABC. Travolta was not yet a movie star, but he was clearly a big draw on television, and that made the movie more valuable to ABC. Along the way, we learned several lessons. One was the power of a new face. An established movie star can help create a box office "floor" for a movie, but often a ceiling as well. In effect, the audience has already cast its ballot on the star—for and against—just as they do for certain best-selling authors whose novels consistently sell in the same range. A new star or author is someone the entire moviegoing audience can discover together, which is what happened with John Travolta, much as it would two decades later with Leonardo DiCaprio in *Titanic.*

I still remember the moment when I realized that *Saturday Night Fever* was going to be not just a critical and commercial success but a cultural phenomenon. In mid-December 1977—a week after the movie premiered—I was skiing in Vail and I heard the title song, "Staying Alive," playing on a portable radio as I got onto the chairlift. Two runs later, I heard the song again when I got off at the top of the mountain. Later that day, I heard it a third time in the warming hut. "Jane," I said, "something's going on here." *Saturday Night Fever* was released at Christmas, just as disco had begun to sweep the country. Both the movie and the Bee Gees soundtrack became giant hits—an experience we would repeat in movies ranging from *Grease* to *Flashdance* to *Footloose.*

In the case of *Saturday Night Fever*, it was Stigwood's company that put together the soundtrack. The music became another way to promote the film, just as the film's success brought more attention to the album. It was my first and nearly my last experience at Paramount with the power of synergy. In this instance, it was almost wholly unplanned and unexpected. But to my never-ending astonishment and frustration, every subsequent effort I made to cross-promote and cooperate with other divisions at Gulf & Western was rebuffed. In particular, Barry and I tried to work with Simon & Schuster, believing that some of their books could likely be adapted into movies. Unfortunately, Dick Snyder's job was to maximize profits for Simon & Schuster, not Gulf &Western. As a result—and perhaps because of his competitiveness with Barry and me—he often permitted other film studios to see Simon & Schuster manuscripts before we did.

Over the years, Barry and I tried unsuccessfully to persuade Charlie to let us place promotional flyers for our upcoming movies into the paychecks of Gulf & Western's 100,000 employees. We also sought without satisfaction to convince the executives at Simon & Schuster, or Kayser/Roth, or Madison Square Garden, or the New York Knicks and Rangers—all of them owned by G&W—to help promote our products or to accept our help in promoting theirs. (I never did have an idea for Gulf & Western's coffin-manufacturing division!) Each business in G&W operated as a separate fiefdom. We tried to exploit the success of the brand names we developed at Paramount. *Happy Days* and *Laverne and Shirley*, for example, were the two highest-rated shows on television when I got to Paramount. I urged that we launch a 1950s-style restaurant chain and build a series of *Laverne and Shirley* bowling alleys. But these suggestions fell on deaf ears. To nearly everyone at G&W, including Charlie, Paramount meant production of television and motion pictures—period.

The biggest wild card in my new job turned out to be Charlie himself. Less than two months after my arrival at Paramount, Barry suggested that Jane and I and our children come to the Dominican Republic for Thanksgiving. This would be a good chance, Barry said, for me to get to know Charlie, who had vast holdings there, including the giant resort Casa de Campo. Jane was cautious. "I'm not sure that the Bluhdorns really want two little children intruding on their holiday," she said. I knew she was right that others might not appreciate a three-year-old with a constantly running nose nor a six-year-old who never seemed to stop running. But I wasn't about to leave our kids at home, and this invitation seemed to be a command appearance. The four of us flew commercial to Miami, where I assumed we would connect to

Santo Domingo. Instead, the G&W corporate Gulfstream was waiting when we arrived. Small planes made me very nervous, but I had my children with me, and fathers are supposed to be brave. I boldly entered the plane. The flight was uneventful—and very convenient. We landed on a small runway at Casa de Campo, right alongside the fairway of the golf course. Charlie was waiting on the tarmac, and when the door opened, he immediately bowed dramatically and dropped to his knees. "My saviour has come, my saviour has come," he said, as we walked down the steps. I can't imagine what my children thought.

Charlie had arranged to put us up at Oscar de la Renta's house, and we were taken there by golf cart. Breck and Eric were in heaven. Jane and I felt embarrassed. When we arrived at the house, we looked for the other guests we had been told would be joining us there, including Barry and Diane Von Furstenberg, his girlfriend at the time; Dick Snyder and his then wife, Joni Evans; and the agent David Obst and his then wife, Lynda, an editor at *The New York Times Magazine*. The first person we ran into was Diane, who happened to be sunning herself topless by the pool, as waiters walked back and forth and armed guards patrolled the house to protect us from some undisclosed threat. Diane greeted us all warmly, and unself-consciously. Breck and Eric stared at her until we took them off to unpack. That evening we had dinner at Casa Grande, the main house, where Charlie lived. When Breck wandered off and managed to drive a golf cart into the pool, Jane's worst fears came true.

But mostly things went very well. Charlie loved sitting in an icy spa and talking. Having been through this ritual several times before, Barry disappeared for most of the weekend. I spent hours with Charlie discussing movies. He was an endless fount of ideas, some of them utterly outlandish. At one point, he told me about a concept he had for a film in which Sitting Bull meets Hitler. "We ought to get Dustin Hoffman involved," he said. At another point, he suggested a *Bad News Bears* sequel set in Cuba, in which Castro hits the winning home run. I replied that the American kids probably ought to win the game, and that in any case, Castro might be a little old to play baseball. Undaunted, Charlie insisted that he was going to call Castro himself and pitch the idea.

No sooner did we return to Los Angeles than Charlie began to call me regularly. (He never mentioned Castro again.) Barry probably would have preferred to manage Charlie and me separately, without any communication between us, but he soon realized that wasn't going to be possible. Charlie refused to accept any traditional corporate lines of authority. He was the founder, and founders are not bound by rules. He could talk to any servant in his empire whenever he felt like it, and that was that. When Barry understood that I wasn't using my relationship with our boss to gain any advantage, handling Charlie drew us closer together. It became our shared challenge.

Each time I finished talking with Charlie, I would pick up the phone to tell Barry exactly what had happened. We laughed, plotted, and commiserated. Charlie could be brilliant, entertaining, and passionately supportive one moment, and then mercurial, arbitrary, and paranoid the next. There was always an aura of intrigue about him. Born in Vienna in 1926, he had arrived in New York as a refugee in 1942, telling some people that he was Jewish and others that he was not. His first job was as a cotton broker, and his skills trading commodities made him wealthy by his early twenties. Persuasive and entrepreneurial, he convinced banks to lend him the money to begin buying up companies in the mid-1950s. Gulf & Western grew into a conglomerate made up of companies ranging from Jersey Zinc to the Consolidated Cigar Corporation, the Collyer Insulated Wire Company to Paramount—none of which had much to do with each other. Charlie was also an exceptional trader. The stock portfolio he built at G&W was worth just over $1 billion when he died and would be worth many times that today.

For all his brilliance, Charlie mistrusted nearly everyone and made life chaotic and very difficult for his top-ranking people. He would regularly take calls from outsiders complaining about Barry and me, for example, believing every word he had just heard—until he talked to the next person. Early in my tenure, he would phone and try to get me to be critical of Barry, abandoning the tactic only when he realized that I always told Barry everything that he said to me. On this subject, Barry and I learned from Charlie by reverse example. Publicly and unequivocally supporting the people who work for you, we both came to understand, is sound management. It's also the right thing to do.

Whenever I failed to take one of Charlie's calls immediately, he became very upset and sometimes even a little hysterical. On one occasion, he called while I was in a meeting with Robert Redford, and I told my secretary to say I would get back to him. Over the next hour, he phoned several more times. When my meeting finally ended, I called him, and he began yelling at me: "I'm the chairman, how dare you not take my call?" I tried to soothe him, but he was furious. After we hung up, he called Barry and complained some more. Then Barry phoned me and tried to negotiate a truce. Charlie, in his incredibly melodramatic way, took to his bed for the entire next day. Finally, under prodding from both Barry and Charlie's wife, Yvette, I gave in and called to apologize. It was impossible to outlast Charlie, even when he behaved like a child.

Barry had his own temper and volatility, and he could be curt and harsh with the people who worked for him, particularly when he sensed any weakness or uncertainty. I soon began to serve as something of a buffer between him and the other executives at Paramount, as I had done to a lesser degree at ABC. Barry was far kinder to those who stood up to him, which I'd done ever since our first days working together. I assumed something of a mother's role now, protecting the children from a brilliant and powerful but difficult and demanding father—much as my mother had done in our family. As for my own relationship with Barry, it was far closer than people imagined. Barry was explosive where I was more even-tempered. (At least that's my view. He would probably argue the exact opposite.) He looked at the world darkly and saw trouble at every turn, while I was upbeat and optimistic. He was single, childless, and highly social; I was married with a family and barely social at all.

But in many ways, the superficial differences masked the deeper similarities. We were both driven, compulsive, and hugely competitive. We were both risk takers creatively and risk-averse in business. When it came to choosing movies, we were each drawn to story above all other factors. I often functioned as the enthusiast and Barry as the skeptic. If I tended to fall in love with projects, he looked instinctively for where they were likely to go wrong. As he once put it, "I will focus on all the negatives, but with the comfort that Michael is pushing to go forward." His style was to make absolute pronouncements about why something wouldn't work. Mine was to question his certainty—and to stand up for my passions.

"Why won't it work?" I might ask. "Am I supposed to accept what you say as some vision from God and leave it at that?"

But at other times we reversed roles. If Barry became too enthusiastic about a project, I reflexively turned my attention to its liabilities. We operated as an instinctive check and balance to one another. It was true that Barry preferred to think of himself as the auteur, with classier and higher-minded tastes than mine. I earned the reputation—partly promoted by him—for having more commercial, mass-appeal tastes. Even that was misleading. Barry did embrace *Reds* and *Atlantic City*, while I loved *Flashdance* and *Footloose*. But it was also true that I championed *The Elephant Man*, while he made the decision to buy *Friday the 13th*. We were equally enthusiastic about films ranging from the pure popcorn of *Grease* to the Academy Award–winning *Ordinary People*. Our shared priority was making successful movies. As Barry once put it, "There are rare times when the material you read in a script plays better on the screen, but generally it gets worse. Only if you keep the selection process clean—in the mainstream of your interest—have you got a prayer of success."

Barry and I made it clear to our production people that they had to be willing to fight for the projects they believed in. I hate having executives agree with me nearly as much as I hate having them disagree with me. I want them to have no fear of being fired for what they say, but never to take their jobs for granted. I always straddled this fence myself. "I'm just going to say exactly what I think," I would tell myself in my early years. "I have ability and I can always get another job." But then, just before I spoke, I'd find a polite way to couch it, in order not to unnecessarily antagonize my boss, choosing a middle ground between self-assertion and self-preservation. Over time, I discovered that a similar approach was effective as a boss. When I respond to someone's work, I try my best to focus first on something positive, to be complimentary and encouraging before I mention what's missing or needs further work. I've learned that it's never the first effort, or the second, or even the third that results in excellence. The best work requires the willingness to go the extra mile even after you feel that you've just completed a marathon —to exceed what you consciously believe is possible.

Barry shared this passion. As he once put it, "Our process is advocacy and yelling." So we debated, and disagreed, and even fought. In the end, we agreed on nearly everything. When it came to dealing with the creative community, we traded back and forth the roles of good cop and bad cop. Our common goal was to resist the constant seductions, hype, and the temptation to overspend. I'm not certain that either of us could have succeeded alone, but by sharing the same agenda, we were able to hold the line. Our biggest bond was that we trusted and respected each other more than we did nearly anyone else. Together, we brought to Paramount the financial discipline that we had learned during a decade of working in television. There were no comparable limits in the movie business when we began. You could spend $8 million on a film and lose it all, but you could also spend $50 million and earn a profit of $100 million. I still remember the first time I discussed a deal with Richard Zimbert, head of business affairs at Paramount, with whom Barry and I had worked back at ABC. I told Dick I wanted him to buy a script from a certain writer.

"Great. What do you want to pay him?" he asked.

"Whatever's normal," I replied.

"There is no normal in the movies," Dick said.

With Barry's support, we began to establish guidelines. One of our first challenges was to find a way of making movies that minimized our exposure. Neither Barry nor I was inclined to swing for the fences —whether that meant investing in high-cost movies, going after the highest-priced stars and directors, entering into bidding wars for "hot" scripts, or paying a premium for "packages" put together by agents who then took a substantial fee off the top.

In contrast to the blockbuster mentality that prevailed at most of the other major studios, we evolved the concept of hitting for singles and doubles. That meant making movies for modest budgets based on strong ideas that we developed ourselves. Profligacy and irresponsibility about money were frequently mistaken in the movie business for style and daring. Our inclination was to treat the company's money as if it were our own. We took a certain pleasure in resisting the lemminglike tendency to overpay for stars, or to approve budgets that made no sense.

Michael Ovitz and I were friends outside the office, for example, but I consistently resisted paying the astronomical fees he sought for packaging his clients in projects. Sue Mengers, then one of the most successful agents in town, made no secret of her frustration with me. "I find Eisner the toughest person I negotiate with, and I don't mean that as a compliment," she once told a reporter. "He simply must win." Barry was more willing than I was to compromise in order to get a deal done. During one of my first weeks on the job, I received a call from Swifty Lazar, the legendary agent. He had a book he wanted to sell us, which I was eager to buy. During our conversation, Swifty mentioned that he would have to be made a producer on the project. I balked, knowing that Swifty had neither the interest nor the experience to function as a producer and was simply asking for the title in order to be paid more money. After we finished talking, I called Barry and explained the problem.

"You're right," he responded, "but with Swifty you just have to do this."

"Then I'm in the wrong business," I replied. In this case, I prevailed on Barry, and we didn't buy the book. In the process I incurred Swifty's eternal wrath. He never again offered me another project. I was also perhaps the only major studio executive in Hollywood who never received an invitation to his annual Academy Award party at Spago.

Within a year or so of my arrival, we began to enjoy considerable success with reasonably budgeted movies, including *Foul Play, Heaven Can Wait,* and *Grease.* I also devoted considerable time to our television division. In the fall of 1978, we produced what may have been an unprecedented three half-hour comedy hits in one season. The biggest was yet another spin-off from *Happy Days.* Garry Marshall had long wanted to build a show around an unknown stand-up comedian who had made a one-time appearance on *Happy Days,* playing the role of an alien. Marcy Carsey, then running ABC's comedy department, pushed the idea, and *Mork & Mindy* was born. It didn't take a genius to recognize that Robin Williams was a genius. When the show taped each week, the script became almost incidental. Using his remarkable gift for improvisation, Robin would fire off a barrage of imaginative, topical one-liners about sex, drugs, politics, and the culture in general. Many of his best lines were too graphic to get past network censors, and the result was that the live taping of the show became the hottest ticket in town. Meanwhile, Garry came up with yet another hit series that season, *Angie,* about a blue-collar waitress in Philadelphia who falls in love with a blue-blood Main Line pediatrician. It starred Donna Pescow, whom Marshall had spotted when she played a John Travolta groupie in *Saturday Night Fever.*

The third successful show we produced for ABC that season was *Taxi,* conceived by Jim Brooks. Both Barry and I were big fans of Jim's work, most especially *The Mary Tyler Moore Show,* which he and

Allan Burns created for CBS in 1970. Jim had a deal with MTM—the television production company named after Mary Tyler Moore and run by her husband, Grant Tinker—but Barry and I began looking for ways to attract Jim to Paramount. Eventually, we offered an opportunity that MTM couldn't: to write and direct feature films. As part of the deal, he agreed to produce at least one television series for Paramount. Jim and his collaborators managed to gather an exceptional cast for *Taxi*, including Danny DeVito, Marilu Henner, Christopher Lloyd, Tony Danza, Judd Hirsch, and the late Andy Kaufman. A top ten hit in its first year, *Taxi* won the Emmy as the best comedy in each of its first three seasons. Paramount, in turn, enjoyed an amazing run. At our height, we had five of television's top ten shows— *Taxi*, *Happy Days*, *Laverne and Shirley*, *Angie*, and *Mork & Mindy*.

The other initiative we launched shortly after I arrived was the Paramount Television Service. ABC, NBC, and CBS remained virtually the only outlets for original programming on television. Both Barry and I believed that there was room for a fourth network to compete with the three majors. Our notion was to build a new network out of the growing number of independent stations that weren't affiliated with the big networks. We wanted to start with a single night of programming and then add others over time. It was Art Barron, Paramount's chief financial officer, who suggested that we lead off at 8:00 p.m. with a new one-hour version of the series *Star Trek*, to which Paramount already owned the rights. *Star Trek* was a brand-name franchise, and we were confident that we could follow it with a strong slate of original TV movies from 9:00 to 11:00 p.m.

To head the new network we hired Rich Frank, a charming, funny, energetic salesman who was then running KCOP, an independent television station in Los Angeles. Rich chose an aggressive young Paramount marketing executive named Jeffrey Katzenberg to work under him. Jeffrey was just twenty-six years old at the time—a decade younger than me. Although he grew up just a couple of blocks from me on Park Avenue, his route to Hollywood was very different from mine. He began his career in politics at age thirteen, the same summer that he was thrown out of Camp Kennebec when he was caught playing poker for M&M's. Returning to New York, he volunteered as a gofer in John V. Lindsay's first campaign for mayor. In the fall, Jeffrey returned to Fieldston, a prestigious private high school in the Bronx. But while he eventually managed to graduate—and even put in a year of college at New York University—Jeffrey devoted most of his energy to working in the mayor's office over the next eight years. He was nicknamed "Squirt," but the sobriquet referred to his size and his youth, not to his talents. In fact, he managed to carve out a significant role for himself as an assistant to top Lindsay advisers Richard Aurelio and Sid Davidoff.

At the age of twenty-one, Jeffrey decided to shift fields. His first job in the entertainment business was as a production assistant on a movie being produced by David Picker, a friend of Mayor Lindsay's. When the movie wrapped, Picker brought Jeffrey to Paramount. When Picker left, Jeffrey went to work for Barry, who quickly discovered that Jeffrey never had to be given detailed instructions or asked to do something twice. The problem was that he often ran roughshod over people and made enemies in the process. As Barry put it to a reporter years later, "He was so aggressive and impossible, he ruffled so many feathers, that I could not keep him [in the job]." After several months, Barry offered Jeffrey a choice. "If you stay here," he told him, "I will eventually have to fire you. The other option is to put you in the marketing department, where you can learn how to function in an organization." Jeffrey resisted at first, but eventually agreed. As usual, he proved to be a quick study.

It was in his new marketing and publicity job that I got to know Jeffrey. Even physically, he was efficient. His diminutive frame and lean, long face made him look as if all excess had been burned away, leaving only glasses and teeth. He was someone who came to work early, left late, and made things happen. Occasionally, people succeed because they are brilliant and visionary; mostly, it's because they work harder than everyone else. Jeffrey was certainly smart and he grew creatively. But above all, he was focused, driven, and relentless.

With Barry's and my support, Rich put Jeffrey in charge of a two-hour *Star Trek* movie that we'd conceived as a way to launch the ongoing series on our new network. A year into the planning, Charlie Bluhdorn suddenly decided to pull the plug on the whole network. "I'm just not willing to risk $100 million when there's no clear evidence it's going to work," he told us. Ten years later, Barry would successfully launch a fourth network at Twentieth Century Fox, but at the time there was no convincing Charlie. Since we were well into building the permanent sets for *Star Trek*, we decided to go ahead and make it instead as a feature film. Jeffrey kept the job of overseeing the movie, which now became a much more expensive production. It was painful for all of us. The first person Jeffrey hired to handle special effects spent millions of dollars on effects that we ultimately had to throw out. Then, in order to secure large upfront guarantees from theater owners, we committed to a specific release date for *Star Trek*. Inexperienced and under huge time pressure, Jeffrey simply spent whatever it took, running up large costs in postproduction. The final budget for the movie was $35 million—astronomical at the time. However, he did manage to get it done on time. By doing so, he saved our guarantees from theaters. When the movie became a hit, we eked out a small profit.

Barry felt that Jeffrey deserved a bonus for meeting his deadline. I felt that he had allowed the movie's budget to spin out of control. We decided to give him a mixed message: a bonus in pennies delivered to the front door of his house. The real value of the experience was learning from our mistakes. When it came time to make a sequel to *Star Trek*, we turned to our television people, who were accustomed to squeezing high production values out of very tight budgets. By this point in 1980, our head of television, Gary Nardino, had decided to leave his job to become a producer. Rich Frank replaced him and we assigned the *Star Trek* sequel to Gary as his first project. He brought it in for $13 million. The film was not as lavishly produced as the original, but it was certainly strong enough to release theatrically. At one-third the cost of the original, the sequel earned nearly four times the profit.

Barry and I had begun to run Paramount like a real business. It wasn't possible to pick hits every time out, but it was possible to protect ourselves financially. Barry and Art Barron engineered the tax shelter deals that helped us to achieve this goal. Our movies were financed by doctors and dentists and lawyers, most of them in New York, Los Angeles, and Chicago. Later, when the tax laws no longer permitted such deals in the United States, we followed the tax shelter money to England. We also began pre-selling our movies to the television networks. Between our pre-sells, our tax shelter financing, and our focus on keeping production costs below the industry average, we almost never lost money on a film.

As for Jeffrey, in 1980, we decided to make him a production executive under Don Simpson. Opposite as they were in temperament, it seemed like a complementary fit. Don was immensely creative, but he was disorganized and had little interest in being a manager. He was also erratic in his work habits, sometimes not showing up for work at all after a weekend, and rarely arriving before ten or eleven in the morning. Jeffrey was meticulously organized and exceptionally hardworking. His days began by 6:00 a.m., and rarely ended before 10:00 p.m.

Jeffrey recognized the value of putting himself at the center of the flow of information. The result was that he knew more than any other executive in town about what was going on in the business. As for our working relationship, we developed a shorthand. I could say a couple of words to Jeffrey about a problem in the third act of a movie or about the sort of deal I had in mind on a given project and he would simply make it happen. "I just can't take him anywhere," Don Simpson would complain. "He's so aggressive that when we walk into a dinner, he's all over the director or the star before we even begin." But Barry and I recognized that this persistence often paid off. Jeffrey was absolutely unfazed by rejection, and if it was necessary to rein him in occasionally, that seemed a small price to pay.

At one point, I heard that Jeffrey had complained to someone outside Paramount about my management style—and in particular, his belief that I was slow to deliver answers. This time I called him into my office. "You can say anything you want directly to me," I said, "but talking about me in public is another thing." I have no tolerance for an executive who disparages his boss to outside parties. Inside a company, dissent and debate and self-criticism are essential. In the broader marketplace, a company's success depends on a sense of shared mission and a united front. Public dissension only benefits one's competitors.

To Jeffrey's credit, he absorbed the lesson of this early confrontation. Over the next dozen years, he frequently disagreed with my views, sometimes adamantly, but never once did I hear that he was saying negative things about me. He also came to understand that when I didn't give him answers as quickly as he would have liked, it had nothing to do with my ability to make decisions. It was actually a conscious negotiating tactic. Patience is almost always rewarded in the entertainment business. In the heat of excitement and competitive frenzy over a project, it's easy to overpay for a script, or an actor, or a director. By simply waiting a little longer you usually end up with a better and more reasonable deal. In some instances, that means you end up preempted on a script, or lose an actor or a director you were after. And, of course, we were scarcely right in every choice we made, no matter how confident we were about a given project. I'm the guy who passed on a script called *Private Benjamin*, believing that it lacked a strong third act—meaning a compelling final half-hour. What I totally underestimated was the appeal of Goldie Hawn playing a soldier. But I never dwelled for long on missed opportunities. It isn't the movies you pass on which determine success and failure, but the ones you choose to make.

Around this same time, Mel Brooks sent me a script. He explained that he wanted to make a fairly inexpensive movie right away. I was excited. "I'm not in it and I'm not directing," he said. "I'm just producing." My interest began to wane.

"It's not a comedy," he continued. Now all I wanted to do was end our conversation as quickly as possible.

Mel convinced me to at least read the script, which was called *The Elephant Man.* I was mesmerized by the story of a grotesquely deformed man who is shown compassion for the first time in his life by a London doctor—a relationship that transforms them both. After talking with Barry, I called Mel back and told him we were prepared to make the film, depending on who he had in mind to direct.

"David Lynch," he replied. "You've never heard of him, but I think he'd be great." Mel then sent me over *Eraserhead,* which was Lynch's surreal and visually repulsive, but also riveting and brilliant student film about a nearly mute misfit, his spastic girlfriend, and their barely human children. I asked Mel to set up a meeting. I envisioned Lynch as a gnomish man—unkempt, unbathed, and uncontrollable. For all his obvious brilliance, I was concerned tht such a person would never follow the more traditional narrative of *The Elephant Man* script.

The meeting at Mel's office at Fox included several investment banker and lawyer types, who I assumed were Mel's financial backers. There was no sign of Lynch. Then Mel introduced me to the best-dressed, most lawyerly looking person in the group. Naturally, it was Lynch. The meeting went well. Afterward, I accused Mel of reaching out to central casting for an actor to play the role of Lynch. In fact, Lynch was utterly in control, and he did a brilliant job on *The Elephant Man*, which became both a critical and a commercial success. It taught me what an extraordinary combination it can be to marry a highly experimental director to a strong script with a conventional narrative.

Whatever choices we made, we were determined to have fun in the process. Our meetings were loose, informal, and enjoyable, a legacy from our days at ABC. Back then, we were so far down that it made no sense to take ourselves too seriously. Laughing a lot became a way to make it through the day. We were serious about the work we did, but relaxed about the way we did it. All that continued at Paramount, not least because Charlie himself wasn't much given to codes of conduct. The collegial style we adopted probably would have gotten us thrown out of a bank or a law firm, perhaps even a CBS or a Universal. But it worked at ABC and then at Paramount, and in time we would adopt much the same style at Disney.

Because we insisted on being closely involved in the movies that we made, we became known in the creative community as a difficult place to do business. "Paramount is the studio," the joke went, "that gives you a green light and then dares you to make the movie." I myself was sometimes accused of giving an "elastic go" to projects—meaning that I allegedly made firm commitments only to reverse them the next day or the following week. I believe this was mostly an unfair rap, but, in retrospect, I think I understand why I got saddled with it. My natural inclination has always been to respond to ideas that I like with enthusiasm and excitement. "Great, let's do it," I might say, after a meeting with a writer or a producer about a project. I never faked enthusiasm, but I also never assumed that saying, "Let's do it" was synonymous with "Let's do it, no matter what." Committing to produce a movie, and to a lesser extent a television show, involves many variables. There's the budget, but also the cast, the director, the timing, and the eventual quality of the script itself. To make an intelligent deal requires weighing all these variables and then coming up with a reasonable offer. Often a project made sense at one price, but not at another.

Paramount was scarcely a monopoly, and no one was forced to do business with us. They chose to do so because our track record was so strong. The odds of having a successful film were simply higher at Paramount than they were elsewhere. In 1977, for example, Robert

Redford came to the studio wanting to direct his first film, based on a novel by Judith Guest, *Ordinary People*. It was a difficult, downbeat story, focused on an emotionally constricted married couple who wrongly believe that their son is somehow responsible for his brother's death. The boy ultimately tries to commit suicide and is saved through therapy with a heroic psychiatrist. Barry and I both loved the script, and we were willing to bet on someone whose talent we believed in. But it was scarcely a surefire hit, and we insisted that Redford agree to the same minimum scale fee that we paid to all first-time directors—at the time approximately $50,000. In my view, directors, like actors and writers, should be paid based on how their movies perfom.

Redford finally accepted our offer, and we were able to keep the budget for *Ordinary People* very reasonable. Barry liked the finished film so much that he decided to reward Redford, even before its release, with a bonus of $750,000. He thought it was the right thing to do, and he also believed that it would endear Redford to us. I believed that the principle and the precedent mattered, and I would have stuck by our original deal. At a minimum, if Barry was determined to give Redford a big bonus, I thought it ought to occur after the movie became successful. Sure enough, *Ordinary People* did become a huge commercial hit and it also won the Academy Award in 1980. But Barry's generosity didn't win us any extra points from Redford. He acknowledged Barry at the Academy Awards, but he never did another project at Paramount.

We took a different sort of measured risk during this same period with a trio of completely unknown aspiring directors. One night in 1979, Jane and I were having dinner with a childhood friend of mine named Susan Baerwald, who happened to read scripts for the United Artists story department. She mentioned a script she found hilarious but that most other studios, including UA, had read and rejected. A send-up of airline disaster movies, it was based on a 1957 movie called *Zero Hour*, in which the pilot and co-pilot eat bad fish and it's only a matter of time before they're too sick to fly the plane.

We had learned at ABC how popular the disaster genre was with audiences, and the idea of a parody was intriguing. Excusing myself from the table, I called Don Simpson at home. "You've got to put your hands on this script immediately," I said. I had long since learned not to delay or debate when something sounded right. A good idea is mean-

ingless unless you do something about it. My catharsis comes from taking action. If I don't, it gnaws at me. Often, people assume that somebody else has thought of an idea first, or find some other reason to give
up on a project before they start. I learned this lesson early, driving in
New York City. Jane and I would circle the block looking for a parking
space near our apartment on 64th Street. When we happened to find
one nearby, Jane would immediately suggest moving on, assuming that
if a coveted space was free, there must be something wrong with it.
"No," I would say. "Maybe someone just left." More often than not, the
spot proved to be legal.

By the following Monday morning we had bought *Airplane!*
and agreed to a unique deal. David and Jerry Zucker and Jim Abrahams
had only one previous writing credit, a cult comedy called *The Kentucky
Fried Movie.* None of them had any directing experience, but we agreed
to let them direct *Airplane!*—together. In return, the Zucker brothers
and Abraham agreed to work for scale, and to make their movie for a
budget of just $6 million. At that price, our risk was negligible. *Airplane!*
ended up earning $83 million at the box office and became one of our
all-time most profitable movies.

As hard as we fought to keep down our costs at Paramount, that
didn't preclude occasionally violating our own rules. We weren't averse,
for example, to paying a high price for something we believed had great
merit and a huge upside. *Raiders of the Lost Ark* was one example. Don
Simpson heard about the property, and Steven Spielberg and George
Lucas brought it to us jointly in 1979. I still remember sitting in my office on the day the script arrived. I began reading, and as soon as I finished a page, I handed it to Don, across the desk. The opening scene, in
which Indiana Jones runs out of the cave with the giant ball gaining on
him, was both captivating and daunting. "This scene alone reads like a
ten-million-dollar extravaganza," I told Don.

"Yeah," he replied, laughing, "but it's fantastic."

The rest of the script was every bit as compelling. It was clear
that the movie had huge potential, not least because Spielberg and Lucas
were two of the most successful and talented people in the movie business. Even so, it wasn't an easy decision to go forward. Spielberg's last
movie, *1941*, had failed at the box office and Lucas's *Star Wars* sequel, *The*

Empire Strikes Back, had gone far over budget. Lucas and Spielberg were asking for an unprecedented deal. In addition to very high fees, they were seeking a large percentage of the box office receipts. In short, they wanted Paramount to assume all the risk and then to share gross revenues even before we recouped our costs. Universal, with whom Spielberg had a close relationship, had already passed on these terms, and so had Warner Bros.

I knew Spielberg, but I'd never met Lucas, so I decided to go see him at his ranch outside San Francisco. I half-expected to meet a William Randolph Hearst character at the equivalent of San Simeon. The Skywalker Ranch turned out to be beautiful but not ostentatious, and Lucas himself was soft-spoken, shy, and low-key. Before I could say anything about *Raiders,* Lucas began to talk about exactly how he intended to make the movie. "Let's take the scene where Indy gets on the plane to go to Nepal," he told me. "Now we can build the entire plane, or we can build a piece of the wing, use one engine, and add the roaring sound effects. We'll get just as effective a result. That's how I want to do the whole film."

Barely pausing, George launched into a broader lecture on his philosophy of moviemaking. "It isn't necessary to make a perfect movie; that's just a formula for going broke," he explained. "You have to make the movie good enough to achieve the desired magic. There's a difference between magic and perfection. Magic is sleight of hand, and so is moviemaking. We're not trying to paint a picture, we're making a film. There are twenty-four pictures per second. Too many directors make movies for the eyes and ignore the ears. Sound can create just as much magic, and far more inexpensively." In less than ten minutes, George Lucas won me over, describing a philosophy of moviemaking to which I had long subscribed, but never articulated as clearly as he just had.

Don and I began to chase the project. Barry was just as drawn to it as we were, but even more fearful of the costs. We spent hours discussing how to construct a deal that we could all live with comfortably. One of the ways was to negotiate in advance the terms for any potential sequels. The executives at Twentieth Century Fox had been so focused on securing the music rights to *Star Wars* that they permitted Lucas to retain rights to all the movie's sequels. It was a classic example of managers looking only at their short-term interests—knowing that by the time the sequels were made, they would probably be long gone. The failure to take a longer view ended up costing Fox nearly $600 million.

The deal that we finally struck with Lucas and Spielberg gave us the right to share in the music revenues and the sequels. Our original choice for the Indiana Jones role was Tom Selleck, but neither CBS nor Warner Bros., the producer, would give him time off from his TV series, *Magnum, P.I.* Instead, we cast Harrison Ford, fresh from his success in *Star Wars*, which helped drive the cost of the film up to $25 million, a big budget then that seems a pittance by today's standards. It proved to be an excellent investment. *Raiders* opened in 1981 to terrific reviews and eventually earned more than $250 million domestically. Three years later, the sequel, *Indiana Jones and the Temple of Doom*, did nearly as well.

The other big bet we made during this period was on *Reds*, a brilliant script with less obvious box office potential than *Raiders*. *Reds* was the true story of the American journalist John Reed's political involvement with communism during the Russian Revolution, and his romantic relationship with Louise Bryant. In some ways, the most extraordinary thing about the project was that we could do it at all. No government authority ever objected to our producing a movie about an American whose idealism leads him to become a communist. It's this sort of creative license—made possible by the enduring power of the First Amendment—that sets American movies apart and helps to account for their popularity around the world. Never in thirty years of making movies and television have I worried that a mayor, or a congressman, or even a president might try to act as a censor or impose a point of view. To be able to make choices purely on the basis of their artistic merit is a precious and often underappreciated freedom.

In this case, Barry was the primary champion of *Reds*. It was one of the few times that I felt he was significantly swayed by something other than the idea itself—in this case, the charisma of Warren Beatty, who eventually co-wrote, produced, directed, and starred in *Reds*. Barry liked being associated with Warren and with such a high-minded project. I liked the script, too, and believed in Warren's talent, but I had significant doubts that *Reds* could earn enough to justify its considerable cost.

To reassure himself, Barry decided to have Warren present the project directly to Charlie Bluhdorn. Early in 1980, Barry, Warren, and I flew to New York and went together to Charlie's office. Warren and I sat across from Charlie, while Barry squeezed himself so far into a corner that he was almost invisible. Warren then proceeded to put on a show, simultaneously playing the roles of passionate filmmaker, historian, movie star, and courtier to a corporate king. It was an Academy Award performance, and midway through, Charlie spontaneously jumped up, grabbed Warren in a bear hug, and shouted, "Let's do it!" Barry smiled faintly from the corner, I sighed, and we all went out to dinner. The next day, Charlie called Barry and asked how we could get out of the deal. Barry told him that it was too late.

Barry himself started to have doubts as soon as shooting began. After five days, the film was five days behind schedule—no small feat—and costs were escalating. Charlie kept haranguing Barry to take his losses and shut down the film. Instead, Barry took steps to limit Paramount's financial exposure, bringing in Barclay's Bank as a partner, in a clever, complicated tax shelter deal. In the end, Warren made a wonderful movie. *Reds* did reasonably well at the box office and brilliantly with the critics, and Warren went on to win an Academy Award for Best Director in 1982. With that boost, the movie finally earned a small profit. Equally significant, perhaps, was that even on an expensive, relatively esoteric movie, which went significantly over budget, Barry never put the studio at serious risk.

It was the experience of *Reds* and *Raiders* that prompted me, in late 1981, to write a long memo to members of our Paramount motion picture team. I felt compelled to raise a red flag. We were coming off yet another highly successful year, but the numbers were misleading. Nearly all our profit in 1981 had come from *Raiders*, an expensive blockbuster that wasn't the kind of movie we ordinarily did. The rest of our slate had performed marginally at best. Barry supported the idea of rethinking our priorities, and eventually the memo ran to twenty-one pages. "Success in the motion picture business is highly prone to prompting complacency and recklessness," I began. "Often the big win comes with a single smash movie. The intoxication of a blockbuster hit can lead to an easy sense the luck will keep striking. Over the past five years, Paramount has either been number one or two in the motion picture business. Success tends to make you forget what made you successful, and just when you least suspect it, the big error shifts the game. Will success lull us into the fatal bad play?"

It was critical, I argued, to remember that movies are a business. "If show business weren't a business, it would have been called 'show show,'" Woody Allen once said. I exaggerated to make the same point: "We have no obligation to make art. We have no obligation to make history. We have no obligation to make a statement. But to make money, it is often important to make history, to make art, or to make some significant statement. . . . In order to make money, we must always make entertaining movies, and if we make entertaining movies, at times we will reliably make history, art, a statement, or all three. We may even win awards. . . . We cannot expect numerous hits, but if every film has an original and imaginative concept, then we can be confident that something will break through."

I also reiterated the tenets of smart moviemaking, and the kinds of mistakes it is all too easy to make: "An apparently no-risk deal is never a valid reason to produce a mediocre movie. A low budget can never excuse deficiencies in the script. Not even the greatest screenwriter or actor or director can be counted on to save a film that lacks a strong underlying concept. And we should generally resist making expensive overall deals with box office stars and top directors, because we can attract them later with strong material." Above all, the purpose of my memo was to reinspire our team at Paramount to return to the approach that had made us successful in the first place.

One of the first opportunities came in the spring of 1982, when Larry Gordon appeared in my office. A producer with an ongoing deal with Paramount, Larry was also one of my few close friends in the business. A quintessential Hollywood character—brash, blunt, fast-talking, street-smart—he grew up in the only Jewish family in Belzoni, Mississippi. I found him entertaining and funny, and I supported him first as a television producer at ABC and then as a movie producer at Paramount. On this occasion, we were looking for a project for Nick Nolte, with whom we had a deal that was about to run out.

"Do you have anything that might be good for Nick?" I asked. Larry mentioned a script called *48 Hours*, which had a wonderfully accessible one-line concept: A cop springs a con from prison to help track down a killer, and along the way these two sworn enemies become best buddies.

"Could you have it in the theaters by December?" I asked. Larry said he could, and we committed to the project the next morning. To play the role of the con, we went after Richard Pryor, Bill Cosby, and Gregory Hines, but none of them was available. Finally, someone suggested the name Eddie Murphy. (It's impossible to say exactly who. Half of Hollywood has since taken credit for the idea.) Murphy was a young stand-up comedian who was just beginning to attract attention on *Saturday Night Live*. He'd never been in a movie before, and he happily accepted a modest fee, which helped to keep the budget down. Within a couple of weeks of shooting, it was clear that we had stumbled on a huge star.

Barry agreed that we should try to sign Murphy to an exclusive contract before *48 Hours* came out. We sent one of our business affairs executives to see his agent. "Don't leave until you've got a signed contract," we told him. Making big deals typically takes forever, but sometimes, by acting early and decisively, the endless back and forth can be avoided. In this case, the deal was consummated that very evening—for Murphy's next three movies.

On *48 Hours*, we argued and fought with Larry Gordon and the director, Walter Hill, over everything from how best to showcase Eddie's talents; to the marketing campaign; to whether or not to preview the film before a live audience before making any decision on a final cut. For all the conflict—perhaps partly because of the conflict—the result was a wonderful movie that reaffirmed the value of a strong story, and made Eddie Murphy into a star. Produced for $10 million, it earned $76 million at the box office, a huge sum in 1982. We renegotiated Murphy's contract, and his next two movies were even more successful. *Trading Places* and *Beverly Hills Cop*—the idea we began developing when I arrived at the studio in 1976—eventually became two of Paramount's biggest hits ever.

Doing business with your friends is always tricky. The entertainment business so dominates West Los Angeles that almost everybody you know is somehow involved in making movies and television. I'm not counting the dentist who hands you a script just before he injects the Novocain, or the doctor who wants to discuss an idea for a television series while doing a hernia test. I'm referring to friends like Larry, who have kids in the same school as yours, and also have film and television projects at the network or studio where you happen to work. Much as I prefer not to do business with friends, sometimes it can't be avoided—and sometimes it leads to disaster.

Soon after *48 Hours* came out, Larry found a script that he wanted to make as his next movie. It was titled *Brewster's Millions*, and the premise was appealing: a man is given one month to spend a million dollars. The problem was that Larry wanted to make his directing debut with the film and no one was willing to back him. Universal was eager to make *Brewster's Millions*, but not with an inexperienced director. Although the original movie had been remade several times, the project intrigued me.

"We'll do it with you," I told Larry, and then I asked Jeffrey to handle the negotiations. As with Redford and all other first-time directors, we insisted on paying scale. We also wanted the right to replace Larry if the budget went over a certain figure—a relatively standard form of protection, given his inexperience and our commitment to keeping costs down.

In the meantime, however, Larry went back to Universal and told them what had happened. To avoid losing the project, Universal reversed field and agreed to let him direct. They also offered him a much more lucrative deal than ours. After talking to Jeffrey, Larry decided to move the project. Larry insisted that Jeffrey had given him permission to take it to Universal, and had promised that there would be no hard feelings. I was enraged. In my mind, Larry had taken advantage of our offer. We made it when no one else was willing to bet on him, and I believed he had used it to extract a better deal at Universal. Almost nothing upsets me as much as feeling betrayed—and in this case by a close friend.

The next morning, I set out to sever Paramount's ties to Larry, and ordered that the furniture from his office be loaded onto a truck and removed from the lot. He responded by going to court and winning a temporary injunction halting the move. In the end, ironically, he decided not to direct the movie after all, and Walter Hill did so instead. *Brewster's Millions* flopped at the box office. As for Larry, our rift took a long time to heal. I pretended not to see him at restaurants and hid when he came to pick up his kids at our house. At one point we both happened to be visiting our children at Camp Keewaydin. I was standing at the end of the dock in my bathing suit, when I saw Larry coming toward me. Instinctively I dove into the water and swam away, still wearing my sneakers. My wife, children, and parents all believed I was overreacting, and they were probably right, but I stubbornly held my ground. The rift even inspired me to commission a script, *Worst of Friends*, which I still think would make a great black comedy. Unfortunately, we never got it quite right. The passage of time did eventually make it all seem less important, and Larry and I became friends again. We haven't made any more movies together—but I don't rule it out for the right idea.

The biggest personnel issue we faced during this period was Don Simpson. He'd done a great job in helping to hammer the screenplays for *48 Hours* and *An Officer and a Gentleman* into shape. But his creative contributions were increasingly erratic. Don's modus operandi had long been to make notes into a voice-activated tape recorder as he read a script. Ricardo Mestres and David Kirkpatrick, two executives who worked with me on my memo, would then take the fifty-page Simpson transcripts and edit them into pithier five- to eight-page memos that a writer or a director could actually use. At his best, Don was brilliant at structure and character, and at identifying the key dramatic moments that make movies memorable. But he could also lose focus, offering up tirades, circumlocutions, and philosophical asides rather than cogent insights.

Although he never discussed it with me, Don's struggle with drugs and alcohol was becoming debilitating and distracting. He started missing more days of work, returning fewer phone calls, and ignoring more of his responsibilities. I deeply valued his loyalty and his skills, and I was more tolerant of his lapses than my colleagues were. But by the spring of 1982, I too recognized that something had to give. In May, we decided to name Jeffrey Katzenberg the president of production and to make an independent production deal with Don. Jeffrey was plainly more suited to running a large organization, but Barry and I were still convinced that Don could make a contribution, freed of the responsibility of running the whole studio. For his first project, we assigned him to *Flashdance*, a troubled script based on a promising concept.

In turn, Don hooked up with Jerry Bruckheimer, who had just produced *American Gigolo* for us. Low-key, meticulous, and highly organized, Jerry was a perfect complement to Don.

Flashdance had originally been championed by Dawn Steel, a young woman whose first business success was selling toilet paper that carried the Gucci label—until the Gucci company intervened. Art Barron had hired Dawn in film merchandising, and her energy, creativity, and sense of humor convinced us that she would make a strong production executive. *Flashdance* began as a movie about models who do tabletop dancing at night in a bar in Canada. That story had a certain tawdry commercial appeal, but Dawn was convinced it had greater potential. When Simpson and Bruckheimer came aboard, they hired Joe Eszterhas, an ex-journalist, to rewrite the script, long before he became the highest paid and most controversial screenwriter in Hollywood. Even in the most explicitly commercial movies, the lead character needs to have a goal with which the audience can identify. In *Warriors*, Walter Hill's movie about street gangs, we insisted that the lead gang members be intelligent and have some sort of direction. Much later, when we did a movie called *Cocktail* at Disney, we argued that the bartender character played by Tom Cruise needed at least the ambition of owning his own bar and attending night school. Under Simpson and Bruckheimer's direction, *Flashdance* grew into a tale of a beautiful young woman who works as a welder in a steel mill by day, dances in a bar by night, but continues to pursue her dream of studying ballet in a classical academy.

For the lead, we cast Jennifer Beals, an exotic beauty with no previous professional acting experience. She also happened to be an undergraduate at Yale, a background we knew we could market very effectively. As it turned out, Jennifer only had limited skills as a dancer. We ended up reshooting her ballet school audition at the end of the movie using four different stand-ins—among them the best leaper and the best pirouetter we could find, as well as a male street dancer who wore a wig and was filmed mostly from behind, spinning on his back. Produced for less than $7 million, *Flashdance* earned $94 million and was one of the first successes to come out of our rededication to making more reasonably priced movies.

Sometimes this commitment required difficult and painful decisions. In 1981, for example, Jim Brooks came to us with the idea of turning Larry McMurtry's novel *Terms of Endearment* into a movie. Barry and I both had great faith in Jim, and the script he had written was intelligent, funny, and moving. I also loved the idea of having the telephone play a central role in a movie. In Jim's script, the two main characters—mother and daughter—talk and gossip and argue with each other constantly by phone, much as I remembered my own mother and sister doing over the years. Still, both Barry and I had doubts about the broad box office prospects of a script built around an attractive young woman who discovers she has cancer and ultimately dies, leaving behind a grieving husband and two young children. Jim was understandably frustrated by our ambivalence. "How can you feel this is a risk because it's about death?" he said. "Paramount is the company that made *Love Story*. You guys made *Brian's Song* at ABC. I've got a great deathbed scene. What more do you want?"

We finally agreed to make *Terms of Endearment*, but with the stipulation that Jim bring it in on the $7 million budget that we believed the movie could safely earn back. Jim tried to cut costs everywhere he could, but with a cast that included Jack Nicholson, Debra Winger, Jeff Daniels, and Shirley MacLaine, he never could get below $8 million—an unimaginably modest figure today. Finally, Jim managed to convince his old employer, MTM, to kick in the last million and we went forward with the movie. In retrospect, we vastly underestimated its appeal. *Terms of Endearment* won five Academy Awards in 1984 and eventually earned $108 million. Even so, I believe that rigorous financial discipline can have a positive creative impact on a movie by forcing a certain kind of leanness and efficiency. Jim Brooks certainly had moments of despair dealing with us, but when the movie came out, he concluded that our toughness had been mutually advantageous. "When the studio decides to get behind you—and God help you if they don't—they can be very helpful," he told a reporter. "The truth is that *Terms* probably wouldn't have been as good if we had made it on a higher budget."

Our success at Paramount didn't go unnoticed, and in time I began to receive inquiries about other jobs. Only two of them even tempted me. One was heading Walt Disney, the only studio in town with a brand name and a unique franchise among kids. The other was running CBS, which I'd come to admire after competing against the network during my ten years at ABC. Under William Paley and Dr. Frank Stanton, CBS embodied not just success, but style and class.

Shortly before my contract at Paramount was up, Bill Paley called. He was nearly eighty, and had been talking about retirement on and off for nearly a decade. At least one of his heirs apparent, Arthur Taylor, had already come and gone. A second, John Backe, was in place, but Paley showed no signs of giving up control. I had little desire to move from Los Angeles to New York, and I remained happy at Paramount. Even so, I felt flattered that Paley knew who I was, and I couldn't resist the opportunity to meet a legend and test the waters. CBS had recently dropped to third place in prime time, which meant that Paley might feel compelled to take a chance on a "creative" type like me, who lacked traditional business credentials.

The only business course I had ever taken was accounting at NYU during the early 1960s when I worked at CBS. I never took an economics course during college. After moving to ABC, I was too busy to take any further classes. At one point, I did convince Jane to take a course in finance so that she would know "things," some of which I hoped might rub off on me. Pregnant at the time, and not much interested, she eventually dropped out. At Paramount in the late 1970s, I read about a three-day seminar at a local hotel called "How to Manage a Company in a High Inflation Era." I never told Barry or anybody else at the studio where I was during those three days, and the course itself proved to be fairly thin. The one value was that I could now impress Barry and Charlie Bluhdorn with some new vocabulary and the sort of minimal knowledge that can be dangerous.

As my contract with Paramount neared its end, I decided to take a course in accounting at UCLA. I suspected that I might someday have to be able to read a balance sheet properly, but I didn't want to go to school alone. Once again, I convinced Jane to enroll with me—in this case to share the pain. Our kids loved watching us. All Jane and I did on weekends and plane trips was homework. We felt the same panic about exams that we had twenty years earlier. We were as competitive as two high school seniors trying to make honor roll. The final was a killer. Jane was so upset about hers that she refused to hand it in and got an F. I was sure I'd done poorly, but I figured it was so difficult that the professor would have to curve the results. Sure enough, I received an A, although I'm sure on any absolute scale I would have failed. Afterwards, I looked at Jane's answers and, as usual, she'd done better than me. But I was the one with the official A. I still remind her of my victory. She reminds me of my endless competitiveness.

I met with Paley in his CBS office and at his Fifth Avenue apartment, both of them exquisitely filled with Picassos and Giacomettis and Klines. His wife, Babe, had died recently. He seemed to have time on his hands, and it was fun to sit and talk about CBS, shows and scheduling, theater and art, and his amazing life. Above all, I was struck by how much Paley enjoyed talking about ideas and stories. I found myself in awe that the chairman of a company could be so involved creatively, and so passionate about the process. Paley wanted me to work both for him and for John Backe. The suggestion disappointed me, but I agreed to meet with Backe. As I feared, all Backe wanted to talk about was budgets, reporting structures, staff meetings, and organizational plans. I returned to Paley and told him diplomatically that I was disappointed by Backe's single-mindedness.

"You should come here anyway," Paley said. What he didn't tell me was that he was on the verge of firing Backe. Several months later, when he made the move, he didn't call me back. Instead, he hired Thomas Wyman, an executive from Polaroid, who, like Backe, had no previous experience in entertainment. Wyman, too, was eventually pushed out. Paley never hired anyone who shared his creative strengths.

My conversations with CBS had one unexpected benefit. Along the way, Charlie Bluhdorn learned that Paley was courting me. Charlie heard it through Bob Evans, who still had a producing deal at Paramount. In a classic Hollywood story, it turned out that Evans was dating a young woman whom Paley was also pursuing, his romantic appetites undiminished by his advanced age. I didn't know the woman personally, but she touted me to Paley, perhaps after a discussion with Evans. He then told Bluhdorn, who called me the moment he heard the news. I happened to be in New York at the time.

"How could you do this?" he asked when he reached me on the phone. "We have to sit down and talk right away." With my contract up for renewal, I was already in a strong negotiating position. Paramount had become the most successful studio in town. Revenues tripled between 1977 and 1982, while profits increased from $13 million to more than $100 million. Nonetheless, neither Barry nor I had shared in the success to any significant degree. These were the days before executives received large performance bonuses and significant stock options. But with Paley after me, I was suddenly in a position to push for a more favorable deal. Charlie was eager to keep me at Paramount—and Barry was happy to see me do well. Whatever arrangement I made, he would receive more, as chairman.

"I don't really want to go to CBS," I told Charlie, honestly. "But I *am* going to leave unless you make a fair deal with me."

"What do you have in mind?" Charlie asked.

I knew he wouldn't consider a significantly higher salary, since Barry and I already earned more than most other executives at G&W. He wasn't going to agree to any substantial stock options, either. Instead, I suggested that G&W lend me the money to buy a house—whatever house I chose. In addition, if I was ever fired, G&W would have to forgive the loan.

"Fine," Charlie said, to my surprise. As soon as I left his office, I called Jane at home in Los Angeles. "I want you to go and find us the most beautiful house you can," I told her. "Price is no object." My main priority was a backyard big enough to play football on with my three young sons (Anders, the youngest, was born in 1978). The next day, as I walked off the plane from New York, I heard an announcement calling me to a red courtesy phone.

"I've found a house," Jane said. "You have to meet me there right away. The one problem is that we can't go inside and look at it." The owner, it happened, was a corporate executive who had just been indicted on charges of bribery in Japan. Apparently, he was too embarrassed to see anyone. I rushed over anyway and fell in love with the house from the outside—especially its large, flat backyard. We made an immediate bid at a price I never would have considered if Charlie hadn't agreed to finance the purchase. When the bid was accepted, I called Charlie to tell him the news.

"No one spends that much on a house," he told me.

"Fine, then just be nice about it and let me go to CBS," I said, only half-teasing him. Charlie blustered some more, but he stuck by his promise, because in the end he was both pragmatic and honorable, and he didn't want to lose me. He also agreed to create a bonus pool to reward Barry and me and our top studio executives based on performance. I signed a new two-year deal in mid-1982, excited about our strong slate of upcoming movies. It included *Flashdance*; *Terms of Endearment*; *Indiana Jones and the Temple of Doom* (the first sequel to *Raiders*); *Beverly Hills Cop*, produced by Don Simpson and Jerry Bruckheimer; and *Witness*, a story about a detective, played by Harrison Ford, who investigates a murder in Amish country. Directed by the Australian Peter Weir, it remains one of my favorite films. As I looked ahead, it seemed completely plausible that both Barry and I would remain at Paramount for the next decade.

In fact, the end was near. Although I didn't recognize them at the time, there were already signs that not all was well with Charlie. Late in 1982, we noticed that his hair seemed very different. We wondered if he had begun wearing a wig, but he emphatically denied it. Around the same time, it became impossible to reach him in the mornings. Finally one day in early February 1983, Barry and I were in New York, and Charlie called us up to his office. In the course of our conversation, he asked us, mysteriously, to please look out for his son, Paul, who was then working at Paramount. Neither Barry nor I knew quite what to make of it. We would learn later that Charlie had leukemia, and that he had kept it secret from nearly everyone while he underwent chemotherapy.

During the second week in February 1983, Charlie flew down to his home in the Dominican Republic, ostensibly for a vacation. Days later, on February 19, he died of a massive heart attack, with his personal physician by his side. For reasons I never understood, the official story was that he had died on the flight home. It was an eerie, upsetting end to an extraordinary life. As for Barry and me, the death of Charlie Bluhdorn changed everything overnight. Nothing, we would learn painfully, lasts forever.

CHAPTER

5

Keys to the Kingdom

ALTHOUGH PARAMOUNT WAS MORE SUCCESSFUL THAN EVER IN THE year following Charlie Bluhdorn's death, that didn't endear us to his successor. It was years before I fully understood why, but only a short time until we felt the consequences. A few days after Charlie's fatal heart attack, Martin Davis was named chairman of Gulf & Western, following a brief but fierce internal battle for the job. All I really knew about Marty was that he began his career at Paramount and served as G&W's chief administrative officer. I hadn't met him more than three or four times, usually when I was in Charlie's office. "Get out of here, Marty," Charlie would bark, waving his arms, all mock gruffness. "I don't want anybody from Gulf & Western around when I talk to the president of Paramount." I was amused by Charlie's histrionics but also embarrassed for Marty.

Barry worked hard to forge a friendly professional relationship with Marty, to protect both himself and Paramount. Their connection proved to be critical for another reason. Both Marty and Barry were close to the Bluhdorn family. At Charlie's death, Yvette, his wife, was named to the board. As might be expected, Yvette had considerable influence in choosing her husband's successor. Barry strongly encouraged her to cast it for Marty, believing he was the best available choice. Yvette followed Barry's advice. In return, when Marty set about reorganizing the company, he gave Barry broader responsibilities, including oversee-ing Simon & Schuster and Madison Square Garden, both of which G&W owned. Still, the decision to support Marty Davis was one that Barry—and Yvette—would come to regret.

My own relationship with Barry changed almost immediately. We had always been collegial and open with one another. We went out to dinner together intermittently, and while we were never close friends, I felt relaxed and comfortable with him. Now a chill set in. After years of discussing everything together, he suddenly began to exclude me. I went from being his partner to his employee. He refused to acknowledge that anything had changed, so I just assumed that his jungle instinct had kicked in and he was moving to consolidate his power.

Only much later did Barry acknowledge what had really hap-pened. It was Marty Davis, he told me, who had moved to consolidate power, in part by trying to create rifts among the top executives within each of G&W's subsidiaries. Marty would deny a lot of it, but Barry ex-plained that within a few months of taking over, Marty called him and said, point-blank, "I have to be comfortable with the executives in this company, and I don't like Eisner." Barry was dumbfounded, since Marty barely knew me, and Paramount was headed toward another record year in profits. As they talked, it dawned on Barry that Marty wasn't looking for a way to be more comfortable with me.

"If what you're saying is that I should fire Michael, then you're going to have to toss me first," Barry said. To which Davis responded, without hesitation, "I'm quite prepared to do that." Barry told me that over the next few months Marty would force the chief executives of many of G&W's divisions to replace their seconds in command. As Barry interpreted it, this was Marty's method of asserting total control over his top people—taking away their most valued lieutenants and humbling them in the process. Barry decided to resist the pressure but without revealing to me what had happened. Years later, he told me that he had considered it his problem to resolve, not mine. My own inter-pretation is that Barry feared—rightly—that I would immediately begin looking for a new job if I knew that Marty had it in for me. Barry tried to run interference, but he also felt a growing resentment toward me for having to do so. For the first time in more than fifteen years of working together, we became estranged.

The first hint I had about Marty's attitude came in the fall of 1983, eight months after Charlie's death, when Jeffrey Katzenberg made a visit to New York. Jeffrey decided to stop in to see Marty, fully expecting a warm welcome, given Paramount's continuing success. Instead, Marty launched into a tirade about the shortcomings of Hollywood generally and our team at Paramount specifically. "You're all overpaid and spoiled," he said. As for Jeffrey himself, Marty was merciless. "I consider you a little Sammy Glick," he said, and then went on to share his primary concern: "I've heard that all of you have been plotting to get the board to throw me out." When Jeffrey called me to report on the meeting, he was in shock. So was I.

I continued to hear stories about Marty's harsh management style and his often inexplicable cost-cutting measures. The most egregious example was with Yvette Bluhdorn, to whom he literally owed his job. Although Yvette remained a member of the board and a major stockholder, Marty decided to take away her company car and driver, remove the telephone tie-line between her house and G&W, and reduce support for one of the Bluhdorn family's favorite philanthropic projects, an arts center they had founded in the Dominican Republic. In the wake of Charlie's death, Marty began to treat Yvette as someone who got in the way and was now expendable.

I also heard that Marty was going around saying negative things about me. Early in 1984, I finally brought the subject up with Barry. "What has Marty got against me?" I asked bluntly. "We've barely met. Why don't you explain to him that I'm not some Hollywood producer who wears tutus, snorts coke, and goes to wild parties?"

Barry minimized the problem. "You're too sensitive," he told me. "Just let me handle it. The important thing is that he's leaving us alone."

I still found it hard to believe that my job was in jeopardy, but Barry's reassurance wasn't very comforting. For the first time, I began thinking seriously about other options. The company I felt most drawn to was Walt Disney. Ever since I first took Jane to see *Pinocchio* at the drive-in on Bruckner Boulevard, I had been fascinated by the unique niche that Disney occupied in the entertainment world. When Jane and I moved to California, we began taking our kids to Disneyland, and I was impressed by the enormous attention to quality and detail throughout the park. I still knew relatively little about Walt himself, who had died in 1966, but I admired his creativity, his commitment to excellence, and his fierce independence from the other Hollywood studios. Disney remained not just the premier name in family entertainment but the only true brand name.

My first dealings with the company were in 1980, when Barry and I went over to the Disney lot in Burbank to try to make a deal. We met with Card Walker, the chairman of the company, who had begun at Disney as a messenger after graduating from UCLA in 1938, and with Ron Miller, a handsome ex–University of Southern California football player who was married to Walt's daughter Diane and now served as president and COO. Our idea was to bring Disney in as our financial partner on two films we had in production that were proving more troubled and expensive than we had anticipated.

Popeye, starring Robin Williams and directed by Robert Altman, was in production on the island of Malta in the Mediterranean. Barry and I had just come back from visiting the set and meeting with the most interesting (and in this case, free-spending) individuals since St. Paul was shipwrecked on the famous fortress island in A.D. 59, on his way to be tried in Rome. We left Malta feeling very concerned. Meanwhile, *Dragonslayer* was being produced by George Lucas at high cost. As usual, Barry wanted financial protection for our company, and I agreed. Both movies were aimed at a family audience, and we believed that the Disney name was still valuable enough to help generate box office overseas. To our delight, Card and Ron quickly agreed to take on the international distribution and to assume half the costs of both movies.

Two years later, as Paramount's success in the movie business continued to grow, Ron Miller called me. As president of the company, he was clearly Card's heir apparent as chairman. "I want to know if you would be interested in running our studio," he said. I explained that I was already president of a very successful studio. I listened sympathetically as he talked about making movies for a broader audience beyond families with young children. I also encouraged him when he spoke about launching a second non-Disney label to produce more contemporary films aimed at an adult audience.

"If Disney really wants to be competitive in the family movie business," I said, "you're going to have to start attracting top outside talent and compensate them at the same level that other studios do. You've never replaced Walt creatively, and people like Steven Spielberg and George Lucas have become the Walt Disneys of our time. They've taken away your franchise." A second non-Disney film label, I told Ron, wouldn't simply be a way to broaden the company's business, but also to forge relationships with the best filmmakers. "They have children of their own, and once you're in business with them, they'll do Disney family films for you, too."

Finally, I returned to my situation. "If you're asking me to come and do the same job that I've been doing at Paramount, then reluctantly I'll have to decline," I said. "What does interest me is a job that includes running the studio and overseeing the theme parks." It was a brazen suggestion—essentially I was asking for his job—but I figured I had nothing to lose. It was no great surprise when Ron politely demurred. Instead, he thanked me for my ideas and asked what I thought about some other candidates he was considering to run the studio. I strongly recommended against the ones he mentioned. Within weeks, he went ahead and hired them anyway. A short time later, he launched a non-Disney label for more adult movies. It was called Touchstone.

In the fall of 1982, at the opening of the company's newest theme park, Epcot Center, Card Walker announced plans to retire during the next year. He also made it clear that Ron Miller would become the new chief executive. The company itself was continuing to struggle. Cost overruns building Epcot, the second park at Walt Disney World, forced the company to take on substantial debt. Profits were down, the studio was still developing only a handful of feature films, and Disney had dropped out of the television business altogether. Sensing that Ron might be more amenable to help in his new role, I brought up the issue the next time we had occasion to talk early in 1983. This time I cut to the chase so quickly that I even surprised myself.

"What if I came over as president," I said, "and you became chairman?" I was aware that Ron might have trouble convincing Card and other members of the Disney board that I should run the whole company. Instead, I suggested that I would concentrate on movies and television while he continued to oversee the parks. So long as I was president of the whole company, I believed that I could eventually broaden my responsibilities. Ron was interested, but he was also concerned about selling the idea. Card continued to dominate the company completely, and it was clear that any decision about my role would be his.

Ron managed to arrange a meeting for the three of us, and sure enough, Card took over. Tall, handsome, and silver-haired, he was an impressive man in many ways. He had devoted his entire life to the company. Although he mostly left the creative decisions to others, Card had strong business instincts and he pursued them confidently and aggressively. He had permitted Ron to start Touchstone, which would soon release its first hit movie, *Splash*. He was also preparing to launch the Disney Channel on cable. His biggest achievement, however, was to build Epcot, Walt's dream community of the future, and to create Tokyo Disneyland. At the same time, he was aware that the company stood to benefit from more creative leadership and he was more receptive to my coming over to Disney than Ron had anticipated. By the end of the meeting, we were talking as if we had a done deal. Just as I was preparing to leave, Card made a strange comment.

"I suppose that you would want a press release announcing the job," he said. Suddenly, I realized that Card saw me as a Hollywood type from the other side of the hill—slick, self-promoting, and obsessed with power and status. I considered myself none of these things, but Card's comment caught me off balance for a moment.

"I think that if I'm going to be made president," I finally replied, "a press release would probably be appropriate." Card nodded and we all shook hands. Card told me that Disney's head of business affairs, Ron Cayo, would get in touch with my lawyer to discuss terms. After the meeting, I met up with Jane, and we went out for pizza on Ventura Boulevard. I recounted what had just happened. By the time I finished, I had talked myself out of the job.

"I'm not going to take it," I said. "They're just not ready for an outsider, no matter who it is." Jane agreed, and I decided I would call Ron Miller to tell him so. He ended up reaching me first. No sooner had I left than Card expressed second thoughts about hiring me. Ron was embarrassed and apologetic, but he was merely confirming my own instincts. (Of course I would have loved him to talk me out of those instincts!)

Card continued to believe that Ron needed help in his new job. In the fall of 1983, when Card officially retired, Ray Watson was named chairman of the company. An architect, developer, and longtime consultant to Disney beginning in Walt's era, Watson was recruited by Card to compensate for Ron's lack of business experience. It was a move that may well have saved the company. Ron continued to run Disney day to day, while Ray focused on the rising tide of outside predators who were increasingly interested in taking over Disney and selling its assets off in parts. Ray's strongest suit was his sound judgment and his equanimity under fire.

Several months later, I found myself in another discussion about going to work at Disney, this time with Roy Disney, Walt's nephew and lookalike and the largest shareholder in the company. Gentle and soft-spoken, Roy was easy to underestimate, and for years that's exactly what Card Walker and Ron Miller seemed to have done. Roy's style belied a sharp mind and a dry sense of humor. He also had a fierce passion for the company that his father had co-founded, and a quietly intense drive to see it grow and prosper, both creatively and financially. Like Frank Wells, Roy was an adventurer—in his case, a sailor and a pilot. His passion for Disney was fueled in part by his wife, Patty. Effervescent, acerbic, and outspoken, Patty was an avid reader and knowledgeable on a range of subjects. She and Roy operated entirely as a team. Each day, no matter what he was doing, Roy returned home to have lunch with Patty. They were inseparable.

In 1977, a year before Card became chairman and named Ron as president, Roy's frustration with Disney finally boiled over. Unable to influence the company's direction, Roy decided to leave the company for which he had worked since his early twenties. "The creative atmosphere for which the company has so long been famous and on which it prides itself has, in my opinion, become stagnant," he wrote in his resignation letter to Card. Roy remained on the board of directors, but his unhappiness only increased as the years went by—above all when the value of his stock began to erode in 1983. Not long after, he resigned from the board of directors, with secret plans to try to wrest control of the company.

I first met Roy in 1980 when I joined him on the board of the California Institute of the Arts, the arts school founded by Walt Disney in 1962 as a training ground for animators and other artists. I agreed to serve on the board largely because it was such a refreshing contrast to the world of popular entertainment and commerce that I lived in every day. Based in Valencia, thirty miles north of Los Angeles, CalArts was a place that Walt envisioned as having no walls between artistic disciplines— where filmmakers and musicians and painters and dancers could inter- mingle and inspire one another. Among its many distinctions, CalArts became a primary feeder school for Disney animated artists.

Roy had just resigned from the Disney board when we had a telephone conversation in the spring of 1984. I didn't feel comfortable asking him the reasons for his move, but I knew about his dissatisfaction with the company's management from several previous conversations. I asked what was going on at Disney. He didn't say much, but he asked me a provocative question: "Are you under contract to Paramount?"

"Yes," I told him, "but it's up soon."

"I hope you won't sign anything new without talking to me first," Roy replied. "I'm not in a position to offer you anything at this point, but I'd like to stay in touch."

In the meantime, our accelerating success at Paramount was at- tracting more attention than ever. In April 1984, *Terms of Endearment* won five Academy Awards, including Best Picture. Over the next three months, laudatory articles about the studio ran in *BusinessWeek, The Wall Street Journal, Newsweek,* and *New York* magazine. All this media at- tention only made Marty Davis unhappier. He was especially incensed by the *New York* article, which featured Barry and me on the cover in a story entitled "Hollywood's Hottest Stars." Later, Marty complained to reporters that the article gave too much credit to the two of us and too little to the rest of our Paramount team — especially the marketing department, run by Frank Mancuso. There was one statement of mine in the article that irritated both Marty and Frank. "It's great to have good marketing, and I think we have the best," I was quoted as saying, "but you don't need it to sell *E.T.* and it won't help if you're selling *The Pi-*

rate Movie. This is a business based on ten to twelve decisions a year. They are very important. Nothing else is close." Mancuso circled the quote and sent copies to Jeffrey, Barry, and me, with a sarcastic note attached. I still believe what I said, but at the time it only made things worse with Marty and Frank.

Barry, meanwhile, was spending less and less time at the studio. His contract with Paramount was up on September 30, and he hadn't made any moves to renew it. Sometime during the summer, I finally confronted him. For the first time, he acknowledged that Marty had been pressuring him to fire me. I found this hard to believe.

"How is it possible, no matter what he feels about me personally?"

"I don't know," Barry replied. "Marty's an idiot, but it's true."

What Barry didn't tell me was that he had already begun negotiations to leave Paramount in order to take over Twentieth Century Fox. Early in 1984, he'd been approached by the Denver oil tycoon Marvin Davis. No relation to Marty Davis, Marvin had purchased Fox for $722 million three years earlier. The studio had been hemorrhaging money ever since and Marvin now wanted Barry to run Fox.

In July, shortly after my conversation with Barry, Roy Disney called me at Camp Keewaydin, where I was visiting my kids. Roy and I hadn't spoken for three months, during which he had been quietly looking for ways to wrest control of the company. Like most readers of the business pages, I was aware of an escalating drama at Disney. During the previous year, the company's earnings had fallen by 7 percent, following a nearly 19 percent drop in 1982. Construction overrun costs for Epcot were a key factor, and so was lower than expected second-year attendance at the new park. Compounding the problem were high start-up costs for the Disney Channel and a continuing lackluster performance in the film division. Even so, because Disney had relatively low debt, an exceptionally valuable film library, and parks that generated $1 billion a year, the company's assets were worth considerably more than the $2 billion market valuation based on its depressed stock price. That disparity made Disney a prime takeover target.

Saul Steinberg was the first to put Disney in play, when he began buying up its stock in March 1984. He quickly acquired nearly 10 percent of the outstanding shares, and in early June, he made a tender offer for the rest. His plan was to sell off Disney's assets individually as a way to maximize his profit. On June 9, Disney agreed to pay "green-mail," buying back Steinberg's holdings at a premium of $7.50 over the market price. For his ninety-day investment, Steinberg earned a profit of nearly $32 million. By then, other interested buyers and investors were circling Disney, including the Minneapolis raider Irwin Jacobs and the arbitrageur Ivan Boesky. The other significant investors were considered friendly—most notably the Bass brothers of Fort Worth, Texas, whose real estate division, Arvida, Disney had agreed to buy during this period in an effort to take on debt and make the company less attractive to potentially hostile buyers. Nevertheless, Disney's independence was clearly at risk, and employees at every level were deeply worried.

What I didn't yet know was what role, if any, Roy was playing in the drama. Only later did I learn that he was among those actively seeking a way to buy control of the company. When I called him back, he simply explained that he was actively pushing for a management change at the top. He also said that he now had some leverage. In return for agreeing to come back on the board of directors the previous month, he had been given two additional seats—one for his brother-in-law, Peter Dailey; and the second for his close friend, lawyer, and business partner, Stanley Gold. He also mentioned that Frank Wells was part of the team that he and Stanley had put together to plot strategy. The Disney board was scheduled to discuss the issue of management at a mid-August meeting, Roy told me, and it looked as if Ron Miller would be asked to resign.

"I'm just calling to see if you're still interested in coming to Disney," Roy said. "If you are, I would like to have Stanley call you." I told him that would be fine.

I was aware by this point that my situation at Paramount was building toward a breaking point, but I viewed it all with more curiosity than alarm. It was as if I were watching an exciting drama on stage, and just happened to be one of the principal players in it. Mostly, I continued doing my job. Finally, on the evening of Sunday, August 19, nearly a month after Roy called me at Keewaydin, I received a call at home from Frank Wells, who was at Stanley Gold's house.

"Could you drop by tonight?" Frank asked. I still knew him only slightly, through our occasional industry encounters. My longest conversation with him remained the one we had had over dinner in Vail a couple of years earlier. Having succeeded in scaling the highest mountains on six of the seven continents around the world, he was now back at Warners as a consultant.

I soon discovered that Frank had once been something of a mentor to Stanley at the law firm of Gang, Tyre & Brown. They remained good friends, and it was Stanley who suggested to Roy Disney that they bring Frank in as an adviser in their efforts to force a management change at Disney. Frank and Roy had attended Pomona College together. Stanley himself was a larger-than-life character. Hyperactive, barrel-chested, and forever successfully dieting, he commanded attention the moment he entered any room. But if he was flamboyant—elegant custom-made suits, monogrammed shirts and suspenders—Stanley was also a conservative and methodical lawyer, investor, and businessman. Highly successful in his own right, he served as Roy's financial adviser, chief tactician, and unofficial spokesman. Both Patty and Roy held him in high regard.

Stanley sought Frank out for his expertise about management and the movie business. They spent their first lunch together talking about the strengths and weaknesses of Disney's current executives, and then turned to potential alternatives for the top job. It was a perfect opportunity for Frank to make the case for himself, but he didn't. "I'm going to give you the best advice you've ever had on the subject," Frank told Stanley, according to John Taylor, whose book *Storming the Magic Kingdom* is an exhaustive account of the battle for Disney. "Whatever else you do, get Michael Eisner. He ought to be running that company. He's hot. He's got a track record. You do everything to get him and I'll help." It was an extraordinarily selfless act. As I soon came to understand, it was also completely characteristic of Frank.

At the same time, Stanley pushed Frank's cause, first by trying to convince Ron Miller to bring him over as part of the current management. Frank went to see Ron, whom he knew socially and considered a friend, but nothing came of it. Then, in early August, once again at Stanley's urging, Frank flew to Nantucket to spend three days with Richard Rainwater, a partner of the Bass brothers, who were now among the company's largest shareholders. Frank and Rainwater got along famously. They were both runners, both loved to talk about business, and both had broad outside interests. The problem was that neither Rainwater nor the Basses were yet in a position to substantially influence the choice of the next chief executive at Disney.

When I arrived at Stanley's house, he and Frank filled me in on recent events. Earlier that same day, under growing pressure, Disney's board of directors had met to consider replacing Ron Miller. At the end of the meeting, a special committee was formed to review Miller's performance. Stanley, who now sat on the board with Roy, said that he expected Miller to be asked to leave within the next couple of weeks. At that point, the board would begin looking for candidates to replace him. Already one Disney board member, Philip Hawley, the chairman of Carter Hawley Hale Stores, had suggested Dennis Stanfill for the job. Stanfill had been the head of Twentieth Century Fox until Marvin Davis bought the studio, at which point Davis replaced him with Stanfill's own second in command, Alan Hirschfield. Now, Davis was on the verge of replacing Hirschfield with Barry Diller. Stanley explained that he wanted the board to consider Frank and me for the top jobs, suggesting that I would concentrate on the creative side and Frank would focus on business affairs.

We didn't discuss who would be the chief executive in such a scenario, but I knew that I wasn't interested in being number two again, nor did I believe it would work to share the top title. I just told Stanley and Frank that I was enthusiastic about coming to Disney. We spent the next several hours talking about the company. The more we discussed the possibilities, the more excited I became.

"What do we do?" I asked finally. "Submit resumés and then wait to see if they call us?" I was only half-kidding. Stanley said that he would arrange for us to be interviewed.

It was time, I realized, to confront Barry. The next morning, I went to see him and asked point-blank whether he intended to sign a new contract at Paramount. I had sensed for months that he was considering leaving, but for the first time he acknowledged the possibility. "It's fifty-fifty," he said, but refused to provide any more details. He didn't ask me if I had any plans and I didn't reveal any. It was an awkward period for both of us. We were each now in the midst of active negotiations to leave Paramount, yet we had to make decisions every day as if we intended to stay. I continued, for example, to negotiate a new, long-term deal with Jim Brooks—even though I would obviously have preferred to have him at Disney if I ended up there, just as Barry would want to have him at Fox. As a matter of professional pride, I continued to give 100 percent of my energy and commitment to Paramount. On another level, I was in denial. I still couldn't accept that Marty Davis didn't want me to be part of Paramount's future.

It was two weeks before Stanley could arrange for me to be interviewed by Ray Watson, who was leading the Disney board's search for a new chief executive. Gracious, even-tempered, and unflappable, Watson prided himself on building consensus and getting along with everyone. On Saturday, September 1, he drove up to interview me at my house. We settled in my living room, and I felt immediately comfortable with him. We talked about our mutual interest in architecture, and went on to discuss the situation at Disney briefly. Then I launched into my vision of the company's future. I took Ray through my own career, talking in particular about running children's programming at ABC, my introduction to Disney animation through *Pinocchio*, and all the opportunities that I saw for the company to leverage its name and reenter the business of movies and television. At one point, I picked up a pad and a pencil and drew a chart for Ray. It began in 1977 and continued through to 1984, depicting Paramount's sharp rise in earnings over the seven years that Barry and I had been there. Our operating profits had increased from $17 to $145 million. But it was unlikely, I explained, that we could sustain such an extraordinary rate of growth so long as we were confined to our existing businesses.

"A studio can only make between twelve and fifteen movies and still give them the close attention that they require, both creatively and in marketing," I told him. "We're already doing that at Paramount. There isn't a lot of upside left. Gulf & Western doesn't want anything more from Paramount—no parks, or restaurants, or new ventures." Disney was another story. "You guys are ripe to be turned around in movies and television. You're in the same position that Paramount was when I started there, and ABC before that. Disney is making only a handful of features, one animated movie every four years, and no television at all. There are enormous opportunities to ramp up production." Unlike Paramount, Disney was already in other businesses—theme parks and consumer products—with obvious cross-promotional potential. "The Disney brand name," I concluded, "is still a unique, largely untapped asset."

By the end of our meeting, I felt confident that I'd made a good impression on Ray. As he left, I mentioned that time was probably of the essence. Marty Davis was planning to come to Los Angeles the following week and I fully expected to start negotiating a new contract with Paramount. I had no idea what to expect from Marty, but so long as I could legitimately hold out the possibility of making a new deal with Paramount, I had greater leverage with Disney.

The next day—Sunday, September 2—I received a call from Frank Wells. Ray had just finished interviewing him. In their talk, Frank said that he'd emphasized his credentials as a lawyer, a dealmaker, and a businessman. He felt that their meeting had gone well, but when it ended, Ray acknowledged that the company was really only looking for one chief executive. "Then get Eisner," Frank told me he'd said. "You need creativity more than anything else." Ray had concurred. "I think you've got the job," Frank told me now.

In part, Frank may have been expressing his own doubts about taking the top job. Although he had succeeded at every stage of his life with a blend of raw brain power, incredible drive, and hard work, I always sensed a degree of uncertainty beneath his charismatic persona. Much later, when I knew him better, Frank would tell me that he never felt comfortable or confident in the creative role he was called on to play toward the end of his tenure at Warner Bros. He was undeniably a leader, but I don't think he preferred to be the ultimate leader. He would have taken the top job at Disney if it was offered, but in the end he was prepared to put aside his own ambitions for me—on the grounds that he believed Disney needed my skills more than his. Everything else, including his own future, was secondary.

It was coincidental that Marty Davis chose this moment to make his first visit to Paramount since taking over as chairman of Gulf & Western eighteen months earlier. He arrived in town on Labor Day, two days after my meeting with Ray Watson and one day after Frank's. By this point, Barry had vaguely shared his plans with me but he still hadn't been specific. On Tuesday, September 4, Barry picked Marty up at the Beverly Wilshire Hotel and brought him to the Paramount lot. They met for more than an hour, and Marty pressed for a renewal of Barry's contract, now due to expire in less than thirty days.

Marty made it clear that he felt Barry and I received too high a percentage of the bonus pool arrangement in our current contracts. He also told Barry that before any new deal could be made, they had to settle the issue of "reorganization." Specifically, he wanted to increase Frank Mancuso's responsibilities and no longer have him report to me. Aware that I would consider such reorganization unacceptable, Barry refused to discuss it with Marty. As for negotiating his own new contract, he parried the issue. Barry and I talked after his meeting, but only generally.

That afternoon, Marty asked to speak to me in the guest office he was using. He had made no effort to set up a meeting in advance and he was scarcely welcoming now. "You and Barry are getting too large a split of the executive bonus pool," he began, much as he had with Barry earlier in the day. What most galled Marty, I guessed, was that both Barry and I were due to earn more in 1984 than he was, by virtue of Paramount's performance. Our conversation was brief and inconclusive.

Next, Marty went in to see Jeffrey Katzenberg. Bizarrely, he took back all the criticisms that he had made of Jeffrey at their meeting months earlier in New York. "They were unwarranted," Marty told him. "I relied on third parties, who did a very effective job of downgrading you. Now that I've had a chance to make my own judgment, I realize I was misled. I withdraw the negative things I said. I think you have a superb future." Jeffrey called me as soon as Marty left, as bewildered by the effusive praise as he had been by the earlier criticism.

On Tuesday evening, hours after my meeting with Marty, Ray Watson called and asked if he could come to see me again. Only much later did I learn that following our first meeting he had returned home and written a six-page memo to the special committee of the board charged with choosing Ron Miller's replacement. In it, he laid out his conviction that if Disney were to successfully fend off a hostile takeover and remain an independent company, the directors needed to act quickly to find a new and credible chief executive. Then he made his case for me, first by mentioning that Ron Miller had previously suggested bringing me to Disney. "Eisner is one of the top two or three executives in the industry," Watson wrote. "If we could attract [him] to

Disney, it would instantly provide us with the substance and image to show to the world we mean business when we say we are going to turn this company around." The memo was hand-delivered to committee members on Monday, September 3, the day after our meeting. Unfortunately, it failed to convince several board members, including Philip Hawley.

Ray returned to my house on Wednesday morning, along with an attorney named Joe Shapiro. I asked my own lawyer, Irwin Russell, to attend the meeting. Ray began by asking whether I would consider the number two job at Disney. I demurred, as I had earlier with Ron Miller. "I'm already number two at Paramount," I said. "Why would I make a lateral move?"

We began to discuss other options. "I don't have to be chairman as long as I'm president and CEO," I told Ray. In that case, I would effectively be running the company. I later learned that Ray had raised this same suggestion, with himself as chairman, in his memo to the board. I liked the idea of Ray's staying on. He had a connection to Disney's past, and I also felt that he would be supportive of growing the company. I worried that Frank might be getting the short end of the stick, but I also realized that the call was ultimately Stanley's and Roy's—not mine. When I talked to Frank, he was enthusiastic. "Just go for it," he said.

That evening, Watson called me at home to say he was going to recommend that the board name me chief executive at the special meeting scheduled for later that week and that he would offer to stay on as chairman. "I've got a pretty independent board," he said. "They might ask for an interview or for time to study the issue. But I'm very impressed with you. I'm going to try to put it to bed." When I called Frank to describe the day's events and solicit his reaction, he was unequivocal. "If they offer you the job," he said, "take it."

The next morning—Thursday—the outside directors met to seal Ron Miller's fate. It was, by several later accounts, a highly dramatic meeting. Feeling betrayed, Ron prepared a written defense of his tenure and ended up making an emotional appeal to each of the board members, one by one. After he left, however, they voted unanimously to ask him to resign, just as Ray Watson had predicted. A full board meeting was set for the following day to ratify the decision and to consider his replacement.

For my part, I arrived at work Friday morning fully expecting to be offered the Disney job before lunch. I arrived at my office at Paramount around 9:00 a.m. At ten, Marty Davis once again unexpectedly summoned me to his office. He wanted to talk further about my future at Paramount, but I decided that I had an obligation to be straight about the situation. I also enjoyed the idea of finally being able to turn the tables on him. "I think that I'm about to be offered the job as president and CEO of Disney," I said, before he began. Davis was stonefaced at the news.

"I won't stand in your way," he replied. The rest of our brief conversation was polite and perfunctory. As I left his office, my main feeling was one of relief. I wasn't going to have to work any longer for someone who seemed so utterly unappreciative of my contribution to the company.

I returned to my office to await word from Disney, where the board of directors was scheduled to begin its meeting at 11:00 a.m. I felt anxious and distracted, but forced myself to go about my normal business, making calls and holding meetings on several projects. By 1:00 p.m., the phone hadn't rung. I still wasn't alarmed because I assumed that the meeting might run long. But as time kept passing, I grew more and more concerned. By 3:30 p.m., I knew something was wrong. Finally, sometime after 4:00, the phone rang. It was Frank.

"How do you feel?" he asked.

"Why?" I replied. "How should I feel?"

"Hasn't anyone called you?" he said.

"Nope," I said, trying to be casual. Frank was obviously embarrassed, and he tried to cover up, telling me he'd just heard the news himself from Stanley. "The board ratified the resignation of Miller," he said, "but they tabled the discussion of his replacement and decided to establish a search committee instead." Suddenly, I had a bad feeling in the pit of my stomach. All my working life, I had been careful about not overplaying my hand. Now I realized that I'd made a terrible mistake in disclosing so much to Marty Davis that morning.

I would later realize that by acting cautiously and deliberately, Disney's board was also acting responsibly. The most important job for any board of directors is to hire and monitor the performance of the chief executive. Forcing the resignation of Ron Miller—Walt's son-in-law and Card Walker's handpicked choice as his successor—was an act of independence and even courage by the board. Making the right choice in replacing Miller was critical to the company's future and probably deserved separate consideration. But for me, the board's decision to take more time was frustrating.

I had little choice that evening but to attend a party in Marty's honor. Earlier in the week, Marty had told Barry that he wanted to meet with all of the top Paramount executives informally, and Barry had agreed to invite them to his home for a buffet dinner. The event was almost as awkward for Barry as it was for me. At one point during the evening, he pulled me aside and acknowledged that he intended to make a major decision about his future that weekend. I no longer remember, but he may even have said that the new option was to head Twentieth Century Fox. In any case, he said that we should keep in close touch. As I mingled uncomfortably at the party, several people came up and told me that Marty had been singling out for praise the one top Paramount executive who wasn't there: Frank Mancuso.

The next morning, I drove our middle son, Eric, to San Bernardino to play in his first tennis tournament. During the game changeovers, I slipped off to a pay phone to check with Barry for status reports on his mysterious negotiations. By the end of the match, Barry had closed his deal. "I'm going to be taking the job as chairman of Fox," he told me. On its face, it seemed like a lateral move. But life with Marty had become untenable for Barry, too, and when I learned that Marvin Davis had agreed to give him large stock options and a percentage of any increased value in Fox, I understood the attraction of the offer.

"Do me at least this favor," I said. "Don't tell Marty about your plans for a few days, so that I have time to consider my options."

Barry told me that he was planning to tell Marty Davis in person the following Tuesday in New York. But by Tuesday he'd received a call from Marvin Davis at Fox, who explained that Hirschfield had just leaked the fact that he was leaving, and that Marvin was going to have to announce Barry's appointment right away. After hanging up the phone with one Davis, Barry dialed the other. He reached Marty late that day in New York and resigned over the phone. Then he tried to reach me, but didn't succeed. I was sitting in a dentist's chair in Beverly Hills with a drill in my mouth.

By the time I finally got back home, there were several messages from Marty Davis. He had requested that I call back no matter when I came in. I felt like a hunter's prey. Shortly after 8:00 p.m.—11:00 p.m. New York time—I called Marty back. "I'd like you to fly in tonight and meet me at my office tomorrow morning," he told me.

I had long ago vowed to myself that if the time ever came for me to be fired, I wanted to be at home with my family. Being fired from a job running a movie studio didn't strike me as shameful. It was part of the risk you took and it had happened to plenty of talented people. Still, I hated the idea of flying across the country to receive bad news, and then returning afterwards to an empty hotel room. I decided to buy some time.

"I can't come tonight," I told Marty. "It's my son's first day of school tomorrow." That was true, but it wasn't the whole story. Taking the "red-eye" overnight was exhausting, and I wanted to arrive at the meeting sharp and focused. More important, I had my own meeting scheduled at 8:00 the next morning with Ray Watson and Philip Hawley, and I wasn't about to cancel it. Finally, if Marty had already made up his mind about Barry's successor, there was no point in making the trip at all. Rather than confront him head-on, I raised the issue indirectly. "Are you going to ask me to report to Mancuso?" I asked.

"I haven't made any final decisions," Marty replied.

I had no choice but to accept his statement. I agreed to fly out by early the next afternoon, and to get together when I arrived that evening. After I hung up, I called Barry and described the conversation.

"Don't make the trip," he counseled. "It'll only be an embarrassment. Marty has no intention of making you the chairman."

But there were other considerations. The contract I had signed with Charlie Bluhdorn two years earlier included a clause requiring that I be offered the job as chairman of Paramount if it ever became available. If that didn't happen, I was entitled to receive all of my deferred compensation immediately, and to have the loan on my house forgiven. Refusing to go to New York might constitute insubordination, and I didn't want to give Marty any excuse to withhold money that I believed I was owed.

At 8:00 a.m., Wednesday, the next morning, I sat down for breakfast with Watson and Hawley. I knew that I had to win Hawley over if I was going to get the Disney job, and I made much the same pitch to him that I had twice before to Ray Watson. Several times Hawley hinted that he had doubts about my credentials as a business executive. By the time we got up, I sensed that I had failed to win him over. I didn't have much time to worry about it. Shortly after noon, I left for the airport with Jane and Jeffrey, whom Marty had also summoned to New York. We spent much of the flight strategizing about the upcoming meeting.

"My best alternative," I concluded, "is to force Marty to breach my contract by not offering me Barry's job." Jeffrey's best move, we both agreed, was to make no commitments to Marty of any kind.

When we landed shortly before midnight, Jeffrey and I were driven directly to the Gulf & Western headquarters. While he waited outside the office, I went in to meet with Marty. He got right to the point. "Would you be willing to report to Mancuso?" he asked.

"I already told you that I wouldn't," I replied. "The only job I'm interested in is Barry's." He asked if I would be interested in a deal to produce movies for Paramount. I told him that I wouldn't. The meeting was over in five minutes.

"I'll have to sleep on it," Marty told me. "I still haven't made any decisions. I'll give you an answer in the morning."

When I emerged, it was after 1:00 a.m. Several of Marty's lieutenants were hanging around outside his office, and while Jeffrey went in, I sat with them, making jokes about the cloak-and-dagger drama of it all. Marty, meanwhile, pressed Jeffrey to extend his contract past its expiration date in December. Jeffrey refused to make any commitments.

Sometime shortly before 2:00 a.m., Jeffrey and I left the building together. We shared a cab, and he dropped me at the Mayfair Regent before heading on to the Regency, three blocks south. A half hour later, as I was getting into bed, the telephone in my room rang.

"I've got something to read you," Jeffrey said. He had noticed a pile of the next morning's edition of *The Wall Street Journal* as he entered the lobby of his hotel. He was calling now to read me an article on the second front page about the unfolding events at Paramount. The article quoted unnamed "G&W executives" as saying that Frank Mancuso would be named chairman of Paramount later that day. The *Journal* is printed in the early evening, so it was obvious that the story had been given to the reporter, Laura Landro, sometime during the previous day. Contrary to what Marty told me, that meant he made his decision on succession before Jeffrey and I boarded the plane in Los Angeles. It was clear now that my contract had been breached.

The article went on to quote Marty directly about his dissatisfaction with Paramount's recent performance. He began by complaining that we weren't producing enough movies: "It's a diminishing business and market share is the key to success. We're not getting enough of it." In fact, profit, rather than market share, is what truly matters in the movie business. Still, my pride was hurt. I knew that we had done well, but hearing Marty's comments at this moment was upsetting—and only more so because they were so misleading. He went on to express disappointment that our television division hadn't sold more prime-time series to the networks during the past couple of years. There was a grain of truth in this, but what he didn't say was that two of our ongoing series—*Cheers* and *Family Ties*—had just been sold in syndication for huge sums, and that the studio itself was earning record profits.

It was nearly 3:00 a.m.—midnight in Los Angeles—by the time Jeffrey finished reading me the story. I couldn't resist calling Diller at home. He was awake, and I ran down the basic details of the *Journal* story for him. "Well, I guess Marty's going to try to rewrite history now," Barry said. "Last month, he was singing our praises to the shareholders. Now, suddenly, we aren't so great after all."

That same day, Thursday, September 13, I met with Marty for a second time shortly after noon. I insisted that he invite G&W's counsel into the meeting, in order that a witness be present. When I confronted Marty, he denied that he had been the source for the *Journal* story, even though it was obvious that only he could have authorized the leak. "I have decided on Mancuso," he told me, "and I want to know if you are willing to stay on and report to him."

"No, I'm not," I said. Instead, I asked that in accordance with my contract, a copy of which I had brought along, a check for my incentive compensation be drawn immediately. I also asked for a letter confirming that the loan on my house had been forgiven. Davis said that would be fine. He handed me a press release and asked me to sign off on it. "I want my letter and the check for what I am owed before I approve any press release," I told him.

Marty balked. "I can't get you a check on such short notice," he said.

I told him that was ridiculous, and that unless he did so, I was not going to approve his statement of my resignation. Twenty minutes later, I had my check. "I'll be back in an hour," I told Marty. He looked at me as if I were crazy, but I excused myself and walked five blocks with Jane to the main branch of the Chemical Bank at 47th Street and Park Avenue. There, I found Bill Turner, a banker I'd known since 1964, when I began working at ABC.

I walked into his office, handed him the check, and asked that he deposit it as cash immediately. He told me that was impossible. It would take three days for the check to clear. I pointed out that the check was written on G&W's Chemical account and that Chemical was also my bank, as it had been my parents', my grandparents', and my great-grandparents'. He left Jane and me for a few minutes. When he returned, he said that the deposit had been made to my account—as cash. In retrospect, I realize that there was no chance Gulf & Western would have canceled payment on my check. I was reacting instead to a feeling of betrayal. I had always known I was in a volatile profession and that my job was no more secure than a baseball manager's. But when the firing finally came, I was totally unprepared for it.

Up to this point in my career, I had been judged on my merits and well rewarded for my successes. Now I had my first important brush with the fact that life isn't always fair. After leaving Marty's office, I went back to my hotel and spent the rest of the day returning phone calls. One of them was from Barry, who immediately suggested that I come and join him at Fox. I was amused by his sudden renewed interest in me. During the past few weeks, we had once again found a common adversary, and he had finally begun talking to me more honestly and openly, after more than a year of shutting me out. I knew in my heart that our time had passed, and that I should probably move on and be my own boss. But I was unemployed and decided it was best to keep my options open.

"Let's sit down and talk when I get back," I said.

I had planned to return to Los Angeles that evening, but in midafternoon, I received a call from Arthur B. Krim, the chairman of Orion Pictures and the former head of United Artists, whose entire top management had resigned six years earlier to protest interference from its parent corporation, Transamerica. UA was never the same. "I can sympathize with what you've just gone through," Krim told me. "I'd love for you to come to dinner tonight." I admired Krim, and I couldn't resist the opportunity to compare notes.

At 8:00 p.m., Jane and I joined him and his wife, Mathilde, at their East Side town house. For the first part of the evening, we talked about Paramount, United Artists, and Orion. Krim made it clear that he was interested in having me run Orion. Midway through dinner, the conversation shifted to the research that Mathilde Krim, a research scientist, was conducting into AIDS. The disease had only recently reached epidemic levels and begun to penetrate the national consciousness. Krim herself had been studying it since the earliest cases were discovered. Now, in response to my questions, she helped me understand for the first time the scale and horror of the disease. It was a wake-up call far more important than the one I had received from Marty Davis earlier that day.

The next morning, Friday, September 14, Jane and I flew back to Los Angeles on Regent Air, the gaudy, short-lived experiment in a super-luxury service between New York and Los Angeles. On one level, I felt that I had badly misread my situation at both Paramount and at Disney, and I was certain that I'd never get a desirable job again. At a deeper level, I believed I had done nothing wrong, and there was no way I could have affected the outcome at either Disney or at Paramount. I felt betrayed and abandoned yet also strangely relieved and released. For the first time in fifteen years, I was taking a plane trip in which there were no scripts to read, no reports to write, no ratings to pore over or ideas rattling around in my head that needed to be committed to paper. No one was waiting for an answer to a question that would affect their career and livelihood. There was nothing I had to do.

As it happened, a reporter who had been covering the unfolding story had managed to book himself into the airline seat across from mine. Ten years later, Tony Schwartz would become my partner in writing this book. At the time, he was a staff writer for *New York* magazine. At first, I considered refusing to talk to him. Then I realized we were stuck together for the next five hours, and I decided to take the opportunity to tell my side of the story. I spent most of the flight reconstructing the events of the past several weeks. Jane, forever protective, kept looking over to remind me silently that I was talking to a reporter.

As we got off the plane, an airline agent handed me a slip of paper with Stanley Gold's name on it and a number to call. Stanley didn't have encouraging news to report. As I suspected, I had failed to win Hawley over during our Tuesday breakfast meeting, and Frank had done no better in a meeting that followed mine. Hawley told Ray Watson afterward that he was still concerned about our lack of "corporate experience." As for bringing more creative leadership to Disney, Hawley was dismissive. "We can always buy creative talent," he said.

Still, Stanley hadn't given up. As John Taylor recounted it in *Storming the Magic Kingdom*, Stanley told Hawley, "Every great studio in this business has been run by crazies. What do you think Walt Disney was? The guy was off the wall. His brother Roy kept him in check. . . . Clean out your image of crazies. We're talking about creative crazies. That's what we ought to have. We can always buy MBA talent."

But Hawley wouldn't budge.

"I just can't bring myself to accept that," Taylor reported him as replying. "Eisner and Wells are very, very impressive, but they're divisional. They've never run anything but a division." It didn't seem to matter to Hawley that the "divisions" Frank and I had run, at Warner Bros. and Paramount, respectively, each had revenues in excess of $1 billion—not much less than the entire Disney Company.

At midday on Sunday, September 16, two days after my return from New York, Frank called to ask that I meet him again at Stanley's house. When I arrived, they had a new plan, which Frank presented. "We will be co-chief executives," he said. "You'll handle the creative side. I'll handle the business side. But we'll be equals."

Stanley's notion was that putting Frank and me together as a team might make us more acceptable to Hawley and to some of Disney's outside investors. I didn't believe that such an arrangement would work. It was vague and sloppy. It was also a political solution and political solutions rarely succeed.

"I'm not willing to be co-CEO," I heard myself say. "And in any case, I don't think that kind of arrangement makes sense. We have to tell the employees, the creative community, and Wall Street that this company is headed by a creative executive." I surprised myself by taking such a strong stand. I had no desire to live in New York and work for Orion, nor to work under Barry and Marvin Davis at Fox. Being co-CEO of Disney was a wonderful opportunity. But deep down, I must have truly doubted that it would work. For a brief moment, I wondered if I had made a fatal mistake. Then Frank spoke.

"Okay," he said. "I'm fine with that. You can be chairman and chief executive officer and I'll be president and chief operating officer, so long as both of us report directly to the board."

"Sounds good to me," I said.

Stanley was growing impatient with the back and forth. "I just want to know," he finally said to me, "will you commit? Do you want to be chairman and CEO of Disney? It's the best job in the world. You can't just wait for this to come to you. You have to go get it."

In that one moment, everything changed. This was no longer a casual effort to persuade Disney to embrace Frank and me. With Stanley mapping our battle plan, it became an all-out war. The Disney board was scheduled to meet and make their choice the following Saturday—just six days later.

On Monday, September 17, Frank and I launched an intense campaign to win the seven votes we needed among Disney's thirteen directors. Stanley drew up a chart that included each director, as well as the names of their friends, colleagues, and clients. Frank and I began to visit them, one by one—and to urge them to call individual directors on our behalf. We also set out to win support from the major investors who were still battling for control of the company.

Saul Steinberg was no longer in the picture, but Irwin Jacobs and Ivan Boesky remained major shareholders, along with the Bass brothers and Richard Rainwater. With all the investors, raiders, and arbitrageurs still circling the company, it wasn't even certain there was going to be a Disney left to run. Nearly all of the potential buyers were still rumored to be considering breaking up the company and selling off the assets, including the theme parks and the film library. Our job was not just to convince everyone that Frank and I were the best choices to run Disney, but that under our management the company as a whole could be more profitable than its component parts.

In between my calls and visits to lobby for the Disney job, I kept a few other balls in the air. I had agreed, for example, to sit down with Barry and Marvin Davis, to discuss the offer to come to Fox. Mostly the meeting gave me an excuse to see Marvin Davis's giant, lavishly decorated house, which had previously been owned by Dino De Laurentiis, and before that by the singer Kenny Rogers. The whole scene was surreal. At midafternoon, we sat down in a living room the size of a football field, and servants immediately appeared carrying mounds of Beluga caviar and long, fluted glasses of champagne. (I had a Coke.) I finally felt certain that this wasn't the job for me—or for Barry. I sensed he was once again placing himself under a difficult owner, and that, if I came along, I was destined to be a perpetual second in command.

At midweek, Ray Watson called Stanley Gold. Ray told Stanley that he admired our campaign, and still supported me as CEO, but that his ultimate interest was in consensus. At least nine of the thirteen directors, he said, were now prepared to vote for Dennis Stanfill—Phil Hawley's candidate. If that happened, Ray said, he would cast a tenth vote for Stanfill. Later, Ray would explain that he had exaggerated the bad news in order to stoke Stanley's competitive fires. Stanley did emerge from the meeting determined to turn up the pressure.

"What we have to do now," he told Frank and me, "is win support from the Basses, Irwin Jacobs, Ivan Boesky, and the other major shareholders. That will give us a huge piece of leverage." As Stanley saw it, the board wasn't likely to go against the direct wishes of the shareholders who effectively controlled the company.

We set our sights first on the Basses, who Stanley believed held the most sway with their fellow shareholders. Neither Frank nor I had yet met Sid Bass, but Frank had formed a strong bond with Rainwater over the summer in Nantucket. Rainwater was also friendly with George Lucas, who had called to support my candidacy, telling Rainwater that I was much more creative than Stanfill, and clearly the better choice.

Sid Bass had read the *New York* magazine cover story earlier in the summer, and concluded from it that I would make a strong executive. Later, he told me that he was particularly influenced by one of the pictures accompanying the article. It showed me standing in front of my house with my wife of fifteen years and our three sons. The photograph reassured him that I didn't fit the stereotype of a wild, partying Hollywood executive. The irony was that Jane had refused to be part of the picture until the very last minute, on the grounds that she didn't want her privacy invaded. She joined us only when she realized that I intended to go ahead without her, and that by not participating it would appear that we were divorced.

Even with the family portrait, both Sid and Richard Rainwater had lingering doubts about whether I had the business credentials to be a CEO—and whether Frank might not be more qualified. On Wednesday morning, September 19—three days into our campaign—I was sitting in my kitchen having breakfast when I looked up and saw Frank and Stanley jogging up my driveway.

"It's over," I said to Jane. "It's not going to happen." My instincts weren't completely off. When I met them at the door, Stanley delivered the verdict.

"The Basses have decided that they can't live with you as chief executive," he said. "They want Frank to be chairman and you to be president." For one fleeting moment, I wondered if perhaps Frank and Stanley agreed with the Basses.

"Why don't you call the Basses and make your own case?" Frank suggested.

Stanley concurred and at that point, I realized my concerns were completely groundless. We went into the den and put the call on a speakerphone, so that everyone could hear the conversation: Jane and I, and Stanley and Frank, who were still in their sweaty running clothes. In Fort Worth, the Basses put their own contingent around a speakerphone: Sid, Richard Rainwater, and Al Checchi, another of their top lieutenants.

I launched immediately into my own version of Stanley's speech about why I ought to be running Disney. "Companies like Disney are always founded by creative entrepreneurs," I said, "but eventually the founder dies or gets pushed out, or moves on to something else. Inevitably the businesspeople take over—the managers—and they focus on preserving the vision that made the company great in the first place. They don't have any creative ideas themselves and they end up surrounding themselves instead with analysts and accountants to try to control the creative people and cut costs. In the process, they discourage change and new initiatives and reinvention. In time, the company begins to ossify and atrophy and die. It's important to have financial parameters and never to bet the house, which is how we always protected Paramount. But in a creative business you also have to be willing to take chances and even to fail sometimes, because otherwise nothing innovative is ever going to happen. If you're only comfortable running a business by the numbers, I can understand that. But then you shouldn't get involved with a creatively driven company like Disney."

I was taking a chance by being so blunt, but I felt that I had nothing to lose. I was surprised at how clear and unequivocal I'd been. I could just as easily have done a lot of stammering. In any case, when I finished speaking, there was a beat. Before I had time to worry, a voice came on the line.

"Okay," Sid Bass said, "you're right. We're with you."

I was dumbfounded. Only later did I discover that this was typical of the Bass style: decisive, to the point, with a minimum of discussion. With the Bass group behind me as chairman and Frank as president, the tide suddenly turned. For starters, we could count on at least one more vote. Chuck Cobb ran the Arvida real estate company that the Basses had sold Disney, and they assured us that Cobb, who was now on the Disney board and had lobbied for the top Disney job himself, would vote their interests. That gave us at least four of the seven votes we needed: Cobb, Roy, Stanley, and Peter Dailey. Ray Watson was now officially uncommitted, but I believed that he would end up voting for us. I was about to learn—for the first time, but far from the last—what a powerful ally Sid Bass can be.

Sid had grown up in a legendary Texas family, and he was introduced to the world of business and investments at a very early age. His great-uncle and namesake, Sid Richardson, was a colorful character who became a Texas legend. Between wildcatting and trading cattle, he became a millionaire twice and went broke twice in his twenties, before discovering so much oil in the 1930s that it was nearly impossible to go broke a third time. Perry Bass, Sid's father, was an only child whose father had died when he was just eighteen. Sid Richardson became something of a surrogate father to Perry, and eventually they went into business together.

The oldest of four children, Sid was ten when his father took him to see the New York Stock Exchange for the first time. By fourteen,

Sid was reading the stock pages, and by eighteen, he was experimenting with different investment strategies using an initial $1,000 stake his father had given him. After graduating from Andover and then Yale, he considered going to art school and becoming a painter. Instead, he went to graduate school in business at Stanford. In 1968, when Sid turned twenty-six, his father handed over the family business to him. Rather than investing in several dozen stocks, as the high-profile mutual fund managers were doing, Sid limited himself to a few companies which he came to know very well.

"I just simplified the rules," Sid told me, soon after we first met. "My first rule was that I wouldn't buy any shares of a company unless I would have been happy to own all the shares. If the price went lower, that was good news, because then it was even more of a bargain than when you first decided to buy it." Over the next decade, Sid and his three brothers and their small team made a modest number of very successful investments in companies ranging from Church's Fried Chicken to Marathon Oil and Texaco.

The second tenet of Sid's philosophy was that he never sought to take over the companies in which he invested. Rather than pay a large premium to win control, he was content with a minority position, which he could acquire, quietly, at market prices. Nor was he interested in serving on any company's board of directors, or involving himself in day-to-day management. He preferred the freedom to serve as a sounding board for the CEO of any company in which he had a substantial investment. Sid had no tricks up his sleeve. He was simply tough-minded and patient, low-key and no-nonsense. By the age of thirty, he had amassed a considerable fortune of his own. "It tells you something about the value of insider information that I never had any," he once told me.

Having cast his lot with me and Frank, Sid now offered to make the case for us to the other major shareholders, and then to Ray Watson directly. That same afternoon, he called Irwin Jacobs and Ivan Boesky and managed to line up both of them. Dennis Stanfill chose the same day to call seeking the Basses' support. Sid explained to him that after much deliberation, he was going with Frank and me. Stanfill bristled, and suggested that he already had the votes of a majority of the board.

"What happens if I win the vote on Saturday?" he asked.

"Then we'll start a proxy vote on Monday," Sid replied. "We'll replace the board and appoint new officers."

Despite Sid's efforts and our own, we had only four sure votes out of the seven by Friday, September 21. The most powerful swing vote belonged to Card Walker. The reason was that at least two other board members — Donn Tatum, the chairman of Disney before Card, and Richard Nunis, who ran the theme parks—could be expected to vote with Walker. Those three would give us the seven votes we needed. We agreed that Frank should make the pitch directly to Card, who happened to be on a family vacation at Lake Powell, in Arizona. Frank flew there in Roy Disney's corporate jet. I remained in Los Angeles, to meet two other board members. In the morning, I drove downtown to lobby Sam Williams at his law firm. Then Jane and I drove to Newport Beach in the afternoon. While she remained in the car, I went into Nacho Lozano's house to make my case. On the way back home, I telephoned Stanley. I wasn't certain that I had managed to convert either Williams or Lozano.

"It doesn't matter," Stanley told me. "We've won." Just five minutes earlier, Frank had called from the plane to say that Card had not only agreed to support us but that he was prepared to make our nominating speech at the board of directors meeting the next morning. It turned out Card had been prepared to support us all along and just hadn't been asked. Perhaps it was my alliance with Frank that made him comfortable with my becoming CEO. I never found out for sure.

Stanley requested that Frank and I meet at his house at six o'clock the next morning, Saturday, to try to agree on a compensation package. Irwin Russell picked me up at 5:45 a.m. I wasn't especially concerned with salary, and I told Irwin that I was happy to be paid as chairman of Disney what I had earned as president of Paramount. What interested me more was the opportunity to be rewarded—through stock options and incentive bonuses—if Frank and I succeeded in significantly turning the company around.

I asked Stanley if he had an annual report for Disney. When I opened it, I saw that the highest net income Disney had ever earned was $100 million. Irwin and I suggested to Stanley that I receive a bonus of 2 percent of any profit the company made in excess of $100 million. If we managed to increase profits by 50 percent, for example, I would earn an additional $1 million—scarcely outrageous for that level of success. Irwin also asked that I be given options on 500,000 shares of Disney stock, which was selling at slightly under $60 a share. That meant I could exercise the right to buy those shares for $60 each beginning at a specified date in the future. Once again, I would be rewarded only if we increased the value of the company for all shareholders, rather than being given restricted stock, or guaranteed bonuses, or any other form of compensation that wasn't dependent on how well the company did.

Frank turned out to be even less concerned about salary than I was. He quickly agreed to a deal structured like mine. The entire negotiation took twenty minutes. Ultimately, we would use much the same formula for all of Disney's top executives—eschewing guarantees and high salaries, and instead focusing on bonuses tied to individual performance, and stock options whose value depended on the company's overall success.

After our discussion, Stanley left for the board meeting. Frank and I went back to our houses to await word. This time, the phone rang at noon, before we had a chance to get worried. "Congratulations," Stanley said. "You got it." In the wake of Card Walker's nominating speech, the board's vote had been unanimous. Even Phil Hawley finally took our side. Now, he took the phone from Stanley to say that he thought the outcome was "terrific" and we had his full support. When Stanley got back on, he asked that Frank and I meet with him, Roy Disney, and the other directors at the Lakeside Country Club in Toluca Lake for a celebratory lunch.

Jane and I were both stunned that it had all worked out. There was nothing to say. We simply looked at each other and hugged. Then I ran upstairs to change out of my blue jeans and into a suit. From the upstairs phone, I called Barry Diller with the news. I felt that it would be wrong for him to hear about it on a car radio or the evening news. He was almost certain to be disappointed and even angry that I wouldn't be joining him at Fox, but I felt certain he would recognize what an extraordinary opportunity it was to run Disney. As I told him the news, the impact of it all suddenly hit me and I heard my voice cracking. I was slightly embarrassed and hoped Barry didn't notice. I hadn't felt so emotional since the day my first son was born.

From our first lunch with the board, it dawned on Frank and me that they represented an extraordinary resource. All too often when new management takes over, they arrogantly assume that they know best and disparage their predecessors. Frank and I agreed immediately that Disney had a legacy which it was critical to protect. The company's past success wasn't an accident, and while it had struggled in recent years, there were still very talented people in the ranks. To this day, our board of directors includes several executives who began at the company under Walt, including Roy Disney, of course, and Ray Watson, and, until very recently, former CEO Card Walker, and Dick Nunis, who served as chairman of the parks division. We continue to draw on their expertise, and their institutional memory. We were in no rush to make wholesale replacements of people in our divisions, either. Today, some fourteen years later, several of those who came to Disney long before we did still occupy key positions in the company. We also derived value from long-standing outside board members, like Nacho Lozano, head of *La Opinion*, the largest Spanish-language newspaper in the country.

The lunch at Lakeside was the last leisurely meal Frank or I would take for a long time. We finally had the jobs we'd lobbied so hard to win, but the company remained very much at risk of being taken over. Our next challenge was to gain some control over Disney's destiny —and our own. On Sunday morning, I awoke early and met Frank to take a tour of the Disney lot in Burbank. Afterwards, we sat down and spent the rest of the afternoon with the group of investment bankers who had been hired by the company to defend it against takeover. Joseph Flom, a senior partner of Skadden Arps Slate Meagher & Flom, briefed us on where Disney stood. Flom focused especially on Irwin Jacobs. Not only was he now the largest shareholder in the company, Flom said, but he was considered the chief advocate for breaking it up. Suddenly, I found myself in a long discussion about subjects I had never spent much time considering: greenmail and arbitrageurs, 13Ds and SEC filings, poison pills and proxy fights. It dawned on me that I was going to have to be a quick study. For all my confidence about Frank's and my capacity to turn Disney around, I had no foundation in finance and limited knowledge of corporate gamesmanship at this level.

On Monday morning, September 24, I drove to the lot to begin my first day of official work. I wasn't even sure where to go, so I decided to use Ron Miller's former office on the third floor of the Animation Building, off Dopey Drive. The office had once belonged to Walt Disney. All this I learned from Lucille Martin, who had briefly been Walt's secretary, and then Ron's, and was now about to become mine. It made sense to have as my secretary someone who truly knew the company. A few minutes after I introduced myself to Lucille, Frank bounded in and sat down across from me. At first, I figured that he just wanted to talk for a few minutes, but then I realized that he intended to stay put.

"Frank," I asked. "Are we going to sit here together?"

"Well, yeah," he said. "I thought we would."

I was amused by his utter lack of guile, but I knew that such an arrangement wasn't ideal. "Look," I said, seeking a graceful solution, "I can't work that way. What am I going to do when I have to discipline one of my sons or argue with Jane about something? Why don't you take this office, and I'll find another place to sit?"

"No, no," he said, and jumped up. "You stay here." Before I could argue, he walked into the conference room next door, where he made himself at home. We both spent much of the morning returning congratulatory phone calls. In the afternoon, we went back to the lot to address hundreds of employees who had gathered. When one of them introduced herself as an assistant manager at BVD, I asked innocently if Disney made underwear.

"No," she said, containing a smile, "BVD stands for Buena Vista Distribution, the division that places our movies in theaters." Obviously I had a lot to learn. Still, Frank and I were heartened by the welcome we received. Whatever doubts the employees may have had, nearly everyone seemed thrilled by the prospect that we might bring new life to a company that had been under siege for so long. It was the first time that I understood how emotional the potential breakup of Disney was to its 28,000 employees. They were loyal and committed, and they had been on the verge of losing their company. Standing in front of Frank and me were men and women who had been worrying about their jobs for months, worrying about supporting their families. We represented the potential for security and stability. We were heroes without being heroic.

Unfortunately, there wasn't much time to get settled in. The next afternoon, Frank and I got on a plane with Mike Bagnall, the chief financial officer under Ron Miller. We were headed to Fort Worth to meet for the first time with the Basses, who had been so instrumental in supporting us for our jobs. I had spoken with Sid by phone the previous day, but Frank and I agreed that it was important to meet him and his partners in person. Sid suggested that he invite Irwin Jacobs to be part of the meeting since Jacobs was the other major outside shareholder.

Bagnall gave us a crash course in each of Disney's lines of business during our flight down. When we landed, we were driven directly to the downtown headquarters that the Basses had built for themselves—two soaring, powerfully striking skyscrapers designed by Paul Rudolph. It was my first visit to Fort Worth, and only later did I learn that Sid and the Bass family were almost single-handedly responsible for the rebuilding and revival of its downtown, much of it designed by a second fine architect, David Schwartz. The Bass offices, on the thirty-second floor, were surprisingly informal. Most of them were separated by glass partitions, so that you could see between them. The atmosphere felt almost like a locker room. The young executives were dressed in suits, but they behaved more like ballplayers, running in and out of offices, high-fiving each other, shouting numbers into phones, and whooping it up about one deal or another.

We gathered in a small conference room, one wall of which was white laminate. Details of the deals that Sid's team were in the midst of discussing were scribbled on that wall in Magic Marker and then erased later. Our meeting included Irwin Jacobs and Sid Bass—along with their associates Richard Rainwater, Al Checchi, Tommy Taylor, and Chuck Cobb. And, of course, Frank, Mike Bagnall, and me. When we walked in, I wasn't even sure who was who until the introductions were made. Polite, soft-spoken, and gentlemanly, Sid looked more like an Ivy League graduate student than a Texas entrepreneur. I'd decided against preparing any formal remarks. After some small talk, Sid simply turned to me and said, "So, how do you see the company?" I stood up, grabbed one of the black Magic Markers on the table, and spent the next half hour writing notes on the walls and talking about Disney's businesses.

I began by describing the creative process, and the primary importance of the initial idea or concept in any form of entertainment. Then I talked about how movies are made, what they should cost, how we protected ourselves financially, and the potential sources of revenue from movies.

"The distribution window after movie theaters will soon be home video," I explained, "followed by cable television and then network." All of these sources of revenue had grown explosively in the last several years. The result was that film libraries now had more value than ever. During the past six months, we had tried at Paramount to put a number on the value of the Disney library, with an eye toward possibly buying it. "The classic animated movies are probably worth at least $200 million in profits over the next several years, and more with better marketing and cross-promotion."

If I'd known how ridiculously conservative that number would turn out to be, I would have considered trying to talk the Basses into buying the rest of the company. Instead, I went on to talk about the television business, and the level of profit it's possible to make once a series has been on the air long enough to go into syndication. "It's a huge opportunity that Disney is missing simply by not being in the television business," I stressed. Finally, I spoke about my belief that the theme parks could be used more effectively to promote Disney's movies, and how characters from movies could become the basis for new attractions in the parks.

When I finished, Sid didn't say much, but Rainwater and Checchi were full of questions. "What about going into business with George Lucas?" Richard asked me. "I assume you're planning to make movie deals with people like him."

"Well, I don't know if that's the best way to go," I replied. "You see, George has already made *American Graffiti* and *Star Wars* and *Raiders of the Lost Ark*. He can now command a giant piece of the gross profit on any movie he makes, plus an upfront fee of $5 million or more. The real challenge is to find the *next* George Lucas, or Steven Spielberg, or Francis Coppola, and develop relationships with these filmmakers before they become high-priced stars themselves. I would rather make a deal with Lucas for the theme park rights to *Star Wars* or *Raiders of the Lost Ark*, and convince him to create a new ride based on those films, which his company can probably do better than anyone. That would be more profitable for Disney than having him make movies right now." I knew I was treading in dangerous territory, since Richard and George were friends. But he had asked me the question point-blank. I wasn't about to start our relationship by trying to tell him what I thought he wanted to hear, if I didn't believe it myself.

After about a half hour, Richard stood up to take a phone call and Sid left the room with him. We didn't know it at the time, but as soon as they walked out the door, Sid turned to his partner.

"I like what I'm hearing," he said.

"I'm with you," Rainwater replied.

"Let's go back and tell them we're in for the next five years," Sid said.

Sid later told me that was the sum total of their conversation. In less than half an hour, Sid and Richard had concluded that they stood to earn more by keeping their money in Disney while we sought to turn it around than they would by allowing it to be sold off in parts. Before returning to the conference room, Sid called Irwin Jacobs out, and they had a brief meeting in his office. "These guys know what they want to do with the company," Sid said. "It's not often that you see management being so open, people who will talk like that to shareholders." Then Sid suggested that they should both consider not just holding on to their Disney stock but buying more. Jacobs responded favorably.

When they rejoined us, the tenor of the discussion shifted palpably. They didn't yet divulge the decision they had just made, but they began to talk as if we were their partners. Sid and his group had a number of ideas about how to enhance the company's value, most of them related to developing the vast real estate that we owned at Walt Disney World. Al Checchi was especially knowledgeable about the hotel business, having worked previously at Marriott, the hotel company. He had even helped to conduct a study of the Orlando market during a period when Marriott was considering making its own bid for Disney.

Al pointed out that Disney owned just three major hotels on its property in Orlando, and that the company hadn't built a single new one since 1973, even though the existing hotels operated at nearly 100 percent occupancy. In the meantime, more than 250 hotels had sprung up all around Walt Disney World, taking advantage of the more than 10 million guests who visited the park each year. Al's study revealed that guests far preferred to be inside Walt Disney World than outside it, and that there was more than enough demand to build several thousand new hotel rooms on the property. Al pointed out that comparable hotels out-side the property were actually charging higher prices for rooms than we were inside the park. Our conversation went on for more than three hours. By the time we broke up, we were all feeling enthusiastic.

"We're in for five years," Sid told us as we left for the airport. "We'll stand pat for at least that long before we sell off any of our holdings."

A week or so later, we received word that the Basses had dra-matically upped their holdings again. After surmising that Ivan Boesky might be looking to unload his 1.5 million shares of Disney, Sid had a broker call Boesky immediately and offer to buy his stake. They agreed on a price of $60 a share—meaning virtually no premium over the mar-ket. No sooner did the news of this large transaction hit the Dow Jones wire than Irwin Jacobs phoned Sid. He was upset at being left out of the purchase. Hadn't Sid implied that they do any further purchase of stock together, he asked.

"I just told you I thought the stock was a good investment," Sid replied. "I never promised you anything." Realizing that he was in dan-ger of being marginalized, Jacobs offered to buy all of Sid's stock for $65 a share. That would have given the Basses an instant profit on their shares of between $5 and $15 a share, or somewhere around $40 million.

"It's not for sale at any price," Sid responded. Then he coun-tered by offering to buy Jacobs out. Clearly, Sid now had the leverage. The following morning, he offered Jacobs $60 a share for his 8 percent stake, and settled at $61—$4 a share below what Jacobs had offered Sid the day before. That gave Jacobs a profit of nearly $30 million on his year-long investment in Disney, but it was probably one of the most costly financial decisions Jacobs ever made. Had he simply held on to his Disney stock over the next ten years, his gains would have exceeded $2 billion.

As for the Basses, within several weeks, they bought up all the stock they could put their hands on, increasing their holdings to 25 per-cent of the company. That made them by far the largest shareholders and insured that Frank and I would have the time we needed to turn Disney around. It was both exciting and daunting. At long last, the ball was in our hands.

CHAPTER

6

Big Screen, Small Screen

No challenge that Frank and I faced when we arrived at Disney was more critical than reentering the movie and television business. We had nowhere to go but up, and I had been through this before —both at ABC and at Paramount. In network television, Disney had dropped out of the business altogether. In live action, not a single project in development seemed worth making. There were a couple of animated projects under way, but no new animated movie had been released since *The Fox and the Hound* three years earlier. We were confident that we could become players again. What we couldn't have anticipated was how dramatically our fortunes would rise and fall over the next eight years.

Hiring Jeffrey Katzenberg to run the studio was the most important initial decision that we made. Marty Davis tried to persuade Jeffrey to stay at Paramount, holding him under contract until it ran out in the late fall of 1984. But Jeffrey and I had agreed that we intended to keep working together, wherever that turned out to be. The weekend that Frank and I were named to our jobs, Jeffrey came to my house so that we could begin to talk about how to rebuild the Disney studio. A couple of weeks later the three of us met at a bungalow at the Beverly Hills Hotel, where Jeffrey had his first real introduction to Frank. Renting a Beverly Hills Hotel bungalow was something Frank had been introduced to back at Warner, and he felt it would add a sense of drama and excitement to the occasion. His enthusiasm, it turned out, was matched only by his appetite. After devouring his own Cobb salad in record time, he leaned across the table and began consuming Jeffrey's salad just as voraciously. Jeffrey looked at Frank curiously, and then turned to me for an explanation.

"He gets very hungry when he starts talking about deals," I said, shrugging my shoulders.

Jeffrey's voracious appetite was for work. He had already proven his ability to ferret out material, attract talent, keep the process moving forward, and get movies made at reasonable prices. There was, in those years, no fiercer team player than Jeffrey. From the day he arrived, his interests and Disney's became one and the same.

The most powerful way to restore the luster of the Disney name and promote the brand to a mass audience, we agreed, was to revive a Disney franchise in prime time. Walt's original TV series, *Disneyland*, went on the air in 1954. It moved among all three networks and several name changes, and eventually became the longest-running series on prime-time TV—twenty-nine seasons. The show grew out of Walt's insatiable creative appetite and his attempt to raise money to build the theme park that would become Disneyland. No one had ever before spent $17 million to build a park—and not a single bank was willing to provide financing. Walt's solution was to turn to the young television networks for help. Each of the network heads was hungry for a weekly Disney-produced series. Whoever truly wanted the show, Walt decided, would have to agree to invest in Disneyland. Both David Sarnoff at NBC and William Paley at CBS turned him down. Leonard Goldenson at ABC was Walt's last best hope. Goldenson still had only fourteen affiliates and he desperately needed programming to compete more effectively with the far more powerful NBC and CBS.

ABC finally agreed to invest $500,000 in Disneyland and to guarantee loans up to $4.5 million. In return, the network got a 34 percent stake in the new park and all of the profits from concessions for ten years. Walt agreed to produce a weekly, one-hour Disney show for ABC. In addition to a $5 million budget for the series, the network agreed to provide Walt with one minute of commercial time within each show to use as he pleased. It was a spectacular deal for Disney. Every one of the other movie studio chiefs remained wary of competition from television; Walt immediately saw how to use the medium. Above all, it became a way to reach a mass audience with Disney-style programming and to experiment with new dramatic forms, such as nature documentaries. While no one yet called it "synergy," Walt recognized intuitively that the weekly show could be used as a platform to familiarize viewers with Disneyland, Disney movies, and the Walt Disney name. "Television," he explained to an interviewer, "is going to be my way of going directly to the public."

Naming the new series *Disneyland* helped to make the theme park a household word even before it opened. Walt's decision to host the weekly show himself became a means of humanizing the company that bore his name. The fact that he spoke with a midwestern twang and lacked a professional actor's polish only made him more appealing to the audience. The show's premiere was a special entitled *The Disneyland Story*, about the making of the park. Several weeks later, there was a documentary about the filming of *20,000 Leagues Under the Sea*, Disney's next live-action movie. The biggest hit of the season was an original movie called *Davy Crockett*. Starring Fess Parker, the three one-hour shows about a rugged American populist hero attracted huge ratings, spawned a number one hit song, "The Ballad of Davy Crockett," and prompted a licensing bonanza for Disney in coonskin hats and dozens of other products. The show also won an Emmy in 1956. As for the *Disneyland* series, it continued to serve as Disney's primary face to the world long after Walt's death in 1966. Finally, in 1983, Card Walker decided to take it away from the networks, fearful that a weekly Disney series would cut into the audience for the recently launched Disney Channel.

Frank and I believed just the opposite was true. The Disney Channel was aimed at viewers who wanted access to Disney all the time. A Sunday-night Disney movie on one of the major networks was an unparalleled opportunity to showcase our company's renewed commitment to high-quality family programming. As it had been for Walt thirty years earlier, it was also a way to bring attention to other initiatives in the company. I first broached the idea of reviving the Disney movie with Fred Pierce. We were headed up the chairlift together in Aspen over Christmas vacation in 1984. Fred had continued to run ABC ever since

I left a decade earlier. My idea was to put the Disney franchise show up against CBS's *60 Minutes* on Sunday nights. ABC had yet to produce a successful show in that time slot, and the networks were now required by the FCC to run either news or family programming during the 7:00–8:00 p.m. hour. By the time we stepped off the chairlift, Fred was enthusiastic about doing the show with Disney. I was elated. I also felt a little shameless, selling an idea at 10,000 feet during a vacation.

The first meeting to discuss ideas took place in the early spring of 1985, over a weekend in Palm Springs. As I had during my first week at Paramount, I gathered our Disney creative group for a marathon meeting. In time, those events came to be known as "Gong Shows." All of the people who attended were encouraged to suggest even their most unlikely and outrageous ideas. The understanding was that most of them would get "gonged"—with no hard feelings. In most companies when you hold a large ideas meeting, the contributions are safe and familiar. Only when people are tired enough, loose enough, and sufficiently free of inhibition do they start to think more imaginatively. Gong Shows can be painful but they're also fun. And usually they're productive.

The first idea that caught on was a modern twist on the classic immigrant's tale. It was a true story about a mother and her children who make a harrowing escape from Cambodia during the Vietnam War. After hiding under their seats during their first airplane trip, they land in America and are sent to a makeshift refugee camp. The mother manages to secure a job, and through her persistence, she eventually finds the family their own housing. By the end of the movie, not only are each of the kids excelling in school, but the oldest daughter, with all the drama of a Super Bowl victory, wins a national spelling bee. It was this story that I told over dinner the next week to Jane, Fred Pierce, and his wife, Marion. When all four of us got tears in our eyes, I felt certain we should go forward. Not all of our movies were equally stirring, but *The Girl Who Spelled Freedom* set an impressive standard.

Even as the series began to come together, the unresolved issue was how to create a sense of continuity for viewers of a weekly anthology show that lacked ongoing characters. The comfort factor in television is extremely important. The most successful series are built around the kinds of people that viewers want to bring into their homes each week. That was true of Danny DeVito's Louie DiPalma in *Taxi*, Henry

Winkler's Fonzie in *Happy Days,* Ted Danson's Sam Malone in *Cheers,* and Tim Allen's Tim Taylor in *Home Improvement.* Successful anthology and variety shows have had their own familiar characters—whether it was Walt Disney himself with the original *Disneyland* series, Ed Sullivan hosting his own variety show, or Alfred Hitchcock introducing his movies. Just the previous year, Steven Spielberg had produced an anthology show called *Amazing Stories* on NBC. Although most of the individual episodes were well done, the series failed to attract a large audience, at least partly because there was no sense of continuity from week to week.

We spent months searching for the right host. Early in 1985, we offered the role to Cary Grant, who turned it down. We went on to discuss other potential hosts, including Ron Howard, Dick Van Dyke, Julie Andrews, and even Paul Newman. In the end, we concluded that none of them had a clear, strong connection to Disney (nor was it clear that any of them would have accepted the job). Finally, around midyear, I began to talk with Frank Wells about hosting the series myself. My wife and my children immediately opposed the idea. "Dad, you'll totally embarrass me," my oldest son, Breck, said. "You'll be like Frank Perdue hawking chickens." Jeffrey and most other executives at Disney were equally discouraging.

As with so many other risky decisions during the next decade, Frank Wells and Sid Bass were the only ones who encouraged me to move forward. They shared my view that the chief executive of Disney would have more credibility than anyone else playing the host's role. Doing so was also a way of demonstrating that there was someone at the helm of Disney other than the ghost of Walt. I wasn't likely to be a smooth performer, but at a minimum, my passion for the project would come across. In the meantime, the critiques of my liabilities only mounted. I committed to buy a new wardrobe, lose fifteen pounds, nurture a suntan, and rehearse as long as it took to improve my skills. To direct my brief host spots for each week's movie we hired Michael Kaye, who had previously produced brilliant political advertising for such candidates as Bill Bradley and Ted Kennedy, and had the ability to be both serious and funny. I also liked the fact that Michael had no connection to Hollywood, didn't frequent the town's trendiest restaurants, and wasn't likely to gossip about how I was doing in my new role.

Filming the spots was even more unnerving than deciding to do them in the first place. On December 30, 1985, the night before my first shoot, I went to bed at 10:00 p.m. Just as I had the night before my SATs back in high school, I ended up staring at the ceiling for most of the night. At 5:45 a.m., I woke up for good, shaved twice, tried on the new suit I had just purchased, and tied the best Windsor knot I could manage. Between 7:30 a.m. and 10:30 a.m., we ended up filming nineteen takes. "You did great," Michael Kaye reassured me when we finished. I felt relieved. Perhaps it wasn't going to be so bad after all. That evening, I left for Palm Springs to spend New Year's Eve with my parents. By the following day the calls started to roll in. "You were a little stiff." "You squinted." "You emphasized the wrong words." When Jeffrey called, he was even more blunt. "It just didn't work at all," he said.

I went to sleep that night wondering why I was putting myself through such unnecessary torture. By the time I awoke, rested, I felt ready to return to the battle. In the end, the criticisms only made me more determined than ever to prevail. Sure enough, over the next decade I went on to do more than three hundred one-minute host spots, working with Mickey, Minnie, Pluto, and Goofy, as well as snakes, elephants, tigers, and monkeys. I did my spots against backdrops ranging from the White House to our own theme parks. My performance improved only marginally over the years, but I did become familiar to our audience. At a minimum, my presence gave the show—and our company —a sense that someone was at the helm, steering Disney's ship.

Help Wanted: Kids, our first movie, premiered on Sunday, February 2, 1986. It starred Cindy Williams, from *Laverne and Shirley,* and her husband, Bill Hudson, in a movie about a married couple who lose their jobs, only to be offered new positions at a company in which employees are expected to have children. Because they have none of their own, they hire two kids to play the role. It was a sweet, funny, topical movie that was ideally pitched to parents and young kids. We drew nearly a 30 percent share of the viewing audience—a huge improvement over ABC's past performance in the same time slot. The ratings remained strong, particularly with kids, for the rest of the season and into the next one. More important, *The Disney Sunday Movie* helped to demonstrate that Disney could be inventive and contemporary and fun. It put us back on the map.

We faced a different set of challenges in our attempt to become a player in prime-time television for the networks. Our first gambit was a big success. In the spring of 1985, we received a call from Bill Haber, who ran the television department at CAA. He represented Susan Harris, the writer-producer who had created *Soap* back when I was at ABC. Along with her partners, Paul Junger Witt and Tony Thomas, Harris had created a new show for NBC titled *The Golden Girls*, about four women in their golden years living together in a Miami house—including a mother and daughter. Haber was looking for a studio as a partner to finance the difference between what NBC was willing to pay for the show and the cost of actually producing it. All of us had some skepticism about whether a show built around four senior citizens could attract a broad audience.

When we questioned Susan about the age appeal of the show, she pointed out that a mother-daughter conflict between an eighty-year-old mother and a sixty-year-old daughter—in this case Estelle Getty and Bea Arthur—is fundamentally no different than the one between a thirty-five-year-old mother and a fifteen-year-old daughter, except it's funnier. I remembered the Shirley MacLaine–Debra Winger relationship in *Terms of Endearment* and realized that Susan was absolutely right. Moreover, nearly all of us have a grandparent who occupies a special place in our hearts. We finally made an exclusive, long-term deal with Harris, Witt, and Thomas. *The Golden Girls* became the highest-rated new show of the 1985–86 television season and remained a top ten hit for the next five seasons. Harris went on to create *Empty Nest*, set in the same Miami neighborhood as *The Golden Girls* and built around a widowed pediatrician whose two grown daughters move back in with him. It, too, became a hit. In our non-network business, where we syndicate shows directly to independent stations, we had a couple of successes, most notably *Siskel & Ebert at the Movies* and *Live with Regis & Kathie Lee*—both produced at a modest cost.

Our one mega-hit in prime time was *Home Improvement*. We discovered Tim Allen in stages. First, Dean Valentine, the young executive we had recently put in charge of television under Rich Frank, became interested in a tape of Tim's stand-up comedy act. Around the same time, Tim Allen's manager sent another tape of the act to Jeffrey. All the networks had passed on Tim, and no agency had expressed an interest in representing him. Jeffrey looked at the tape anyway, thought

Tim was very funny, and decided to set up an outing to go see him perform his act live at the Improv. He invited Dean, me, and several other Disney people to come along. We all agreed that Tim's iconoclastic, ironic "real man" act would translate perfectly to a TV series.

Matt Williams was a writer with whom we had an exclusive deal. In addition to working on *The Cosby Show*, he had developed its successful spin-off, *A Different World*, and created *Roseanne*. Plainly, he was capable of writing for big, bold personalities. Tim had the idea of doing a show-within-a-show based loosely on the earnest PBS home improvement series *This Old House*. As he later put it, "I wanted to be Bob Vila with a bad attitude." The pilot drew mixed responses, especially from women, but soon after it went on the air, *Home Improvement* took off. It reached number one in the ratings, and in 1995, when we sold reruns in syndication, they commanded one of the highest prices ever.

In the movie business, Frank and I shared the view that we needed to protect our financial downside even as we moved forward aggressively. By raising financing from outside sources, our balance sheet could be protected from any sudden, significant losses in the event that we had a bad run with our movies. Unfortunately, the tax-shelter money that we raised so successfully at Paramount had essentially dried up, largely because the IRS codes permitting such investments had been significantly tightened. It was Frank who found an alternative. Silver Screen Partners was a limited-investment partnership run by a gruff, charming former lawyer from New York named Roland Betts, and his partner, Tom Bernstein, who had once been a camper at Keewaydin. In partnership with brokers from E. F. Hutton, Betts and Bernstein sought money from individual investors across the country. By the fall of 1985, Silver Screen had raised more than $200 million to finance our movies. In effect, we had interest-free financing, which allowed Frank and me to sleep better at night. Silver Screen's investors split revenues on the movies. When we did well, Roland, Tom, and their partners did well.

Creatively, we began with a piece of very good fortune. During our first week at Disney, I received a call from the agent Sam Cohn in New York, who had a script that he thought might interest us. Universal owned it but had decided not to make the movie. A remake of an early Jean Renoir film titled *Boudu Saved from Drowning*, the script was written by the director Paul Mazursky, who moved the setting from

Paris to Beverly Hills. His version was a clever contemporary comedy about a bum who is literally saved from drowning by a wealthy couple whose pool he falls into—only to move in with them and take over their lives. We were immediately drawn to the project, even though we knew that it would almost surely earn an "R" rating—something that Disney, even under its Touchstone label, had never before permitted. Mazursky himself was considered by some a quirky director, and he had a mixed track record at the box office. But the script was strong, the deal was reasonable, and I admired much of Mazursky's previous work, especially *An Unmarried Woman* and *Moscow on the Hudson*. Eventually we renamed his new script *Down and Out in Beverly Hills*.

Rather than cast expensive stars for the lead roles, we opted for actors whose work we admired but whose careers were in temporary downswings. I first became interested in Bette Midler after I heard about her nightclub act at the Continental Baths when I was at ABC in the 1960s. For twenty years, I tried unsuccessfully to do business with her. The roadblock was her manager, Aaron Russo. Way back in 1967, he answered an ad that Jane and I put in the *New York Times* to rent the other apartment in our brownstone. A pleasant but disheveled and somewhat overweight young guy showed up with his beautiful, blond, perfectly put-together wife, and they promptly fell in love with the apartment and agreed to rent it.

As he was leaving, I asked Russo what he did for a living, and he told me that he managed rock groups. That night, Jane and I decided it was a mistake to rent the place to him. When I called to tell Russo, he begged and begged, saying that his marriage depended on it. He and his wife came over again, and I finally relented. Soon after, Jane and I had second thoughts for a second time. I was amazed at how badly I was handling this personal business, given how well I was handling business at the office. (Fortunately, I couldn't be fired from my own life.) This time when I called Russo back, he was less friendly. "I'm going to kill you," he joked.

Several years later, I was called into a meeting at ABC to try to close a deal with Bette Midler for several network specials. There, across the table, was Aaron Russo. I had no idea that he managed Bette, and I pretended not to recognize him. But after a few moments he stood up, walked over, and looked me right in the eyes. "You're the guy, aren't you?" Sheepishly, I acknowledged that I was. None of the eight other people in the office knew what was going on. Aaron simply walked out of the room. The deal was off. In the years that followed, I sold the brownstone, Russo was divorced from his wife for reasons that had nothing to do with the apartment, and we became friendly. Aaron changed careers and eventually ran for governor of Nevada.

As for Bette, her movie career had stalled after she starred in *The Rose*. When we offered her the role of the rich wife in *Down and Out in Beverly Hills*, she accepted it immediately. Richard Dreyfuss did the same, but based on a very different career trajectory. I'd first seen him at ABC in the 1970s, when he performed brilliantly as the star of a terrific pilot based on Joseph Heller's *Catch-22*. For reasons I can't imagine, we didn't pick up the series. For Richard, the rejection proved to be a blessing. Disappointed by television, he went on to star in *Jaws, Close Encounters of the Third Kind,* and *The Goodbye Girl*. Along the way, he began a long battle with drugs, during which he virtually stopped working. He had just emerged from rehabilitation when we decided to take a chance and cast him opposite Bette. For the part of the bum, we went after Nick Nolte. Although his career was in its own dry spell, he had been successful in every project we had done together, from *Rich Man, Poor Man* at ABC, to *North Dallas Forty* and *48 Hours* at Paramount. Using these three first-rate actors, we were still able to make the movie for a modest $14 million.

Important as it was for our first movie to be successful, *Down and Out in Beverly Hills* was at least equally significant as a statement to the creative community about our intentions. In the years since Walt's death, Disney had become something of a filmmaking backwater—so old-fashioned that it was increasingly difficult to attract good writers, directors, producers, and actors to work for the company. We no longer had Walt, and the only way to replace him was to nurture new talent, pay them at rates competitive with other studios, and offer them the opportunity to do the projects that most interested them. Ron Miller's launch of the Touchstone label in 1983 began the process. For the first time, the company was able to produce films aimed beyond the traditional Disney audience of families and kids. *Splash* attracted Ron Howard and Tom Hanks to our lot and became Disney's biggest hit in years.

With its "R" rating and adult subject matter, *Down and Out in Beverly Hills* represented another leap. Back at Paramount, I might have considered asking Mazursky to make a small number of changes such as dropping a handful of four-letter words and a moderately explicit sex scene. But by giving Mazursky more rope, we sent a message that Disney was prepared to support talented filmmakers and to make movies that dealt frankly with contemporary adult life. Attracting actors such as Bette Midler, Richard Dreyfuss, and Nick Nolte had a similar impact. Nearly overnight, Disney went from nerdy outcast to leader of the popular crowd, from "out of it" to "cool." The immediate value was that we were able to draw on a stronger talent pool. Once a good actor or director came into the company to work on a non-Disney project, there was a better chance that he or she would ultimately be convinced to do a Disney-label project aimed specifically at the family audience.

By producing projects like *Down and Out in Beverly Hills*, we also ran the risk of alienating our core audience. It wasn't easy sitting next to Patty and Roy Disney during the first public screening. We'd explained in advance why we'd made the film, and won their support. Even so, after each increasingly vivid expletive I felt a drop or two of sweat forming somewhere, until by the end of the screening I was drenched. In fact, the movie became successful not just at the box office but among critics, and prompted no backlash.

In time, many actors became part of an extended Disney family, particularly when they had kids of their own. Bette, for example, went on to do the voice of Georgette in our animated film version of *Oliver & Company*, and later starred in Disney's *Hocus Pocus*. Robin Williams first came to us in the Touchstone film *Good Morning, Vietnam* and *Dead Poets Society*. Subsequently, he agreed to serve as the robotic host for our *Timekeeper* attraction at Walt Disney World; provided the voice for the Genie in *Aladdin*; and most recently starred in Miramax's *Good Will Hunting* and Disney's hit remake of *Flubber*—directed by Les Mayfield, who first came to us to direct the Touchstone film *Encino Man*. Nearly a decade after *Splash,* Tom Hanks returned to provide the voice of Woody in *Toy Story*. Tim Allen, who did the voice of Woody's counterpart, Buzz Lightyear, began at Disney by starring in the Touchstone television series *Home Improvement*. He also went on to star in the Disney hits *The*

Santa Clause and *Jungle 2 Jungle,* and he wrote his first best-seller—*Don't Stand Too Close to a Naked Man*—for Hyperion, Disney's book publishing imprint.

Success in the movie business often feeds on itself, not just by attracting better talent to projects but by raising your own team's level of confidence and passion for the process. Jeffrey's film group began arriving as early as he did— 6:00 a.m.—and rarely left before nine or ten in the evening. We all worked long hours, often seven days a week. "If you don't come in on Saturday," Jeffrey allegedly told his troops, "don't bother coming in on Sunday." That was a joke, of course, but it did reflect the level of our commitment. Perhaps nothing is more exciting than creating something from the ground up. We were a small team at the start and we shared a missionary zeal about rebuilding Disney.

Jeffrey ran the movie division day to day, but during that early period we remained very much partners in the process. We were making only a dozen movies a year, and each one assumed great importance. Just as we had at Paramount, we developed our own ideas, insisted on being closely involved in the creative process, and produced movies for less money than our competitors did. To a modest degree, we tried to re-create the old studio system, signing up young writers to exclusive deals —often in return for offering them a chance to direct. Actors returned to do other Touchstone films, even before we recruited them for Disney projects. After *Down and Out in Beverly Hills,* Richard Dreyfuss starred in *Stakeout,* about a cop who falls in love with the woman he is assigned to spy on. Bette Midler played Danny DeVito's wife in *Ruthless People* and then starred alongside Lily Tomlin in *Big Business* and Shelley Long in *Outrageous Fortune.* Unlike most studios, we were more than willing to use actors whose only previous work had been in television. We knew Danny DeVito from *Taxi,* and we became familiar with Shelley Long through her role in *Cheers.*

None of our early comedies better proved the power of a strong idea than *Trois Hommes et un Couffin.* I saw it for the first time in the fall of 1985, while negotiating with the French government about building a new theme park near Paris. The movie was already a giant hit in France. I was trying to learn French at the time, so I liked the idea of attending a movie on the Champs-Elysées. I understood perhaps a third of what I heard, but responded to all of the visual humor. You didn't need to understand the dialogue to recognize that this was a very funny women's revenge movie—three bumbling bachelors left with a baby to care for and no clue how to do it. The mostly female French audience with whom I saw it never stopped laughing. We agreed that Jeffrey should make a substantial offer to the producers and the director, Coline Serrau, for rights to remake the film under the English title, *Three Men and a Baby*. Several other studios were also interested in the project, but we simply refused to let go.

By one view, we were investing an undue amount of effort on a single deal. But at the time we had yet to release a single movie of our own, and we believed that *Three Men and a Baby* had the potential to be our first blockbuster. It reminded me of our efforts at Paramount to buy *Raiders of the Lost Ark*. "They are asking for a ludicrous deal," I wrote in a memo during the *Three Men and a Baby* negotiations. "If you add in the cost of a star, you are in the mega-cost picture and maybe we should forget it. On the other hand we could be at the threshold here, if we don't go forward, of passing on the equivalent of *Stripes* or *Tootsie* or one of those movies. The only thing I know is that this movie will be vastly and wildly and spectacularly commercial." (I actually made that prediction before we bought the script. I've chosen not to mention my similarly optimistic predictions about movies that subsequently failed.)

We finally offered the filmmakers $1 million outright—an extraordinary sum at the time for remake rights to a foreign film. We seriously considered stars for the title roles, and negotiated with Michael Ovitz for two of his biggest CAA clients, Dustin Hoffman and Bill Murray. Either one would have literally doubled the price of a movie that we were convinced was going to work on its own merits. Instead, we produced *Three Men and a Baby* for a very reasonable budget with a cast that included two TV stars—Tom Selleck from *Magnum, P.I.,* and Ted Danson from *Cheers;* Steve Guttenberg, an actor of moderate renown; and a director, Leonard Nimoy, whose only previous directing credits were TV episodes of *Star Trek*. Even pulling together that cast required herculean efforts by Jeffrey. Danson turned our offer down three times before Jeffrey finally prevailed on him. "I have rhino skin," Jeffrey later told a reporter. "Rejection is part of the process. If I took it personally, I wouldn't know how to get up in the morning." We took another calculated risk by opening *Three Men and a Baby* over Thanksgiving in 1987, hoping to beat the annual glut of high-budget holiday movies. It became by far our biggest hit to that point.

By producing a series of accessible, mainstream movies for moderate prices, we enjoyed an extraordinarily consistent run in a business where failure is far more common than success. Beginning with *Down and Out in Beverly Hills,* twenty-seven of our first thirty-three movies were profitable over the next three years, including nineteen in a row. More than a half dozen earned a profit in excess of $50 million. This early run of success was built to a significant degree on commercial, "high concept" comedies. Perhaps as a result, a certain backlash set in. Some critics derided what came to be called "Touchstone comedies" as slick, superficial, and formulaic. We never consciously set out to make a certain kind of movie. Adult comedies simply filled a void in the marketplace when we entered the business. They were a way to set ourselves apart from our competitors. As Dick Cook, then our head of distribution, later put it: "If everyone wanted to go right, we went left." The irony was that by the time these comedies prompted the critical reaction they did, we had already moved on to other kinds of movies.

Our success emboldened us, for example, to take chances on several more ambitious, less obviously commercial movies. *Good Morning, Vietnam* was based on a true story about a U. S. armed forces disk jockey named Adrian Cronauer. Jeffrey found the project languishing at another studio. Vietnam was scarcely an issue when I went before my own draft board in 1964. Five years earlier, during my senior year in high school, I had walked into my midterm exams just before Christmas and suddenly felt the worst headache of my life. By the time I arrived home that afternoon, I could hardly stand up. Within two days, I was in the hospital with the case of viral meningitis that nearly killed me. Miraculously, two weeks later, I had fully recovered. Ironically, the illness may ultimately have saved my life. I wasn't highly political at the time, had no inclination to dodge the draft, and probably would have served if I had been called. But based on my meningitis, my draft board classified me 4-F and I was excused from service. A short time later, I went to work for ABC and was soon immersed in Saturday morning children's television and soap operas. The troop build-up was just beginning under Lyndon Johnson, and war in Vietnam seemed very far away.

Much the same was true for the main character in *Good Morn-*

ing, Vietnam. Only after the Tet offensive in February 1968 does Adrian Cronauer realize that war isn't one big joke after all. *Good Morning, Vietnam* was an opportunity to do a movie about a major historical event through an accessible coming-of-age story. Barry Levinson agreed to direct, and we decided to take a chance on another hugely talented actor whose career was in a temporary lull: Robin Williams. He had appeared in several forgettable movies and later acknowledged that he'd struggled with his own drug problem. It was Williams who would later joke that Disney cast its movies by hanging out at the back door of the Betty Ford Clinic. Released just a few weeks after *Three Men and a Baby* in 1987, *Good Morning, Vietnam* became a huge critical and commercial hit. Together, the two movies took in nearly $300 million domestically, making Disney the number one–ranked studio at the box office for the first time in its history.

Our big movie in 1988 was *Cocktail*, with Tom Cruise. In 1989, we had another one-two success with two completely contrasting movies written by Tom Schulman. *Honey, I Shrunk the Kids,* nurtured and championed by Touchstone president David Hoberman, was in many ways the perfect Disney family movie—a very funny fantasy for kids but sufficiently clever to attract their parents. The second hit was *Dead Poets Society*—perhaps the most ambitious and least obviously commercial movie we had yet attempted at Disney. I had been pushing for years for a movie built around an inspiring teacher. Even so, it's difficult to imagine three less obviously commercial words for the title of a movie than "Dead," "Poets," and "Society," or a less likely hero than a poetry-loving prep school teacher.

Dead Poets Society worked for all of the right reasons. It had a great script, for which Tom Schulman eventually won the Academy Award; an emotional story about a charismatic teacher who convinces his young students that each of them has the capacity to "seize the day"; characters that the audience could root for; and first-rate acting and direction. Peter Weir had done a brilliant job directing *Witness* at Paramount, and he brought the same blend of texture, passion, and a faint touch of melodrama to *Dead Poets Society*. Robin Williams gave a bravura performance. In releasing the movie, we took our biggest scheduling risk yet—once again by "counterprogramming." Traditionally, no studio released an adult drama at the beginning of the summer, for fear that it would get buried under the avalanche of youth-oriented, block-buster star vehicles. The summer of 1989 seemed particularly daunting, with a lineup that included *Batman, Lethal Weapon 2, Ghostbusters II,* and the second *Indiana Jones* sequel. "There's no movie for grown-ups," Dick Cook argued. "Let's take a shot." We opened *Dead Poets Society* in June, directly against *Batman,* and both critics and audiences loved it.

It was during this same summer that we made a badly misguided strategic decision prompted both by personnel considerations and by the arrogance of success. From early on at Disney, Jeffrey and I met for dinner nearly every Monday night at the restaurant Locanda Veneta, to discuss business. One of our discussions focused on what to do about David Hoberman and Ricardo Mestres, the two top executives at Touchstone. Increasingly competitive, each one wanted more independence and authority. "If we don't do something to solve the problem, one of them is going to leave," Jeffrey told me one evening.

During the past decade, Jeffrey pointed out, the number of theaters had nearly doubled, fueled by the growth of multiplexes. That meant more outlets than ever for movies. We both knew that it was difficult for any one studio to produce more than a dozen or so films and still give each of them close attention. "What we could do," Jeffrey suggested, "is launch a second separate studio. Hoberman could run one, Mestres the other." This was a way, Jeffrey argued, to accommodate the ambitions of both executives and to potentially double our film production. Frank consistently opposed any increase in production. Other studios, he argued, had tried the same approach—Columbia by launching Tri-Star, United Artists by merging with MGM—and all had essentially failed. But Jeffrey convinced me, and Frank finally relented. In February 1989, we launched Hollywood Pictures, and we put Ricardo in charge. Within three years, we more than doubled our production—from a dozen movies to nearly thirty. We grew too big for our own good—and we paid the price.

The first signs of trouble arose in 1990. For the fifth year in a row, live action produced record profits, but for the first time the results were based largely on the performance of a single movie. *Pretty Woman,* which became our biggest hit ever, began as a far darker script, entitled *3000.* It told the story of a callous businessman who picks up a street prostitute, mistreats her, and then discards her. We read the script, and I had only one note for Jeffrey: "Let's not make *Taxi Driver*. This has to be a modern Doris Day movie. Make the lead the only virgin woman-of-the-night in Hollywood." Jeffrey agreed. He offered the project to Garry Marshall, who had moved on from his success producing shows like *Happy Days* and *Laverne and Shirley*, to directing films, including *Beaches*, with Bette Midler, and *The Flamingo Kid*. Garry rewrote the *3000* script as a modern *Pygmalion*. The notion of a love story between a businessman and a Hollywood prostitute was far-fetched, but in Garry's hands it turned into a very appealing fantasy.

One reason was casting. Around this time, I happened to be seated next to Sally Field on a flight to Los Angeles. She told me about the film she had just finished, *Steel Magnolias*, and mentioned that it included a fantastic young actress named Julia Roberts. We ought to take a look at her, Sally told me. I called Jeffrey as soon as I arrived in L.A. Over the years, I've made similar urgent calls on dozens of occasions. The vast majority of them go nowhere, but along the way I've learned that following up every idea and piece of advice—particularly from someone who expresses it with passion—is what leads to the occasional breakthrough. Jeffrey managed to sign Julia for *Pretty Woman*, which made both her career and our movie.

The problem was that we had only one other hit that year. *Dick Tracy* bore certain similarities to our experience with *Reds*, at Paramount. In this case it was Jeffrey, rather than Barry Diller, who dealt with Warren Beatty on an ongoing basis. Once again, we committed to a highly expensive project, although this one had more obvious commercial potential than *Reds*. Also, we managed to earn a significant profit with *Dick Tracy*—in part because it was so well produced by Warren and in part because we supported it with such a massive marketing campaign. Still, it was perfectly reasonable to ask whether the rewards were worth the enormous effort expended on the project. "We got into the movie star business, and we tried to create a phenomenon," argued Terry Press, our head of publicity at the time. "Making that kind of big blockbuster film is not what we do very well, or feel comfortable doing." She was exactly right.

The rest of our slate fell short in 1989, and Jeffrey treated our painful experience with a run of failures as a wake-up call. Recognizing that we had slowly but inexorably veered off course, he began working on a memo reaffirming the fundamental tenets I'd described in the memo I wrote at Paramount ten years earlier. Jeffrey's, finished early in 1991, and written by Dan Wolf, a speechwriter in the company, ran to twenty-eight pages. It faithfully reiterated the philosophy that Barry and I had evolved at ABC and refined at Paramount.

"Our initial success at Disney was based on the ability to tell good stories well," the memo began. "Big stars, special effects and name directors were of little importance. Of course, we started this way out of necessity. We had small budgets and not much respect. So we substituted dollars with creativity and big stars with talent we believed in. Success ensued. With success came bigger budgets and bigger names. We found ourselves attracting the calibre of talent with which 'event' movies could be made. And more and more, we began making them. The result: costs have escalated, profitability has slipped and our level of risk has compounded. The time has come to get back to our roots."

The memo went on to reemphasize the fundamental importance of the idea and the script. *Dick Tracy* was used as an example of how we had violated our basic tenets. By Jeffrey's reckoning, we'd been drawn to a huge talent—Warren Beatty—paid a very high price to sign him, and then devoted enormous time and energy to the project in part to justify our investment. What we overlooked, Jeffrey argued, was the fact that the movie lacked an emotionally compelling story and characters that the audience could truly care about.

I really liked *Dick Tracy*, but I agreed with nearly everything else in the memo. "This is an excellent analysis of where we are today and where we should go in the future," I scribbled on the copy of the memo he sent me. "I applaud the intelligence and the perception you have put into this paper." Then I warned him about its potential dangers: "I would demand that this paper never get into any hands outside our company, especially the press, but agents and lawyers as well. Nobody needs to read it so long as Ricardo [Mestres] and David [Hoberman] understand."

There was no need to share our analysis of the business, which was precisely why I'd never allowed my Paramount memo to get out. In Jeffrey's case, there was another, more obvious reason to keep his memo confidential. He named names, most notably Warren Beatty's. Making the memo public could only serve to antagonize Warren and other big-name talent in town, for no good reason. No sooner did I scribble my warning, however, than Jeffrey's memo had found its way to virtually every journalist who covers Hollywood. Suddenly it was news in the *New York Times*, the *Los Angeles Times*, and the Hollywood trades. Jeffrey did end up receiving wide recognition for the memo, but it wasn't the sort that he'd been seeking. What should have been a useful internal brief about how to return to smart, prudent moviemaking instead eventually came to be seen as self-important and self-serving.

The smartest move we made in the movie business during this period was the purchase of Miramax in 1993, an idea initiated by Jeffrey. Based in New York and run by the Weinstein brothers, Miramax had long acquired and distributed high-quality independent films. Four years earlier, it had jumped ahead of other independents by releasing *sex, lies, and videotape, Cinema Paradiso,* and *My Left Foot* in one year—three low-budget films that not only won critical praise and a slew of awards but also did strong business at the box office. Over the next few years, Miramax continued its dominance among the independents with acclaimed films, including *Like Water for Chocolate* and *The Crying Game.* Even in success, Harvey and Bob remained quintessential New Yorkers: blunt, passionate, exuberant, and combative. They prided themselves on their Queens background and utter lack of affectation, but they were also well read and had an encyclopedic knowledge of film. They also loved what they did—always a big plus for me.

With its focus on unconventional, often controversial films aimed mostly at a sophisticated adult audience, Miramax wasn't an obvious fit with Disney. In fact, we were surprisingly complementary. The Weinsteins' primary focus was on the idea itself, and they resisted paying for big stars and directors. "Our whole company has been built to be successful by hitting singles, not home runs or grand slams," Bob explained in an interview. "Why do we need that pressure? It goes against the whole grain of what we do, which is to make movies economically and have them turn a profit."

Ultimately, we were able to buy Miramax for approximately the cost of a single high-budget studio film. In return, we got not just the talents of Bob and Harvey and their proven ability to identify hits and market them effectively, but also a film library with a wide range of titles. This would prove especially valuable in creating packages that included our own Disney and Touchstone films and selling them overseas.

In addition, Miramax increased Disney's access to a group of artists who might not otherwise have considered working for us. What we brought to Miramax was a source of financing, as well as greater clout in the marketplace. Until we acquired the company, Miramax had mostly served as a distributor for other people's films. We immediately increased their budget for buying product, and also agreed to finance any film that Bob and Harvey wanted to produce, up to an agreed price. Within a short time, they went from producing 10 percent of their own films to 40 percent. Disney's financing also allowed them to make long-term deals with young filmmakers rather than lose these artists to bigger studios after a first success with Miramax.

Pulp Fiction was a good example of how the deal worked. Bob and Harvey loved the script and were eager to bet on Quentin Tarantino, the young writer-director whose first film, *Reservoir Dogs*, they had discovered at the Sundance Film Festival. With our financing, the Weinsteins were able to underwrite the production of *Pulp Fiction*, an ambitious film with an unusual narrative structure and a campy attitude toward violence that probably wouldn't have been appropriate even for Touchstone or Hollywood Pictures. The obvious strength of the script attracted stars including John Travolta, Samuel L. Jackson and Uma Thurman. *Pulp Fiction* became one of the best reviewed movies of the year and earned more than $100 million at the box office around the world, a record for an independent film at the time. Disney's strength in foreign distribution helped to double the film's box office overseas, while our home-video division turned it into one of the most successful rental films of all time. John Travolta came back to Disney two years later to star in *Phenomenon*, and the relationship we developed with Quentin Tarantino was useful when we needed a dialogue rewrite on *Crimson Tide*, our big summer movie in 1995.

Because Bob and Harvey had built their company on a willingness to be daring in their choice of material, being in business with them also meant enduring some difficult moments. But far more often than controversy, Miramax's films generated critical praise and well-deserved honors. In 1994 alone, for example, Miramax had four films competing at the Cannes Film Festival: *Pulp Fiction*, which won the prestigious Palme d'Or award; *Mrs. Parker and the Vicious Circle; Red;* and *Queen Mar-*

got. At the same time, by the second year of our acquisition, Miramax's profits had increased tenfold.

We were far less successful with our own movies. In the three years following Jeffrey's memo, we failed almost completely to live by his clear restatement of our philosophy. As we launched a new label in Hollywood Pictures and significantly increased production in live action, we devoted less time and attention to each film than we had in the past. The impact was dramatic. Having spread ourselves too thin, we made far too many movies without a strong premise and a real reason for being. During all of 1993, only two live-action movies—*Homeward Bound* and *Cool Runnings*—could be considered genuine hits. Meanwhile, we seemed to be releasing one instantly forgettable movie after another—*Life with Mikey, My Boyfriend's Back, Indian Summer, Father Hood,* and *The Program.*

In retrospect, a big part of the problem was that my partnership with Jeffrey, which had worked so well in our early years at Disney, was no longer as effective as it had been. Strong partnerships create an environment in which one person's enthusiasms and prejudices are forever tempered by another voice and subjected to another opinion. Most successful movie studios and television networks have had at least two strong executives at the top, supporting and counterbalancing one another. At ABC, I worked with Fred Pierce and then with Fred Silverman, and at Paramount with Barry Diller. At Universal, Lew Wasserman and Sid Sheinberg were an enormously effective team for nearly two decades. Our most consistently successful competitor at Disney was Warner Bros., run in a truly equal partnership by Bob Daly and Terry Semel. NBC had a long run at the top during the years that Grant Tinker and Brandon Tartikoff worked together. And of course there are the Weinstein brothers.

But Jeffrey increasingly wanted his independence, and I was probably too willing to turn my attention to the many other demands on my plate. To be effective, executives must be organized, keep their desks clean, answer their mail, return their calls, and remain sufficiently calm to put out each day's small fires before they spread. I spend probably 75 percent of my time on these tasks. If I don't get them done, there is no way I can comfortably focus the rest of my attention on what matters most—namely, trying to add value to the creative process. As Disney grew, even my creative energies were divided between more divisions, and more initiatives. Partly because I had less time, and partly to placate Jeffrey, I agreed when he requested that I stop attending the weekly creative meetings where scripts and ideas are discussed. "Having you there is undermining my authority," he complained. Although I believed I still provided a useful voice, I acceded to his sensitivity and settled instead for being filled in at our weekly dinners together. At the same time, Jeffrey began to hold regular screenings of the rough cuts of upcoming movies without me. What we lost was an objective voice in counterpoint to his.

In March 1994, Frank presented Jeffrey and me with a memo that painted a detailed—and devastating—portrait of the course of our live-action performance over the past decade. During our first five years, Frank reported, all but a handful of our thirty-five live-action films were successful. Exclusive of animation, we earned an average profit before overhead of nearly $200 million a year, as strong a performance as any studio in Hollywood. During the subsequent four years—spurred by the launch of Hollywood Pictures—we released seventy-six movies, nearly double our previous output, and only thirty-three were profitable, or barely more than 40 percent. After figuring in our overhead costs, we actually lost money. Frank's conclusion was blunt: "It's not worth being in the business at anything like this profile."

The statistics spoke for themselves. Bad movies lose money no matter how little they cost and no matter how many new ancillary markets emerge. I said as much in my Paramount memo, and Jeffrey echoed the same sentiment in his. Frank had a simple, logical solution: Make fewer movies and give each one more attention. "I really believe the two of you, working in partnership as you did the first four years, can make 15—plus or minus—movies a year and have spectacular results," he argued. "But I'm very concerned about going much beyond 15. . . . I seriously do not believe that the true head of production (that is Jeffrey—let's be real clear) can manage more than 15 pictures per year and give each one the individual attention it requires. Particularly as Jeffrey moves into broader responsibilities, we should all agree, starting now, that Michael becomes a true partner in the creative process."

In the meantime, failure—like our earlier success—had begun to feed on itself. For years at Paramount and later at Disney, our toughness about not overpaying, our resistance to agents and hype, and our stubborn focus on the basic premise for a movie had worked effectively. Leslie Dixon was a good example. A talented young writer, she had her first hit with us on the comedy *Outrageous Fortune*. We had the contractual right to another screenplay from Dixon, and despite her resistance to taking an assignment from us, we essentially insisted that she come in and do a rewrite on *Big Business*. It, too, turned into a hit, and Dixon became hotter than ever. Still, she vowed never to work for Disney again, literally comparing the experience to indentured servitude. In time, she found that success wasn't so easy to come by elsewhere and decided that perhaps we hadn't acted so unreasonably after all. Two years later, a reporter asked her to describe her feelings about working at Disney. "Was [it] a good experience for me?" she replied. "No. If I were them, would I have done the same thing? Probably. Would I write for them again? Well, let me just say that time and wisdom have made me miss their marketing department with every fiber of my body."

When our movies began to fail, it became more difficult to stand up for doing business our own way. Jeffrey backed off a bit and the agents quickly smelled blood. "Listen to me," they would say to him. "You guys have a terrible reputation. You have to embrace talent. The best people don't want to be in business with you anymore. So what if Star X wants $9 million instead of $8 million for his next movie? It's only an extra million and it will send the right message to the creative community." Jeffrey's solution was to adopt a kinder and gentler mode. He would, he announced, give his own executives more rope and seek to be more "talent-friendly." The problem was that agents typically don't care how much a movie costs. Their goal is simply to get the highest price possible for their clients. When you begin to make decisions based on a desire to please others, you cease making them for the right creative and economic reasons. Before long, you stop making good movies, and you also stop making a profit.

Frank's memo ended with two main recommendations. One was to give up trying to make two dozen movies a year. The second was for Jeffrey and me to recommit to renew our partnership in live action. I agreed with Frank that something had to change, although I knew that it would take time to ramp down. I also knew it that would be difficult to return to my earlier arrangement with Jeffrey as the company continued to expand, and I highly doubted that he would willingly agree to it anyway.

Journalists covering Hollywood continue, even today, to measure success in the movie business primarily by box office revenues. By that measure, we continued to finish among the top studios, in large part because we now released so many movies. In reality, all that finally counts is net profit—after the costs of production, marketing, and overhead. Those numbers rarely attract much attention. If they did, it would become clear that relatively few movies actually earned a profit in the early 1990s. Without the occasional blockbuster, many studios would have been hard-pressed to stay in business. Production and marketing costs had simply ballooned too high, and the number of movies being released exceeded the capacity of the market to absorb them.

Our own troubles in live action were largely hidden by virtue of our huge and growing success in animation. This included not just our new films but the re-releases of the animated classics produced by Walt beginning in the 1930s. Unhappy as Frank and I were about our live-action results, it was impossible to fault Jeffrey's overall performance running his division. In 1993, despite significant losses in live action, animation and home video produced record overall profits of $622 million for filmed entertainment. Animation had turned into a huge business—and that success eventually began to prompt a different set of problems.

7

Animation

No one deserves more credit for focusing our attention on animation when we arrived at Disney in 1984 than Roy Disney. In the days before Frank and I were named to our jobs, we asked Roy what he wanted to do, assuming that we took over. "Why don't you let me run the animation department?" he asked. "I suspect I'm the only guy around who has an understanding of how it works." We agreed immediately. The golden years of animation under Walt had clearly passed. Since his death, the department had slowly contracted from a high of 650 artists to fewer than 200. Several of the brightest stars had left Disney in frustration. One of them was Tim Burton, who went on to direct live-action movies ranging from *Beetlejuice* to *Batman* at other studios, before returning to Disney to direct *The Nightmare Before Christmas*, in 1993. The most high-profile loss was Don Bluth, who quit in 1979, taking with him seven other animators and four assistants. "We felt like we were animating the same picture over and over again, with just the faces changed a little," Bluth told a reporter at the time. In 1986, his new group's successful animated feature *An American Tail* — produced by Steven Spielberg's company, Amblin—became the first successful non-Disney animated film. Suddenly it seemed possible that the unique franchise Disney had pioneered and dominated for more than fifty years might be usurped and overshadowed.

While animation was critical to Disney's future, both symbolically and substantively, we knew that we could make our mark in live action more quickly. Soon after Jeffrey arrived in the fall of 1984, he came to me and said that he wanted to move our animation group off the lot and fill their offices instead with the film producers, directors, and writers we were beginning to sign to long-term contracts. Roy didn't strongly object. I went along, and we relocated the department in nearby Glendale. On one level, it might have appeared a shortsighted decision. The animation group had been in the studio building that carried their name for more than forty years, the first twenty of them under Walt. Animation represented the heart and soul of Disney, regardless of whether it ever became a significant business again. But it was also true that animation needed a shake-up. Relocating its headquarters had a more galvanizing impact than we anticipated. Fearing wrongly that the move meant we were considering shutting down their whole operation, the animation group suddenly felt an urgent need to prove themselves.

One month or so after our arrival, Roy invited Frank, Jeffrey, and me over to look at the storyboards for an animated movie that was well along in development. Storyboards are a series of comic book–style drawings that visually depict what the movie is about. The movie had been tentatively titled *Basil of Baker Street*, and it focused on a mouse who lived beneath Sherlock Holmes's flat in London. Eventually, it would be renamed *The Great Mouse Detective*. The directors who conceived the project were Ron Clements and John Musker. Both had come to Disney back in 1975, John following graduation from CalArts, and Ron after being accepted into a Disney-run training program for aspiring animators. Having slowly worked their way up from story artists to lead animators, Ron and John were now part of an unofficial splinter group of young artists who had grown dissatisfied with the department's main project, *The Black Cauldron*. A dark and lugubrious sword-and-sorcery tale, this film had already been nearly a decade in the making. As Ron later told me, the unofficial Disney credo in animation had become, "We may bore you, but we will never shock you."

The one notable breakthrough in *The Black Cauldron* was Disney's first use of computer-generated images in several scenes. The innovators were Glen Keane, who would go on to draw many of our most memorable characters, and John Lasseter, who would later direct *Toy Story,* the first fully computer-animated movie, for us. But Ron and John were committed to projects that were more contemporary and daring than *The Black Cauldron.*

For *The Great Mouse Detective,* Ron and John took us through the storyboard panels onto which drawings and bits of accompanying dialogue are pinned. I had a torrent of questions. At one point, Ron and John showed us a sequence of Holmes and Watson in an old Victorian bar. "Michael Jackson has just agreed to produce a 3-D film that we're going to use in the parks, called *Captain EO.* Maybe we could get him to do a song for this bar scene," I suggested. Ron and John both looked at me as if I'd lost it.

"If you don't like the idea," I said, "just throw it out. Your job is to keep us from ruining your movie." In fact, the two young artists were feeling neither disdain nor skepticism, but astonishment that we'd consider trying to involve a contemporary performer like Michael Jackson in one of Disney's timeless animated movies.

Much as I admired what we were shown, the movie still lacked a well-told story, with a beginning, a middle, and an end. This was the area that Walt had handled almost single-handedly for thirty years. After he died, no one had filled the void, and story had lost its priority in Disney's animated films. "If we're going to produce new classics," I told Ron and John, "then we have to begin with a script, just the way we do with the rest of our movies." I didn't realize it then, but with that single, casual statement, I was proposing to fundamentally change the way that animated movies had been put together at Disney for fifty years.

The history of animation can be told almost entirely through Walt Disney's biography. The true measure of greatness is the capacity to exceed oneself over and over again. Walt's career was marked by a series of creative breakthroughs and an extraordinary run of classic films. Born in Chicago in 1901, he grew up on a small farm in Marceline, Missouri, where his father moved the family in 1906. Little about Walt's childhood was easy. His father, Elias, struggled hard to make ends meet and often took out his frustration on his four sons. Even so, Marceline became the source of Walt's happiest memories. It was there that his imagination was awakened, and that he began to draw. Legend has it that his parents went off to town one day and Walt and his younger sister came upon a bucket of tar in the yard. Walt suggested they get some sticks and paint with the tar, using the side of the house as a canvas. He proceeded to draw a series of houses, a bit of mischief that became an enduring legacy.

Elias Disney moved the family several times during Walt's childhood, and Walt lived in both Kansas City and Chicago. At the age of sixteen, he falsified his age in order to enroll in the Red Cross ambulance corps. He spent a year in France driving an ambulance and chauffeuring Army officers at the end of World War I. Restless and ambitious when he returned, Walt joined his brother Roy in Kansas City and took a job creating newspaper ads. Soon he began freelancing on the side, producing short cartoons for a company that owned three local movie houses. By mid-1922, he was sufficiently successful to quit his day job and launch his own business, hiring five other artists to help produce longer cartoons based on fairy tales. *Little Red Riding Hood* was the first. When it was finished, Walt made the first of many distribution deals he would come to regret, this one with a small New York company that agreed to pay $1,800 per cartoon—and then failed to pay up. Before long, he was forced to let his employees go. Penniless, he began sleeping nights in his tiny office. A job producing a short film about dental hygiene, *Tommy Tucker's Tooth*, put him back in business.

Walt's next project was *Alice's Wonderland*, a blend of live action and animation in which a six-year-old child model was hired to act out stories against a background of cartoon figures that was drawn in later. Before he could finish, he ran out of money again. Roy, suffering from tuberculosis, had been assigned to a Veterans Administration hospital in Los Angeles. He urged Walt to file for bankruptcy and head west. By the time he paid for his one-way train ticket to Los Angeles, Walt was down to his last $40, a single suitcase containing his life's belongings, and a print of the unfinished *Alice's Wonderland*.

Walt started trying to peddle his short film once he arrived in L.A. To his astonishment, a New York distributor named Margaret Winkler offered him $1,500 for *Alice*—and committed to buying another dozen at the same price. Walt rushed to Roy at the hospital with the news. "I need your help," he said. More conservative than Walt, Roy asked a series of pointed questions about costs and delivery dates. Walt insisted he could make the films at a rate of one a week for $750, leaving a profit of $750 on each one. Walt's enthusiasm finally prevailed, as it would countless times during their careers. Roy even agreed to invest $285 from his own savings. In return, Walt made him an equal partner, handling the financial side of the business. Roy checked out of the hospital the next day, against his doctor's advice. He and Walt rented a small storefront in Hollywood, stenciled a sign in the window that read: DISNEY BROS. STUDIO, and their business was born.

Winkler continued to pay for the *Alice Comedies*, but she pushed Walt hard to improve the quality of the animation. "Everyone around here agrees your ideas are brilliant, but your execution lacks something," she wrote him early on. Long aware that his storytelling and filmmaking skills exceeded his drawing ability, Walt managed to convince an old colleague from Kansas City, Ub Iwerks, to move to L.A. and join the company as its chief artist. At the end of 1926, Winkler's new husband and partner, Charlie Mintz, visited the Disneys with the news that Universal Pictures was looking to create a new cartoon series. Walt and Iwerks produced some sketches, Mintz came up with the name "Oswald the Lucky Rabbit," and a cartoon series based on the character turned into an overnight sensation. Two years later, when the contract for the Oswald series came up for renewal, Walt traveled to New York with his wife Lillian to negotiate in person with Mintz. He received a rude shock. Rather than offering Walt a raise, Mintz announced that he intended to cut the Disneys' fee. When Walt balked, Mintz revealed that he had already secretly made deals to hire away all of Walt's animators on *Oswald* but Iwerks.

"Never again will I work for anyone else," Walt told his wife.

The idea for Mickey Mouse apparently occurred to Walt during the train ride back to California. With so many hours to kill, Walt decided to sketch. The story goes that he soon had a character who looked a lot like Oswald, except that Walt had transformed him from a rabbit into a mouse. Lillian came up with the name "Mickey," rejecting Walt's choice—"Mortimer"—as "too stuffy." I love the idea of a Mortimer Mouse. Today we're working on making him into a new character—Mickey's cousin, who we can allow to be mischievous in ways that Mickey was fifty years ago, but can't be anymore. He's simply too beloved and idealized.

Once Walt arrived back in Los Angeles, Ub Iwerks joined in the effort. He took over the animation while Walt focused on the story. Inspired by Charles Lindbergh's recent transatlantic flight, the first Mickey cartoon was titled *Plane Crazy*. It failed to attract a distributor, as did a second cartoon, but Walt was undeterred. Encouraged by *The Jazz Singer*, which became the first "talking" movie when it debuted in October 1927, Walt decided to synchronize his third Mickey cartoon to sound. He called it *Steamboat Willie*. Roy balked at the added cost, but Walt insisted. The film was released on November 18, 1928, at the Colony Theater in New York and the response was rapturous.

"Sound effects and talking pictures are more than a mere novelty," he wrote Roy after the preview. "I am convinced that sound on film is the only logical thing for the future." By early 1929, Mickey Mouse had become a national sensation and a marketing bonanza. Even so, Walt continued to face obstacles. Despite his vows of independence, he made a series of deals with studio heads and distributors who subsequently stole his artists, fought for control of his properties, and reneged on their promises. Walt's experiences only fueled his passion for control over his work and his desire for independence from the Hollywood establishment.

Perhaps the biggest breakthrough in Walt's career was his decision to produce *Snow White and the Seven Dwarfs* as the studio's first full-length animated feature. In mid-1934, at the end of a workday, Walt gathered together his top animators to share his dream. They included four of the key artists who would help to create most of the classic Disney animated films over the next four decades: Ward Kimball, Marc Davis, Ollie Johnston, and Frank Thomas. All of them are still alive today. *Snow White*, as Walt explained it to his group, had all the elements of a great drama: an appealing heroine, a scary villain, humor, and an archetypal story. For the next two hours, Walt literally acted out the film he had in mind, including a rendition of each of the seven dwarfs. By all accounts it was a bravura performance—and one that would be repeated in countless variations over the years. "Walt could have you in tears or rolling on the floor," Frank Thomas told me decades later. "He could act out literally anything—even an inanimate tree or a stone—and somehow make it come alive."

Walt told Roy that he estimated *Snow White* would cost $500,000 to produce, nearly twice the cost of the average live-action

film of the day. Roy objected—the company had finally become profitable through the Mickey cartoons—but as he usually did, Walt eventually prevailed. The project would take over three years to complete.

"One of Walt's greatest gifts was his ability to get you to come
up with things that you didn't know were in you and that you'd have
sworn you couldn't possibly do," Thomas told me. "Everything had to
get better and better. We had no idea that Snow White would be as good
as it turned out to be. Walt just kept at us. He would say, 'Don't you think
we're missing something here? I'm not getting involved in this scene,' or,
'I don't care enough about the characters here.' He would wait for you
to say something. When you did, he might reply, 'Yeah, that could work.'
Other times, something you suggested would give him a new idea and
he would build on it."

Walt once characterized his role at Disney in a way that's very
close to the way I see my own, although it almost certainly understated
his contribution and overstates mine. "Sometimes I think of myself as a
little bee," he told a young boy who asked him what exactly it was that
he did. "I go from one area to another, and gather pollen, and sort of
stimulate everybody."

As Snow White neared completion, rumors swirled that the project was out of control. Such a case could certainly be made. Walt had
launched the project with a handful of animators. After three years, more
than 750 people were involved. Its budget had tripled to $1.4 million—
astronomical at the time. In the end it was Roy who secured the Bank
of America loans that made Snow White possible. The film finally opened
on December 21, 1937, at the Carthay Circle Theater in Hollywood, and
early in 1938 at Radio City Music Hall in New York. From the first day,
it drew sell-out crowds. The New York Times rated Snow White as one of
the ten best films of the year, while the New York Herald Tribune called it
"one of those rare works of inspired artistry that weaves an irresistible
spell around the beholder."

The film went on to win a special Academy Award, Walt was
featured on the cover of Time magazine, and he was celebrated with
honorary degrees from both Harvard and Yale. Snow White became the
highest-grossing film of all time in its first year, taking in $8.5 million at
a time when a child's ticket cost just 10 cents. For the first time, Roy felt
comfortable committing to build a new studio on fifty acres near Grif-

fith Park in Burbank—our current location. The film single-handedly transformed the Disney brothers' small cartoon company into a major Hollywood studio. Based on 1998 dollars, *Snow White* is by some estimates the most successful movie of all time.

Walt's next animated films were *Pinocchio* and *Fantasia*, both released in 1940. Neither one was as commercially successful as *Snow White*, but each represented a huge leap in technical virtuosity. *Bambi* came out two years later, a beautiful, emotionally ambitious film, but the war then slowed production. It was eight years before Disney produced another elaborate full-length animated feature, and the company began to struggle once more financially. *Cinderella* revived its fortunes. Released in February 1950, it cost nearly $3 million to make but earned more than $20 million worldwide.

Cinderella's success emboldened Walt to push forward on two more artistically risky projects: *Alice in Wonderland* and *Peter Pan*. Roy fought against both films, and he was especially frustrated about *Alice*, which was subtle, episodic, and sometimes esoteric.

"You're just trying to impress the critics," Roy complained. In fact, the critical response to *Alice* was mixed at best when the film opened in 1951. Years passed before it won a large audience. Several more animated classics were produced under Walt's supervision, including *Peter Pan* in 1953, *Lady and the Tramp* in 1955, *Sleeping Beauty* in 1959, *101 Dalmatians* in 1961, and *The Jungle Book* in 1967. However, in the aftermath of Walt's death at the end of 1966, the quality and quantity of the animated output dropped precipitously.

As part of our effort to revive animation, we not only accelerated production on *The Great Mouse Detective* but began actively developing new projects. The first idea we put into production was Jeffrey's—remaking *Oliver Twist* as an animated musical, featuring songs by well-known pop stars. Jeffrey had suggested the idea as a live-action film back at Paramount, but I was never very excited about remaking the original British version. Now, we were eager to put another animated movie into production. A contemporary *Oliver & Company* would send an immediate signal inside and outside the company that we were prepared to move beyond the animated movies aimed mostly at very young children which Disney had been producing since Walt's death. A modern musi-

cal with a strong story line set in a gritty, urban environment seemed like
a good way to start.

Jeffrey evinced little interest in animation at first, but it wasn't
long before he became more involved. Both *The Black Cauldron* and *The
Great Mouse Detective* did modest business at the box office and drew
limited critical attention. For *Oliver & Company*, Jeffrey managed to
convince pop stars ranging from Billy Joel to Bette Midler to serve as
the voices of the main characters. In addition, he put together a soundtrack that included Joel, Midler, Huey Lewis, Barry Manilow, and Ruth
Pointer. The combination of recognizable pop names and a well-known
story gave us two strong marketing hooks. To some degree, the movie
lacked the powerful emotional core and the blend of physical and verbal
humor that would become hallmarks of our later animated movies. Nor
did it have a singular musical sensibility. Despite these limitations, *Oliver
& Company* was lively, accessible, and fun. Released in November 1988,
it took in over $50 million at the domestic box office, the strongest
performance for a Disney animated film to that point, eclipsing Spielberg and Bluth's *Land Before Time*. It also provided the first clear evidence
that animation had the potential to become a highly profitable business
once again.

The other event that helped to relaunch animation was a technological innovation called CAPS, an acronym for Computer Animation Production System. Its initial champions were Roy Disney and
Peter Schneider, whom we hired in the fall of 1985 to run animation
under Roy and Jeffrey. Peter came from a background in theater, having
managed and directed at a series of theaters in New York and Chicago.
In 1983, he moved to Los Angeles to help run the arts festival planned in
conjunction with the Olympics. Peter was recommended to us through
his friendship with Bob Fitzpatrick, then head of CalArts, on whose
board both Roy and I served. With his slender frame, impish features,
and casual style of dress, Peter has a Peter Pan look, even now in his mid-
forties. He proved to be driven, passionate, and completely devoted to
the artists who work for him. In time, he chose as his deputy Tom Schumacher, who had begun as a producer on *The Rescuers Down Under* and
worked his way up to head of story development before he turned
thirty-five. Tom had great taste, a droll sense of humor, and an easy, re-

laxed charm. His most distinctive feature was a swath of hair with a cavalier's swoop as theatrical as Tom himself.

One of the first projects that Peter involved himself in when he arrived in October 1985 was CAPS. The chief architects of the process were Lem Davis and Dave Inglish, who had earlier approached Roy Disney about it. Roy enlisted Peter in the cause. This new technology, Lem argued, had the potential to revolutionize animated movies, both by creating efficiencies and by giving artists a new range of creative capacities that were the equivalent of moving from writing by hand to using a personal computer. Peter and Roy, in turn, began trying to sell the idea to Jeffrey, Frank, and me. The estimated cost was $12 million. That sum hardly sounds overwhelming today, but at the time it struck us as a very big investment in a fledgling business with uncertain profit potential. Frank was especially skeptical. "We're not an R&D company," he argued. "It's going to cost twice as much as they say, and I don't believe that it will ever save us a dime."

But there was another issue at stake. "Roy wants to do this, and he believes in it," I finally told Frank. "I think we have to take a deep breath and say yes." Frank agreed, and we approved the purchase. His prediction turned out to be exactly right. CAPS didn't save us any money, in part because its cost quickly rose to $30 million. But it did open up vast new avenues for our artists. For example, CAPS allowed them to digitize hand-drawn images into the computer, which gave them the power to manipulate and three-dimensionalize characters and scenes in entirely new ways. It also dramatically enriched their color palette. In a short time, CAPS technologically and artistically revolutionized the archaic method by which animated movies had been made since *Snow White*.

The creative process itself evolved in a remarkably democratic way. "Cultural Darwinism" was the phrase Tom Schumacher came up with to define it. By that he meant that "good ideas are welcomed, no matter who they came from," including the most junior people in the department. Ideas that didn't measure up soon died on the vine, even if they had been championed by executives at the highest levels, including me. "Because these movies get produced over several years," Peter Schneider later said, "every creative decision gets visited and revisited, challenged and scrutinized, worked and reworked." We began develop-

ing two other animated movies after committing to *Oliver & Company*—
Who Framed Roger Rabbit and *The Little Mermaid*. Each would prove to be
groundbreaking.

Who Framed Roger Rabbit was an attempt to blend live action
and animation in a uniquely sophisticated way. Based on Gary S. Wolf's
film-noirish novel *Who Censored Roger Rabbit?*, it told the story of a
comic strip character who teams up with a hard-boiled Los Angeles detective to solve a murder mystery involving his wife and the man with
whom she has a romance. Our predecessors had seen the story's Disneyesque potential, and nearly a dozen drafts of a script had been written by the time we arrived at the company. Still, the project had never
been put into production. Steven Spielberg had long been interested in
it, and in early 1986 we recruited him as our partner, fresh from his success with Don Bluth's *An American Tail*.

To direct, Spielberg brought in his friend Robert Zemeckis,
who was coming off his own huge fantasy hit, *Back to the Future*. Zemeckis had once been offered the film by our Disney predecessors but
turned it down. "They just didn't have the energy to pull together a
movie this massive," he later explained. Because *Roger Rabbit* was so innovative creatively and technically, we knew that it would be expensive.
The deal reminded me of the one that we had made ten years earlier
with Spielberg and Lucas for *Raiders of the Lost Ark*. In this case, we gave
Spielberg and Zemeckis a significant percentage of the profits and creative control of the project. We insisted on retaining all of the merchandising rights, much as Walt had always done. Nothing had more
potential value to our company than the creation of new animated characters like Roger Rabbit. Consumer products could be based on such
characters and they could also become the basis for new attractions in
the parks.

At first, Spielberg and Zemeckis pushed to cast Harrison Ford
in the detective role. When he wasn't available, we chose Bob Hoskins,
a wonderful British character actor. Hoskins's deft, understated performance allowed the animated Roger Rabbit to be the true star. The production was an even greater and more expensive challenge than we had
anticipated, in part because of Spielberg and Zemeckis's perfectionism
and in part because no one from Disney was really overseeing the production day to day. The movie was shot in London, and costs skyrock-

eted above the initial $30 million budget—already more than we had spent on any previous movie at Disney. Although Peter Schneider had been flying to England once a week and reporting back on the growing problems, Jeffrey never said anything about them to me, which was unusual. He knew that I preferred to hear bad news right away.

Hiding a problem doesn't make it go away. From the time that Frank and I started at Disney, I would inform board members regularly between meetings to keep them up-to-date on our activities. I paid particular attention to problems and what we were doing about them. Both Frank and I did the same thing at our meetings, never sugarcoating. In return, the board was relentlessly honest with us—polite, but firm and direct. I myself am never in any great rush to hear good news. By contrast, learning bad news early on can help avert a disaster or prompt a change in strategy and salvage a situation in midcourse. Nothing upsets me more than finding out about a problem when it's too late to do anything about it. That didn't happen in this case, but only because I finally brought up the subject with Jeffrey myself. As he had a decade earlier on *Star Trek* at Paramount, but with considerably more experience now, Jeffrey stepped aggressively into the process and essentially took over the production. The movie was better creatively for his intervention, and it was finished on time.

Because *Roger Rabbit* was sophisticated and sexy, we had hoped to distance it from the Disney brand by releasing it under the Touchstone label. But even that didn't help. One week before the movie opened in June 1988, *Newsweek* ran a cover story entitled "Spielberg and Disney Take a $45 Million Gamble." Nearly all the critics referred to it as a Disney film. Fortunately, the reviews were so glowing that they subsumed any potential controversy over the content. *Roger Rabbit* also became our first big success in cross-promoting a movie. By the time it premiered, we had licensing agreements for over five hundred products, ranging from Jessica Rabbit jewelry to Roger Rabbit talking dolls to computer games, which was a business by itself but also a way to extend the movie experience for the audience. Both McDonald's and Coca-Cola created massive promotional tie-ins. The movie's success also inspired us to build Mickey's Toontown, a new attraction at Disneyland based not on the movie but on our historic characters. Intended as a temporary exhibit, it proved so popular that we turned it into a permanent addition. Nine months after its release, *Who Framed Roger Rabbit* won four Academy Awards, more than any Disney movie since *Mary Poppins*.

Our next animated release, *The Little Mermaid*, played an even more profound role in the turnaround at animation. The premise emerged during our first animation Gong Show in mid-1985. We asked everyone to bring in at least a half dozen ideas. Ron Clements, still in the midst of producing *The Great Mouse Detective*, suggested adapting the Hans Christian Andersen fairy tale. I had always loved the idea of setting an animated movie underwater, but both Jeffrey and I were concerned that this idea sounded too much like the live-action *Splash*, which Disney had released early in 1984, six months before we arrived. Ron Clements had written a two-page synopsis of his idea, and we agreed to read it overnight. Andersen's *Little Mermaid* is a dark, downbeat story in which the mermaid Ariel dies at the end. In Clements's version, it became a story about how Ariel longs to be human so that she can marry her Prince Charming, Eric. To fulfill her wish, she must give up her voice to the witch Ursula, only to regain it—and the prince—at the end. It was a happier ending, and in some ways a more compelling allegory. The next morning, Jeffrey called me first thing. "We've got to do this one," he said, and I agreed.

The most important creative decision we made on *The Little Mermaid* was to work with the lyricist Howard Ashman and his composing partner Alan Menken. This idea came from David Geffen, by then one of Jeffrey's closest friends and advisers. Geffen had been highly successful in the record business, while also dabbling in movies and theater. Most recently, he had co-produced the off-Broadway cult hit *Little Shop of Horrors*, which was written and composed by Ashman and Menken. Peter Schneider met Ashman while serving briefly as company manager on the show. Early in 1986, Jeffrey sat down with Ashman and tried to interest him in a series of animated projects that we had in development. *The Little Mermaid* was the one that most sparked his interest, and Ashman agreed to write the score with Menken.

It was then that the true renaissance of Disney animation began to take shape. The artistic hothouse was animation's relocated home, a bland, unmarked building in Glendale that became our very own suburban Tin Pan Alley. Ashman and Menken flew out from the East Coast and began writing their songs in one office. Next door, Clements and Musker worked away on their script and storyboards. The animators, led by two of our most talented artists, Glen Keane and Mark Henn, worked in adjacent offices. They all played off one another. Ashman and Menken would write a new verse of a song, play it for Ron and John, who would then take a different approach on a particular scene. The animators wandered in and out of both offices, returning to their cubbyholes with fresh ideas. "It was a wonderful, incredible, unique time," Alan Menken would later tell me. "Nothing can ever compare to that first experience of working together." Jeffrey himself began devoting more and more of his time to animation, including at least one two-hour creative meeting with the animation executive team each week.

The process was entirely collaborative, but if any single person made a critical difference, it was Ashman. A Disney aficionado from his childhood, he knew more about our early animated classics than virtually anyone in the company, and he also had a rich sense of theater history. As a writer, Ashman was evocative and accessible but also edgy and irreverent. It was his idea to transform the witch Ursula into a larger-than-life character, as well as to turn Sebastian the Crab, Ariel's guardian, into a clever, wisecracking Trinidadian. The latter decision introduced humor to the movie and also made it possible to add reggae, calypso, and even doo-wop to the score, giving the classical fairy tale a more contemporary feel.

Ashman and Menken had collaborated before, but at Disney they seemed to find their metier. Having grown up in musical theater, Alan was comfortable working in a range of musical styles. By temperament, he was as upbeat and direct as Howard was moody and complex. Alan could write catchy, distinctive melodies virtually on demand. He sometimes described his style as "expansive pastiche," but that understated his talent. In fact, he could take a very basic song form and thread it into a more ambitious, sophisticated, and original piece of music. Although I was removed from the day-to-day process, I still remember coming in midway on *The Little Mermaid* and hearing the song "Under the Sea." It's easy to claim in hindsight that I knew we had a hit at that moment—I've often felt that way about songs, only to be proven wrong —but this was truly one of those occasions.

Excited as we were, nearly all of us believed that the core appeal of *The Little Mermaid* would be to young girls. However, from the very first screening on the Disney lot, the film played strongly to all segments of the audience, including adults. It contained all of the elements that would become signatures of our subsequent animated movies: great original music; clever lyrics; a wry sense of humor; a strong, evocative story; and dazzling animation. When *The Little Mermaid* opened in November 1989, it quickly became our most *successful* fully realized animated film ever, earning more than $84 million at the domestic box office. The movie also won the Academy Award for Best Score and the Caribbean-lilted "Under the Sea" went on to win for Best Song. Suddenly, our animated movies were competing in a whole new league.

The box office success of *Oliver & Company, Roger Rabbit,* and *The Little Mermaid* was enough to turn animation into a very big business. The decision to begin releasing Walt's classic animated films on videocassette also fueled the division's reemergence. For years, at periodic intervals, Disney had re-released movies ranging from *Snow White* to *Bambi* to *101 Dalmatians* for relatively short runs in theaters. This proved to be a steady source of income for the company. Even before our arrival, for example, *Pinocchio* had been slotted as the Christmas animated re-release for 1984. Never the most popular of Disney's classics, the film still earned more than $26 million over the holidays. The question now was whether we ought to follow up the theatrical run for *Pinocchio* by releasing it on home video—and then do the same with the other animated classics.

Home video was still a relatively small business. Disney had earned revenues of about $70 million from video rentals the year before we arrived, much of it from old cartoons and live-action movies. None of our classic animated films had ever been released on video, out of a belief that doing so risked diluting their proven value in theatrical re-release. Jeffrey, for one, shared this skeptical and conservative view. "If we start releasing the classics now and it means that future generations won't pay to see them in theaters, then we're ultimately hurting the franchise," he argued. Mike Bagnall, our CFO at the time, put it even more bluntly: "We could be killing the goose that lays the golden eggs." Hard as it seems to imagine today, it wasn't even clear yet that any significant demand existed for children's films on video. The market in the mid-1980s remained overwhelmingly oriented to rentals. As far as most video store owners were concerned, children's titles were likely to be rented only on weekends.

Early in 1985, we convened the first of a series of marathon meetings to debate whether or not to release *Pinocchio* on home video that summer, and if so, at what price. It was Frank who set the tone for the initial discussions. "There are overwhelming arguments not to do this," he said, "but it's still important to have the debate." As everyone had already discovered, Frank loved the process of debate. In his mind, the more you talked, the more you were in a position to make an informed decision. Even if he didn't agree with you, Frank could be counted on to make your case at least as effectively as you could yourself. If too much consensus developed too early, he would jump in and play devil's advocate.

"Can't I get anyone to disagree?" he would ask, waiting a beat to see if there were any takers. "Well, fine, then, I'll take the other side." He was insatiable. Frank believed, as I did, that you never knew who might add a fresh insight or come up with a new idea.

Nearly everyone on our team had a story to tell about receiving a phone call from Frank in the middle of the night. He never stopped working, nor did he pay attention to time zones during his frequent travels. If he was awake, he figured everyone else was, too. When you picked up the ringing phone at 3:00 a.m., still three-quarters asleep, Frank was all solicitousness: "Oh, did I wake you up? Why don't you pull yourself together and I'll call back in five minutes."

Sometimes the issue Frank had on his mind was genuinely important, but just as often the call might be similar to the one that Roy Disney received at home one night around 4:00 a.m. "What was Goofy's original name?" Frank asked. Roy took a moment to orient himself and responded, "Well, Goofy used to be called Dippy Dawg." Frank thanked him and hung up and Roy went back to sleep. He never found out the reason for the call. Looking back, I think Frank's style sent an important message to all of our team. His relentless round-the-clock questioning reflected his total commitment to the job. Sometimes that frustrated executives who worked for him, but it also kept them on their toes.

If Frank took one side of an issue, I often instinctively took the other, only to reverse roles somewhere during the debate. We were a remarkably complementary fit. Frank was brilliant at putting all the evidence on the table, but he often found it hard to make the final decision. I never tried to come to a conclusion by logically weighing the pros and cons. Instead, with Frank's help, I kept accumulating evidence until I reached the point where a certain choice instinctively felt right. At that point, I simply followed my gut—and rarely looked back.

The most persuasive advocate for releasing the animated classics on home video was Bill Mechanic. At Paramount, Bill had helped us to build the most successful pay-television division in Hollywood, selling our films to cable networks for unprecedented prices. With his longish hair and bushy mustache, Mechanic scarcely looked the part of a traditional corporate executive, and his real dream was to work on the creative side of the business. At Disney, his first job was producing specials for the networks, but he also happened to be an astute businessman—sarcastic, opinionated, charming—and we continued to call on him in those areas.

One key argument against releasing our library on video was that we would lose control of major assets of the company by putting them permanently in the homes of millions of Americans. Here my own experience as a parent of three children was helpful. I was painfully aware that no toy lasted even a year in our house, much less the seven-year intervals that we planned between any re-release of a given classic animated film. I'm not sure what happens to children's "things" in a house, but I do know they disappear. Our home-video people disagreed. They believed that people would make our videos collectors' items. We ended up compromising on a conservative approach in the summer of 1985. Rather than offering Pinocchio at the affordable price of $19.95 or $29.95, which we had set for some of Disney's old live-action titles, we decided to sell it for $79.95. The idea was to encourage customers to rent Pinocchio rather than purchase it, thereby minimizing the chance that it would remain permanently in people's homes. In fact, sales of the movie to video stores fell below our expectations, and so did the initial revenues.

In August, we officially named Bill Mechanic head of home video, and one of his first moves was to convince Jeffrey and the rest of us that it made sense to lower the video price for Pinocchio to $29.95 as a way to generate more sales. During the next few months, we sold more than 600,000 cassettes of the film, with only moderate marketing.

For the first time, it became obvious that children and their mothers represented a large, mostly untapped market for videos—at least when it came to the animated Disney classics. The reason, we soon discovered, is that children simply are far more likely than adults to watch videos multiple times. It made more economic sense for parents to buy their children's favorite films at $29.95 than to rent them over and over.

In November 1985, when it came time to decide how to handle our next re-release, *Sleeping Beauty*, we gathered for another big meeting and debate. Bill had prepared two large white poster boards, which he placed on easels at the end of a long table. He started by unveiling the first board, which was entitled "Emotional Issues." These included questions like, "Could releasing the animated classics on video undermine their uniqueness by making them too widely available in viewers' homes?" and, "Might such a move cheapen Disney's image and undermine the brand?"

Once we had exhausted ourselves on these sorts of questions without any clear resolution, Mechanic unveiled another poster board entitled "Economic Issues." The key question was how to derive the most value from a particular asset, in the near future and over the long term. With that in mind, Bill had run a series of comparative financial calculations. His figures showed that if we released *Sleeping Beauty* four more times theatrically over the next twenty-eight years (at our traditional interval of once every seven years), we were likely to generate a total of $125 million in box office revenues. By contrast, he estimated that the very first home-video release of *Sleeping Beauty* would earn at least $100 million in sales. It was here that I appreciated the importance of net present value (NPV). First drilled into my head by Charles Bluhdorn back at Paramount, NPV is simply a way of estimating the current value of income that is earned over time. Because inflation progressively reduces buying power, the value of earning a dollar seven years from now—much less in fourteen or twenty-eight years—is far less than earning the same dollar today. In addition, any money earned today can be reinvested immediately, either in new product or to generate additional income.

"The net present value of earning $125 million from *Sleeping Beauty* over the next twenty-eight years in theaters is less than $25 million," Mechanic said. "It makes a lot more economic sense to earn $100 million from home video during the next six months." At this point, even Frank began to lose patience with more debate. "An asset isn't an asset if you don't use it," he said. "What the hell are we waiting for?"

By the end of the meeting, we had decided to go all-out on *Sleeping Beauty*. When it was released in the fall of 1986, we had put together an unprecedented $7 million marketing effort for the video, priced at $29.95. Built around the theme "Bring Disney Home for Good," the campaign helped to sell 1.3 million copies of the cassette. That more than doubled the performance of *Pinocchio* and made *Sleeping Beauty* one of the largest-selling videos of all time. The initial fear of diluting the value of our classics in future theatrical release began to pale beside the enormous profits we could earn immediately through home-video sales. Nor did it cheapen Disney's image in the marketplace. The best possible impact on our brand turned out to be having our classic films in people's homes, where they were watched over and over.

The next giant leap in sales occurred in 1988, with *Cinderella*. For the first time, we reached out aggressively beyond video stores, to big mass-merchant retailers who had never before been in the home-video business. Our initial deal was with Target stores, but other chains, including Caldor and Wal-Mart, soon followed. Over the previous Christmas holidays, *Cinderella* had earned a highly respectable $34 million in theatrical release. Six months later, the video—buoyed by far wider distribution and our biggest marketing campaign yet—sold nearly 6 million copies, generating revenues of nearly $100 million.

The following year, we made another leap by eliminating the middlemen, or rack-jobbers, and taking over home-video distribution ourselves—echoing Walt's decision to launch Buena Vista Distribution for feature films back in the 1950s. By working directly with large retailers, we not only eliminated substantial overhead costs but were able to create joint marketing campaigns, and establish direct computer links that made it possible to keep daily track of our stock. In 1991, *The Jungle Book* became our first independently distributed animated video. It eventually sold almost 9 million copies. In 1992, *101 Dalmatians* sold more than 14 million copies. It was a measure of Bill Mechanic's success that he was tapped to run the movie division for Twentieth Century Fox in 1993. By then, fortunately, Bill had trained two excellent successors in Ann Daly, who took over the domestic home-video business for the next three years, and

Michael Johnson, who later ran home video worldwide and now serves as president and managing director of Walt Disney International Asia.

Roy Disney was among those who initially worried that the release of any of the classic animated films on video would dilute their value. Over time, as both their enormous profitability and their ability to enhance the brand were demonstrated, he too supported the strategy. Still, Roy continued to hold out on releasing two of Disney's greatest classics, *Snow White* and *Fantasia*, which he put in a special category. So did I, not just because both films were so special, but because I had looked into their fascinating histories. In the case of *Fantasia,* Walt had intended it to be a living, breathing entity to which he would add new sections of music and animation every few years. "*Fantasia* is timeless," Walt said, even before its release. "It may run 10, 20, or 30 years. I can never build another *Fantasia*. I can improve. I can elaborate. That's all." The film was released for the first time in 1940, and it was a breakthrough cinematically and in the quality of the sound. Typically, Walt recognized its unique qualities before others did. Not long after the video release, when the film became a smash financially (although fifty years late), I called Walt's widow, Lillian, to tell her of the success. "I always hated that movie," she told me. "But as always, Walt was right."

But World War II interrupted Walt's dream of adding more musical pieces to the film. I grew convinced that we should take on this challenge. At one point, in 1990, I thought of including Beatles music, and arranged to discuss my idea with Leonard Bernstein. Jane and I went to a rehearsal of the New York Philharmonic at Lincoln Center one afternoon. Bernstein conducted brilliantly for two full hours, until the orchestra suddenly stopped two minutes from the end of the piece. Bernstein was furious, but union rules prevailed. Having just conducted with the energy of an athlete in his prime, he hobbled off the stage like an injured quarterback. He made his way back to his dressing room through a mass of adoring fans, mostly older women, who treated this classical icon like a rock star. By the time Jane and I arrived at his dressing room, Bernstein had transformed again, this time into an old man draped in a cape, smoking a cigarette in between shots from his asthma inhalator. He loved the idea of working with us on *Fantasia* and using Beatles music. Then I talked enthusiastically about using the entire Philharmonic Orchestra and what a great job they could do. "Mr. Eisner," he said, looking at me over his glasses, "we only need four musicians."

Bernstein died within the next six months from lung cancer, and I was never able to find another conductor to embrace my idea of joining the Beatles with Tchaikovsky, Stravinsky, and Beethoven. Years later, I was shown projections for the potential profit to be derived just from releasing the original *Fantasia* on video. The numbers were so astronomical that I decided to set up a meeting to discuss the issue with Roy, Patty, and their four children at their home. I reminded them that *Fantasia* had never made a profit in theatrical release, nor had it been as widely appreciated as it deserved to be.

"Releasing *Fantasia* on video will finally give it the broad exposure it deserves," I argued. I also pointed out that because of the film's age, only three of every twenty-four frames still retained their initial color. By reshooting each frame with modern computerized technology, we were in a position to restore perfect color to the other twenty-one frames and make the quality of the home video better than it could ever be on the original film. We could use the profits from the release of the original *Fantasia*, I suggested, to finance a new one—which Roy would oversee.

The family unanimously agreed on the plan. *Fantasia* sold nearly 15 million copies in its first release in 1991, vastly increasing its audience. When it came time to broach the release of *Snow White* with Roy a year later, the issue was far easier. It happened that the film was in danger of moving into the public domain in Italy. If we chose not to release it on video, there was a risk that pirates would quickly do so. I had a thirty-second call with Roy, and he agreed that we should go ahead. In its first release, *Snow White* broke all records for our classics, selling nearly 50 million copies worldwide. Ultimately, we were also able to extend our copyright.

The enormous video market for our animated films prompted a second epiphany, namely, the huge potential upside to be realized in stepping up production of new animated films. When we arrived at Disney, one new animated movie was being released approximately every four years. In the aftermath of *Oliver* and *Roger Rabbit*, we set a goal of producing one every twelve to eighteen months. In Jeffrey's shorthand, the chant became "Bigger, better, faster, cheaper." The tension level at animation rose perceptibly. Artists trooped into Roy's office, complaining that Jeffrey was a "slavedriver." Roy came to me directly and expressed his concern that greater volume would occur at an expense to excellence. Increasing our output, I felt, had the potential to improve not just our profits but even the quality of our films. Endless time isn't necessarily a good thing. Deadlines, pressure, and exhaustion often lead to breakthroughs as artists are forced to exceed what they believe is possible. Increasing our production also forced us to seek out new talent.

In December 1989, Peter Schneider wrote a long memo summarizing the state of animation. It was possible, he argued, to be bigger, better, and faster with our animated movies—to break ground with each one, and to produce more of them—but it wasn't possible to do so more inexpensively. "If cheaper means not squandering money," he wrote, "we are making strides to improve the efficiency and better manage the process. If cheaper means smaller budgets for our movies, then this is in conflict with 'Bigger, Better.' With Jeffrey and Roy's desire to make truly top production value movies, it will cost more money. In my opinion, the reason that Disney animated movies were and can again be great is the ability to throw out and redo and make it better. The money spent during the making of *Mermaid* made a good movie into a great movie."

As *The Little Mermaid* prompted our feature-animation business to explode, we enjoyed a parallel success reviving television animation. For the first time, Disney emerged as a major player in Saturday morning children's television—and without relying on the mindless violence that characterized the low-cost, low-quality shows from nearly all our competitors. We were even more ambitious about producing animated shows for weekday afternoons. By the fall of 1990, we'd created four half-hour shows that we began selling as a group called the *Disney Afternoon*. It quickly became the most profitable part of our television division, consistently earning more than $40 million a year. As with most programming success, however, it was not destined to last forever.

The competitor primarily responsible for the eventual decline of the *Disney Afternoon*—Barry Diller and his Fox Television Network—had initially been its strongest supporter. Within six months after Barry took over as chairman of Twentieth Century Fox, Rupert Murdoch purchased the studio from Marvin Davis. With Rupert's backing, Barry was finally able to realize the dream we had first conceived together back at Paramount: launching a fourth television network. Fox began running its first shows in 1986. When we decided to launch the *Disney Afternoon*, Barry committed on the spot to run it on all his Fox-owned stations. Fox-affiliated stations eventually comprised more than 80 percent of the stations that carried the *Disney Afternoon*.

Still, my relationship with Barry wasn't free of conflict for long. Virtually from the moment that he took over Fox and I moved to Disney in 1984, we had a series of disagreements over various business deals. None was quite so dramatic as the one that emerged over the *Disney Afternoon*. It began in late 1988, when we purchased KHJ, an independent television station in Los Angeles, renamed it KCAL, and began looking for ways to improve the station's performance. One obvious move was to take the *Disney Afternoon* away from Fox's station and put it on KCAL.

This decision infuriated Barry. Having supported *Disney Afternoon* from the start, he believed that he was entitled to continue running it on his flagship Los Angeles station. "I helped bring you to where you are," he told Rich Frank and Jeffrey, "and you can't just take the shows away from us." I certainly understood his feelings, but there was no way for us to justify depriving our new station of highly desirable Disney programming.

Barry responded by immediately canceling the *Disney Afternoon* on his other six stations. Then he made a decision that would ultimately prove even more devastating to us: producing his own children's television programs. Much later, I would learn that this idea was conceived by several Fox affiliates. In any case, before very long we began to hear from our salespeople in the field that Fox was putting intense pressure on its affiliated stations all across the country to carry the network's new programming. If they didn't agree to replace the *Disney Afternoon* with Fox's new children's programs, they were told, then they risked being dropped as affiliates.

In February 1990, we filed a lawsuit against the Fox Broadcasting Company, charging it with contract interference and an unlawful attempt to monopolize children's TV. One of our most valuable assets was now in jeopardy. If you don't respond aggressively when that occurs, your competitors soon learn that they can run over you, and ultimately your shareholders are hurt. Because of my long relationship with Barry, the battle immediately took on an added personal dimension. He felt betrayed that we hadn't left the *Disney Afternoon* at KTTV. I was angry that he seemed to be urging the Fox affiliates to dump our programming in favor of his.

In the meantime, Barry moved ahead to produce his own slate of children's programs. They became his best revenge. The *Power Rangers* series emerged as the hottest children's show on television, and Fox began to dominate afternoon children's programming as we lost outlets. In the wake of our lawsuit, Fox probably proceeded more cautiously with affiliates than it might have otherwise. As a result, the *Disney Afternoon* stayed on the air in enough markets to remain highly profitable for another two years. Finally, in early 1992, we dropped the suit, in part because the dispute made it difficult for us to do any other kind of business with Fox and its parent, News Corp., around the world. Barry and I have long since reconciled, making new deals and fighting over others.

Even at its height, the profit from television animation paled against what we were earning in filmed animation. Over time, this business occupied more and more of Jeffrey's attention, not just because it was such a huge profit center but because it proved so well suited to his temperament. In live action, authority had to be shared with — and sometimes ceded to — strong producers, powerful directors, and big-name actors. This wasn't true in animation. Peter Schneider ran the operation day to day, keeping a huge and still-expanding group of artists working effectively together. Roy talked regularly to Peter, maintaining contact with key artists, and also screening and providing notes on the rough cuts of each of the new films. But it was Jeffrey who served as conductor of the animation orchestra and commanded center stage.

An animated movie took four years to produce, and Jeffrey drove his team relentlessly. He didn't always have a solution to a problem, but he was very good at spotting them. "If you showed Jeffrey a piece of material," Alan Menken later told me, "he always had an immediate gut reaction. You might agree with him or disagree, but he always provoked you." Jeffrey worried over the details on a daily basis. I came in at longer intervals and tried to focus on the big picture. Was a certain character's action credible? Did a particular scene evoke the intended emotion? Did the third act really work? Jeffrey sought and received more independence and authority, but I still believed I added an important perspective. In animation, we released only one movie a year, and each one took on enormous importance.

After each rough-cut screening, we all gathered together—producers, writers, and directors—to discuss our movies. I also continued to speak intermittently to Peter, Tom, and other creative executives beneath Jeffrey, much as I did to people at various levels in Disney's other divisions. It was a way to stay truly connected to the process.

The only significant artistic misstep we made during the first several years in animation was *The Rescuers Down Under*. Released in the fall of 1990, it was the first movie to make significant use of CAPS, and the quality of the animation took a quantum leap—especially in the scene of the soaring flight by the eagle Marahute, drawn by Glen Keane and conceived by Chris Sanders. In retrospect, however, the movie lacked at least three of the ingredients that audiences responded to most strongly in *The Little Mermaid:* great music, a central theme, and a strong, emotional story. It was also a sequel to the original *Rescuers*, released in 1977. However much audiences valued the Disney signature on animated movies, they also came to each one looking for something wholly new and original.

Beauty and the Beast put us back on track, but not before overcoming its own rocky start. The project began as a purely dramatic version of the classic fairy tale. A year of intensive work went into the script. After looking at the first twenty minutes in storyboards, it was clear to all of us that it didn't work. The movie was too dark, depressing, and overbearing. Finally, in the fall of 1989, Jeffrey brought in Ashman and Menken, fresh from their success with *The Little Mermaid*. They reconceived *Beauty* as a musical and began writing songs. The biggest problem was Ashman's health. Though he had suffered from various ailments for some time, he assured his colleagues that they were all stress-related. In mid-1990, soon after Ashman and Menken won the Academy Award for *The Little Mermaid*, Ashman acknowledged to Menken and a few close friends that he'd developed AIDS. When travel became difficult for him, Peter Schneider arranged to move the development of *Beauty* from Glendale to the Residence Inn, in Fishkill, New York, near Ashman's home.

A makeshift workplace was set up in one of the conference rooms, using giant foam boards on which storyboard sketches could be pinned. A Yamaha piano was rented for Menken. Despite his deteriorating health, Ashman once again became the guiding voice. Referring to himself as "the simplicity police," he argued that each scene in a powerful drama had to be both accessible and emotionally strong at its core. He fought to retain the archetypal appeal of *Beauty and the Beast*—a love story built on the premise that a tender heart lies beneath even the toughest exterior—even as he helped to create its distinctive narrative and musical identity.

It was Ashman who first recognized that the story ought to be told not from Belle's point of view but from the Beast's. He also thought of transforming Gaston from a blandly foppish suitor into a wonderfully boorish chauvinist pig. And it was Ashman who had the whimsical but touching idea of giving human voices to the servants who have been reduced by the Beast to inanimate objects, such as a mantel clock (Cogsworth) and a candlestick (Lumiere). Together, Ashman and Menken created the film's extraordinary songs. The first time that they played their opening number for us—"Belle"—we were warned that it ran seven minutes. "You're going to find it too long, too theatrical, and too unconventional," Howard said. In fact, "Belle" was a classic show stopper, which set up the whole movie and worked brilliantly in spite of its length.

Although Ashman's health continued to deteriorate, he insisted on staying at his work, even when he began to lose his eyesight and his voice. He died on March 14, 1991, at the age of forty-one—just six months before *Beauty and the Beast* opened. It was a tragic loss on both a personal and an artistic level. Beloved by those who collaborated with him, he had managed to work at the height of his creative powers until the very end of his life. In the fall of 1991, *Beauty and the Beast* became the first animated movie ever to be screened at the opening night of the New York Film Festival. When *Beauty* opened in theaters two months later, it earned by far the best reviews yet for our animated movies. It also quickly surpassed the previous leader, *The Little Mermaid*, at the box office. *Beauty* ultimately earned more than $145 million domestically. On video, it eventually sold nearly 22 million copies, compared to 9 million for *The Little Mermaid* a year earlier. Most notably of all, *Beauty and the Beast* became the first animated film ever to win an Academy Award nomination for Best Picture.

As Ashman and Menken were finishing their work on *Beauty and the Beast* during 1990, they returned to the songs for another movie that they had temporarily put aside, *Aladdin*. I had always been slightly uneasy about a film set in the Middle East, a part of the world that I didn't know and didn't feel comfortable trying to portray. Nor was I convinced that the story held together until John Musker and Ron Clements, the directors of *The Little Mermaid*, came aboard to produce and direct. In the wake of Ashman's death, Peter managed to broker a new partnership between Alan Menken and the lyricist Tim Rice, who had long been Andrew Lloyd Webber's collaborator. Together, Menken and Rice finished the song score. What made *Aladdin* most distinctive, however, was Robin Williams's brilliant, hilarious, often extemporaneous performance as the voice of the Genie. For all that, *Beauty* seemed like a tough act to follow, and most of us were surprised when *Aladdin* became an even bigger hit during the fall of 1992. In hindsight, the reasons seem clear. *Aladdin* was exotic yet accessible, engaging but also exceptionally funny, a movie that adults could enjoy every bit as much as their kids. It also benefited from the momentum created by *The Little Mermaid* and *Beauty and the Beast*.

Success invariably prompts restlessness. It may even be true that absolute success corrupts absolutely. During 1993, Jeffrey was finishing the third year of a six-year contract. Under its terms, he had the right to exercise an option that September which would permit him to leave a year later. It never occurred to me that he might make such a choice. I knew that he felt some conflict about our relationship and his own stature in the company, but he seemed to love his job. As the year wore on, he made it increasingly clear that he was interested in expanding his role. We agreed to spend time discussing his future in detail during our executive retreat in Aspen later in the fall.

It took me by surprise when I received an official letter from Jeffrey's representative on August 31, confirming that he had decided to exercise his option to leave Disney a year later. "I have no intention of leaving," he told me. "I'm just protecting myself legally, in case you don't come up with new mountains for me to climb." A month later, we finally had a chance at Aspen to talk in more detail about his future. As we set out on a walk downtown after a day of meetings, I began by asking a simple question: "What do you want?"

"I want to be president of the company," Jeffrey said. I felt taken aback. "That job isn't available," I said. "Frank is president."

"But Frank always said he intended to leave at some point," Jeffrey responded. It was true that from the time we arrived at Disney, Frank had left open the possibility that he might one day make a third attempt to scale Mount Everest. But over the years, Frank's wife, Luanne, became more vocal in her opposition to further mountain climbing and he grew more attached to his life at Disney. The result was that we were now well into negotiating an extension of Frank's contract for seven more years at Disney. I told Jeffrey as much.

"But Frank could become vice chairman," he persisted.

"There is no way that I can make you president," I replied. An awkwardness had crept into our conversation, and Jeffrey began to backtrack. I sensed his disappointment, and assured him things would work out.

Much later, Jeffrey would claim that I had promised during our walk to make him president of the company should Frank ever decide to leave. Obviously, I remember the conversation very differently. The only issue in my mind is whether, in my phrasing, or my tone, or my body language, I might have inadvertently given Jeffrey a measure of false hope about someday inheriting Frank's job. What I know with certainty is that neither Roy Disney nor the board was prepared to make Jeffrey president of Disney. I did hold out the possibility—even the wish —in my own mind that he might grow in ways that would someday make it possible to promote him. In any case, I deeply valued Jeffrey as the executive in charge of filmed entertainment, and I didn't want him to leave the company or feel discouraged about his future prospects. I suggested we talk instead about what else we might do to satisfy him. "I need new mountains to climb," Jeffrey said again. I promised to give it some thought.

That evening, I called Frank, who had returned to Los Angeles earlier in the day. I knew he would be surprised by Jeffrey's request; what I didn't anticipate was just how hurt he would be. "Jeffrey really said that?" he responded. "I'm just amazed by his chutzpah." But Frank was also immensely practical, and he too valued Jeffrey's talents. While he was stung by the news that Jeffrey had asked for his job, he quickly managed to put those feelings aside, and we spent the rest of the conversation discussing ways to add to Jeffrey's current responsibilities.

When we arrived back in Los Angeles, Jeffrey continued to work at his ordinary feverish pace and we kept meeting for our Monday evening dinners. The news from animation remained uniformly positive: the success of *Aladdin* in theaters overseas and huge sales for *Beauty and the Beast*, just out in video stores. There was also an overwhelmingly enthusiastic response to the early screenings of *The Lion King*, our next animated movie, scheduled for release in the summer of 1994. Jeffrey and I also discussed the current problems with live action. If anything, his temperament was more optimistic than mine, and he reassured me, as he had many times during the past year, that a turnaround in our live-action films was imminent. "I understand the problem and I've got it under control," he said enthusiastically. "Next summer is going to be giant."

My deepest concerns about Jeffrey had to do with the way he conducted himself, and the degree to which he focused on his own agenda rather than the company more broadly. Early in 1993, for example, Jeffrey had come to Frank seeking permission to launch with his friend Steven Spielberg a restaurant chain to be called "Dive!" Frank acquiesced, and I was loath to overrule him. Still, it struck me as rife with potential conflicts of interest. How could Jeffrey justify launching a highly themed, merchandise-driven restaurant chain, given Disney's involvement in competitive entertainment ventures? How could he enter a partnership with a high-profile producer-director and still feel comfortable negotiating a movie or television deal with him in the future? Above all, how could Jeffrey consider this side venture an appropriate use of his time, given his aspiration to be president of the company?

I was also increasingly concerned about Jeffrey's profile at animation. Each of the animated movies represents a collaboration of more than four hundred people, many of them exceptional talents. Because Jeffrey captured the limelight, his team continued to operate largely in the shadows, and some of them were beginning to chafe at their anonymity. Peter Schneider, for example, was understandably proud of his contribution to our success, and I knew from Roy that he wasn't entirely happy playing a purely supporting role. Peter wasn't alone in his desire for a higher public profile. In the aftermath of *Aladdin*'s enormous success, I picked up intimations that its directors, John Musker and Ron Clements, felt that they, too, hadn't been given their public due. I also knew that Roy was fielding more and more complaints from other artists who felt undervalued. "Jeffrey's style of management," Peter would later explain to me, "is to create a wheel in which all the spokes return to him at the center, but none of them ever intersect."

What worried Frank, and me, was that the simmering resentment toward Jeffrey had the potential to fracture the delicate cooperative spirit of collegiality that had made us so successful at animation for so long. I was also concerned about Jeffrey's continuing lack of recognition for Roy Disney. Roy remained content to play his role largely out of public view, but he had a keener sense of what a Disney movie ought to be than any of the rest of us. He was also the soul of the brand, had a deep commitment to animation, and was understandably upset at being ignored by Jeffrey.

Oddly, the more success and recognition Jeffrey received, the more dissatisfied he seemed to become. In part, the explanation may have been his growing hunger for more independence and authority. Jeffrey was now forty-two—the same age I had been when I left Paramount and took over Disney—and he was no longer so willing to be anyone's subordinate, but especially mine. Over the years he acknowledged to Frank that he frequently wrestled with feelings of envy, which he referred to as "the little green man" inside himself. In animation, it seemed to be expressing itself as Jeffrey's growing need for center stage. In live action, meanwhile, Frank's memo in March 1994 made it painfully evident that our problems there persisted. For all Jeffrey's optimism when we spoke the previous fall, there was little evidence that we were taking the steps necessary to turn the situation around.

Nearly all of the problems that we now found ourselves facing were a by-product of our enormous good fortune during the past decade. In animation, we were being tested on our ability to survive our success—at least as daunting a challenge as overcoming our recent struggles in live action.

CHAPTER

8

Designing Parks

DURING OUR FIRST WEEKS AT THE COMPANY BACK IN 1984, FRANK and I devoted many hours to walking through Disneyland in Anaheim and Walt Disney World in Orlando. On one level, the two parks had a great deal in common. Each was a world unto itself—a uniquely designed blend of rides, parades, shows, and shops that provided a magical experience for visitors. Each park was impeccably run, reflecting Disney's passionate commitment to service and meticulous attention to detail. Finally, each park, after years of sustained success, was suffering from flagging attendance and diminished profits. But at another level, these similarities were misleading. From the start, the two parks had been designed to attract very disparate populations. As a result, they delivered very different experiences and faced distinctive challenges.

Disneyland had always been a local theme park, drawing as much on nearby residents in the Los Angeles area—a population of over 10 million people—as on out-of-town tourists. For most guests, Disneyland was a one-day experience. The most effective way to attract local customers back to the park was to regularly introduce new rides and parades and shows, preferably built around recognizable characters from Disney's recent movies. The problem was that few successful new movies were released during the seventies and early eighties, no broadly popular character had emerged since Mary Poppins, and nothing major had been added to Disneyland for years. Reenergizing the park required not just coming up with several strong attractions, but finding some well-known characters to build them around—until such time as characters emerged from our own new movies.

Walt Disney World presented a very different problem. From its launch a decade earlier, the park had been conceived as a destination resort to which most visitors would travel by car or plane and stay for several days. Walt Disney World included not just the Magic Kingdom—the equivalent of Disneyland—but a small water park (the first in the nation), several hotels, a campground, three golf courses, and Epcot Center, which had opened in 1982. No single new ride, parade, or show could be counted on to prompt families to travel long distances to Walt Disney World. Our immediate need was to market the park more effectively as a full-service resort. In the long run, our challenge was to extend the number of days that guests stayed with us by building more hotels and restaurants, along with new theme parks and nighttime entertainment.

The other key issue at both parks was to find a balance between our creative initiatives and the need to remain profitable. This dilemma, we soon discovered, was nothing new. For more than thirty years, the operators who ran the parks and the artists who designed them, known as Imagineers, had been at loggerheads. The operators focused on keeping costs down and running the parks as efficiently as possible while maintaining rigorous standards of service and performance. Surprise was their enemy. The Imagineers, charged with dreaming big dreams and bringing them to life, took Walt's lead and resisted any compromise that might mean sacrificing quality. Boundaries and limits were their enemy. My challenge and Frank's was to encourage cooperation between the operators and the Imagineers while allowing a certain creative tension to persist—to nurture a form of checks and balances in our system.

These tensions had their origins in the relationship between Walt and Roy Disney. Walt first began thinking about a park as early as 1937, when he mentioned to a colleague at the premiere of *Snow White* that his dream was to build a park for kids scaled down to their size. The idea gained more momentum when Walt began taking his own two daughters, Sharon and Diane, to local amusement parks after Sunday school and was put off by their seaminess. One of them was Beverly Park, where I would someday take my own children before it got torn down to make way for the Beverly Center, a giant mall.

In 1948, Walt put his ideas for a "Mickey Mouse Park" into a memo. "I want it to be very relaxing, cool and inviting," he wrote. His notion was to create a miniature town with a range of attractions that would appeal to all members of a family. With the company still beset by enormous debt, Roy refused to take Walt's musings seriously. "He is more interested, I think, in ideas that would be good in an amusement park than in running one himself," Roy said at one point.

In fact, Walt had simply decided to pursue his dream independently. For seed money, he borrowed on his life insurance and sold the vacation home he had built in Palm Springs. Then he made a decision that led to perhaps the most serious and lasting rupture in his relationship with his brother. In 1952, Walt told Roy that he wanted to create "Walt Disney, Inc." as a privately held company, which would own the rights to his name and earn between a 5 and 10 percent royalty on its use. Roy's son, Roy Edward, believes that Walt came up with the arrangement partly as a way to guarantee economic security for his family but mostly as a vehicle to finance the theme park he would eventually name Disneyland.

"My father was pretty sore," Roy told me. "He thought it created a terrible appearance for the shareholders. But Walt's lawyer came to my dad and said, in effect, 'If you don't make this deal with Walt, he's leaving and will find work somewhere else.'" Three outside board members resigned, but Walt's sole concession was to change the name of his company to WED—for Walter Elias Disney—in order not to be accused of commandeering the company name. The bitterness of the battle prompted a long feud between Walt and Roy that lasted much of the next decade. For more than two years, they stopped speaking almost completely, communicating mostly through their wives and secretaries.

Walt refused to be deterred. He assigned a small group of artists, animators, and art directors to work on a detailed five-foot-square model of the park. He and his team began visiting amusement parks everywhere—from the Los Angeles County Fair, to carnivals to Coney Island in New York. For the most part, Walt hated what he saw: the tawdriness, the seamy characters who ran the rides, the greasy food, the rip-off games, and the absence of anything for adults to do. The one exception was the Tivoli Gardens in Copenhagen, where he was delighted by the spotless surroundings, the beauty of the landscaping, the modestly priced food, and the courtesy of the Danish employees. When he realized there was not enough space to build his own park across the street from the Disney studio in Burbank, he eventually settled on a 160-acre orange orchard in the small town of Anaheim, 38 miles from Burbank.

Walt planned Disneyland as a fully self-contained world. In an effort to command the immediate attention of visitors, for example, he insisted on a single entrance to the park, opening onto Main Street—an idealized version of Marceline, Missouri, the town in which he grew up. His dream was to build everything in miniaturized scale to make it more appealing and accessible to children, but in the end he chose a more practical compromise. All of the buildings on Main Street were roughly seven-eighths size on the first floor, with each higher floor proportionately smaller. The train circling the park was done on a five-eighths scale.

By creating a berm or protective barrier around Disneyland, Walt ensured that the experience would be totally undisturbed by urban life on the outside. Employees were called "cast members." They wore costumes rather than uniforms and were encouraged to think of themselves as actors once they got "on stage," leaving behind their problems and real-life identities to perform whatever role they'd been assigned. Walt envisioned an experience at once nostalgic and futuristic, blending fun and fantasy, entertainment and education. Disneyland became not just a park but a vehicle through which to bring to life beloved film characters, including Mickey Mouse, Donald Duck, Snow White, and Peter Pan. For the first time, Disney audiences could enter the world of their favorite movies and animated films. Disneyland gave Walt's characters a whole new life.

The park was also an unexpected triumph of architecture and design. In 1963, the noted city planner James Rouse used Disneyland as the centerpiece of his commencement speech at the Harvard School of Design. "I hold a view that may be somewhat shocking to an audience as sophisticated as this," he declared, "namely that the greatest piece of urban design in the United States today is Disneyland. It took an area of activity—the amusement park—and lifted it to a standard so high in its performance, in its respect for people, in its functioning for people, that it really became a brand-new thing." More recently, the eminent architectural historian Vincent Scully, Jr., went even further, maintaining that Disneyland is "the most complex and compelling structure of myth and dreamwork that American architecture, perhaps any architecture, has ever achieved."

Disneyland opened as scheduled on July 17, 1955, an event televised live by ABC and hosted by several actors, including Ronald Reagan. The park was an instant hit. Built at a final cost of $17 million, it attracted 1 million guests within 7 weeks, and the company was able to pay off all its bank loans. In 1960, Walt and Roy exercised their option to buy back ABC's 34 percent share of Disneyland for $7.5 million. At the time, Walt resented paying such a huge premium over ABC's initial $500,000 investment. Today, that share would be worth more than $500 million.

Even with the park's huge success, Walt kept looking for ways to improve it, a phenomenon that came to be known as "plussing." Having built himself a small apartment above the firehouse on Main Street, Walt spent many days and nights there, walking the grounds at all hours. "The thing will get more beautiful year after year," he told a reporter soon after the opening. "And it will get better as I find out what the public likes. I can't do that with a picture. It's finished and unchangeable before I find out if the public likes it or not."

Walt's biggest regret about Disneyland was that he only had enough money to purchase 160 acres in Anaheim—although he did manage to double the acreage in his lifetime. As the park grew more popular, a raft of fast-food restaurants, bars, T-shirt outlets, and inexpensive motels sprouted up all around it. By 1963, Walt was actively scouting for an East Coast location—determined to prevent it from suffering a fate similar to Disneyland, and this time with Roy's support. He settled on Florida almost immediately, drawn by its warm climate. At the time, Orlando was a sleepy, undeveloped town of fewer than 90,000 people, surrounded by forest and swamp. To avoid attracting speculators and inflating prices, the company began acquiring land under assumed names. Ultimately, Walt was able to buy 27,000 acres of undeveloped land for just $5 million—an average of less than $200 an acre. On November 15, 1965, Disney publicly announced plans to build its second theme park near Orlando, along with Walt's newest and fondest dream: Epcot, short for the Experimental Prototype Community of Tomorrow, which he envisioned as a real-life model city of the future.

Tragedy cut his plans short. By early 1966, Walt was suffering from a series of symptoms—pain in his back and legs, a chronic sinus problem, a kidney ailment. On Wednesday, November 2, experiencing shortness of breath and disabling pain in his left leg, he checked into St. Joseph Hospital for tests. Surgery was scheduled for the following Monday. When he arrived with his wife and daughters, he learned that he had lung cancer—he'd been a chain-smoker all his life—and that the prognosis was poor. The lung was removed, but he told almost no one how sick he really was. "Walt always thought that if anyone knew he was ill, the stock would go down," his secretary, Lucille Martin, later told me. His condition deteriorated fast. On the morning of December 15, 1966, ten days after his sixty-fifth birthday, he died of acute circulatory collapse.

Walt's death made the front page of the *New York Times*, but his funeral arrangements could hardly have been more modest. He was cremated, and the ashes were buried at Forest Lawn Cemetery in Glendale. Because the arrangements were so private, a rumor persisted for years that his body had been cryogenically frozen. Ever curious, I eventually drove over to Forest Lawn to see Walt's burial site for myself. In a cemetery full of huge memorials, Walt's grave was impossible to find without help. It turned out to be a small monument on a tiny, overgrown plot. I'm convinced that if it had been up to Walt—the consummate showman—his funeral would have been marked by a giant parade up Main Street at Disneyland.

Roy was seventy-three years old at Walt's death, and he had been intending to retire within the next couple of years. Now, he vowed to carry forward his brother's last project. He even insisted on calling it *Walt* Disney World. Although Roy chose not to try to build Epcot, many of Walt's ideas for it were incorporated into the Magic Kingdom. Ten acres of service facilities were built into underground corridors. Pneumatic tubes were constructed to deliver garbage directly to a central deposit a mile away. The waste water treatment system removed solids and filtered the water before it was dumped into adjacent basins. A silent, futuristic monorail became the primary means of transporting guests around the park.

Built at a cost of $400 million, Walt Disney World opened as scheduled on October 1, 1971. Roy was at long last free to retire and relax after five exhausting years of work on the project. Eight weeks later, he made plans to take his grandchildren to Disneyland in Anaheim on a Sunday. At the last minute, he decided to stay home, complaining that he wasn't feeling well. When his family returned early in the evening, Roy had suffered a massive cerebral hemorrhage. He died the following day.

Disneyland and Walt Disney World remained immensely popular and successful long after Walt's and Roy's deaths. Unlike movies and television, which needed to be virtually re-launched from scratch, when Frank and I arrived, all the parks required was updating, expansion, and renewed excitement. We turned our attention first to Disneyland, where it seemed possible to make a difference most quickly and easily. One of the first calls I made was to George Lucas. No moviemaker had a more original blend of storytelling skills and technological imagination. Our idea was to recruit George to help us produce new attractions, building them around the immensely popular characters from movies such as *Star Wars* and *Raiders of the Lost Ark*.

George was instantly enthusiastic, partly because this was a way to reintroduce the movie characters he'd created to young audiences, but mostly because it would give him the chance to experiment with new forms of three-dimensional storytelling. He quickly set his sights on an Imagineering project based on NASA-developed flight simulation technology. Using the *Star Wars* characters, the ride was designed to create the feeling of a wild trip through the universe. George had the idea that the spaceship ought to be flown by a psychologically unbalanced rookie pilot named Rex—making it plausible for a series of disasters to occur in the course of the flight.

Frank and I arrived at Imagineering one day to see an early version of the ride, which we were calling *Star Tours*. We were dressed in business suits but ready for thrills. At this stage, the outside of the ride was little more than a giant box on stilts. I was completely intimidated by its long legs and the shaky ladder we'd have to climb to get into the box. Frank led the way. I followed reluctantly, along with two or three Imagineers I hoped could double as paramedics. When the ride began, we rocked to *Star Wars* music. We rolled to a comedy soundtrack. We tossed and we turned. When we emerged, I felt elated. I had just experienced a genuinely new kind of ride. Frank had turned a pale shade of green and looked as if he was about to faint. Based partly on this experience, we modified the ride so that not even queasy or nervous riders would get flight sickness. *Star Tours* was launched in 1987 and Disneyland experienced an immediate boost in attendance. As Walt had many years earlier, we soon discovered that a thrill ride, unlike a movie, can be adjusted and rejiggered long after it opens.

A second new Disneyland project was Videopolis, a vast outdoor dance amphitheater with dozens of monitors playing music videos. This attraction was aimed directly at teenagers—a group that tended to lose interest in the parks until they grew up and had children of their own. Videopolis opened in June 1985 and immediately became a popular draw, especially in the evenings.

What Frank and I didn't know was that Disneyland had a longstanding policy prohibiting same-sex dancing. Very quickly, a series of gay organizations organized a protest. My instinct was that no one comes to Disneyland to dance cheek-to-cheek and that the protesters merely wanted to make a statement. I prevailed on Dick Nunis, the head of our parks, to allow same-sex dancing. The first night, a handful of same-sex couples danced cheek-to-cheek. No one made a fuss, and we never saw any same-sex dancing again. In the absence of rigid rules, people feel much less compelled to act out. It was a lesson I'd learned countless times as a parent. There are times when it pays to lighten up.

The third early idea we came up with for Disneyland was to create something with Michael Jackson, who appealed to teenagers, but also to young kids, and even their parents. Jackson was a huge fan of our parks, sometimes visiting several times a month, in and out of disguise. Our notion was to put him in an extended 3-D music video. George Lucas happened to be one of Jackson's heroes, and provided another lure. Ultimately, Lucas decided to produce the video and recruited Francis Ford Coppola to direct.

With three strong creative voices involved—Lucas, Jackson, and Coppola—it was no surprise that the seventeen-minute film we called *Captain EO* ran over budget. The biggest factor was special effects, some 150 of them, more per minute than Lucas had used in *Star Wars*. The final cost reached $17 million, the same sum that it cost to build Disneyland. But the result was worth the effort and the expense. *Captain EO* was hugely popular from the moment it opened at Disneyland and at Walt Disney World in September 1986.

Perhaps the most ambitious project we undertook at Disneyland was a water ride we eventually named *Splash Mountain*. It grew out of a visit to Imagineering that Frank and I made with my son Breck, then fifteen, on a Saturday afternoon just weeks after our arrival at Disney. Over the years, I've often ameliorated my guilt at being away from home on a weekend by taking one of my sons with me to work. I enjoy talking with them about their lives as we drive somewhere, and rehashing whatever we've seen on the way home. I taught them to be polite on these outings, to shake hands firmly when introduced, and—remembering my own childhood—to let me know if they had to go to the bathroom. I also taught them to hold their criticisms until the car ride home.

In this case, we were met by Marty Sklar at an Imagineering warehouse in Glendale not unlike the one that housed animation. With his passion and unending flow of ideas, Marty embodied the Disney spirit. Having begun by doing publicity for Walt at Disneyland, Marty had been running the creative side of Imagineering for a decade when we arrived. In a huge loftlike room, he had laid out a presentation of all the Imagineering projects. Everywhere we looked there were elaborate scale models, artwork, and storyboard displays, many of them dazzling. For several hours, Marty escorted us through the room and we listened to a series of artists and designers describe their favorite ideas, most of which had been lying fallow for years. Among the most promising was a pavilion for Epcot devoted to the history of movies and featuring Audio-Animatronics figures—lifelike replicas of famous actors re-creating memorable scenes from their movies.

"That's one we'd like to see you develop further," Frank and I told Marty, not realizing that the idea would soon evolve into a third, completely separate theme park at Walt Disney World.

As for Disneyland, no project was more immediately compelling than the elaborate scale model we saw for a flume water ride, climaxing with a steep drop down a waterfall. It had been designed by Tony Baxter. Like so many of our cast members, Tony began his career by working at Disneyland right after high school—in his case selling ice cream in the Carnation store on Main Street, not unlike ex–cast member Steve Martin, who rode his bicycle over from Garden Grove each day to work in a magic shop or Kevin Costner, who met his future wife, Cyndi, when they both appeared as characters in the daily parade along Main Street. Tony was hired at Imagineering when he was twenty-two, based on a highly sophisticated model of a ride that was a precursor of *Big Thunder Mountain Railroad*, which eventually got built at all of our parks.

Tony's water ride had the potential to be what Walt originally called an "E-ticket" attraction. In Disneyland's early years, visitors purchased ticket books, and E-tickets were required for the best rides. The E-ticket was eventually abandoned, but the term stuck and became synonymous with a top-drawer experience. It had even seeped into the broader culture. When Sally Ride, the first woman astronaut, returned from her first space excursion, she summed it up for reporters as "the ultimate E-ticket ride." To me, an E-ticket became synonymous with "Disneyesque." It meant emotional and exciting, amusing and awe-inspiring, the highest quality and the most amazing. Above all, it meant what my young children used to call the "funnest." *Splash Mountain* seemed especially E-ticketish. In addition to a 45-degree waterfall drop, it took guests in a hollowed-out log through the backwoods and bayous of the old Disney movie *Song of the South,* where they could meet characters like Brer Fox and Brer Rabbit.

Approving an E-ticket thrill ride, we quickly discovered, is a decision equivalent to greenlighting a high-budget movie: both risky and expensive. It was here that we first came up against the historical conflict between our Imagineers and the operators. Dick Nunis, longtime head of the parks, loved the idea of a water ride, both for its marketing value and as a way to cool off visitors in the summer heat of Orlando and Anaheim. But his team also immediately raised questions about Walt Disney Imagineering's budget for *Splash Mountain*. It's impossible to make an $80 million budget look reasonable when it generates no specific return, but the Imagineers made the case that these E-ticket attractions were the key to keeping up attendance levels by constantly reinventing the park.

Instead of trying to cut back on the ride, Marty and his team said they could save a small fortune by moving the Audio-Animatronics characters from an attraction called *America Sings*, which was growing old and tired. We were still naive about costs, loved the ride, and accepted the argument. In fact, it saved only a fraction of the eventual budget. While Frank and I often instinctively favored the more creative (and costly) solution to a problem, we learned not to choose sides too quickly, and to let the battles play out. The result is usually the best possible ride at the most reasonable cost. *Splash Mountain* also led to new rules about my own role in the process. After my son Anders and I were the first humans to try the new attraction, and were nearly decapitated by a board resting across the track on the final drop down the waterfall, I was no longer permitted to talk the construction supervisor into letting me test new rides whenever I felt like it. Now I make my preopening visits incognito.

Much as E-ticket attractions matter, small details also add up. Early on, Frank instituted a special fund from our corporate budget specifically earmarked for improvements at Disneyland and especially at Walt Disney World. Once a year, a group of us walk the parks with Marty Sklar and his Imagineers and agree to replace concrete benches with more comfortable ones, or repave certain areas, or change paint colors, or build little fountains for kids to play in. These changes don't bring any direct financial return, and they aren't promotable, but they do subliminally make the experience more appealing.

At Walt Disney World, our most immediate task was to promote and market the resort more effectively. To our amazement, Frank and I discovered that almost no money had ever been spent on advertising. Instead, Disney relied on stories written by reporters who were invited down for the openings of new attractions or anniversary celebrations. "You can see how much we've accomplished without advertising," Walt Disney World's marketing chief Tom Elrod told us soon after we arrived. "Just think what wonders we could do with it." We gave him an immediate go-ahead. Elrod's group came up with a series of highly emotional spots built around a theme we'd discussed—"The family that plays together stays together." This was a way of promoting Walt Disney World as a full-service resort and a logical vacation destination. It also addressed an issue that many modern families faced.

My own best memories from childhood were the family vacations that we took together—whether it was a buggy ride in Williamsburg, Virginia, playing skeetball in Atlantic City, hiking in the

Adirondack Mountains, or skiing together in the Laurentian Mountains of Quebec. When Jane and I had our own children, we found ourselves re-creating our childhood vacations. By the 1980s, when two-career parents were increasingly commonplace, vacations represented a more precious time than ever for families to be together.

The most powerful and controversial spot we ran began with a family rushing to get off to work and school, only to realize that they've left the baby all alone in his high chair in the kitchen. "We need a vacation," the mother says, and the next scene shows everyone in the family having a great time at Walt Disney World. It was a very powerful message, but eventually we decided it was just too guilt-provoking and took it off the air. However, others with similar themes proved effective, including a series starring the Huxtable family from *The Cosby Show* on NBC. During the first year the spots ran, long before any of our new attractions debuted, attendance at Walt Disney World rose more than 10 percent.

No campaign we undertook achieved more visibility than our "What's Next?" ads. Early in 1987, Frank and I had a dinner inside Disneyland with George Lucas and several celebrities we'd invited to promote the opening of *Star Tours*, among them Jeana Yeager and Dick Rutan. The couple had made headlines a month earlier by piloting a single-engine plane around the world on one tank of gas. At some point in the evening, my wife turned to Rutan. "Now that you've flown around the world and done the most adventurous thing imaginable," Jane asked reasonably enough, "what are you going to do next?"

"Well, we're going to Disneyland," he replied sincerely. As soon as she had a chance, Jane pulled me aside and described the exchange. "This would make a great advertising campaign," she said. By the middle of the night I was addicted to the idea. The next morning, I called Tom Elrod. Two weeks later, at the Super Bowl in Pasadena, the New York Giants overwhelmed the Denver Broncos. As the Giants' quarterback walked to the sidelines, he stopped for the camera crew we had waiting. "Phil Simms, you've just won the Super Bowl," an off-camera voice asks. "What are you going to do next?" He looked at the camera with a big smile and replied, "I'm going to Disneyland." We had arranged for Simms to spend the next day at the park with his wife and young children, appearing in our parades, taking his kids on rides, and making a slew of media appearances—each using Disneyland as a backdrop.

To our amazement, the campaign acquired a certain icon status. World-famous athletes were suddenly eager to have the "What's Next?" ad on their resumés. At major sports events, we would typically make provisional deals with each of the athletes most likely to emerge as the game's standout. During the past decade, we've produced dozens of spots at major events. We've used the campaign not just to honor athletes ranging from John Elway to Michael Jordan but to celebrate others who've achieved something outstanding. The campaign has given our parks and the company enormous visibility, but it also has a subtler effect: powerfully identifying Disney with excitement and achievement, triumph and joy.

The other immediate challenge at Walt Disney World was to build it out. Fewer than 3,000 of the 28,000 acres Walt originally purchased had been put to use. Even with more than 7,000 acres devoted to conservation and water management, there were still nearly 18,000 left to dream about—a stretch of property two-thirds the size of the city of San Francisco. No initiative had more promise than building new hotels. Within a few weeks of Frank's and my arrival, Chuck Cobb, then in charge of our real estate, told me that a deal was in place with the developer and builder John Tishman, whose company had built Epcot, to construct two new hotels. I instantly hated the designs. I associated Disney with fun, theatricality, magic. These were perfectly serviceable buildings, but they were bland, boxy, and completely unimaginative—typical of the hotels that large chains have put up all across America. "The doctor can bury his mistakes," Frank Lloyd Wright once said, "but the architect can only advise his client to plant vines." For me, approving these hotels and having them on our property seemed an equivalent to the "A" that Hester Prynne wore in *The Scarlet Letter*: a constant public reminder of my transgression.

The intensity of these feelings took me slightly by surprise, and I was relieved when Frank immediately agreed with me. As a young man, I couldn't have articulated my feelings about design, but even without a formal education in architecture, there were buildings all around me that silently shaped my perceptions of the world. Still, if you had asked me about Le Corbusier, I would have assumed you were talking about Marie Antoinette's hairdresser. If you mentioned a pediment, I would have said it was something that got in your way.

Eventually, I became more sophisticated. At the age of eighteen, I took a backpack trip to Europe. When I arrived in Rome, our family friends Victor and Sally Ganz had left for the weekend. I was able to use their suite at the Hassler Hotel and take a hot shower for the first time in weeks. After they returned, I moved to the Y but politely agreed to let them feed me for the next two days. I hadn't anticipated that they'd also set out to feed my mind. In a whirlwind tour, Victor took me to see every statue, church, museum, and landmark he could fit into forty-eight hours. What I absorbed from the experience was my first conscious feeling of awe about architecture and its power along with a new respect for the idea of permanence. I'd never before imagined that every square, every building, every fountain, had a story behind it, a reason for being, passions that prompted its creation. Victor talked about architecture the way my college fraternity brothers talked about girls and football. He made it exciting.

At the end of our second week at Disney, Frank and I convened a dinner to meet with the executives in charge of developing real estate. They included Cobb, Marty Sklar, and Wing Chao, our chief in-house architect, who was born in China and trained at Harvard. "How about designing a hotel right here in Burbank shaped like Mickey Mouse?" I said, launching the conversation. For a moment there was a shocked silence. Then ideas began to fly back and forth. Much later, Wing Chao told me that it was as if "a big bomb had been dropped in our laps." My purpose was to stress the importance of theatricality and innovation. In my heart, I knew that a hotel shaped like Mickey, with one foot on the east side of the street adjacent to the studio and the other on the west side, probably was going too far. I gave it up as soon as Wing raised a practical concern: where to place the elevators. Still, by pushing the envelope and suggesting the impossible, a lively debate was sparked. Several people at the table—most obviously Wing and Marty—left feeling enthusiastic about bringing more ambition to our design.

Elsewhere in the company, there was support for taking a safer, more conventional route. Among the strongest of these voices was Al Checchi, who had once been treasurer of the Marriott Corporation, and whom we had first met when he was working for the Basses. When Al expressed a willingness to move from Texas to California, we offered him an office and an unofficial role as an adviser to Disney. Brilliant and exuberant, he punctuated every proclamation with a tone that suggested absolute certainty. It was also Al who undertook to provide me with a crash tutorial in business. He handed over his Harvard Business School texts and I crammed every evening. The next day, he quizzed me on terms, and explained the more arcane concepts.

One of the first deals that Al suggested was to go into partnership with Marriott, having them build and operate all of the new hotels and convention space we needed. In Al's view, which he had first voiced when we met at the Bass offices and his colleagues had shared, Disney was a mediocre hotel operator. By contrast, he argued, Marriott had a worldwide reservations system, unparalleled experience in the convention business, and a deservedly superb reputation as an operator.

In the winter of 1985, Al arranged for Frank and me to meet Bill Marriott at his company's headquarters in Washington, D.C. Listening to Bill describe his company turned out to be like having a biology teacher describe the anatomy of a frog. He knew every detail, down to the sheets and pillowcases. But when we arrived at Marriott's design center, my enthusiasm began to wane. What we saw was extremely functional, but uninspiring. It seemed unlikely that Marriott's team would ever embrace my more ambitious and theatrical ideas about design. Also, it was hard to imagine meshing Marriott's button-down operating style with Disney's more freewheeling culture.

The unexpected bonus of our trip was meeting Gary Wilson. We had been looking for a chief financial officer for several months without success. Gary was Marriott's executive vice president for finance and development. Virtually every executive recruiter told us that what we needed was a CFO like Gary Wilson—tough-minded, financially innovative, and astute about managing risk. No one suggested that Gary would consider returning to such a job himself. They made him sound like a wise elder statesman, and I simply assumed that he was in his midsixties. Instead, he turned out to be in his early forties. When he walked into the room, it was as if a spotlight shone down on him. Nattily dressed in a dark, highly tailored suit, with a monogrammed shirt and a handkerchief, Gary had a magisterial style. His insights about Disney were sharp, but my main response was that I had a good time talking with him

—a very different experience from all the other stuffy CFO candidates I'd been meeting. I took Frank aside and said, "This is the guy we should hire."

After a difficult negotiation, Gary came aboard. He quickly emerged as a very astute strategic thinker, with a rare capacity to analyze the value of any potential deal. He also introduced strong financial disciplines to Disney. At ABC, I'd learned to operate in what later came to be termed a "financial box," an economic model that forecasts costs, revenues, and profits for any business venture. At Disney, Gary and Larry Murphy—recruited by Gary from Marriott to run our strategic planning group—took this process several steps further. They initiated the concept of five-year plans, requiring each division to lay out clear, long-term financial objectives and expectations, and to plan their budgets within that framework. Five-year plans don't guarantee performance, but they do force executives rigorously to assess their businesses and to be accountable for their claims.

In turn, Gary introduced to Disney our 20/20 goals—aiming for a 20 percent annual growth in earnings as well as a 20 percent return on equity, a key measure of return on our investment. By achieving these two markers, which we did over the next decade, Disney came to be seen by investors as a growth company. That helped our stock to command a high multiple over our earnings, and to rise in price at a rate that far exceeded most companies'.

In the aftermath of our visit to Marriott, John Tishman learned about our proposed partnership and was outraged. "You can't do that," he called to tell me. "It's a breach of my agreement with Disney." By Tishman's reckoning, he had negotiated with Disney's previous management the exclusive rights to build any new convention hotels on our property for a period of at least ten years. Our lawyers believed that his claims were questionable, but Tishman began threatening a lawsuit if we went ahead with the Marriott deal. The irony was that neither deal—with Tishman or with Marriott—appealed to me.

Meanwhile, work was continuing on a luxury hotel called the Grand Floridian, which had been conceived before Frank and I joined the company and was designed largely by our own Imagineers and the firm of Wimberly, Allison, Tong & Goo. Before we approved the start of construction, we wanted to see what the rooms might look like.

In October 1985, we asked Wing Chao to put together a presentation. When we walked into Imagineering, we were stunned. Wing's team had created two completely finished model rooms, including beds and bedspreads, bureaus and nighttables, carpeting, light fixtures, bathroom towel racks, door handles, even art on the walls—all designed around the hotel's turn-of-the-century Victorian theme. These were vastly more attractive hotel rooms than I'd ever seen in a Marriott or a Hilton or a Sheraton, and they'd been produced on short notice for a reasonable budget by a creative group new to hotel design.

Frank and I were awed, and made a final decision on the spot. "Obviously, we don't have the experience of a major hotel company in building and running hotels, but the fact is I've never much liked partnerships," I told our team. "I don't want to be in a position where every time there's an artistic decision or a design choice we have to consult with a partner, or ask for approvals and make compromises. Here's what we're going to do instead: We're going to build up the Disney Development Company. We're going to hire the best people in the industry. We'll make mistakes along the way, but they'll be our mistakes and we'll learn from them."

My resolve only intensified in the weeks ahead. "If we're going to imprint our stamp on the world," I wrote in a memo to Frank in late 1985, "if we're going to do something more than help people have a good time with Mickey Mouse, if we are going to make aesthetic choices, then we've got to upgrade the level of our architecture and try to leave something behind for others. This is going to be highly charged politically inside the company. There is definitely going to be a problem trying to make some of our executives understand that we're not going to just be concerned about the bottom line, we're not going to do schlocky architecture, and we are going to try to make a statement—to make some history. There are some who feel it's going to cost us additional money. I don't think it has to, but even if it costs a few dollars more, I think it's well worth it."

Early in 1986, we let Tishman know we weren't prepared to go forward with his hotels, having delivered the same message to Bill Marriott about our proposed partnership several weeks earlier. On February 4, 1986—the day before our annual meeting—Tishman and his partners filed suit against Disney, seeking damages of over $300 million.

The timing was clearly an effort to prompt shareholder unrest and thereby attract maximum media attention, but the lawsuit received only minimal coverage. Within a few months, we came up with a solution: offering Tishman a better location for his hotels, in return for permitting us control over design, and the obligation to live by the same service standards we set throughout the rest of the park. Over dinner in New York the next week, I laid out our proposal. Tishman agreed, with one caveat: that our right to control design not force him to increase his construction budget. Here, finally, was an opportunity to test whether much more ambitious design could be accomplished economically.

By this stage, I'd already spent nearly a year becoming informally educated about modern architecture. Wing Chao helped to familiarize Frank and me with the work of a dozen important or promising architects. I had also turned for advice to Victor Ganz, our old family friend and my longtime mentor. Victor was on the board of the Whitney Museum in New York, and it happened that Michael Graves had just done a controversial design for the museum's planned expansion. At Victor's suggestion, I met with Graves as well as with Robert Venturi—two of America's most imaginative postmodern architects. I also went to see their work.

The idea of holding a design competition for the Tishman hotels intrigued Frank and me. We both liked the idea of having multiple options, and it was also an opportunity to broaden our education in architecture. I never thought of us as patrons or clients. To me, a client needs a lawyer and a patron needs a wheelchair. Instead, I saw us as collaborators, playing an active role in the dialogue with the architect. Graves and Venturi were our two choices for the first competition. At Tishman's request, we agreed to include Alan Lapidus, whose father, Morris Lapidus, had designed the most famous Miami hotels, including the Fontainebleau. Our Imagineers also eventually asked to be part of the competition. Less than three months later—in July 1986—I joined Frank, Tishman, Victor Ganz, and the rest of our Disney group for a presentation in a conference room next to my office in the Animation Building. We began in the early afternoon, and it turned out to be an unexpectedly long day.

Venturi, Lapidus, and the Imagineers all presented their models, but Michael Graves's model was diverted en route to Burbank by thunderstorms in the Midwest. The WDI model looked like a giant mountain, with all the parking in the middle. It was wonderfully whimsical—but totally impractical. Lapidus produced a kind of modern Crystal Palace in the style of the Miami Beach and Las Vegas hotels he ordinarily designed—not right for Disney. Venturi had designed two graceful, crescent-shaped buildings facing a semi-circular area that we liked very much. As we waited for Graves's contribution to show up, we spent the next several hours trying to humor Tishman, who was growing impatient. After a long day, everyone was exhausted, anticipatory, and creatively and emotionally on edge. Shortly before midnight, Graves's model arrived in four huge crates covered with frost, apparently from the altitude. When the model was put together, I felt immediately that the wait had been worth it.

The long-standing rule at Walt Disney World was that no building should create a visual distraction for guests inside our parks. But Graves had produced one building twenty-seven stories high, in the shape of a classical pyramid, and a second one of twelve stories, shaped like a vault with a curving roof designed to echo the adjacent lake. He also added several extreme design elements, including a fountain across the top of the pyramid that he called "the birdbath." For me, the basic concept had an almost mythical power. My concern was not that Graves had gone too far—excess can always be scaled back—but that for Disney the buildings remained a bit too serious and foreboding looking. My note to Graves was simple: "Lighten them up." Tishman looked genuinely ashen. "This design is outrageous and impossible," he insisted. "The buildings make no sense practically or economically."

"Don't worry," I said naively. "We'll get this built on time and on budget. It won't cost us more than the hotel you had in mind."

Graves responded to my concern by adding icons to the top of his buildings: two huge swans for one and two dolphins for the other. The idea of using these creatures—icons that had classical antecedents but were also lighthearted and accessible—seemed a perfect solution for a Disney hotel. As for the height issue, the hotels turned out to be visible only from a small section of Epcot.

Early in the design process, I discovered that it was crucial to ask Graves what he had agreed to cut out since our last meeting. In an effort to make peace with John Tishman and our Disney operators, Graves often ended up editing himself—something I would discover that most architects do. As often as not, my role was to reinstate a design element and let others figure out how to make it work financially. At one point, for example, the pyramid shape of the Dolphin was eliminated in the course of what's called "value engineering," the systematic process by which costs are brought down to meet a budget. The change would have cut out the building's heart and soul. When I showed the revised plans to Victor Ganz, he had a pithy response: "You've castrated it." The pyramid was restored.

The Swan and the Dolphin did end up costing a little more than the average, cookie-cutter hotel. But we felt confident that the distinctive design justified charging a higher-than-average room rate. We also believed that the hotels would provide one more reason for people to visit Walt Disney World. Even Tishman became something of a believer. Hard-nosed and skeptical as he was at first, Frank and I appreciated his willingness to be drawn into the creative process and his desire to get it right. Once he had committed to our approach, he built two great buildings.

The Swan opened in 1989, and the Dolphin a year later. Frank and I had insisted that Graves be permitted to design not just the buildings themselves but their interiors, something very rare at the time. Far better, we felt, to have one vision and sensibility inform the project all the way through. Graves proved to be just as startling and distinctive in his interior choices as he had in the hotels' design. Painted parrots and macaws were perched on the chandeliers, and emblazoned cut-out dolphins, swans, and other exotic creatures adorned the backs of all the chairs. These basic themes were carried into every aspect of the design, from ceilings to carpets. From that point on, every architect who designed a building for Disney also worked on its interior design.

The tenets we had evolved working on the Swan and the Dolphin would guide us as we moved ahead to build our own hotels. Above all, we learned that good design didn't have to cost significantly more than bad design. In part, that required being tactical in the use of materials and avoiding high-cost items where they didn't clearly add value. We also believed that great architecture could be lighthearted, colorful, and metaphorical, in marked contrast to the cold, abstract modernist idiom. Design was enriched, not undermined, by drawing on the narrative devices that I'd first learned by studying literature in college. It was possible to tell a story even through an inanimate object. Attention to small details, inside and outside the buildings, was what created an over-all impression of care and excellence. The best design, like the best of any art, needs to be challenging and provocative, even a little threatening at first. At the same time, we tried never to take ourselves too seriously. As important as it was to design buildings that were aesthetically pleasing, they also had to be fun and entertaining.

By the end of the 1980s, we had a full-scale building pro-gram under way. Wing Chao and Peter Rummell oversaw all design and construction. Design is fun, clean and exciting; construction is dirty, frustrating, and expensive. I prefer the former. Wing, who had been recruited to Disney straight out of architecture school, focused on our relationships with the architects we hired and on the design process. Peter, who came from a background in real estate development, also appreciated good design and had long experience dealing with the chal-lenges of large-scale construction. Over the next decade Peter and Wing would manage to bring in fifty-eight buildings on time and on budget. In that period, we would build eleven hotels with some 14,000 rooms. Aimed at every price level from budget to luxury, each was designed by a notable American architect and each told its own themed story. In every case we sought, as Walt had done at Disneyland, to create a unique, self-contained environment—to use architecture and design to prompt an emotional response from our guests.

Our hotels became experiences and entertainments in them-selves. My own favorites range from Peter Dominick's Wilderness Lodge, reinterpreting with remarkable attention to detail the great national park lodges found in the American Northwest, to Robert A. M. Stern's evocative Yacht Club and Beach Club, adjacent hotels inspired by turn-of-the-century East Coast resorts. Successful as our hotels are in artistic terms, the simplest tribute to them comes from our guests. To this day, the occupancy rate at each one of them runs in excess of 90 percent —the highest in the world.

We also discovered that attention to design could affect our own work spaces at Walt Disney World. Soon after we arrived, we realized we needed a new building in which to hire cast members. By that point, we were conducting nearly 100,000 interviews a year to fill openings for a cast that exceeded 25,000. Most of these interviews were being held in trailers scattered around the "backstage" areas of the property. Competition for good workers had grown more intense than ever, in part because Disney's success had attracted so many other tourist-related businesses to Orlando. It seemed important to design a building that provided a feeling for who we were—and communicated the sense that Disney was an appealing place to work.

It was here that we first worked with Bob Stern. My connection to Bob went back many years. When my parents moved out of their Park Avenue apartment into a smaller apartment, they hired Bob, then just thirty-three. He designed a strikingly dramatic space for them by ripping off the roof, replacing it with glass, and building a greenhouse-like structure that evoked a sense of country in the city. Bob went on to acclaim for his wonderful shingle-style beach houses in East Hampton, as a professor of architecture at Columbia, and as the host of an eight-part public television series about architecture in America, *Pride of Place*. At my urging, Wing Chao first approached Bob in 1987 about designing a "Casting Center" where we could hire new employees. Bob's exuberance, his knowledge of architectural styles, and his instinctive feel for the Disney culture led to his designing several more buildings for us during the next decade. It was Bob who coined the memorable Disney design tenet, "Form follows parking." With the death of Victor Ganz, Bob became my main adviser on architecture, and in 1991 we made him a member of our board of directors. It is important to have a board that is diverse not only ethnically and in gender, but professionally. Reveta Bowers, for example, is perhaps the only elementary school principal on a major corporate board, but she provides an important voice in a company whose primary constituency is children.

Our idea was to locate the Casting Center on I-4, the main interstate that passes by Walt Disney World. Because we rarely use billboards, the center was destined to become what Stern described as "the only building identifying Disney in the public realm." He designed a model that we all loved immediately: a long, low-slung structure with cupolas on either end and a yellow and white triangular pattern on the front that he referred to as "argyle socks." Inside, the ceilings showed Peter Pan and his merry band of friends, while the walls featured murals of Disney scenes. The cumulative effect was to give prospective employees a humorous evocation of the Disney culture before they faced the more serious drama of a job interview. The Casting Center also demonstrated that good design not only can be aesthetically pleasing but also can enhance function. In the first year after it opened in 1989, applications for jobs at Walt Disney World increased dramatically.

We brought this same attention to detail (and fun) even to our office buildings. Early in 1993, Jeffrey told me that he was planning to move animation, which had grown exponentially, into a high-rise office building in Burbank. The notion of housing this extraordinary group of artists in a boxy, modern glass tower somehow seemed wrong. Instead, we decided to build them a new home and agreed that Bob Stern would be ideal for the project. He worked quickly and had proved that he could produce Disneyesque buildings on a tight budget. Above all, we wanted to create an open, airy work space without pretension or lavish accoutrements. Bob ended up designing an alluring, lighthearted building with forms and shapes that recalled 1940s Art Deco Hollywood. The interior was graceful but informal, with walls where artists could hang their drawings and storyboards, large presentation rooms, wide hallways, and loosely designed work spaces. It was a casual, understated environment conducive both to creativity and to collegiality.

Several other buildings were especially striking. For the Team Disney executive offices on our Burbank lot, Michael Graves produced a headquarters that is at once elegant, classical, and playful. One of my favorite elements was his idea of using Disney's Seven Dwarfs atop the front of the building—with Dopey apparently holding up the roof. The Team Disney building at Walt Disney World became perhaps the most acclaimed of all our design efforts. In this case, we approached the Japanese architect Arata Isozaki, who had designed the Museum of Contemporary Art in Los Angeles. Isozaki produced three separate designs, and we chose a long, sleek, multicolored, low-slung structure, both peaceful and compelling. Ultimately, it would win the National Honor Award from the American Institute of Architects.

The other remaining challenge at Walt Disney World was to find a strong theme for a third park. No single venture had a greater potential to extend the number of days that visitors stayed in our hotels and restaurants and shops. The idea for a movie pavilion at Epcot had come up during our first Saturday visit to Imagineering. But the more we talked about the attraction, the more we recognized that it had the potential to become a separate, gated park. Over the coming months, Imagineering began to work on developing the concept. Under the direction of Bob Weis, who had joined Disney right out of college, the Imagineers developed a series of attractions, beginning with the one that had sparked the park in the first place: *The Great Movie Ride*, which covered the history of the movies. They also designed an Indiana Jones stunt show, drawing on Lucas's *Raiders of the Lost Ark*; a studio in which guests could star in their own television shows; and a studio tour ride culminating in a stop at Catastrophe Canyon, complete with simulated earthquake, oil-rig fire, and flash flood. The overall design for the park was an attempt to evoke old Hollywood, rich in detail and atmosphere. Architecturally, we drew on the graceful curvilinear style of the 1920s—Streamline Moderne, an offshoot of Art Deco—in part by re-creating Hollywood landmarks ranging from the Brown Derby restaurant to Grauman's Chinese Theater.

In March 1985, Frank received a call from Frank Rothman, an old lawyer friend who had been hired to run MGM/UA by its owner, Kirk Kerkorian. MGM/UA was losing money, and Rothman's mandate was to sell off valuable assets, including parts of its library, while actively seeking a buyer for the company. Rothman was calling Frank because we'd indicated that we were considering moving our movie lab work from MGM/UA to Twentieth Century Fox. "We very much need you to keep your business with us," Rothman explained to Frank.

Frank and I quickly recognized an opportunity. In exchange for leaving our lab business with MGM/UA, we would ask for the right to license their name and call our new park the Disney-MGM Studios. While MGM's best days had clearly passed, few studios had such an illustrious history or a more extraordinary library of classics, ranging from *Gone With the Wind* to *Mutiny on the Bounty, The Wizard of Oz* to *Singin' in the Rain*. Disney, by contrast, had virtually no profile as a live-action movie studio at the time. Our animated classics were certainly valuable, but our library of other kinds of films was sparse. Rothman was receptive, and we immediately began a negotiation.

Less than four months later, in June 1985, we signed an agreement that gave us most of what we sought, including perpetual rights to use much of MGM's library and its logo for a very modest fee. For reasons that remain a mystery, Kerkorian was told about the deal only as it was being signed. Much later, it would become clear that he had been upset by the news, particularly when he discovered that we planned to shoot movies and television shows at the studio and that our rights to build studio tours using the MGM name weren't limited to Walt Disney World. Suddenly, we were showered with calls from MGM executives seeking a way out. When we declined to renegotiate, they eventually decided to sue, claiming that we didn't have the right to film movies or shows at the tour. We suspected that the lawsuit was designed to extricate MGM from a deal they didn't like.

It was during this case that I first observed Sanford Litvack in action in court. A former partner at the law firm of Dewey Ballantine in New York and a former assistant attorney general in the Carter administration, Sandy had a reputation as a superb trial lawyer. We hired him as our general counsel in 1991, and he took on the MGM case. The trial finally took place in the summer of 1992, and the key moment occurred when MGM's general counsel took the stand. She'd been involved in negotiating the deal. Under Sandy's relentless questioning, she did something that until then I thought only happened on episodes of *Perry Mason*. She became tearful, broke down, and reluctantly acknowledged that her superiors had indeed wanted to get out of the deal. We eventually won the case, and Sandy became my hero.

The other company that wasn't very happy about our plans for a new park was Universal, which already operated its own studio tour theme park in Los Angeles. For more than three years Universal had been trying without success to raise the financing to build a second studio tour park in Orlando, just a few miles from Walt Disney World. In this case, the conflict took on a personal resonance. The day before it was announced that Frank and I would be going to Disney in 1984, I received a call at home from Sid Sheinberg, the president of Universal. He'd heard the rumors that I might be headed for Disney. "Taking the Disney job is the stupidest thing you could possibly do," he told me. "It's still in play. Eventually, it's going to be taken over by one of the raiders. You'd be crazy to go there." I thanked Sid for his thoughts, but I doubted that he believed what he was saying. At a minimum, his perspective wasn't entirely objective. If I did accept the Disney job, Sid knew that we would be very aggressive competitors with Universal not just in movies but in theme parks.

A couple weeks after Frank and I began at Disney, Sid called again, this time with his chairman Lew Wasserman on another phone extension. "Let's get together on a studio tour in Orlando," Sid suggested. "We tried with your predecessors, but they were unresponsive. We think we can help you." By this point, Frank and I had given Imagineering the go-ahead to expand their Epcot tour idea.

"We're already working on something of our own," I explained. Although they didn't say so at the time, Sid and Lew were outraged. By launching a studio tour at Walt Disney World, Sid would later argue, we were invading Universal's turf. "Do you really want a little mouse to become one large ravenous rat?" he said to one reporter. It was the sort of catchy quote that guaranteed headlines, but it begged the real issue. In fact, it was Universal that was seeking to capitalize on Disney's efforts, by proposing to build a theme park in Orlando just a few miles from Walt Disney World. It was obvious that they'd chosen their site in an effort to feed off the millions of visitors who were already traveling to Orlando to visit our parks.

We moved quickly to begin construction on our new park. Sensitive to the cost overruns at Epcot, we decided to build Disney-MGM Studios with a much smaller capacity, while leaving room to expand in the face of demand. The heart of the park was a working studio, which meant that it could be less finished in its look than our other two parks. Building two sound stages for actual production and creating a working animation studio was a way to make the experience more authentic, but these decisions would also serve our production needs as they grew. Jeffrey and others argued that artists would never be interested in moving to Orlando, and certainly not to work in what would begin as a demonstration animation facility. I wasn't so sure. Some artists, I thought, would jump at a chance to relocate. By comparison with Los Angeles, Florida offered less expensive housing, no state income tax, and a more relaxed lifestyle.

Florida was already the fourth largest state in the country, a new melting pot with a richly diverse population, particularly in big cities like Miami and, increasingly, Orlando. Bob Graham, then the state's governor, told me during one of our meetings about Disney-MGM that three things had dramatically changed Florida over the past few decades: air conditioning, emigration from Cuba, and the launch of Walt Disney World. All three caused the state's population to jump. Much as we had taken advantage of this pool to hire our cast for the parks, now we had the opportunity to tap into it as a source of new artists in front of and behind the camera.

Disney-MGM was scheduled to open on May 1, 1989. As the date drew near, we focused on a companywide marketing and advertising effort. In April, we received a big boost when *Newsweek* ran a cover story about the park entitled "Mickey's New Magic." The night before the opening, NBC aired a two-hour special based on the making of the Disney-MGM Studio, and *Time* magazine wrote a glowing advance review of the overall experience. Jeffrey helped to convince a dozen stars from our movies—including Bette Midler, Robin Williams, and George Lucas—to participate. Three thousand members of the media accepted our invitation to the festivities, assuring worldwide press for the event. Our biggest problem was dealing with demand. Within several hours of opening the gates for the first time, we reached capacity and had to begin turning people away from the parking lots.

In a month, the park's success had helped push Disney's stock up more than 20 percent. After three months, we announced our intention to double its size over the next few years, based on plans developed as part of our initial design. In Disney-MGM's first half year, overall attendance at Walt Disney World rose by more than 5 million visits—most of them from guests extending their stays. It increased another 3.5 million the second half of the year. By the end of 1990, operating income from the parks had reached $800 million, up from $250 million when we arrived in 1984.

Even so, we couldn't afford to ignore the competition from Universal. For a long time, I had doubted they would secure the financing to build their theme park in Orlando. At one point, my assistant Art Levitt and I climbed over a fence at three in the morning to see if any dirt had actually been moved at their site four miles from Walt Disney World. All we saw was a small construction permit sign in the middle of the property. As we stood talking, a guard began to walk slowly across the property toward us. We took off at full speed, scrambled back over the fence, dove into our car, and headed back to Walt Disney World. In the end, Universal did get its financing, construction began, and I resigned myself to the fact that the prospect of an aggressive competitor was an incentive to redouble our own efforts and not take our success for granted. "Competition," General Sarnoff once said, "brings out the worst in people and the best in products."

By the early 1990s we faced other competition for our core family audience. Club Med responded to the aging of the baby boomers by turning much of its focus from singles to families. Las Vegas began trying to attract families for the first time, while Branson, Missouri, emerged as a fast-growing resort destination focused on country music. The cruise business boomed, in part by broadening its appeal beyond its core audience of senior citizens. To make matters even tougher, the economy fell into a recession early in 1991, prompting many families to vacation closer to home and for shorter periods. The recession hit especially hard in Europe. Foreign visitors accounted for 20 percent of Walt Disney World's guests, but suddenly, they had less income to spend. In early 1991, the ominous threat of a Gulf war with Iraq further dampened international travel. The war also affected domestic travel, as Americans became concerned about the price and availability of gasoline.

Taken together, these factors led to a drop in attendance at Walt Disney World of nearly 5 million guests in 1991, our lowest level in three years. Disneyland suffered an equally significant fall-off. In addition to the problems of increased competition and the recession, we faced other issues. One was that by 1992 the introduction of high-profile new attractions had slowed to a trickle at Disneyland and Walt Disney World. The second was that the thousands of new employees didn't all reflect the standards that were second nature to our longtime cast members—a problem to which Judson Green, the new president of Walt Disney Attractions, turned much of his attention. Nothing so visibly defines Disney's parks as the warmth and commitment of our cast members over the years, and the appreciation that guests feel for the way they're treated. Judson and his team set out to reaffirm these values. I was first impressed with Judson when he worked with Gary Wilson on the negotiations with John Tishman. He had a long and varied history in the company, including a stint as CFO. While he had a classic business and finance

background and a genuine enthusiasm for operations, I liked the fact
that he was also an accomplished jazz pianist.

Our long run of success at the parks inevitably prompted management to become more ingrown and bureaucratic, more protective of
the status quo and more arrogant. It was at the parks, in particular, that
we felt we should do everything ourselves. We were the experts, and no
one could do it as well as we could. I was as guilty of this "Let's do it all
ourselves" attitude as anyone else. When we were offered the chance to
bring the Hard Rock Café onto our property, for example, we passed.
"We can do our own rock'n'roll themed restaurant," I told our group.
Instead, the Hard Rock made a deal at Universal Studios, just down the
street, and it became a smash hit. Making a mistake once is painful, but
there has to be room for failure, or no one will ever take chances. At the
same time, it's critical not to make the same mistake twice. When the
opportunity arose subsequently to sign a deal with Planet Hollywood at
Walt Disney World, we gave up our stubbornness, went forward, and it
became a huge success.

An even more dramatic example of the perils of trying to do
everything the same way was Pleasure Island, the nighttime entertainment complex that we opened in 1989, at the same time as the Disney-
MGM Studios. On paper, it seemed like a terrific way to provide
another amenity and to build a whole new business. From the time
Frank and I first began visiting Walt Disney World, it had gnawed at me
that there was virtually nothing to do at night. What happened, I always
wondered, to those visitors who weren't satisfied to watch TV after dinner and go to sleep early? After several false starts, our team came up
with the idea for a complex of restaurants and clubs—everything from
comedy to dance to rock'n'roll to country and western—to be located
on a small island adjacent to the Disney Village shopping area. We took
the name "Pleasure Island" from *Pinocchio*.

The first problem was that we went over budget and spent too
much on the facility. Beyond that, our theme park operators had never
before tried to create entertainment for a more sophisticated young-
adult audience. Pleasure Island lacked any kind of excitement or edge.
After months of hectoring park executives about the problem, I decided
to send Art Levitt down to Orlando. Art lacked any operating experi-

ence, but he had credentials that Frank and I considered more important. He was single, thirty years old, and actually enjoyed going out at night. We decided to take a chance on him, not least because neither of us knew anyone else young and single who might run this business. "If I'm not hearing from our parks guys that they want to fire you," I told Art, "then you're not screaming loud enough."

Art had terrific promotional instincts and a willingness to take risks. He quickly added street games and outdoor entertainment to Pleasure Island, and instituted a New Year's Eve celebration every night. He arranged to have the comedian Howie Mandel arrive one evening on a horse and ride through the complex. He brought well-known rock musicians in to play at the clubs and spin records as guest deejays. To create a sense of glamour and excitement, he hired drivers to park their white stretch limousines out front—ostensibly waiting for guests they'd dropped off. He even hired local models to come and hang out at Pleasure Island, until it became a hip enough destination that it was no longer necessary to pack the house. When Art pushed too far for Disney —hiring dancers just a bit too scantily clad, for example—we reined him back in. I've always found it easier to pull back an overly enthusiastic executive than to inspire a passive one to take action. Most of Art's ideas were on the mark. As the crowds at the clubs grew, we moved forward on an idea that had first been raised several years earlier: enclosing the attractions and charging a single nightly admission, the way we already did at our other parks. By the time Art moved on in 1993, Pleasure Island was making a solid profit.

In spite of this turnaround, attendance at both Walt Disney World and Disneyland remained flat through 1992 and 1993. It was certainly easy—even reasonable—to attribute much of the blame to factors such as the Persian Gulf War, the economy, and the chilling effect of the murder of several foreign tourists in South Florida, which attracted worldwide media attention. Although none of the killings took place within 250 miles of Orlando, the reverberations reached us and foreign bookings at Walt Disney World declined precipitously. *Saturday Night Live* even did a parody in which the late Phil Hartman played me doing an advertisement for the parks, in which I stood before a map of Florida and tried to convince viewers of the vast distance between Miami and Orlando—"as far as from Paris to Madrid." I appreciated the help. At

Disneyland, attendance was undercut by the riots that followed the Rodney King verdict in Los Angeles in 1992, and then by the Northridge earthquake in early 1994. But ultimately we weren't sure which factors had stalled attendance growth. One possibility was that our theme park business had simply reached maturity and costly new attractions could only produce small gains in attendance—a no-win strategy.

The two people who advanced this position most vocally were Richard Nanula and Larry Murphy, who together took over Gary Wilson's role after he left the company in 1989. Gary had been a possible candidate to replace Frank Wells in the event that Frank followed through on his plan to make another attempt to climb Everest. But when Frank decided to stay at Disney, Gary began looking for other opportunities. In the summer of 1989, together with Al Checchi, he engineered a leveraged buyout of Northwest Airlines. Over the next five years, they turned the airline around and became very wealthy in the process. More recently, Al turned his attention to California politics—running unsuccessfully for the Democratic nomination for governor in 1998.

Larry Murphy's responsibility was for strategic planning. With his dark hair, dark Armani suits, and dark temperament, Larry was viewed by some in the company as a naysayer who stood in the way of their entrepreneurial initiatives. Frank and I saw it differently. We believed that Larry acted out of what he believed was best for the company, and that he could be counted on to be totally honest in his assessments, even when they weren't what any of us wanted to hear. Larry's integrity and his sharp analytic skills made him an effective critic, if at times an unnecessarily harsh one. He did oppose many potential acquisitions and new businesses, but always for sound reasons. At the same time, he could be a highly persuasive ally when he got behind an idea or a new venture. Larry was a guiding force behind several major initiatives, including our decision to enter the cruise business.

It was Larry who hired Richard Nanula straight out of Harvard Business School in 1986, where we all met him when he led a presentation by his fellow students evaluating a new business we were considering at the time. Richard soon became a rising star at Disney. In 1991, when he was just thirty-one years old, Frank and I decided to name him CFO—making Richard not just the youngest CFO in a Fortune

500 company but one of the highest-ranking African American corporate executives. His natural charm and quick sense of humor disarmed people, but he was every bit as financially tough-minded and unrelenting as Larry. Together, Richard and Larry assumed the financial oversight role for Frank and me that Roy once played for Walt. They provided another check and balance in our system. Without that, Disney couldn't have continued to grow at a rate of 20 percent.

The immediate focus of their attention at the parks was on our latest E-ticket attraction—*The Twilight Zone Tower of Terror*—which was scheduled to open at Disney-MGM in July 1994. The final cost of the ride would exceed $100 million. Richard and Larry argued that it would be far more prudent to make this level of investment in something that promised a more direct and predictable return. I shared their concern about the escalating cost, but the *Tower of Terror* seemed to me so special that it was worth the investment—in part because the Disney-MGM park very much needed an additional thrill ride to round out its offerings.

The "Tower" referred to a classic abandoned Hollywood hotel, where guests were directed through the lobby and told the scary tale of its demise. Then they boarded a creaky elevator, which climbed up to the thirteenth and top floor. After several small drops, it falls suddenly to the ground—at a speed exceeding gravity. At first, my impulse was to take the concept to its logical extreme by building an actual hotel around the ride and having the elevator literally drop into the middle of the lobby. As with the Mickey Mouse hotel and other outrageous ideas over the years, I let myself be overruled — on the grounds of cost and practicality. But the *Tower of Terror* was still a spectacular ride that seemed certain to have a huge impact on attendance at the Disney-MGM Studios.

During this same period, we faced a similar decision on a far bigger investment in Walt Disney World's future. For more than four years, we'd been developing plans for a fourth park, to be called the Animal Kingdom. It was an undeniably ambitious and expensive undertaking—at least $850 million—and Larry and Richard's concerns about the risks involved were shared by many of our executives.

"I just don't believe that adding another park is going to prompt our guests to extend their visits with us another day," Richard argued.

"At a time when we're already struggling, the much greater possibility is that it will cannibalize attendance from our other parks" Intellectually, I understood this view, but emotionally I disagreed. Typically, and predictably, companies will commit to a new venture during boom times only to find themselves opening for business two or three years later when the economy has moved into a down period. Investing aggressively in a new business during hard times is more daunting. The key is to do it in a core business and to believe deeply in what you're doing. If we moved forward with the Animal Kingdom, our best hope was that it would open in the middle of a full-scale boom. But, regardless, the most compelling reason to do it was that the project was unique and yet very much in the Disney spirit. For all the risks, it had the potential to be to old-fashioned zoos what Disneyland became to amusement parks—a quantum leap.

In more than a decade running the company, I'd seen scores of ideas for new parks, and the Animal Kingdom was one of the few that I considered outstanding. Even at this early stage of planning, the proposed park included unusual elements. At 500 acres, it was four times the size of the Magic Kingdom, with room enough for two full-fledged safari experiences. With attendance still flat at Walt Disney World in early 1994, we deferred giving the Animal Kingdom a final go-ahead, but I knew it was only a matter of time. For better or for worse, Frank and I remained optimists. Standing still was not an option. Either you take calculated risks to grow, or you slowly wither and die.

9

Broadening the Brand

I'D NEVER HEARD ANYONE TALK MUCH ABOUT "THE BRAND" BEFORE Frank and I arrived at Disney. To me, a brand was a marking that you put on horses and cattle. Brand management sounded very austere and serious—something that people did at Procter & Gamble, perhaps, but not in a creative business. Way back in my first job at CBS, I'd been intrigued by the slogan, "If it's Mattel, it must be swell." But it was the rhyme that appealed to me, not the concept. If there was anything swell about Mattel, it was products like Barbie, not Mattel itself. ABC and Paramount succeeded because we made movies and TV shows that people wanted to see. No one I knew felt any loyalty to the Paramount "brand."

But Disney was different. The name plainly stood for something. Walt's genius had been to make Disney synonymous with the best in family entertainment—whether it was a theme park or a television show, an animated movie or even a Mickey Mouse watch. Customers did seek out Disney products, just as they were drawn to Disney animated movies, or visited Disney's Magic Kingdom. The name "Disney" promised a certain kind of experience: wholesome family fun appropriate for kids of any age, a high level of excellence in its products, and a predictable set of values. By the time Frank and I took over, nearly two decades after Walt's death, Disney had begun to seem awkward, old-fashioned, even a bit directionless. But that was misleading. The underlying qualities that made the company special lived on, just the way a person's character endures. Our job wasn't to create something new, but to bring back the magic, to dress Disney up in more stylish clothes and expand its reach, to remind people why they loved the company in the first place.

Strengthening the Disney brand, Frank and I soon recognized, wasn't something that could be achieved in a single broad stroke. We came to think of Disney as a canvas on which many artists paint in pointillist style—one dot at a time. If each of these dots is executed with precision, imagination, and an awareness of the whole, the painting becomes richer, more vibrant and multidimensional. Walt Disney and his team created such a masterpiece. When a new group of artists comes along, the risk is that they'll bring a diminished commitment to excellence, or a lack of attention to the whole. Then the opposite process can occur. Point by point, stroke by stroke, the masterpiece deteriorates into something mediocre and commonplace, even ugly, until eventually it's destroyed altogether. A brand is a living entity, and it is enriched or undermined cumulatively over time, the product of a thousand small gestures.

In addition to emphasizing to Disney's artists and cast members our own firm commitment to excellence, Frank and I undertook a series of specific initiatives to encourage teamwork and enhance the Disney brand. The most practical had to do with compensation. We both believed that the best way to reward and encourage executives was through incentives rather than high salaries. Above all, we created a very generous stock option plan. This was a way of tying compensation for our executives not just to the performance of their own divisions but to the company's — to encourage their investment in Disney's performance. At companies composed of diverse, unrelated businesses, stock options may not serve much purpose. But at Disney, our goal was to increase the interdependence of our divisions. Too often, I believe, people take competitive pleasure in seeing one of their colleagues fail. By tying every top Disney executive's compensation partly to the company's performance, Frank and I were determined to reward cooperation and collegiality— not least because such an atmosphere made coming to work each day more enjoyable.

The next initiative we launched was a weekly lunch of our top corporate executives and division heads. Attendance was mandatory, even though we rarely had a specific agenda. Instead, we wanted to create a forum in which our executives talked about what was going on in their divisions, and then looked for ways to enhance one another's businesses. The lunches were also a way for people doing very different jobs to become more comfortable with one another and more familiar with each other's work. So long as cooperation was a priority for Frank and me, it was likely to be so for others. And once our executives began to interact in this informal setting—something that might never happen in the ordinary course of a day—they were more likely to seek each other out on their own.

In a similar spirit, we launched "Disney Dimensions." Like so many of our initiatives, this one grew out of something that Walt had pioneered. In 1955, Disney University was launched at Disneyland to teach Walt's philosophy of service and to communicate his values. Over time, it became a way to introduce new hourly and middle management employees in all divisions to the Disney corporate culture. Because Disney was so widely respected for its commitment to quality and service, other companies began sending their own middle managers to take the courses offered by Disney University. Frank and I were both struck that these companies never sent their top executives. If they had, they would have discovered that certain simple tenets are every bit as relevant to CEOs and vice presidents as they are to middle managers.

Walt Disney, for example, always bent down to pick up stray trash in the parks. Frank and I took our cue from Walt. The one catch was that when we flew down to Walt Disney World for our first visit, I had thrown my back out and couldn't bend over without pain. But when I came across trash during our tour of the parks, bend I did. I hate to oversimplify the Disney magic, but when it comes to service, that was how it worked. There's a value, we realized, in training even the top management of the company to stoop for excellence.

We designed Disney Dimensions as a kind of Hell Week immersion in the Disney culture—nine days during which groups of twenty or so top executives spend full time learning about every aspect of the company. One inspiration for the program was my fraternity initiation at Denison's Delta Upsilon (minus the hazing). The Disney Dimensions programs begin at 7:00 a.m. and end after 10:00 p.m. The executives in charge of each of our divisions provide detailed briefings on their businesses, covering everything from the frequency with which we clean the bathrooms at Walt Disney World (once every thirty minutes) to how we peel potatoes in our restaurant kitchens (with a high-pressure air hose that literally blows the skins off); from the way we choose our movies and television shows to the process by which we analyze potential acquisitions.

Participants also have several hands-on experiences. When they travel to the parks, for example, they put on character costumes and spend time interacting with the guests. Athough there are always objections to devoting nine precious days to the program, every one of our senior executives is required to attend Disney Dimensions. Most of them end up loving the experience—and appreciating its value. What they love first is hating us for making them participate. But after a few days, they embrace the Outward Bound–style camaraderie that grows out of enduring a punishing schedule together. They also appreciate the concentrated education they receive and the relationships they form. When they return to their jobs, and they need help from an executive in another division, they no longer have to call a stranger, but can turn instead to a foxhole companion from Disney Dimensions. The company, and the brand, derive the benefit.

A third way we sought to encourage cooperation was by giving Frank Wells the unofficial title "vice president of *mishegoss*." Very loosely translated, mishegoss is the Yiddish word for hassles and craziness. Frank wasn't Jewish but he was Talmudic, and he became the executive with the authority to settle interdivisional conflicts involving the allocation of costs and any other kind of intramural squabbling. If the success of a film led to large merchandising revenues, for example, the question might arise as to how to divide such profits between the movie division and consumer products. Or if a television network paid us a license fee for a special that we produced about an anniversary at Disneyland, an issue might arise about whether the movie division or the parks division ought to cover any shortfall in production costs. At the end of the fiscal year, it was up to Frank to make these decisions. It was soon obvious to everyone that he thrived on meticulously weighing the merits of any given issue. As a result, we largely avoided the sort of bitterness that might have made divisions less likely to cooperate the next time out.

The final initiative we undertook was to formalize the role of synergy and brand management in the company. In the case of synergy, this evolved serendipitously. A few months after arriving at Disney, I walked into a Knoll furniture showroom at the Pacific Design Center with Jane, looking for furniture for our offices. Art Levitt, then in his early twenties, took care of us. The only salesman wearing a suit, he was exceptionally knowledgeable about his products, and he also seemed to know a great deal about design. I happened to be looking for someone to help us upgrade design throughout Disney. As soon as we left, I said to Jane, "This guy must run Knoll out here and he probably went to Yale School of Design. He also seems to have great people skills. I'm going to try to hire him." When I returned home, I called Art and invited him to join Jane and me for dinner that night. He was a bit startled, but said yes. In the course of our meal, I discovered that Art had actually attended Long Island University and his major was marine biology. After college, he'd lived in Hawaii for two years, studying girls and tropical fish, and he had been working as a Knoll salesman for just four months. Even so, I liked his enthusiasm and his confidence, and decided to offer him a job as my personal assistant.

Art worked closely with me on design and architecture, but he also became the point person in following up on ideas that Frank or I heard about in one division of the company but had the potential to be cross-promoted or extended by another division. In effect, Art was in charge of synergy for two years, until we sent him off to reinvent Pleasure Island. At that point, Linda Warren took over as my assistant, and we formalized the job of overseeing synergy. Linda, too, moved on to Walt Disney World and today she is the resort's senior vice president for marketing. Running synergy has now become a full-time vice-presidential position under Jody Dreyer, who was first recruited through the Walt Disney World college program and went on to work in publicity at the parks. Jody now oversees at least ten major, company-wide synergy initiatives each year, ranging from the launch of an animated movie to an anniversary celebration for Mickey Mouse. Her job is to mobilize each division of the company to make contributions, so that the cumulative effort on a given project far exceeds the sum of the parts. Jody may be the most organized, focused person I've ever met, and she has excelled in every job she's held at the company. No one better embodies the Disney spirit.

Our extraordinary success with synergy prompted the need to pay more attention to protecting the brand. By the late 1980s, we had become so aggressive on so many fronts—movies and television shows and home video, new parks and attractions and licensed merchandise—that the Disney name seemed to be everywhere. If the company was in danger of being dismissed as irrelevant when we arrived, now we faced the opposite risk. Overexposure was threatening to dilute the integrity of the brand. You can never make too many good products, but it is possible to promote and market them too aggressively. For the first time, we began to think rigorously about what represented an appropriate use of the Disney name and characters, and what seemed excessive or gratuitous.

Laurie Lang started out at Disney working for Larry Murphy in strategic planning, and it was soon clear that she had an almost inborn feel for the company and its products. In much the way that Frank unofficially handled interdivisional squabbles, we asked Laurie to oversee the use of the Disney name and the protection of the brand in the marketplace. Reporting to Frank and me, Laurie became the arbiter of where and how to use the name. These judgments applied not just to products and promotions but to evaluating prospective new business ventures. Above all, her job was to ensure that nothing we did would undermine faith in Disney. Every choice we made had to deliver the blend of quality, fun, and imagination that our customers had come to expect from us.

Laurie provided a useful counterpoint to our ordinary decision making. The executives running our divisions were charged with finding new ways to grow and increase their profits, and they were naturally eager to take advantage of the Disney name wherever they could. By contrast, Laurie focused on a single issue: Will this initiative enhance the brand or undermine it in the long term? For Frank and me, the challenge was to find a balance between protecting Disney's core values, and finding fresh ways to broaden and extend our reach. It was never easy. Each time we sought to grow and change we ran up against forces of the status quo—the resistance that arises both inside and outside a company when you try anything different. We undertook many ventures during our first decade, but none had a more powerful impact on the growth of our brand than the Disney Stores, the Disney Channel, and Disney Theatrical Productions. Each one also prompted separate issues.

The Disney Stores grew out of meetings chaired by a young executive with no previous track record launching any kind of business. I agreed to interview Steve Burke back in late 1985 largely because I knew and admired his father, Dan Burke, who was then president of Cap Cities/ABC. It was Dan's partner, Tom Murphy, who called me about Steve. "I know you get these calls all the time," he began, "and I know that Dan would never call you himself, but he has this great son who has a Harvard M.B.A., all kinds of energy, and is struggling with what to do with his life. I know Dan would appreciate your talking with him." Obviously, I wasn't going to turn down the chairman and the president of a television network with which Disney had an important relationship. But I also liked and respected Dan, and I've never accepted the conventional wisdom that the sons and daughters of successful fathers are somehow doomed to apathy or failure. High performers are rare regardless of background, and from the moment I met Steve, I sensed he could be one of them. He still looked like a college freshman, but he was self-confident, ambitious, and enthusiastic.

We sent Steve to several interviews around the company, including one with Barton "Bo" Boyd, our head of consumer products. It was Walt himself who recognized that additional income could be generated by permitting the animated movie characters to be used on consumer products. When Mickey Mouse became a national phenomenon in 1929, Walt made his first merchandising deal, accepting a flat $300 licensing fee to put Mickey on writing pads. In 1932, Walt and Roy hired Herman "Kay" Kamen, a Kansas City advertising man, as a full-time representative to handle their merchandising. The Disneys agreed to share all royalties fifty-fifty and very quickly Kamen made a series of lucrative royalty deals. The first one was with an ice cream company. Ten million cones bearing Mickey's face on the wrapper were sold during the first month. The old-line Ingersoll Waterbury watchmaking company was on the verge of bankruptcy when it signed a deal with Disney to market Mickey Mouse watches—and ended up selling more than 2.5 million. The Lionel Company, also reeling from the Depression, had already filed for bankruptcy when Kamen made a licensing deal for Mickey Mouse wind-up trains that could circle a track. Lionel ended up selling 250,000 of them, propelling the company back into business.

Over the years, Disney licensed its name and characters to a series of companies that were saved or transformed by the deals. Mickey himself endured not just as a symbol—an endearing, plucky everymouse —but as the most popular character at our parks. Disney was paid a royalty by the manufacturer for using Mickey's name, or Donald's, or Goofy's, or Disney's itself, sometimes with a guarantee against future sales. The risks were modest, but so was the upside. In 1984, when Frank and I arrived, operating profits for consumer products were approximately $100 million—a tiny fraction of what the theme parks were earning. Licensing was essentially a passive business. Disney played almost no role in the production, distribution, or marketing of these products. Frank urged Bo to take a much more aggressive approach with our licensees. The result was both an improvement in the quality of Disney merchandise and a leap in the royalties we received from them. By 1994, a decade after our arrival, operating profits in our consumer products division had more than quadrupled, to $425 million.

One reason was the extraordinary quality of the team Bo put together. Executives can be judged on many qualities, but high on my list is how well they hire. Insecure managers invariably choose weak, nonthreatening subordinates. Confident managers hire the best people they can find, aware that improving overall performance will ultimately redound to their credit. Bo was low-key and easygoing, but he had an unerring eye for talent such as Michael Lynton, a young executive who did a superb job of building our publishing business and was eventually named CEO of the publishing house Penguin Putnam. Bo responded to Steve immediately. Lacking a specific job to offer, he made Steve a director of business development—an amorphous title with no specific responsibilities. Steve and Bo immediately decided to launch a companywide contest, offering a free dinner for the best new business idea. To his surprise, five hundred suggestions flooded in, and Steve whittled them down to a dozen. Then, with Bo's encouragement, he called Frank Wells. "Would you and Michael consider coming over to consumer products for a morning to hear a bunch of ideas for new businesses?" he asked.

We ended up spending more than five hours listening to presentations. "Let's just do them all," I said at one point, only half-joking. At the end of the meeting, we agreed to pursue the most promising—book publishing, video games, and retail stores devoted exclusively to Disney products. Steve promised to do more detailed research and come back to us. Three weeks later, he called and arranged a second meeting that included Bo, Frank, and me, as well as Gary Wilson and Larry Murphy. Steve began by presenting a conservative business plan that envisioned rolling out the stores slowly. I continued to find the idea appealing, in part because Disney stores had the potential not just to sell products but to promote our movies, TV shows, and parks. Typically, Frank assumed the role of trying to draw all the arguments out on the table.

Both Larry and Gary pointed out the downside. "This is a small business with relatively low margins," Larry said. "These sorts of stores usually only work in tourist areas. The risk is that if we ultimately build just twenty to thirty of them, it won't have been worth the investment of our time and the diversion of our attention." This was exactly the role that we asked Larry to play—to quantify the downside and keep us out of trouble. On this occasion we put off a final decision.

Within two weeks, Steve was back on the phone saying he had a new business plan and asking if he and Bo could come and see Frank and me again. This time, their pro forma showed a little more upside. Their main argument was that we ought to try one store, see how it performed, and then make a decision about expanding. We spent nearly an hour batting more ideas back and forth, and agreed that if we did a prototype, it ought to be near the studio, so that we could keep an eye on it. Also, by opening a store near Disneyland, we would find out whether there was a market for our products even among customers who could easily visit the park to buy them. "How much do you estimate this one store would cost?" I finally asked Steve.

"We figure we can do it for under $500,000," he said.

I turned to Frank. "I understand all the sophisticated financial analysis that says this isn't going to work," I said. "But can't a company our size try something every once in a while just because it feels right? What if it does fail? It's still not going to cost as much as one expensive hot movie script." Forever the enthusiast, Frank agreed.

RIGHT: With my sister Margot at our family's New York City apartment, 1949.

LEFT: Playing football on the Allen-Stevenson team with my best friend John Angelo in 1954. While I was a good student, school itself was secondary to my central interest: sports. *(Photo taken by John Angelo's mother, Judy Cowen)*

To a remarkable degree, my core values were shaped during summers at Keewaydin. Here I am playing one of my favorite camp sports, tennis, in 1955.

Hiking at Keewaydin, 1956.
(The Keewaydin Collection)

My graduation photo from the Lawrenceville School. Lawrenceville, with its academically rigorous curriculum, remains the most competitive and challenging environment I've ever encountered.

With Jane in 1977. Although she and I come from incredibly different backgrounds, we were compatible and comfortable with each other from our very first date.

LEFT: My parents, Lester and Maggie Eisner, at their Vermont apple orchard around 1984.

BELOW: With my dad in Vermont, around 1961.

RIGHT: With my firstborn, Breck, in 1973.

BELOW: With Jane and our second son, Eric, in 1975.

ABOVE: At Parents Hockey
Weekend, Denver University, 1998,
with Jane and Anders.

RIGHT: Horseback riding at my
parents' farm in Vermont. Riding
was one of my father's favorite
activities, and as a child I would
ride with him on the weekends in
Central Park and at the house in
Bedford Hills.

ABOVE: The Paramount team together during the production of *Escape from Alcatraz* in 1979: Jeffrey Katzenberg, Don Simpson, Charles Bluhdorn, Yvette Bluhdorn, Barry Diller, and me. *(Berliner Studio)*

BELOW: With Sylvester Stallone and John Travolta during the production of *Stayin' Alive* at Paramount in 1983. *(© 1983 Annie Leibovitz/Contact Press Images)*

All together at
Walt Disney World.
Back row *(l to r)*:
Michael Ovitz, Judy
Ovitz, Marilyn
Katzenberg, Frank
Wells, Luanne Wells,
Jane, and me.
Kneeling *(l to r)*: Eric
Eisner, Chris Ovitz,
Jeffrey Katzenberg,
Breck, and Anders.
October 1984. *(Walt
Disney World
Photography)*

My favorite
photo of me and
Frank Wells, stopping
for a break at Walt
Disney World in
1986. *(Walt Disney
World Photography)*

ABOVE: The Team Disney Building in Burbank, which was completed in 1990. The wonderful architect was Michael Graves. *(Gary Krueger/The Walt Disney Company)*

LEFT: With George Lucas at the opening of the Indiana Jones Epic Stunt Spectacular at Walt Disney World in 1989. *(Walt Disney World Photography)*

ABOVE: Our esteemed guest: Ronald Reagan visits Disneyland in 1990 as Grand Marshal for Disneyland's 35th Anniversary. *(The Disneyland Photography Department)*

BELOW: At Walt Disney World with Sid Bass. Bass played a decisive role in bringing Frank Wells and me to The Walt Disney Company, and over the past decade he has become both an invaluable advisor and a good friend. *(Walt Disney World Photography)*

LEFT: A scene from the short film "Michael and Mickey." The film was made at the studios in Burbank to introduce coming attractions at the end of the Backstage Tour at the Disney-MGM Studios. *(The Walt Disney Company)*

BELOW: With Jane and Jeffrey Katzenberg at a premiere party for the movie *The Mighty Ducks* in 1992. *(Eric Charbonneau/The Walt Disney Company)*

LEFT: At a Mighty Ducks game at the Pond in Anaheim, 1993. The team turned out to be a good thing for both Anaheim and Disneyland. *(The Lovero Group)*

With Michael Ovitz and Frank Wells on the Disney Studio lot in Burbank. *(Berliner Studio)*

Tom Murphy and I shake hands at the announcement of Capital Cities/ABC on 7/31/95. With the purchase of ABC, Disney grew to nearly twice its previous size. It was one of the largest acquisitions in U.S. corporate history. *(Ida Mae Astute/ABC)*

ABOVE: Warren and Susan Buffett at the ABC Management Meetings, February 1996. Buffett is the biggest shareholder in Capital Cities/ABC, as well as a good friend. *(Steve Fenn/ABC)*

RIGHT: Watching the dailies of *The Wonderful World of Disney* with Michael Kaye. Kaye was the director hired to work on my brief host's spots before each *Wonderful World* movie. *(Bob Neese/The Walt Disney Company)*

Shooting a *Wonderful World of Disney* host spot. *(Bob Neese/The Walt Disney Company)*

Roy Disney, me, Hillary Clinton, Alberto Cruz, and Governor Lawton Chiles at a Walt Disney World Boy's and Girl's Club Event, 1997. *(Walt Disney World Photography)*

LEFT: With Jane at the White House state dinner for President Jiang Zemin of the People's Republic of China, 1997. *(Greg E. Mathieson/MAI)*

BELOW: At Castaway Cay *(l to r)*: Robert Stern, Jane, me, Mercedes Bass, Luanne Wells, and Sid Bass. The *Disney Magic* is in the background. *(Alain Boniec/The Walt Disney Company)*

The entire family—Anders, me, Jane, Breck, and Eric—at the June 1998 Hollywood Bowl premiere of *Mulan*. *(Berliner Studio)*

At the March 1999 ShoWest *Tarzan* premiere: me, Phil Collins, Joe Roth, Peter Schneider, and Dick Cook. *(Berliner Studio)*

Steve and Bo signed a lease for a 2,000-square-foot space in the Glendale Galleria, a shopping mall ten minutes from the studio. After sending Steve back to the drawing board twice, the store we finally settled on was designed to look like a working movie set, with most of the merchandise displayed on rolling hangers. In the front windows were scenes from our classic animated movies. Throughout the store, television monitors played scenes from upcoming films. In the back was a large projection screen, and a mountain of plush Mickeys and Minnies and Goofys. Although the concept would evolve over time, the first store was lively, colorful, and fun. Steve and Bo managed to build it below the initial estimate—for just over $450,000.

From the first day we opened in March 1987, it was obvious that customers had a huge appetite for Disney products. In its first year, revenues in the Glendale store were $2.4 million—nearly $1,200 a square foot, or more than three times the revenue of the average specialty retail store in the same mall. In July, we opened a second store on Pier 39, in San Francisco, and that November, we opened one in Orange County, even nearer Disneyland than the Glendale store. Neither one had a negative impact on business at Disneyland's shops. We did make one costly mistake with our Pier 39 store. Inexperienced at real estate deals, we agreed to an exclusivity clause for the area around the pier. We simply assumed that one store would be enough. In fact, demand was far greater and our deal held us back from expanding. We never offered exclusivity again.

The rapid success of our first three stores raised another challenge. "Let's go out and recruit a really top retailer to run the stores," Gary Wilson suggested. "We don't have that sort of expertise in the company, and this is a chance to import it."

I called Leslie Wexner, founder and head of The Limited, to solicit his opinion. "When you've got a good concept, you can run it on enthusiasm and energy for the first couple of years," Wexner told me. "But once you hit fifty stores or so it becomes a science. Unless you've got those skills, it will fail. Why don't you let us run them?" I respected Wexner's experience, but I felt much the way I had when Bill Marriott tried to convince me to let his company build and run our hotels at Walt Disney World. We might not have all the expertise, but we knew our company and its culture better than anyone else did.

We gave Steve Burke the job of interviewing candidates to run the Disney Stores. Most of the people he saw had come up through the ranks at other retailers such as Bloomingdale's and Nordstrom. An interesting pattern emerged. Before each meeting, Steve asked the candidate to visit one of the Disney Stores. "Okay, so you've seen what we are doing," he began his interviews. "What would you do differently?" In almost every case, the answers he elicited were variations on the same theme.

"You're devoting your most valuable real estate—the store windows—to your animated movies instead of to your hottest products," Steve was told. Or: "Your employees are wearing costumes and you have all this theming in the stores, which is fine for now, but when you roll out the stores, all that will be too expensive to keep up." Or: "The Disney music you're playing is nice, but if you turn it off, people will buy more." In each case, these executives were reciting the rules of retailing that they'd learned over the years. The problem was that if we did everything they suggested, we'd risk completely undermining the concept we had created. What these candidates failed to appreciate was the unique appeal of the Disney culture. People came to our stores looking to experience a certain sort of magic as much as they did to buy any specific item. After several weeks, we realized that the solution was staring us in the face. Although Steve lacked retailing and creative experience, he could develop the first by hiring experienced managers to work for him and the second by working closely with Frank and me.

We decided to put Steve in the job, but we also focused enormous attention on the stores ourselves. For the first year or so, I looked at designs for dozens of new products, and started paying more attention to our retailing competitors. Each store became a stage. I took to visiting the new ones unannounced, usually over the weekend. Toys and jewelry and clothing had never much interested me, but I tried to put myself in the role of our customers. Without identifying myself, I went into our stores and searched for the cheapest and most unattractive-looking items. Then I brought them along to our Monday staff lunches. The message I wanted to send to Steve and the rest of our team was that I cared about the quality of our products. If the boss cares, I had long since learned, then everyone else cares.

Frank and I also showered Steve with notes based on our experiences. I happened to visit a store the week after we re-released *Cinderella* into theaters. "I was surprised to learn that there was no *Cinderella* promotion, no indication that the film is now playing, nor any specific *Cinderella* merchandise," I wrote him the following Monday morning. "I hope that our stores will cross-promote Disney films, especially animated releases, but also Disney television shows, and big park openings and events." In another instance, I complained about dirty carpets in a store and half-joked, "This is the army." In still another, I suggested that we consider experimenting with the lighting in the back part of a store where the big-screen TV played. "When the light is too high, you can't see the screen," I wrote. "When it's too low, it's difficult to see the merchandise. We've got to find a balance." I'm sure Steve would have preferred it if I'd played golf on the weekends instead of haunting his stores, but I couldn't resist. He also learned, by trial and error, that Frank and I couldn't be "finessed"—meaning sidestepped—when he didn't feel like doing something we suggested. Teaching young executives that it's better in the end to be fully forthcoming is crucial to building mutual trust, and to insuring a team effort.

Frank pushed Steve even harder than I did. At one point, he insisted that Steve create a daily checklist to cover every imaginable aspect of running the store. Even when Steve complained a year later that the form prompted time-consuming paperwork, Frank insisted on its value. Much the same happened in a confrontation over service standards. At first, Steve resisted introducing to the stores some version of the "Disney Traditions" training program given to all new cast members at the parks. Under pressure from Frank, Steve finally took the training himself in Florida and was completely won over. Within a short time, he instituted his own rigorous weeklong in-store training for all new cast members.

We also discovered that guests expected our cast members to know everything about Disney—not just the products in the stores but our movies, television shows, parks, and even the company's history. As a result, Steve went out of his way to hire cast members who weren't just competent and friendly, but also had a special feeling for Disney and a willingness to learn about all facets of the company. At the front of every store, we installed a "greeter"—an idea adapted from Wal-Mart—both to make customers feel welcome and to answer their questions. This attention to service helped to account for one of the more remarkable statistics that regularly showed up in our studies of guests. On average, more than 60 percent of them visited a Disney Store at least thirteen times a year. They did so, they said, partly because they found the experience enjoyable and entertaining. But they didn't simply browse. In virtually every location, our per square foot sales were among the highest for any specialty retailers.

By the end of 1989, we were up to forty-one stores. A year later, we had reached seventy, including our first overseas store, in London. In 1990, an estimated 14 million guests visited at least one of the stores. As the number of stores increased, one of our fears was that they would undercut business for Disney-licensed products in other retail outlets located in the same malls as a Disney Store. "We were catatonic when the stores got launched," Anne Osberg later told me, referring to the film licensing group that she ran for consumer products. Instead, precisely the opposite occurred. "The Disney Stores proved to be such an entertainment showcase for our properties," Anne explained, "that when a Disney Store opened, a store in the same mall would actually see its sales of Disney products go up." Anne would later become president of the division —a tribute to her skills as a manager and a creative marketer. It was Anne, for example, who spearheaded the remarkable growth in sales for Winnie the Pooh products from $390 million to nearly $3.3 billion a year during the last three years.

The segmenting of markets for our products proved to be very effective. Often, a person shopping for presents might buy one or two items in a Disney Store and then a half-dozen others from the wider selection in Sears or Toys "R" Us in the same mall. The stores were also a natural venue in which to promote products from other divisions of the company. Placing a display in the front window of the stores for a new attraction at the parks, or an upcoming movie, or the re-release of an animated classic had a huge marketing value. The success of our new animated films, in turn, had an enormous impact on sales at the stores. Merchandise based on *The Little Mermaid,* for example, accounted for at least 30 percent of total Disney Store sales in the weeks after its release on home video. Much the same was true for the two animated features that followed, *Beauty and the Beast* and *Aladdin.* But even between films, we built a strong, steady business based around our enduring characters, ranging from Mickey and Minnie to Winnie the Pooh to Donald Duck.

By the end of 1991, Steve had overseen the openings of nearly 125 stores, which were generating annual revenues of $300 million. We anticipated doubling our total number of stores within the next two years and reaching five hundred during the next five. For all Steve's success, Frank and I also believed in the value of moving young executives around to broaden their experience. By 1992, we were in the midst of launching Euro Disney, and both Frank and I believed that Steve could strengthen our management team there. We chose as his successor at the stores a fellow consumer products executive, Paul Pressler, who also happened to be Steve's best friend.

A natural, charismatic leader with strong creative instincts, Paul had successfully spearheaded the transformation of our licensing in consumer products. Most important, he'd taken back from our licensees much of the responsibility for designing and marketing products using the Disney name. His experience and good taste seemed ideally suited to what I now believed was the second-generation challenge at our stores: bringing the quality of the merchandise to a new level. Steve's energy had been devoted to launching new stores, operating them efficiently, and creating a strong culture of service. Now it was time to turn more attention to upgrading the products themselves. Partly, we were influenced by the opening of the first of the Warner Bros. Stores, in 1991— itself a direct response to the success of the Disney Stores. We enjoyed an enormous advantage because we could draw on such a beloved group of characters for our product line—not just Mickey and his friends but newer characters, such as Ariel from *The Little Mermaid,* Belle from *Beauty and the Beast,* and Robin Williams's genie from *Aladdin.* Warner Bros. were limited to far fewer well-known characters, from their cartoons. What they did, however, was to focus more attention on higher-cost merchandise, much of it aimed at adult customers.

For Paul, reinventing our product line meant aggressively seeking out and overseeing higher-quality manufacturers and setting high standards. As he had earlier in licensing, Paul focused on a more imaginative and exciting group of products. He achieved this in part by hiring a team of artists to create product lines built not only around individual characters but related story lines. Rather than simply creating a Minnie Mouse doll, for example, an entire line of costumes was created for Minnie's preparation for a ballet performance. The quality of our products soared. Paul's other major challenge was to begin thinking about the next generation of Disney Stores. In many locations, we'd outgrown our space. It made sense to think about a new design.

In November 1993, Paul and his team came to see Frank and me in my conference room, carrying the first prototype that they'd developed. We sent them back several times, as we had Steve four years earlier. What we ended up with was a design that split our new stores into three discrete zones—one for kids, who had been the overwhelming focus in our original stores; another for adults; and a third for more expensive collectible items, such as animation cels and high-end jewelry. Each of the three new areas had its own distinctive look. By using common theming, all of them could still be pulled together for a single promotion around an upcoming animated movie or a new attraction at the parks. Above all, the new store design had the potential to attract a more diverse audience. Sure enough, when the first of the new stores opened in the Del Amo shopping center in Torrance, California, a year later, it immediately generated a 20 percent increase in sales per square foot over our smaller, first-generation stores.

What we set out to achieve with the Disney Stores in the retail marketplace, we aimed to accomplish with the Disney Channel on television—a successful business in its own right, but also one that would enhance the public perception of the Disney brand. Card Walker and Ron Miller had the foresight to launch the Disney Channel as a pay cable network in 1983. When Frank and I joined the company a year later, average monthly subscriptions had reached 1 million. However, losses from the start-up costs exceeded $100 million, and the programming consisted mostly of old cartoons, second-tier Disney movies, and occasional classic animated features such as *Cinderella*. Very little money was spent on original programming. Subscribers were drawn at first to the Disney name, but often grew bored with the programming after a few months. All pay services lose subscribers, a phenomenon known as "churn." But where the industrywide rate was about 5 percent a month, the Disney Channel was losing nearly 8 percent.

The executive who turned the channel around was John Cooke, whom we hired away from the Times Mirror Company in 1985. In the brash, informal Disney culture, John was something of an anomaly. Fastidious and reed-thin, he wore his dark hair carefully slicked back and dressed most days in the same conservative, impeccably tailored style —dark suit, white shirt, and striped tie. In his disciplined, meticulous way, he was highly effective.

"Your job," I told John early on, "is to gradually widen people's perception of what Disney is without ever going too far or losing sight of who we are." He succeeded on several levels. First, he repositioned the Disney Channel as America's family network and built a schedule of programs aimed at different family members. In the early morning, when the audience was mostly young children, the focus remained Disney animated cartoons. In the afternoons, John's team produced a new version of the Mickey Mouse Club, but this one included rap singers, break dancing, and a hipper group of teenage girls and boys playing the Mouseketeers. In the early evenings the emphasis was movies. In the late evenings, the offerings ranged from concerts by pop performers such as Elton John and Billy Joel to a TV version of *Prairie Home Companion*, adapted from Garrison Keillor's popular National Public Radio show. I had been listening to *Prairie Home Companion* and reading Keillor's book when I heard he was doing a show live at Pomona College. On an impulse, I dragged Jane with me and went to see it. Partly, I was curious to see where Frank and Roy Disney had gone to college, but Keillor's show also turned out to be hilarious. It was the Middle America I knew from Denison. He had his finger right on the pulse.

John also commissioned a series of high-quality original movies aimed at families. A history buff, he was especially drawn to historical dramas—among them, *Goodbye Miss Fourth of July*, about a Greek family that immigrates to West Virginia during World War I and confronts a small town's racism; and *Friendship in Vienna*, built around the relationship between a Jewish and a Catholic family in Austria at the time that Hitler came to power. Programs like these won more than eighty Emmy and Cable ACE Awards over the years, and often attracted a family audience equally split between parents and their children.

The Disney Channel also became the primary television medium through which we promoted the growing number of initiatives in the rest of our company. Upcoming movies were previewed in three- and five-minute segments between our regular programs. The channel ran specials targeted to anniversaries at our parks and to openings of new ventures such as the Disney-MGM Studios. We did "making of" documentaries about our new animated movies and major new park attractions. When NBC decided not to renew *The Magical World of Disney,* in 1990, we moved it to the Disney Channel on Sunday nights. Finally, John made the Disney Channel the home for two ventures that made me especially proud: the Disney Young Musician's Symphony Orchestra and the American Teacher Awards. Both became not just high-quality entertainment but a way to ally Disney with the interests of our core family audience.

The earliest inspiration for the Disney Symphony was Stanley Gauger, the passionate music teacher and orchestra leader at Allen-Stevenson for whom I played percussion as a young boy. The more immediate motivation, in 1990, was a growing awareness that cuts in school budgets were taking a huge toll on music programs and orchestras. It was John who enlisted the Young Musician's Foundation to manage a week-long camp for talented young musicians under the age of twelve, which Disney agreed to underwrite. The notion was to bring musicians together each summer, offer top-level instruction and camaraderie, and then have them perform as an orchestra at week's end—taping the program to show later on the Disney Channel. In the course of an hour, we intermingled profiles of young musicians at the camp with the orchestra's performance. It was a way to support and spotlight promising musicians at a very young age, and also make classical music more exciting and accessible to the hundreds of thousands of children who watched the Disney Channel.

The American Teacher Awards were inspired by my early experiences with great teachers and by the term that I spent in the mid-1980s as president of the parents' association at the Center for Early Education in Los Angeles, which all three of my sons attended. During my own term at the center, I understood for the first time how underappreciated and underpaid teachers really are. One night in the spring of 1988, Jane and I went out to dinner with Joel Fleishman, then a professor of law at Duke University. Our conversation turned to teachers.

"There are all these 'Humanitarian of the Year' awards for business executives and politicians who do nothing to earn them except convince their friends to buy tables at philanthropic events where they're being honored," I said. "And then there are the endless award shows for actors and directors and rock stars." Suddenly, I was on a righteous roll. "Why is it that teachers never get publicly honored for their accomplishments? Don't they deserve at least equal recognition?"

"If you feel so strongly," Joel said, "why don't you do something about it?"

We decided to launch our own awards show on the Disney Channel. Once again, John Cooke took charge. Our idea was to model the show after the Academy Awards, bringing together the finalists in a variety of "best teacher" categories to a glamorous venue like the Dorothy Chandler Pavilion in Los Angeles. As with the Academy Awards, we sought out celebrity presenters to hand out awards in front of a live audience. Rather than clips from the best film nominees, we produced short films of each of the finalists at work in their schools and interspersed them throughout the show. We also decided to award cash prizes to the winners and their schools, so that the recognition would be something more than symbolic. John recognized the importance of rallying educational organizations like the National Education Association, the American Federation of Teachers, and the National PTA behind our idea. They became part of an advisory committee, helping to give the event credibility and to increase our access to teachers. Students and school administrators were offered the opportunity to make nominations, and the winners were ultimately chosen by a panel of education experts.

The first show was taped on October 7, 1990, at the Pantages Theatre in Hollywood. I had the privilege of presenting the best overall teacher award, voted on by the gathered nominees. Each teacher who won in a given category became a candidate for best overall teacher. Aware that they were still competing when they accepted these awards, many gave *Stand and Deliver* and *Prime of Miss Jean Brodie*–type acceptance speeches. Often, they were emotional and theatrical and inspiring.

The idea, as with the Academy Awards, was to ensure an exciting conclusion to the show. The first year's winner was Sylvia Anne Washburn, who grew up the daughter of migrant farm workers and triumphed over a legacy of poverty and illiteracy to become a beloved elementary school teacher in Toledo, Ohio. In subsequent years, we honored equally extraordinary winners ranging from Patricia Ann Baltz, an elementary school teacher from Arcadia, California, who had suffered several strokes and still managed to teach while permanently confined to a wheelchair, to Huong Tran Nguyen, a Vietnamese immigrant who fled her homeland during the war and now taught English as a second language at Polytechnic High School in Long Beach, California.

The Disney Channel remained a bit old-fashioned by comparison with the other main children's network, Nickelodeon. That was fine with me. Sophisticated preadolescents and teenagers often chose Nickelodeon, but we wanted young kids and their parents to be comfortable with us. With that audience, the Disney Channel grew into a substantial business. By 1990, we had 6 million subscribers and revenues of nearly $200 million a year, making us one of the most successful pay cable services. It was at this point that John came up with something he termed the "hybrid strategy"—a way of increasing our reach. Rather than continuing to operate as a pay channel with a monthly fee, we decided to offer cable operators the option of carrying the Disney Channel in their basic menu of offerings to subscribers—without an extra monthly fee. Making this transition was no small feat. For the right to carry services such as Nickelodeon and CNN as part of their basic package, cable operators paid these networks an average of 10 to 12 cents a month per subscriber. Now we were asking them to pay $.75 cents to $1 a month per subscriber to carry the Disney Channel. The extra $.60 to $.75 a month was critical to us. Unlike our competition, we were advertiser-free and those fees would be our only source of revenue.

On the face of it, our request was preposterous. Why should cable companies forgo the revenues of $5 to $8 a month they received for carrying the Disney Channel as a separate subscription service in order to pay us to carry it in their basic programming package? The first argument was that having the Disney Channel would give cable operators a strong addition to their basic package of services, which families would welcome. Further, the government had tied the approval of any price increases for basic cable service to the addition of certain kinds of programming. As an advertiser-free children's service, the Disney Channel qualified. Finally, we argued that having the Disney Channel exclusively in a given market was a way to compete more effectively with competitors such as direct broadcast satellite services. John's strategy proved highly effective. By 1994, the number of households that we were reaching had increased from 7.5 to 15 million.

Much as it eventually became necessary to build a second generation of Disney Stores, an update of the Disney Channel's programming increasingly made sense. As a subscription service, the key to success had been appealing to different segments of a given household by providing enough memorable and special programs each month that families would feel compelled to keep the service. Now, like Nickelodeon and other basic services, we faced the imperative of attracting a mass audience for the first time. To do so, we needed to sharpen our identity, in part by developing the sort of regular series programming that has the potential to hook viewers each week. John had built an exceptionally profitable and important franchise. By 1994, after nearly a decade running the Disney Channel, he was growing restless and felt ready for a different challenge. My job was to find a new and substantial role for him, and to find an executive as strong as Paul Pressler at the stores to help us take the next leap at the channel.

The third important expansion of the Disney brand was the one that I felt most cautious about undertaking. Among all the arts, theater had been my earliest passion, but I was also aware of its limits as a business. If you produce a movie, it can open in as many as three or four thousand theaters across the country. Even if it performs poorly, it has other lives on video, cable, network television, and overseas. By contrast, if you produce a full-scale Broadway musical—at a cost not all that much less than a midrange movie—it can close in a single night, forever. Even a long-running hit reaches only a fraction as many people as a successful movie—and typically earns only a fraction of the profit.

During my tenure at Paramount, we became involved in producing two Broadway shows, the musical *My One and Only* and Bernard Slade's drama *Tribute*. *Tribute* lost money even though it was based on a fantastic script. *My One and Only* was moderately profitable, but the investment of time and effort proved far out of proportion to the financial gain. Much as I was drawn to the romance and glamour of the theater, I believed that our early efforts at Disney could more practically and profitably be put elsewhere.

"We don't need to soothe our vanity by becoming Broadway producers," I told Jeffrey when he began pushing to enter the theater business not long after we arrived. "Let's concentrate first on building Disney back into a significant entertainment company." I didn't rule out theater forever, but I was determined to wait for the right moment—and the right project.

Beauty and the Beast was released as an animated film in November 1991 to huge business and excellent reviews. Six months later it won Academy Awards for Best Score and Best Song. Suddenly there was talk, both inside and outside the company, that *Beauty* was an ideal Disney-brand theatrical property. A classic love story, with a built-in audience created by the film's success, it also had Howard Ashman and Alan Menken's highly theatrical songs. Early in 1992, Frank Rich, then the theater critic for the *New York Times*, referred to *Beauty and the Beast* as "the best new musical score of the season." It was clear that Rich meant this partly as a backhanded slap at Broadway's current musicals, but he was also acknowledging the power of *Beauty*'s score. His comment encouraged us to think more seriously about adapting the movie to the stage.

I made two stipulations to Jeffrey. "We must do the show without partners, so that we can retain creative control," I told him, "and we have to use as much of our own talent as possible." We could afford to finance the show ourselves and partners were only likely to prompt disagreements creatively. As for talent, Disney produces more live entertainment in its theme parks than all of the shows on Broadway combined. I couldn't imagine bypassing our best people. I was also determined to produce a show with a Disney sensibility. Jeffrey went along, and we finally agreed that Robert Jess Roth was the best choice for director.

Rob was just twenty-nine years old at the time, and his credits were almost exclusively for shows in our parks, but his talent was unmistakable. He had just created *Mickey's Nutcracker,* a sophisticated rock musical based on the Tchaikovsky ballet music, with tap-dancing wooden soldiers and a rapper as the evil Rat King. Rob had both the technical skills and the theatrical sensibility to bring *Beauty* to the stage. He enlisted two of his regular collaborators, Matt West as choreographer and Stan Meyer as scenic designer. "Go see if you can make this work,"

Jeffrey told them, "and then come back and pitch it to us." I was eager to be convinced, but I fully intended to play devil's advocate until my doubts were erased.

The safest option would have been to mount a modest road show and play it in towns across the country where Disney is beloved and critics are less harsh. But Broadway is the proving ground if you intend to be serious about theater. Commercial success in New York prompts the attention and buzz that then makes it possible to launch road companies in major cities across the country and around the world. The trick was to resist producing a show specifically aimed at pleasing the critics. "It doesn't work to be what you are not," I wrote early on to our creative team. "We are not Stephen Sondheim, or Cameron Mackintosh, or Rodgers and Hammerstein. If we try to be, we will be second rate and we will fail. We are Disney, and that is an asset. It doesn't mean we can't deal with challenging topics, but we must do it our own way, the best we can, and hope that audiences respond."

In July 1992, at the end of one of our annual corporate retreats in Aspen, Rob and his partners flew out to make a first presentation to Jeffrey and me. It included 140 rough sketches, a half-dozen large renderings of how the production might look on stage, and a demonstration of one of the show's best illusions: the real-life head of Chip, a small boy, atop a tea trolley, somehow managing to talk and move around without any visible lower body. After listening for an hour, Jeffrey and I both had plenty of notes and ideas, but we were sufficiently impressed to give the production a go-ahead. Alan Menken was skeptical about working with a team recruited from Disneyland. In the end, he, too, was won over. He agreed to compose the six or seven new songs that a stage version required. For lyrics, he collaborated again with Tim Rice, with whom he'd just written several songs for *Aladdin*. One of the few Broadway veterans we recruited was Ann Hould-Ward, who would eventually win a Tony Award for her brilliant costumes.

The theatrical version of *Beauty and the Beast* also turned out to be Jeffrey's and my last successful collaboration. Although he increasingly resisted my input on our live-action movies, and even in animation, this was Jeffrey's first experience in theater, and he was more open to my involvement. We chose Houston as the city in which to preview the show. It was far enough from New York that we could be free of unwanted attention while we worked on it, but close enough to L.A. that both Jeffrey and I could fly in regularly. As with animation, he oversaw the project day to day and focused on the details. I came in at regular intervals and mostly offered broader notes.

The notion of buying a Broadway theater took shape on a parallel track. Over the years, Bob Stern had often tried to rouse our interest in efforts to revive 42nd Street. I was never able to envision a role for Disney. On one occasion, Jane and I held a small dinner at home to benefit the American Academy of Rome and I sat next to Marion Heiskell, an old family friend who now chaired the 42nd Street Redevelopment Corporation. She spent much of the evening trying to convince me that Disney ought to become involved in Times Square, but again I resisted. As with so many ideas, the key proved to be timing. One Friday afternoon in the spring of 1993, soon after we'd begun to discuss bringing *Beauty and the Beast* to Broadway, I happened to be sitting in Bob Stern's New York office talking about architectural projects. He suggested that we go over together to look at the New Amsterdam Theatre on 42nd Street off Seventh Avenue as a potential home for future theater productions.

For the first time, I was intrigued. Over the years, we'd passed on many opportunities to buy movie theaters. With 35,000 screens available across the country, we had plenty of outlets for our movies, and we could usually negotiate good terms. But the situation was different for Broadway theaters in New York City, where there are too few of them and location is everything. Often, it was difficult to book a theater for a show. Even when you could, it required paying a large percentage of your gross off the top to the theater's owners—mostly the Nederlander and Shubert organizations. In the long run, it was virtually impossible to make money on Broadway unless you owned the theater yourself. I agreed to meet Bob the next morning at the New Amsterdam.

I hadn't walked along 42nd Street for many years. As I approached the New Amsterdam with Jane, Bob, and Anders, now sixteen years old, it dawned on me that I'd attended double-feature films at this same theater as a teenager in the late 1950s. Afterwards, my friends and I would walk over and play arcade games at Fascination on Broadway and 47th Street. It was a more innocent time, when Times Square was still safe and fun. Over the next decade, sleazy X-rated bookstores took over the block, and once elegant theaters began showing pornographic films. In 1969, John Schlesinger's movie *Midnight Cowboy* created an indelible image of the neighborhood's decline, largely through Dustin Hoffman's powerful portrayal of Ratso Rizzo, the sad hustler who calls 42nd Street home. If anything, Times Square had only deteriorated further during the subsequent twenty-five years.

The New Amsterdam mirrored the downward slide. Built in 1903, it had once been known as the jewel of 42nd Street. For fifteen years, in the early 1900s, it was home to the Ziegfeld Follies. In 1915, Flo Ziegfeld had turned the roof garden into the Midnight Frolic, a supper club. In 1937, like so many theaters on the block, it was converted into a movie house. An effort by the Nederlander family to restore the New Amsterdam as a legitimate theater was launched in the early 1980s. After a long battle with city agencies, they halted the renovation midway. Finally, in 1983, the city bought the theater for $283,000. In the interim, the roof had been left partially open and massive interior damage ensued.

As our group walked through the theater, wearing hard hats and carrying flashlights, we could see water leaking from the roof, birds nesting in the ceiling, puddles mingled with rubble on the floor. The interior was badly gutted. Still, the theater's remarkable detailing remained in ghostlike form—its Art Nouveau decor, Wagnerian friezes, and allegorical murals. The once lavish grandeur of this building was easy to visualize, even in its dilapidated state. By the time we left, I felt excited. As soon as we boarded the plane, I called Peter Rummell, who ran our real estate development company, and asked him to follow up with the appropriate agencies.

On Monday morning, Peter began talking with the 42nd Street Redevelopment Corporation about what sort of deal we might make to buy and restore the New Amsterdam. For all the high-level efforts to turn Times Square around, they'd sputtered fitfully for years. A half dozen city and state agencies had a voice in any decisions, and the result had been endless bureaucracy and unfulfilled promises. As for the New Amsterdam, any restoration represented a massive job. "Think of this as the world's biggest kitchen rehab," Peter told me, after taking a look. "It's going to be much more expensive than you think—and a lot of headaches."

The budget for the job came in at $34 million. As a business venture, it was impossible to justify spending that sum on a single theater without some sort of help from the city and state. Fortunately, their incentive was strong. If Disney made a commitment to the New Amsterdam, it was likely to give the Times Square project a powerful jump start. For city officials, bringing Disney to Times Square was the equivalent of landing a prestigious anchor store for a shopping mall—a powerful lure to other businesses. Public subsidies aimed at attracting new business to a given region are commonplace, but they also often generate political controversy. In this case, dissent was surprisingly muted, perhaps reflecting the widely shared hunger to finally turn Times Square around.

By January 1994, we'd tentatively agreed to put up $8 million to purchase and restore the New Amsterdam. The city and state promised to provide low-interest loans for the other $26 million, and in return we agreed to pay them a percentage of our gross revenues from the theater. To minimize the risk of ending up an island in a run-down neighborhood, we reserved the right not to move forward on the New Amsterdam unless at least two other major companies committed to launching businesses along 42nd Street. We were confident that would happen, but the negotiations dragged on for months. By the time they neared completion in the early winter of 1994, we were just weeks away from starting previews for *Beauty and the Beast* in Houston.

The press conference to announce the New Amsterdam deal was scheduled for February 2, 1994, at City Hall. The prospect of Disney's involvement in reviving 42nd Street drew dozens of reporters and television cameras to the tiny press room. The announcement also included Rudolph Giuliani, the mayor of New York, and the governor, Mario Cuomo, both of whom had been instrumental in the deal. Giuliani spoke first, reiterating that Disney's involvement would indeed "jump-start" the redevelopment of Times Square—especially given Disney's reputation as a family entertainment company. "If there were a match made in heaven, this is it," he said. I spoke next and explained that the project not only represented Disney's commitment to New York and to theater but to the viability of entertainment outside the home.

It was Governor Mario Cuomo who delivered the most emotional and personal speech about Times Square and what Disney's involvement meant. Speaking without notes, he lyrically evoked the New

York City of his youth—"egg creams and stickball and lazy Saturday afternoons at the movies on 42nd Street." He talked about the "sleazy sewer that Times Square has become" but also of "the excitement of resurrecting this once great street." He was both nostalgic and inspiring, and had he been running for president that day, I probably would have signed up.

Over the next several months, a remarkable array of companies followed our lead: Tishman Realty, our longtime partners at Walt Disney World, announced a large hotel and entertainment complex along 42nd Street; AMC Entertainment proposed a twenty-five-screen movie multiplex; the London-based Pearson PLC came in with a Madame Tussaud's wax museum; and Condé Nast announced its intention to relocate its headquarters to a huge new office building around the block from the New Amsterdam. The decision to buy the theater now seemed worth the investment whatever happened with our own productions. At the very least, we would play a central role in promoting live theater in New York and helping to revive one of the great streets in the world.

Ten weeks after the press conference, as we continued to negotiate on the New Amsterdam, *Beauty and the Beast* opened in the nearby Palace Theater. As newcomers to Broadway, mostly using our own talent, we didn't expect a warm welcome from the theater community. Just a few days before the premiere, the *New York Times* ran a long Sunday story by Alex Witchel that gave voice to all our detractors. "Money, of course, is a key reason for industry sniping about this show," she wrote. "As is power. And control. And expertise." There were complaints, she reported, about how much we had allegedly spent to produce *Beauty*. Anonymous experts speculated that we'd have a hard time earning our money back, "especially given the Palace's hard-to-sell second balcony." Witchel herself concluded that we'd so far failed to turn the show into a big event. She described our advance sales as "surprisingly low." In addition, she pointed out that we'd produced the show mostly with "amateurs" from Disney, and only a handful of Broadway veterans.

A few of the major critics, including Ben Brantley in the *New York Times*, were hard on the show, complaining that it was too lavish, hyperbolic, broad, and manipulative. But we also earned our share of positive reviews. I loved *Beauty* without reservation. To me, it was entertaining, moving, and musically unbeatable. Theatergoers agreed.

On the day after *Beauty and the Beast* opened, we set an all-time Broadway record by selling more than $700,000 in tickets. The review in *Variety* captured the split between critics and the audience best. "Disney arrives on Broadway with a bang. And a boom and a roar, plenty of fireworks and a fistful of lovely songs," wrote Jeremy Gerard. "It will almost certainly be met with varying levels of derision by Broadway traditionalists. . . . The complaints, however, will be meaningless where it counts, which is at the Palace box office. Disney's first Broadway show will be packing them in—and thumbing its nose at the naysayers—for a very long time." Sure enough, at a time when only a handful of musicals survived at all—Stephen Sondheim's *Passion* opened a few months later to admiring notices, swept the Tony Awards, and then closed after four months—we sold out our eighteen hundred seats night after night. *Beauty and the Beast* became one of Broadway's long-running hits.

During the next several months, we signed deals for road shows in Los Angeles and Chicago and also abroad in Toronto, Japan, Germany, and Australia. For the first time, I felt confident about making a full commitment to live theater. On May 2—two weeks after *Beauty* opened—I sent Jeffrey a memo: "I think we should continue discussing *Aïda* as our next Broadway presentation. It is exactly the risk that interests me. The beauty of the setting and the tragedy of the story may make this very suited to New York. What arrogance. What confidence. What brilliance or stupidity!"

At the same time, we started considering other projects, ranging from *Mary Poppins* to a musical based on *King David*. In June 1994, *The Lion King* opened, and very quickly emerged as the most popular animated film of all time. It, too, was a logical candidate to adapt for the theater. We announced plans to launch a new show each year, beginning in 1997, when the restoration of the New Amsterdam was due to be completed. Whatever we finally chose to do next, we were all determined to take an entirely different approach. It made no sense to try to repeat ourselves. Having been successful our first time out, we now had the freedom to try something riskier and less mainstream.

For me there will always be something special and intensely personal about *Beauty and the Beast*. In many ways, it represented a homecoming—the closing of the circle. I'd grown up with the theater in New York. When I took my first job at CBS, I left theater behind and followed the audience to movies and television. Eventually, I moved to Los Angeles. Success at Disney provided the opportunity to return to a first love. To watch *Beauty and the Beast* become a hit in New York, and later in London, was a thrill. To know that the show is still running in nearly a dozen cities around the world, offering thousands of children their first experience with live theater, is immensely satisfying.

I've lost count of how many times I've seen *Beauty and the Beast*. During the Los Angeles run alone, I went at least a dozen times, mostly sneaking into the balcony for weekend matinees, until I felt a bit like a real-life Phantom of the Opera. The thrill isn't gone. In the fall of 1997, I traveled to the show's opening in Denver, Colorado. Sitting in the audience on a Sunday afternoon, sharing the enchantment of a sea of children seeing the show for the first time, I felt like a child myself, watching my first show on Broadway four decades earlier.

CHAPTER

10

Euro Disney

THE IRONY ABOUT EURO DISNEY IS THAT WE BEGAN MODESTLY. Within weeks of our arrival at Disney, two different groups of executives brought Frank and me separate proposals to build a theme park in Europe. Each group approached us as though they were the only ones working on a European park. Not only was this wasteful, it was odd. We combined the groups immediately. The idea of building a European park had first been raised by Card Walker as early as 1976. Discussions continued intermittently over the years. By the early 1980s, more than 2 million European tourists were visiting Disneyland and Walt Disney World annually, but it was only after the successful launch of Tokyo Disneyland in 1983 that research into potential European sites began in earnest.

Tokyo Disneyland had been more than a decade in the making. At least two Japanese companies approached Disney in the late 1960s, each suggesting potential theme park sites near Mount Fuji. The discussions didn't go very far until the early 1970s, when the Japanese-owned Oriental Land Company came to Disney with a 200-acre site on Tokyo Bay, six miles from the heart of downtown. The talks focused at first on a joint venture, but the rising costs of building Epcot at Walt Disney World dampened the company's enthusiasm for making another major investment in a theme park. Ultimately, the negotiations turned to a licensing deal, under which Disney would design the park and earn royalties based on its performance. Discussions continued for years without any resolution. Finally, the offer got so good that Disney literally couldn't turn it down. Initially, the Japanese had proposed paying a royalty of 2 percent of all gross revenues. The final contract, signed in 1979, gave Disney 5 percent of the gross revenues on all food and merchandise and 10 percent of the gross on admissions, in exchange for a token $2.5 million investment in the park.

On one level, it was a very good deal. Disney not only earned a fee for developing the park but retained complete design control. The best elements of the Magic Kingdoms at Disneyland and Walt Disney World were lifted whole—not just shows and attractions but fast-food outlets and merchandise shops. Disney also retained significant control over park operations through a series of highly detailed manuals that spelled out guidelines for operating the rides, guest service, and even grooming for cast members.

The good news was that the park attracted 10 million guests in its first year, meaning Disney earned $40 million in royalties that went directly to its bottom line. The bad news was that by having elected not to enter into a joint venture, the company sacrificed a potentially far bigger share of the profits as attendance grew. After four years, it reached 12 million guests, and within a decade, it grew to 16 million. Merchandising profits were a key example of what the company had forgone. At the last moment in negotiations, the Japanese offered to give Disney sole merchandise rights at the park for $20 million. Even that sum the company judged to be too costly an investment at the time—perhaps prudently so. But in a country where bringing back gifts from a vacation was the custom, merchandise proved wildly successful. Just one outlet— the 2,000-square-foot Confectionery Shop on Main Street—would eventually produce annual revenues of nearly $100 million. The failure to take an ownership position in Tokyo Disneyland was exceptionally costly. Frank and I were determined to be primary owners if we undertook a new theme park in Europe.

We heard the first joint presentation in the late fall of 1984. It was made by Dick Nunis, head of our domestic parks, and by Jim Cora, who had just finished overseeing construction of Tokyo Disneyland.

They'd already culled through nearly twelve hundred potential sites in Europe, and were leaning toward either France or Spain. When they finished, Cora held up two videotapes. "If either of you wants more detail about what we've just told you," he said, "here it is. You can watch at your leisure."

"What for?" Frank replied. "Let's start negotiating with both countries and find out what they have to offer. See if you can get us a deal."

By March 1985, Cora and Nunis had narrowed the choice to three sites, two in Spain and one in France. The Spanish sites were along beautiful beaches, including one outside Barcelona. The advantage of the Barcelona site was that the local Catalonian government—which operated almost autonomously from the central government—had a highly progressive vision for increasing tourism, and its team made a very polished pitch. The French site was in Marne-la-Vallée, a small farming town east of Paris. After the first site visit, Cora's initial impression wasn't very enthusiastic. His French hosts drove him there by a long scenic route through the countryside. "It seemed like it was in the sticks," he explained. "You couldn't see anything but cornfields around for miles." That perception changed the next day when Cora's group returned to tour the site from overhead, by helicopter. Suddenly, they realized it was only twenty-five kilometers from downtown Paris and that a major throughway—the A-4—ran directly by Marne-la-Vallée.

A debate over the three sites quickly took shape. Nunis and Cora were the strongest proponents for Spain, mostly on the grounds of its more temperate weather, but also because it was clear that negotiations were likely to be smoother than with the French government. But Spain had some obvious drawbacks. It used a different rail line from the rest of Europe, still lacked a countrywide highway system, and the phone service was erratic and frustrating. The Spanish sites attracted a large tourist population, but only in the summer. Nor did it make me feel especially welcome when I received a letter from the Basque opposition threatening violence if Disney came to Spain. But the biggest problem was that Spain represented something of a geographical cul-de-sac, distant from the center of Europe. Preliminary studies showed that we could expect to draw perhaps 6 million visitors the first year to Barcelona—far fewer than we needed for a successful resort.

My heart was with France from the start. I'd spent vacations in Paris during my youth—sipping espresso at cafés and people-watching on summer nights. (All right, I was probably gulping Coke and struggling to understand the conversations I overheard.) In any case, Paris was one of the most beautiful and romantic cities in the world. It was also perhaps the most central of all European cities—a hub through which millions of travelers passed each year on their way to wherever else they might be headed. Nearly 70 million people lived within a three-and-a-half hour drive of the site at Marne-la-Vallée. Paris itself was a year-round tourist attraction. Our own initial projection of first-year attendance for the park was 10 million people. At least one consultant we hired estimated at least 12 and perhaps as many as 16 million in the first year.

The most obvious drawback to the Paris site was the weather. Winters can be cold and raw, not that different from New York, except that it rains in Paris an average of 110 days a year. I never found that concern compelling. Generally, it came from people who'd lived in California for most of their lives. I'd grown up with cold winters in Manhattan and I knew that no true New Yorker is deterred by weather. If it rains in Los Angeles, the city stops. If it's rainy in New York, the city barely notices. I assumed the same was true of Parisians, used to the cold weather, and of the millions of tourists who already visited Paris in the winter.

The only issue that really worried me about Paris was the distance from the closest subway, or Métro stop, to our Marne-la-Vallée site. Once again, I was influenced by my experience growing up in New York. I was taken on the subway to my dentist when I was six years old, and before long, I used it all the time. I grew reluctant to travel anywhere that wasn't near a subway stop. When my dentist moved his office several blocks from the subway, I went to a new dentist. As far as I was concerned, we were doomed to failure if our park was more than six minutes by foot from a subway stop. Extending the Paris Métro right up to the front gate of our proposed park became the number one condition for making a deal. We also made it a priority that the TGV—the French bullet train—agree to put in a stop at the front entrance of the park. Much as the Métro brought day visitors to our park from Paris, the TGV would bring overnight visitors from all over Europe. In a world in which people's time is more precious than ever, the value of convenience was hard to overestimate.

By the fall of 1985, the debate was no longer over which site was preferable but whether we could make a good enough deal with the French government to justify building the resort in Marne-la-Vallée. They had good reason for wanting to make a deal. The park represented a potentially huge economic boon to whatever country we put it in. The French government's projections showed that it would lead to employment for ten thousand people. The 10 to 15 million annual visitors would generate billions of dollars in additional revenue for the French economy. Finally, from an image standpoint, the government, led by Prime Minister Laurent Fabius, could scarcely afford to lose the project to neighboring Spain.

Our primary goal was to control our financial exposure—as we had in Tokyo—and ensure a substantial share of the profits and management control. Dick Nunis led our team of negotiators, and by mid-December 1985, they had pulled together the broad outlines of a deal. First, the French government agreed to sell us approximately 4,400 acres of contiguous land in Marne-la-Vallée at a price reflecting its value as farmland rather than the much higher price it would command once the land was commercially zoned. The government also agreed to lend us $700 million at interest rates considerably below the market, and to finance much of the key infrastructure for the park, most notably extending the Métro, as well as improving the A-4 freeway that ran by the site.

On December 16, I flew to Paris with the intention of signing an agreement for Euro Disneyland, which we soon nicknamed EDL. I arrived in Paris one day before our planned announcement. Negotiations were still continuing. That afternoon I spent several hours meeting with the producers of *Trois Hommes et un Couffin*, as part of our effort to buy the rights to remake the film as *Three Men and a Baby*. At eleven p.m., feeling the effects of jet lag, I returned to my hotel for a meeting with our team, to go over the final points on the Euro Disney agreement. There were still a sufficient number of unresolved issues that we decided to sign a letter of intent rather than a completed deal. Even at that, our announcement the next day outlined an exceptionally ambitious plan for a full-scale resort. In addition to the Magic Kingdom, it included nearly five thousand hotel rooms, a large campground, shops and restaurants, a golf course, convention facilities, an office complex, and a residential housing development. We also said that we would be seeking investors from France and other European countries. In addition to taking an equity position ourselves, Disney would be paid a management fee and royalties based on the park's revenues.

My biggest concern was still the Métro. The government had agreed to the extension. I'd been told that it took less than a half hour to travel from the Arc de Triomphe in downtown Paris to the current terminus of the line, six miles from our site. Once the extension occurred, the ride would require another five to ten minutes. Those thirty minutes or so seemed an acceptable commute, but I had to find out for myself, so I decided to take the Métro ride. If it took much longer than we'd been told, I wouldn't sign the agreement. As it turned out, I reached the Torcy station near Marne-la-Vallée exactly twenty-five minutes after I left the station in Paris. I felt elated—and relieved.

In fact, the negotiations for Euro Disney had only just begun. The letter of agreement was at best a broad working document. We'd expected that it would require three months to reach final terms on a definitive contract. It required more than a year and nearly fell apart on several occasions. Along the way, we negotiated simultaneously with more than a half dozen government agencies. Halfway through, Prime Minister Fabius and his socialist government were voted out in favor of Jacques Chirac and the conservatives. Chirac would prove more sympathetic to our project, but his arrival meant dealing with an entirely new group of government officials.

Frank assumed the primary role in overseeing the negotiations. Even at the early stages, we estimated that the project would cost in excess of $2 billion, which meant that the stakes were very high. The key to succeeding in any difficult negotiation, I've always believed, is the willingness to walk away at any point in the process. It was critical to convince the other side that we were willing to do just that, but also to persuade our own negotiators of the same. For that reason, we regularly communicated to Joe Shapiro, our corporate counsel and lead negotiator in Paris, that almost nothing his team got was enough. If Joe reported back that he had won a certain concession—say a lower interest rate, or a reduction in the price we were going to be charged for land, or an additional tax benefit—Frank, or Gary, or I myself would try to raise the bar.

Because the time difference between Paris and Los Angeles was nine hours and Frank paid no attention to such issues, he frequently called Joe at 2:00 a.m. or 3:00 a.m. in his room. Joe learned to keep a bottle of Coca-Cola by his bed, so that when the phone rang, he could take a quick gulp to jolt himself awake. "We just can't go forward on the project if you don't do better on this point," Frank would tell him. One of our shorthands was to rate what we were after on a given issue on a scale from 1 to 10. In one instance, we urged Joe to push hard for a 10 on a particular point—and to let the other side know that the whole deal was off if they didn't agree to what we were seeking.

"I got a twelve," Joe announced proudly when he called in the next day.

Rather than feeling happy, this news made me nervous. "If you got a twelve that easily," I said, "then you probably should go back and push for a thirteen." In most cases, Joe and his team eventually achieved what we were after. On March 24, 1987, Frank and I finally flew back to Paris to sign the completed deal with the new prime minister, Jacques Chirac, with whom I would develop a close relationship in the years ahead.

By the time we finished our government negotiations, Gary Wilson had begun working to create a way of financing the new resort. Under French laws, no foreign investor could own majority interest in a company. Gary designed a brilliant structure that allowed us to sell shares in the park to the public while retaining management control and a 49 percent ownership stake. We would also earn a percentage of the revenues for managing the resort, as well as royalties from its gross revenues, based on the same terms that we had in Japan. We agreed to make an investment of $100 million ourselves, but most of the money to build the resort would come from the banks and individual investors. Gary's arrangement protected Disney's downside while also creating an opportunity to do exceptionally well if the park became a big hit.

Our confidence in Euro Disney's prospects continued to grow over the next two years. Disneyland and Walt Disney World were achieving record attendance. In May 1989, Disney-MGM Studios opened on time and on budget to crowds that far exceeded our projections. We also opened several thousand new hotel rooms at Walt Disney World, and occupancy rates remained above 90 percent. In the summer of 1989, we arranged to bring several hundred European bankers and stockbrokers to Orlando to experience our Walt Disney World for themselves. Impressed by the size of the crowds, the quality of our operation, and the variety of offerings, they returned to Europe singing our praises. To some degree, we were swept up in the enthusiasm. "A groundswell is developing among analysts that EDL's vision for the future is projected too conservatively," Gary Wilson wrote a short time later in a new valuation study of Euro Disney.

"We must not undersell this issue," I scribbled back in response. "I believe we should get the true value, and not undersell the Disney brand as the company has done in the past."

On October 5, 1989, we took our $1 billion offering public at $13 a share—launching it with an event that featured Disney characters performing at the Paris Bourse, the French stock exchange. The offering was underwritten by a consortium of banks led by the Banque Nationale de Paris. I arrived for the event with other members of our team, in a car driven by Mickey Mouse. Confident and in a great mood, I emerged from the car smiling. Then I walked up to make a short speech from the steps of the exchange, still confident, still smiling. Suddenly objects started flying through the air toward me. When I looked out at the crowd, I suddenly realized that we were in the midst of a demonstration, apparently by critics of the deal the government had made with us for the park. This was definitely a new experience for me. Gary Wilson had an egg thrown at him, I rushed through my talk, and we all ran off the stage, no longer smiling or confident.

Within hours, images of me and other Disney executives seemingly under siege in Paris were flashed around the world. For the first time in my life, I had a sense of what it is like to be a politician during a campaign. Unfortunately, the media coverage of the small protest deflected attention from the fact that our offering was a huge success. By the end of the first day of trading, the price had jumped to $16—some 20 percent. At its height, the stock would sell as high as $30 a share. Nearly 86 million shares sold within days.

While Gary arranged the financing, work began on two separate creative tracks. One was the design of the Magic Kingdom and the other was the plans for adjacent hotels. Both were exceptionally ambitious ventures, but our confidence remained high. "I wish 1988 would never end," I wrote in that year's annual letter to shareholders, "because it has been one of those perfect years for all of us." At the end of 1989, I began my annual letter with a statement that would turn out to be unintentionally prescient: "We had another fantastic year and, like good health, everybody seems to be taking it for granted."

The Imagineering executive we put in charge of designing the Magic Kingdom was Tony Baxter, whose creativity and passion I'd first come to appreciate through his design for *Splash Mountain*. Tony reminded me of the Tom Hanks character in *Big*—a grown-up with a kid's unfettered enthusiasms. In Tony's mind, Euro Disney was a chance both to correct shortcomings in our previous parks and to bring theme parks to a whole new level. "We can't just transplant Tokyo Disneyland to Paris," he argued in one of our first meetings. "We're building a resort next to one of the most sophisticated, cultured cities in the world, and we're going to be competing with the great art and architecture of Europe. We have to do something unique."

I agreed with Tony, but I also believed it would be a mistake to try to create some ersatz version of French culture at Euro Disney. Our experience at our other parks had long been that foreign visitors were eager for the Disney experience, pure and undistilled. At Tokyo Disneyland, for example, our partners had a specific request: "Don't Japanize us." They weren't interested in Disney's building attractions based on Japan, and we took them at their word. Even the signs at the park in Tokyo are in English. One of the few instances in which the Japanese pushed for their own culture at the park was asking us to sell rice cakes in favor of popcorn. We pushed to do it our way, and popcorn, like everything else American at the park, proved to be immensely popular. In France, by contrast, the government was deeply interested in having the country's culture and history interwoven through the park. We made a few concessions, but for the most part we were determined to make EDL every bit as American as Tokyo Disneyland and our domestic parks —meaning fast food instead of smoky bistros, Coca-Cola and lemonade in preference to wine, animated movies rather than film noir.

Our creative meetings on the new park sometimes extended over several days at Imagineering. We probably met on fifty occasions, discussing everything from architecture to ashtrays. We studied every detail of every inch in the park. Unlike producing movies, here we could be producer, director, editor, and even the actors in every foot of the film. Designing parks was more exciting than anything one could do in the proscenium world, where two dimensions was the rule. One of the early discussions was how to handle the entrance. Main Street at Disneyland had been inspired by Walt's hometown of Marceline, Missouri. In fact, its architectural elements originated during the Victorian period in Britain and were translated to an American vernacular, using less expensive materials. Tony's point was that while Main Street seemed quaint and special at our parks in Anaheim and Orlando, it looked a lot like hundreds of small towns and hamlets across Europe. "Why not do something more contemporary and more uniquely American?" he argued.

Tony's design team for Main Street, led by the wildly imaginative Imagineer Eddie Sotto, initially created a street based on the New York and Chicago of the twenties, with speakeasies and jazz clubs, rough-hewn glamour and movie stars. The design was provocative but it seemed wrong for us. Our goal was to transport the Disney brand to our new park, not to dramatically reinvent it. The movie *The Untouchables* opened during this period and it only confirmed my worst fears. "Why export gangsterism and corruption as the essence of American culture?" I asked Eddie and Tony. "I just think it's sending the wrong message." To their credit, they went back and came up with a Main Street that retained a Victorian charm but added a more contemporary dimension of Americana, mostly through graphics, billboards, and signs displayed along the street. The level of detail was stunning. The one problem was that designing two new versions of Main Street made the final result far more expensive than it was at our other parks.

A similar process would be repeated dozens of times for nearly every other aspect of the new park. The castle at the end of Main Street was the quintessential example. In this case, we faced the task of building a castle in a country that was full of spectacular authentic castles hundreds of years old. The Château d'Usse, one of the original inspirations for the castle at Walt Disney World, was barely an hour away from Marne-la-Vallée. The one at Disneyland had been inspired by several German castles. "We can't just do a kitschy rendition of French history right in their own backyard," Tony insisted. "We need something that can stand on its own." Nor did it make sense, he argued, to use fiberglass as a building material when right down the road our guests could visit castles rendered in Gothic stone splendor. As Tony lobbied, it dawned on me that we also faced the daunting task at Euro Disney of trying to compete with Paris itself. In the case of the castle, our solution was to design one based on fairy tales, largely inspired by the castles drawn for Disney's animated classics such as *Sleeping Beauty* and *Snow White*.

Once again, the commitment to wholly original design turned into an enormously expensive undertaking. Instead of columns and arches, we used huge trees whose branches formed the support system for the castle's ceiling, with lights twinkling in the branches. We brought a seventy-year-old English artisan, Paul Chapman, out of retirement to design stained-glass windows in the castle depicting scenes from *Sleeping Beauty*. The basement included a dungeon and an elaborate, fire-breathing Audio-Animatronics dragon. As much as any of our designers, I grew passionate about making every detail count. At one stage, a group of us put in several hours with John Hench—an Imagineer who had worked with Walt and who had an extraordinary sense of color—trying to find the perfect shade of pink for the castle. We ended up repainting the model three separate times before agreeing we had it right. The castle ended up costing millions of dollars more than the one at Tokyo Disneyland.

The other major project that we worked on was a nighttime entertainment complex called Disney Village and loosely patterned after Pleasure Island at Walt Disney World. Several of our team members believed that we ought to hold off altogether, but I disagreed. When several thousand hotel rooms filled with guests, there would be a need to entertain and feed them after the park closed. For the same reason, we designed an elaborate Wild West dinner show. Expensive as it would be to build and to run, it represented a theatrical evening's entertainment. We considered two schemes for Disney Village. One was a New England–style wharf village, designed by a Boston architectural firm. It was adequate, but that was precisely the problem. There was nothing distinctive about it, and given a far more modest budget than we had for the park itself, it would look cheap by comparison.

The second scheme was designed by Frank Gehry, the innovative California-based architect. Rather than a themed complex, he designed a series of unusually shaped buildings pulled together by tall pylons, built out of stainless steel, with a grid of overhead lights that looked almost like stars at night. When we held a vote at one of our final design meetings, it came out virtually unanimously for the New England design. I was one of only two votes for Gehry's alternative. As I'd learned in dealing with Michael Graves's design for the Swan and the Dolphin Hotels, truly original architecture is at once beautiful and a little threatening. In the case of Disney Village, we went forward with the Gehry design. A decade later, I remain its biggest fan.

In the midst of all this intensive work, Jane and I rented an apartment in Paris during the summer of 1988. We would return the following two summers, and so would Frank. We'd been visiting the site frequently, but this was an opportunity to focus exclusively on Euro Disney and expanding our company's operations in Europe. Afterwards, I wrote a letter to the members of our board of directors. It began with a warning about taking the company's recent success too much for granted: "Let's see how we do when the tide turns at Disney. Can we pull ourselves back? The reason I went to Europe was to help keep the tide from turning. Our biggest threat is Euro Disneyland. And it is here that we must be cautious." Then I went on in a more lighthearted vein: "Thirty days is not enough time to learn French, but it's plenty of time to realize how much English grammar one has forgotten. Thirty days isn't enough time to solve our preconstruction Euro Disneyland over-budget items, but it's plenty of time to know they exist. And thirty days is more than enough time to know that thirty days with one's mother, sister, brother-in-law, wife, children, son's girlfriend, and friends of children is thirty full days."

I began each day with classes in French at the Institut Catholique de Paris—the only American in a class of twenty-two students from twelve countries. I learned a reasonable amount of French, but the most valuable aspect of the experience was completely unexpected. I never identified myself, but one day our teacher mentioned, with obvious pride, that he worked part-time translating American TV scripts into French. One of them was *The Golden Girls*. I was taken aback. The teacher did a reasonably decent job with our class, but his English was fractured and awkward. I immediately called Dimitri Agratchev, my Russian-born French translator, and arranged to have him look at a dubbed episode of *The Golden Girls*. Dimitri reported back that the idiomatic expressions in the show had been badly mangled and its humor almost completely lost. Estelle Getty's sweet "I gotta go pee," for example, had been translated as the far cruder "I gotta go piss." Sure enough, *The Golden Girls* had bombed during its first run in France. With a little further research, I found that this sort of dubbing occurred in virtually all our television shows, and even some of our movies.

Almost immediately, we expanded a department called Disney Character Voices. It was overseen by Roy Disney, who was already concerned about the lack of consistency in the voices of our characters in the United States—especially Mickey Mouse. The mandate of the new committee was to review any voice used on a Disney program around the world. Eventually, we redubbed our entire library of programs in more than thirty-five languages. To do so, we set up what is perhaps the most technologically advanced dubbing organization in the world. As part of our new standards, translators had to demonstrate not just their theatrical ability but that they were truly bilingual, meaning at home with idiomatic and colloquial expressions in both languages. In the case of *The Golden Girls*, the redubbed version eventually went back on the air in France and became a bona fide hit.

On weekends during my month in Paris, I recruited as many park executives as possible, along with Jane and other interested relatives, and together we traveled around Europe looking at other theme parks. It seemed critical to see what the competition was doing. We visited parks ranging from Alton Towers in the East Midlands in England, to Gardaland in Verona, Italy, to De Efteling, forty-five miles from Rotterdam in Holland. Several of them were in beautiful settings, and it became clear that in order to make our rural site more attractive, we were going to have to invest a great deal in landscaping. As had once been true for Walt, the best and most beautiful of all the parks we visited was still the Tivoli Gardens in Copenhagen, with its great attention to original detailing in everything from the lighting to the graphics on signs. But many of the others had tried to copy Disneyland and come up considerably short. Not a single one drew more than 2 million customers a year, and nearly all of those came for one-day visits from the local area. One of our mandates was to build a resort that people would view as a vacation destination.

During this month, I also began meeting with Etienne de Villiers, a Rhodes Scholar who Rich Frank had hired away from a South African company to head our international television operations. Our goal was to map out a television strategy for the next five years across

Europe. "This philosophy is all-important if we are to make Europe and its 320 million people a primary market for the next decade for the Disney company," I later explained to our board. "We must be on television in all countries. We must be on television in a regular way. We must consider being in pay television. We must export the Disney Channel. We must produce in Europe. And all this must be going on by 1990, so that when we open our Park in 1992, the frenzy about Disney will already be there." Etienne was laying the groundwork. Disney shows in Portugal and Italy had already achieved number one ratings. We would eventually become partners in GMTV, the dominant British morning television franchise, which runs from 6:00 to 9:30 a.m. seven days a week. On weekends, GMTV runs Disney programs predominately, most of them animated shows for kids. During 1989, Etienne sold most major European countries a daily one-hour Disney Club, inspired by Walt's original Mickey Mouse Club.

Living in Paris for a longer stretch also had a broad strategic value. It was one thing to pop in and out for two or three days at a time. But during this summer stay, Frank and I came to know our European managers, not just at a few meetings but over time. We could stroll around the city on a weekend, walk into a Disney Store unannounced, ask questions about why one street drew more tourists than another, see what kind of movies and shops were drawing crowds. Beyond our immediate business at Euro Disney, there was an enormous value in coming to understand the everyday interests and patterns of people in another country where we did business.

To run Euro Disney, we'd hired Bob Fitzpatrick, whom I first met when he asked me to serve on the board of the California Institute of the Arts in the early 1980s, where he was then president. Articulate, charming, broadly educated, Bob had spent a great deal of time in France, spoke the language fluently, and was married to a French woman. With Frank's support, I took Bob out to dinner one night and essentially offered him the job by the time dessert arrived. While he lacked experience as a businessman, he brought to the challenge great taste and an ability to deal gracefully with many constituencies, as he had done very effectively at CalArts. Under Bob, we installed Jim Cora, who brought to the job his background as a park operator and a reservoir of knowledge about everything from ride capacity to how wide streets ought to be. Jim was blunt, no-nonsense, and so defiantly American that he refused to learn more than a few words of French during his seven years in Paris. Jim and Bob could scarcely have been more different, but their skills seemed complementary. Unfortunately, they didn't get along.

One of the challenges that summer was to bridge the gap between Bob and Jim, and I spent much of my time racing between meetings that ranged from creative to political to financial. The budget was a source of growing concern even before full-scale construction began. "Frank continues to take the lead here, but even he is nervous about how we are going to control costs," I wrote to the board at the time. "We are presently looking at a $300 million over budget situation even before we begin. Of course that is unacceptable, and we are chopping, re-drawing and getting our act together. We are at it early. But it ain't fun."

The other key piece of the puzzle at Euro Disney was the design of the hotels. Gary Wilson was the strongest and most persuasive advocate for building a large enough number of hotel rooms that other operators would be discouraged from competing with us. He never tired of reminding us of what had happened at Disneyland, where there simply wasn't enough land to build hotels, and even at Walt Disney World. "Disney built 2,000 hotel rooms in Orlando," Gary would point out, "and meanwhile 40,000 went up all around the park." This time, we chose to be much more aggressive, aiming for five hotels with 5,200 rooms by opening day. In a country where a 300 room hotel is considered very large, our plan included two with 1,000 rooms. Ambitious as this seemed, it lay at the heart of our strategy to build Euro Disney into a destination resort where guests would come to vacation for several days, just as they did at Walt Disney World. Indeed, the second phase of our plans included a second theme park, to be patterned after the Disney-MGM Studios. "We could wait until the second gate opens to build more rooms," Gary argued, "but by then it would be much more expensive and disruptive. Better to do them all up front."

Just designing a master plan for the hotels proved daunting, in part because we completely shifted directions at the eleventh hour. One Friday afternoon in late March 1988, Bob Stern came out to Los Angeles to check on the progress of the projects he was designing for us at Walt Disney World. He stopped in to see me, and I suggested he visit with Wing Chao, our chief in-house architect, and take a look at the plan for the Euro Disney hotels that Wing and Peter Rummell were developing, and that we were due to submit for approval to the French authorities within a month. Bob looked it over and made no effort to hide his dismay. "It looks like an American subdivision in the French countryside," he told Wing. "You've got these big areas for the hotels and then all kinds of roads but very little integration of the parts. It's very, very suburban."

"I see what you're saying," Wing replied mildly, "but this plan is still in an early stage."

"That may be," said Bob, "but once you start going through the governmental process, it's going to be very hard to change."

Wing decided to immediately pull together a small caucus, including Peter Rummell and Art Levitt, by then a vice president who continued to spend a significant amount of his time on design issues. They discussed their options and Wing mentioned that several prominent architects were gathering for dinner that night at Rebecca's, a restaurant in Venice Beach designed by Frank Gehry. The dinner was being hosted by Elizabeth McMillan, an editor at *Architectural Digest*, and it included Gehry, Stanley Tigerman, Michael Rotondi, and Bob Stern.

"Why don't we try to get all of them to come over here tonight?" Wing said. "We'll serve them dinner while they critique our plan." He was counting on the fact that few architects could resist the opportunity to exert some influence over a project as huge and high profile as the master plan for the hotels at Euro Disney. When Wing called Frank and me, we urged him to go forward and keep us posted. Elizabeth McMillan graciously agreed to give up her dinner in exchange for the opportunity to watch the architects in action.

They gathered at one of our Imagineering warehouses in Glendale and spent the next five hours critiquing our plan over catered Chinese food. They ended by agreeing to meet two weeks later in New York to come up with a new plan. Michael Rotondi dropped out of the original group, but we added Robert Venturi and Michael Graves. It was a truly extraordinary team — Stern, Graves, Venturi, Tigerman, and Gehry—and we immediately dubbed them the "Gang of Five."

At 9:00 a.m. on Saturday, April 2, they gathered at Stern's office. By the time Frank and I showed up at noon on Sunday, they'd considered more than twenty ideas, and had begun developing an entirely new site plan for the resort area. All of the hotels were located around a formally designed lake. The purpose was to create a sense of unity and connection among five hotels that we anticipated would reflect different regions of America and aspects of the American experience.

"Let's have a design competition for the hotels," I suggested to Wing. By midweek, he had begun to gather a long list of top architects from around the world. Nearly all of them expressed interest in the project. The first set of presentations took place just three weeks later at my home in Los Angeles, over a marathon four days. The European architects were inclined to a very stark, modernist vocabulary, which meant designs that were mostly abstract, cool, stylized, and often high-tech. I instinctively preferred to have many styles among the buildings we did at Disney. Also, given the park's focus on fantasy and entertainment, I felt more excited about design that had a certain romance, whimsy, and drama. For EDL, I was especially interested in buildings that vividly evoked America and Americana.

One of the first commissions we gave was to Bob Stern, based on his concept for a hotel conceived as if it were a gold-rush town in the Old West. Eventually we named it the Cheyenne. Later, Bob designed the Newport Bay Club, patterned after the Yacht and Beach Clubs at Walt Disney World. We also responded to Michael Graves's design for what became the Hotel New York, which simulated rows of Manhattan apartment-style buildings abutting one another. Finally, we were taken with an adobe-style hotel by American architect Antoine Predock that drew on the monuments and icons of the American Southwest.

We had more difficulty settling on designs for the other two hotel sites. I believed that we should include at least one European architect—preferably a French one. Ultimately, we chose Antoine Grumbach, who would produce perhaps the most romantic and quintessentially American of all our hotels. His design for the Sequoia Lodge, an inspiration that came to him while vacationing in Montana, evoked the great western lodges, much as Peter Dominick would later do using a slightly different vernacular for the Wilderness Lodge at Walt Disney World. The final hotel at EDL evolved out of a discussion about how to create a more welcoming experience for guests when they arrived at the park. Tony Baxter and Eddie Sotto came up with the idea of building an elaborate hotel façade where guests entered the park, which would actually serve as our ticket center. Eventually, their idea evolved into a real hotel, overlooking the Magic Kingdom. Our Imagineers produced a romantic, Victorian storybook design, with a Beaux-Arts flavor, full of cupolas and spires and balconies. We named it the Disneyland Hotel.

As usual, we invited criticism, both within our own group and from other architects. Frank, for example, worried that guests inside the park would look up at the Disneyland Hotel and see people in underwear and bathing suits through the room windows. Bob Venturi's concern was that the design we had in mind would end up obstructing a view of the park's castle for arriving guests. Tony Baxter disagreed vehemently, and produced a physical model and computer-generated photographs to support his case. The argument grew so heated that they nearly had a fistfight and Tony all but pushed Bob out of the room. We did finally move forward with the Imagineering design. Tony turned out to be right in this instance, and the Disneyland Hotel became the most popular of all our hotels at Euro Disney. As for Venturi and the other architects, they eventually made their peace with our often fractious process—although rumor had it several of them formed a support group to help them through the experience.

The Italian architect Aldo Rossi, who died tragically from injuries suffered in an automobile accident in 1997, found our process especially unnerving. From the first time we saw his work in Europe, we agreed that Rossi was one of the great architects of our time. After much courting, he agreed to design a hotel as part of the EDL competition. We met and remet, he designed and redesigned, until finally he threw up his hands—and wrote me a letter. "Dear Michael, I am not personally offended and can ignore all the negative points that have been made about our project at the last meeting in Paris," he began, seeming conciliatory. In fact, he was only warming up. "The Cavalier Bernini, invited to Paris for the Louvre project, was tormented by a multitude of functionaries who continued to demand that changes be made to the project to make it more functional. It is clear that I am not the Cavalier Bernini, but it is also clear that you are not the King of France. Aside from the differences, I do not intend to be the object of minuscule criticisms that any interior designer could handle. It is my belief that our project, notwithstanding the specialists, is beautiful in its own right and as such will become famous and built in some other place."

I was very sorry to lose Rossi's contribution, but we weren't about to give up on working with him. Even after his letter, we never stopped pursuing him, and eventually I assume he grew tired of our calls. Rossi finally agreed to make another attempt and ended up designing a complex of three office buildings at Walt Disney World. They were simple but arresting, mostly for his use of shifts in perspective and manipulations of space.

Different as the Euro Disney hotels were, the combined efforts produced something extraordinary. But achieving this level of excellence came at a price. The initial hotel plan that Gary Wilson envisioned was put together by Larry Murphy. The vast majority of the rooms were low and moderate price, which was what our marketing studies suggested the majority of guests would be seeking. The first hitch in this plan was that the cost of building the hotels rose substantially—a consequence of dozens of enhancements along the way, whether it was building a formal lake from scratch; or importing hundreds of cedar, sweetgum, and pine trees for the Sequoia Lodge; or insisting on the same level of detail inside our hotels as we did outside. There were occasional voices of caution, but none of them was loud or persistent. If anything, we grew more ambitious over time. When Bob Stern finished his design for the Newport Bay, for example, we convinced ourselves to add another three hundred rooms—thus making it one of the largest hotels in Western Europe. Again, the decision seemed justified. "Once you've got the front desk and food and beverage in place," Gary argued, "those extra rooms are pure profit. If we wait, they will cost us far more to build later." By the fall of 1989, there was widespread sentiment for increasing the prices for rooms.

On one level, it all seemed to make great sense. Given the quality of the hotels we were building—and the fact that so many of them now contained added design amenities and lakefront views—it seemed reasonable to assume we could command another $20 or even $30 a night. In turn, our financial team at Euro Disney progressively raised the estimates of revenues we anticipated earning. It was a self-perpetuating cycle of enthusiasm and optimism. External factors played a key role. The

French economy was booming and unemployment was relatively low. It was unlikely that a robust economy would persist indefinitely, but we didn't focus on that. I believed, as Walt had at Disneyland, that the commitment to excellence would ultimately be rewarded at the bottom line.

In the short term, we made some fundamental errors. One was the way we dealt with the media. In the fall of 1989, after we received our financing, one of our executives did an interview with the French newspaper *Le Figaro Economique*. "There is a world of difference between Disney and others," he said at one point. "There is Disney, Disney, Disney, Disney and the others. We are already the best." When I saw these comments, I responded immediately, sending copies of my memo to all of our key EDL executives: "I think we should change our public strategy, to become much less sure of how much better we are than anyone else. We are setting ourselves up to be killed. We cannot be arrogant. We must say simply, 'We will try hard and we hope you will like us.' I think this is a vital change of direction." Unfortunately, it never occurred. Six months later, another EDL executive was quoted as saying, "We're building something immortal, like the pharaohs built the pyramids." When Euro Disney ran into trouble after its opening, the press would gleefully jump all over comments like these.

As our construction problems mounted, Frank's solution was to bring Mickey Steinberg into the project late in 1988. A big, bluff man with passionate enthusiasms and a quick temper, Mickey had worked with the architect John Portman for twenty-seven years, running his company and overseeing the construction of its hotels. Now he was executive vice president of Imagineering under Marty Sklar. At Euro Disney, Mickey concluded very quickly that our organizational structure was dysfunctional. "You are headed for one of the biggest failures I've ever seen in construction," he told Frank after visiting the site. "Unless something changes, you're never going to get finished on time." As Mickey analyzed it, the firm we'd hired were construction managers. "What we need are project managers who understand the whole process from construction to design to operations," Mickey said. "If you want to spend more on some aspect of design, the project managers' job is to help you find somewhere else to save money. It's all about trade-offs. That's not happening now."

Mickey spent his first six months on the job making lists of unresolved issues. When his analysis was completed, he concluded that the budget for the park had been underestimated, and that it would require an additional $150 million to finish. He also convinced Frank that we needed to bring a far larger contingent of Imagineers over from Glendale. "I'll take responsibility for keeping to the budget you give me," Mickey said, "but our own people are the only ones who have the expertise we need to get this park built." Frank and I went along, but as the opening date grew closer, the pressure of a fixed deadline prompted what is euphemistically termed "acceleration." Put simply, that means doing whatever you have to do to finish the job, including overtime. Solving design and construction problems on an expedited basis was very expensive, but delaying the opening wasn't a viable alternative. The carrying costs of the park were already enormous, and the planned launch date in April 1992 had been chosen to take advantage of the higher attendance we anticipated during the prime spring and summer vacation months.

By far the biggest hidden costs at Euro Disney were those associated with the pre-opening period, including the hiring, training, and housing of some twelve thousand cast members. As our opening date grew closer, it became more obvious that launching such a complex operation from a standing start was a huge logistical challenge. In order to make it happen, we brought in an additional five hundred executives from Walt Disney World for the final five months. They were like a huge army descending on the battlefield. At the same time, work continued on the design and infrastructure for a second theme park at Euro Disney —the Disney-MGM Studios—which we hoped to open two years after the Magic Kingdom. This was all part of a conscious attempt to model the development of EDL after Walt Disney World.

The miracle was that EDL opened as promised on April 12, 1992. In addition to the Magic Kingdom, the resort had six giant hotels; Disney Village, with its restaurants, nightclubs, and Wild West dinner show; the Davy Crockett campsite, which included 400 cabins and 180 campsites; and an 18-hole-golf course. In contrast to the fiasco of Disneyland's opening day, Euro Disney's came off remarkably smoothly. More than twenty thousand people attended, and a television special based on the festivities was beamed to twenty-two countries on four continents. The opening was covered by some five thousand journalists.

Among the stars who showed up to help us celebrate were Candice Bergen, Peter Gabriel, Eddie Murphy, Don Johnson, and Melanie Griffith.

In our initial euphoria, we didn't immediately recognize that we had other, serious problems. Although the park's costs had risen inexorably, we had also revised all of our revenue forecasts upward to reflect our growing confidence. Even so, there were ominous clouds on the horizon. By opening day, Europe generally, and France specifically, had fallen into what would prove to be a deep and sustained recession. The prices that we set for admission, hotel rooms, food, and merchandise were ambitious, but especially so given the poor state of the economy. To make matters worse, the value of the dollar and of several foreign currencies dropped significantly against the French franc during 1992. As a result, the costs at Euro Disney were significantly higher for foreign visitors.

For all that, park attendance was strong enough to make Euro Disney the biggest tourist attraction in Europe virtually overnight. More than 7 million people visited between the April opening and December that year. Operating issues were our primary initial concern. For example, we'd assumed that the French would eat only a light breakfast of croissants and coffee in the hotels. When we discovered that they mostly preferred full sit-down breakfasts, we weren't prepared to handle the demand, and the long lines prompted complaints. We also ran into trouble with a thirty-seven-year-old company policy—no alcohol in the Magic Kingdom. Nearly everyone disagreed with me about this policy for Europe. Marketing studies suggested that we'd sacrificed profits of as much as $11 million a year by not serving alcohol. The press used the decision as a symbol of our alleged insensitivity and even future French president Jacques Chirac kidded me about our barbaric American puritanism.

Over time, these sorts of issues paled in importance. We dealt with the breakfast problem by adding more extensive room service at the hotels, much as we systematically resolved other frustrating but inevitable problems that arise in any start-up operation. As our financial troubles increased, we finally allowed beer and wine. It proved largely irrelevant, generating only a fraction of the revenues that some had envisioned. Much as we'd seen in Japan, the Europeans behaved just like Americans when they came to our parks. Rather than sitting down for extended midday meals, as they might back home in Rome or Paris or Madrid, they bought lunch on the run at our fast-food outlets, and mostly eschewed the beer and wine.

The real problems that we faced were much more fundamental. Initial attendance was only modestly below expectations, but other revenue projections were off more dramatically. Based on our experience at Walt Disney World and our assessment of the European market, we'd estimated room occupancy rates for Euro Disney at 80 to 85 percent. The actual rate turned out to be closer to 60 percent, partly due to the recession, partly because of negative publicity for the park as our troubles mounted. The recession also exacerbated a problem we hadn't fully taken into account—the fact that there is a smaller middle class in Europe than in America, with less discretionary income to spend.

Still, the crowds remained large during the warm months, and none of our Euro Disney executives suggested that we might be headed for serious trouble financially. It was Richard Nanula and Larry Murphy who first began to raise questions about our financial assumptions several months after EDL's opening. In August 1992, Richard wrote a memo making a passionate case for dramatically reducing our costs by making significant cutbacks. The memo was the first clear warning that the park might be headed for a financial crisis. With Larry's support, Richard made the stark point that costs and debt service were outstripping EDL's revenues.

Despite this early warning signal, we moved forward on plans to spend an additional $200 million to add attractions and increase our capacity. Odd as it may seem, this was a prudent move. The first $100 million was spent on new shows and small attractions across the park. With long summer lines, it was clear that we needed more capacity in order to ensure that people didn't wait too long, which would undermine their enjoyment. The second $100 million was for *Space Mountain*, an E-ticket attraction that we believed was critical to creating a second wave of interest in the park after the initial excitement wore off. In addition to providing guests with a strong reason to return to the park, we knew from Walt Disney World and Disneyland that E-ticket attractions are a powerful marketing hook to lure new customers. It would eventually prove to be just that.

In October 1992, seven months after opening, we chose

Philippe Bourguignon to run Euro Disney. Philippe had been oversee-ing development of the hotels at Euro Disney under Peter Rummell. There was a value in having a French executive in the top job, who truly understood the culture, but mostly, he seemed the right executive for the job. Intense and highly emotional, Philippe was also a hardworking, strong leader, as effective with our cast members as with French politi-cians and bankers. It was then that we decided to take Steve Burke out of the Disney Stores and send him over to Paris as Philippe's number two. Steve had already demonstrated his capacity to help build some-thing from the ground up.

Through the fall of 1992, there were still reasons to be hopeful. Europeans were becoming more familiar with the park. Approval ratings from guests were very high, and improving. We expected attendance to jump dramatically during our second summer in 1993. Unfortunately, the bad news continued. As the recession in France deepened, the real estate market collapsed and the potential profits from selling off land evaporated. We'd anticipated that a majority of visitors would make their reservations directly; in fact, only 25 percent did. The rest came through travel agents and wholesalers who were entitled to substantial discounts that reduced our profit margins dramatically. Eventually, bad news, like good news, tends to feed on itself. During the first winter in Paris, the media began to pile on. In addition to continuing to focus on our oper-ational miscues, they now turned their attention to attendance levels, low occupancy rates in hotels, the complaints about high prices, and the continuing hostility to Euro Disney among the French intelligentsia. It didn't help that François Mitterrand, the French president, refused even to visit the park. "It's just not my cup of tea," he was quoted as saying the day before we opened, and then went on ignoring his country's largest new tourist attraction.

In the winter of 1992, Richard and Larry flew to Europe to begin a detailed analysis of our situation at Euro Disney. On an operat-ing basis, it was actually running in the black. The problem was that we also faced the huge costs of servicing a $3 billion debt. Richard and Larry concluded that Euro Disney was literally running out of money. This was a grim forecast, but we continued to hold out hope that atten-dance and hotel occupancy would rise significantly in the summer, and that the economy would finally begin to turn around in Europe. In the meantime, we authorized Larry and Richard to begin working on a turnaround strategy with Philippe and Steve. The task occupied much of the next two months.

On July 23, more than two dozen of our key executives gathered around a large horseshoe table at the Little Nell Hotel in Aspen to discuss Larry and Richard's analysis. I had asked Sid Bass to join us, to draw on his financial expertise. The most pressing decision we faced was whether to continue to develop the Disney-MGM Studios as a second gate. It remained central to our strategy for increasing visitors' length of stay. But the more I listened to the numbers, the harder it became to justify financially. Richard and Larry recommended not just halting work on the second gate but instituting a dramatic set of remedies for the park's troubles. These included a vast reorganization aimed at improving operating efficiency; a shift in marketing and sales strategy to improve the park's image; lowering prices for admission, hotels, food, and merchandise to stimulate demand; and laying off nearly one thousand cast members. The last was especially painful. It was a cutback far bigger than we'd ever before been compelled to undertake at Disney and would cause hardship for a large number of committed people. Even these moves wouldn't be sufficient to fully turn the park around.

"If we successfully implement this strategy," Larry concluded, "we have the potential to increase operating profits by $250 million. Even then, without a substantial financial restructuring, we'll be looking at losses of several hundred million dollars in 1994 and 1995."

Frank and I agreed that the second park would have to be put on hold. We also authorized the launch of what was sure to be a difficult negotiation with the banks that financed Euro Disney about restructuring our debt. All of this would prompt more bad press for Euro Disney —and for Disney generally—and almost certainly further dampen attendance at the park. It was a bitter pill to swallow, but in the end there seemed to be no better alternative. The meeting was especially hard on Philippe and Steve, who now had to go back to Paris and implement the cutbacks. Distressing as I found all these events, there was never a single moment—including that morning—when I lost faith in EDL. We still had a great park at a great location. We faced a business crisis, a blazing one at that, but I'd faced similar crises, albeit on smaller scales, nearly every week for thirty years. Although others at our meeting probably would have disagreed, my main feeling as we ended was one of optimism. I believed that we'd faced the worst of our problems.

The next challenge was dealing with the banks. Almost immediately, we hired Lazard Frères, the investment firm, to help us with restructuring, in large part based on their relationships with the leading French banks in the consortium that had helped to finance Euro Disney. One of the first decisions we made was to have The Walt Disney Company advance Euro Disney a substantial sum to cover the shortfall in operating the park over the next six months while we negotiated with the banks. This decision ensured a substantial drag on our 1993 earnings, but it also put all the pain behind us right away. Taking one big hit, we believed, would protect our shareholders down the road. On the afternoon of Thursday, November 4, 1993, Frank, Richard, and I met in my Burbank office and agreed on a $350 million reserve or write-off against Disney's earnings. Of that, $150 million would go to cover Euro Disney's anticipated shortfall during the next six months and $200 million to cover initial costs for the aborted second gate.

Several days later, I placed a call to Antoine Jeancourt-Galignani, a member of the board of Euro Disney and also the president of IndoSuez, one of the two French banks that led the financing of the park. I laid out the financial situation for him very starkly. "Obviously, we want very much to save Euro Disney," I said, "but we're not prepared to put the Disney company at risk to do so. We're going to need help from the banks." What I left unsaid but implicit was that if the talks failed, we were prepared to let the park go into bankruptcy, or even to close it altogether. I was telling Galignani something that directly affected his own bank's interests, as well as EDL's. Within a day, my news was creating considerable consternation among the executives at the other banks which had lent EDL money. The negotiations were underway.

Because the banks had far more cash invested in Euro Disney than we did, it wasn't in their interests to allow the park to go into bankruptcy, and certainly not to close. For us, the risk was less financial than it was the impact on the credibility of the Disney brand, and our sense of obligation to the Euro Disney shareholders and to the banks. For the shareholders, we could best serve their long-term interests by taking decisive action to put EDL back on sound financial footing. As for the banks, from whom we had borrowed, we felt a responsibility to pay the money back, and fully intended to do so, but we needed some relief in the time frame. If the onus of saving the park was left solely to us, it would require putting Disney into a financial black hole for a decade, and we weren't prepared to do that to our own shareholders. The key was to convince the banks to share the costs of restructuring. It probably helped that I had a reputation for being willing to walk away from deals when the terms didn't seem reasonable. I was reluctantly prepared to do that in this case, if it became necessary, but in my heart of hearts, it was inconceivable to give up on EDL.

In late November, we acknowledged that we had created a reserve and were prepared to fund Euro Disney through March 31, 1994—but not longer without help from the banks. In my annual letter to our shareholders that December, I was direct about the crisis we faced. During a year in which each of our other businesses rated an "A" on a report card, I wrote, "Disneyland in Europe, if only judged by the financial performance, was barely a 'D.'" I also took the opportunity to send a more indirect message to the banks: "We are working with all interested parties to help restructure Euro Disney's financial condition. But as we cannot shoulder the entire burden ourselves, other parties must bear their fair share. . . . We will deal in good faith with our fellow Euro Disney shareholders and Euro Disney creditors. But in doing so, I promise all shareholders of The Walt Disney Company that we will take no action to endanger the health of Disney itself."

The negotiations with the banks went almost nowhere for the next two months. The banks took the hard line that EDL was our problem and our responsibility to remedy. In early January 1994, three months from our funding deadline, Sandy Litvack, our general counsel, entered the picture. He had traveled to Paris to work on a relatively narrow legal issue in the case. Until that point, Sandy had been increasingly frustrated by Frank's failure to increase his responsibilities. As it turned out, Sandy made a strong impression on the banks' negotiators, and they asked him to stay on in a broader negotiating role. If anyone could help to break the logjam, he seemed a likely candidate. In addition to being exceptionally bright and analytical, Sandy has a calm, reasonable way of discussing any given issue.

With help from Richard Nanula, Sandy took over the negotiations for our side. In less than a week, the banks backed off their blanket refusal to consider any sort of compromise, but neither side put a viable restructuring proposal on the table. Sandy, I later learned, felt that he was in an impossible position. From his perspective, he was negotiating with two clients—the banks on one side, and Frank and me on the other— and neither of us was prepared to be realistic. Meanwhile, the clock kept ticking toward the March 31 deadline.

Unquestionably, this high-stakes poker game carried dangers. Sandy referred to them by the abbreviation OBE, short for "Overtaken By Events." The term had evolved during his tenure in the Carter Administration Justice Department. "It refers to a situation in which *both* sides lose control of the outcome and surrounding events take over," he later told me. One possibility was that if we failed to come to an agreement, the issue would be decided in a bankruptcy proceeding. That was especially alarming because this proceeding would take place in the small town of Meaux. Not surprisingly, the town judge had never before handled a bankruptcy—much less one of the largest bankruptcy cases in modern European history. This was a source of concern to both sides, but especially to us. "We are the ugly Americans in this case," Frank told me. "Guess who has the hometown advantage?"

The situation took a turn for the worse on the morning of Thursday, February 17, 1994, when the formal negotiating session in Paris began with an opening statement from a lawyer representing the banks. To Sandy and Richard's astonishment, the thrust of his remarks was that Disney had been guilty of a series of illegal financial maneuvers at Euro Disney. "We are prepared to prove a detailed pattern of fraud and theft," the lawyer read calmly.

Sandy was apoplectic. In his mind we were in the middle of a difficult but good faith negotiation, and suddenly the other side was introducing preposterous claims about criminal activity. When his adversary finished, Sandy stood up and delivered his own terse rebuttal. Then he motioned to Richard and the rest of our group to follow him out of the meeting. "We're cutting off negotiations and going home until such time as we have a full apology," he announced. With that dramatic flourish, he led our team out the door. As soon as he was back in his hotel, Sandy called Frank to tell him what had just happened. Frank loved this sort of intrigue and believed it was all just part of the negotiation, even a sign that things were finally moving. "Just check out of your hotel, so they think you've really gone home, and then move into another one," Frank told him. "I promise you they'll get back in contact with you."

"I'm not going to play games," Sandy replied. "We're coming home." He boarded a plane and, sure enough, within a couple of days he received a call at home in Los Angeles from one of our bankers at Lazard Frères, who had been contacted by the other side.

"They feel we overreacted," Sandy was told, "and they don't understand why you were so insulted. They want to get back together as soon as possible." I was in Orlando preparing for our annual meeting when Frank called on a Saturday afternoon to update me. "This may just be the event that turns the negotiation around," he told me.

Sandy and Richard returned to Paris the next week, but their first meeting proved uneventful. The following Monday, February 28, Sandy was sitting around with David Supino, the head of our negotiating team from Lazard Frères in New York. On an impulse, Sandy wrote down a settlement proposal on a piece of paper, essentially splitting the costs of a restructuring equally with the banks. "There's no way on God's green earth that Michael or Frank would ever let me suggest this," Sandy told Supino, "but what do you think of it?"

Supino took a quick look. "I think it makes sense," he replied. They agreed to ask David Dautresme, the managing partner of Lazard Frères in Paris, to sit down that afternoon with several of the bank's key representatives and make the proposal to them. "We have no permission from our client to make this deal," Dautresme would truthfully say. "However, the hour is late, and we all know what happens if we can't make an agreement. If you say yes to what we are suggesting, we're prepared to go back and fight for it." In effect, this tactic gave Sandy deniability. He could simply drop the proposal if it were not well received—either by the banks or by Frank and me.

In all likelihood, we wouldn't have authorized Sandy to make his offer. It was very close to the deal that everyone on our team had long since agreed would be an acceptable compromise. On the other hand, Frank and I were concerned that the banks might view any proposal we made not as a final offer, but as a new point from which to resume negotiating. In fact, the banks responded favorably to Dautresme's approach, with a few small caveats. While the proposal involved a series of highly complicated financial transactions, it was very simple at heart.

We offered to defer all of our royalties and management fees at Euro Disney for the next five years, and a smaller percentage of them for an additional five years. In turn, we asked the banks to forgive all interest payments on Euro Disney's debt for sixteen months, and to defer principal payments for three years. Under this agreement, we would together pump $1 billion into the park—half of which we would agree to buy if it didn't sell to the public, the other half to be similarly underwritten by the banks. In effect, these transactions would cut the park's debt from $4 billion to $3 billion.

There was just one other problem. By this point, we were deeply concerned about maintaining the security of our conversations. Our suspicions were first aroused when confidential information kept showing up in the press. This led Richard and Sandy to a series of bizarre actions right out of a spy novel. In an effort to find secure telephone lines, for example, they would venture out of their hotel in sweatpants in the middle of the night and call Frank from a pay phone with some particularly important information. When we spoke from hotel or office phones, Frank and I were reluctant to sound too enthusiastic about the deal that Sandy and Richard believed they were on the verge of closing. We still feared that any enthusiasm from us would somehow get back to the banks, leading them to push for tougher terms at the eleventh hour.

In late afternoon on Thursday, March 3, Sandy called Frank again from a pay phone in Paris, and Frank delivered a cryptic instruction: "Close the best deal you can." By the end of the day, Sandy and Richard had reached an agreement in principle with representatives for the lead banks. At 8:00 p.m. Paris time—11:00 a.m. Los Angeles time—Sandy and Richard called Frank and me to deliver the news. We spent the next hour challenging every aspect of the deal.

"It's too generous," Frank said.

"The board will never approve it, and in any case, we'll never be able to sell it to Sid Bass," I warned. By the time the call ended, Sandy was absolutely enraged. What he didn't realize was that we were playacting, just in case anyone was listening in on the conversation.

Later that evening, Sandy called Frank. "I just want you to know how angry I was about your reaction," Sandy said. "We made a good and fair deal, and all you did was criticize it." Frank was distraught but felt he still couldn't risk revealing our ruse. Instead, he tracked down Steve Burke, who happened to be in London on his way back to Paris, and asked him to visit Sandy personally and explain everything as soon as possible. Once again, it became high melodrama. Steve met Sandy and Richard at their hotel, insisted that they walk through the streets of Paris, and only then revealed the true story.

The deal was announced publicly on March 14, the same day as our annual meeting and exactly two weeks before the March 31 deadline we had set. For the first time in two years, we had some breathing room. Rumors that the resort might close had already dampened attendance and cut into reservations for the upcoming summer season. However, the reorganization of the resort was well underway, including price cuts on everything from admission tickets to hotel rooms to food. More than nine hundred jobs had been eliminated, by far the most painful part of the process for Philippe and Steve. The worst was now behind us. At long last, we could focus all of our attention on simply making Euro Disney a great theme park.

We'd built a unique resort. Our commitment to excellence was expensive, and we made plenty of mistakes along the way, but I was more confident than ever that the park would endure and prosper over time. The decision to change its name—something we had been discussing for months—now took on a symbolic importance. As Americans, we had believed that the word "Euro" in front of Disney was glamorous and exciting. For Europeans, it turned out to be a term they associated with business, currency, and commerce. Renaming the park "Disneyland Paris" was a way of identifying it not just with Walt's original creation but with one of the most romantic and exciting cities in the world. As spring approached, we were shedding our old skin and preparing to be reborn.

II

Death in the Family

WHEN FRANK AND I SAT DOWN TO TALK IN MY OFFICE LATE ON FRIDAY, April 1, 1994, we had reasons to feel both hopeful and concerned. Three weeks earlier, we'd finally concluded the Disneyland Paris financial restructuring that had occupied so much of our time and attention during the previous six months. There were undeniably more issues ahead. Attendance at the domestic parks remained flat, and Disney's performance in live action was still poor. We continued to be concerned about a growing blend of complacency and self-satisfaction, and a diminution of the passionate team spirit that marked the early years. No one was more openly restless than Jeffrey Katzenberg. Important as he had been to our success, Frank and I agreed that unless we could inspire Jeffrey to become a team player again, it might be necessary to part ways. What seemed clear was that the time had come to renew the company for a second time—to move some of our young executives around, to rethink our existing businesses, and to explore new ones, despite the short-term pain and dislocation such changes were likely to cause.

The encouraging news was that Disney remained strong on many fronts, and that Frank and I were going to be facing the challenges ahead together. For months, we had been discussing the length of Frank's contract extension, and he'd finally come to a decision. "I'm going to sign on for seven more years," he told me that afternoon. Having put the dream of conquering Mount Everest on indefinite hold at the age of sixty-two, Frank now satisfied his taste for outdoor adventure with smaller expeditions like the one he was just about to undertake—a weekend of helicopter skiing in the mountains of Nevada with his older son Kevin, his friend Clint Eastwood, and several other fellow adventurers. We agreed that when he returned on Monday morning, we'd finalize his contract and turn our attention to the job ahead. It had been a long winter.

Easter Sunday, two days later, proved to be an unexpectedly lovely and relaxed day. For perhaps the third time in twenty-five years, I played golf. Jane and I had lived most of our adult lives in Los Angeles, without ever belonging to a country club. The previous fall we had finally succumbed to the pleas of our two younger sons, who wanted to learn how to play golf, and joined the Bel Air Country Club. And then, of course, I was too busy ever to get there. But this was a beautiful spring day, free of the aftershocks that had punctuated our lives for weeks following the January earthquake in nearby Northridge. On the spur of the moment, Jane, our fourteen-year-old, Anders, and I decided to visit the country club for the first time. I wasn't really prepared to play. My clubs, long abused by my children, were nowhere to be found, and my golf shoes turned out to have been eaten by Cadillac, our longhair German shepherd.

But I borrowed clubs from the club's golf pro and he sent us off with a caddie. I was pleasantly surprised to find I could still hit a golf ball reasonably well, but none of us worried too much about scores. We just enjoyed each other's company. The round took longer than expected, mostly because we each hit numerous shots into the trees, or sprayed them into the waterholes. We were expected at the home of our oldest son, Breck, at 5:00 p.m. He and his girlfriend, Kris Jones, were cooking an Easter dinner for us and for her parents, who were visiting from New York. By the time we arrived, it was nearly 6:00 p.m. Breck was upset that we were late, but he seemed to get over it pretty quickly. Just before 6:30 p.m., we sat down to eat at a dining-room table that had once belonged to my grandmother and that we had recently passed on to Breck. I was struck by the transition this event represented—having my son and his girlfriend serving their parents dinner. Five minutes into the meal, we vaguely heard the phone ring. Breck stood up and when he came back, he said that the call was from Lucille, my secretary. Immediately, I sensed that something was wrong. Lucille was very protective of my rare moments of privacy. For her to call on a Sunday evening, in the middle of a family dinner, was uncharacteristic.

"Michael," she said, as soon as I picked up the phone, "Frank is dead. He was just killed in a helicopter accident."

I felt instantly numb. "What happened?" I heard myself asking. Lucille had only sketchy details. The helicopter carrying back Frank, two of his friends, and a guide from their ski trip had crashed somewhere in the mountains of Nevada. The pilot and all but one passenger had died. Frank's son, Kevin, Clint Eastwood, and several others had been in different helicopters. It seemed impossible to fathom. I told Lucille that I would call her back and took a moment to try to absorb the news. Then I called Jane over, so that I could tell her privately, first. "Frank is dead," I blurted out. She screamed, and everyone at the dinner table jumped up. Jane started crying. I told the others what had happened, and said that I had to return home immediately. Jane came with me.

My reaction in crisis has always been to set my emotions aside and to focus on the issue at hand. It would be weeks before the enormity of the loss really hit me. In the meantime, I operated largely on automatic. As soon as we arrived home, I began making phone calls. I found Sid Bass at a restaurant in Aspen, where he was having dinner with his wife Mercedes and friends. I reached Stanley Gold—one of Frank's oldest friends, and a member of our board—on his car phone. With Lucille's help, I also managed to track down Roy Disney and Irwin Russell, my longtime lawyer, both members of our board. I spoke with each of them about what immediate steps we could take to stabilize the company. We agreed that I should make no dramatic moves. Next, I reached John Dreyer, who handles corporate public relations. "I'd like you to go to the office and start on a press release," I told him. John wrote a first draft, but in this case, I later felt compelled to write my own version, perhaps partly as a way to begin dealing with the reality of Frank's death.

Lucille helped me to reach the other members of our board of directors, as well as Jeffrey and the other key members of the Disney team. I asked each of them to pass on the news through their own divisions. At about 8:00 p.m., Jane and I got in the car to drive up to see

Frank's wife, Luanne, at their beach home in Malibu. Their younger son, Briant, was already there. Kevin, whose helicopter had left just before Frank's, was on his way. We set out on the Pacific Coast Highway and halfway up traffic stopped completely. The highway was blocked off with ambulances, police cars, and an evacuation helicopter. A pedestrian had apparently been hit crossing the highway. Suddenly, it seemed almost surreal—to be stuck in traffic, desperate to see Luanne, detained by another horrible tragedy.

By the time we reached the house, it was crowded with people. Both Briant and Kevin were there. Luanne was in her bedroom with a close friend. Beautiful and elegant, Luanne shared many of Frank's best qualities—kindness, grace, modesty, a strong social conscience. Kevin had hoped to reach Briant so that Briant could be the one to break the news to his mother. But instead, Shari Kimoto, Frank's longtime secretary, heard about the crash from one of our pilots and called to tell Luanne. Shari drove to the house immediately, and others began arriving in a steady stream. As people so often do in the face of tragedy, they wanted to offer whatever help they could. Understandably, Luanne looked overwhelmed.

Jane and I stayed several hours and finally drove home after midnight, exhausted. When I awoke the next morning, I spoke again with Sid Bass, Irwin Russell, Stanley Gold, Roy Disney, and Sandy Litvack. They all agreed that the best course was for me to assume Frank's titles as president and chief operating officer, at least temporarily. We decided to release a statement to that effect later in the day. In part, the purpose was to send an immediate signal to Wall Street and the financial community that business at Disney would continue as usual. Equally important, I wanted to put to rest speculation that anyone was in line to inherit Frank's job.

My immediate priorities were Frank's family, the funeral arrangements and the literally hundreds of condolence calls that were pouring in. It was also important to find a way to comfort and reassure the members of the Disney company family. Many of them were reeling in the face of a loss that was devastating both professionally and personally. Rather than cancel our regular Monday staff lunch, I decided to use it to try to build morale and to make some attempt to carry on business. I hadn't yet found a comfortable way to discuss Frank's death, nor had anyone else. The lunch was awkward and sad. Just as we were about to leave, I announced that I would be taking over Frank's president's title, at least for the time being. I worried about Jeffrey's reaction. The tension between us had grown in the six months since our walk in Aspen. But to my relief, he handled the news gracefully. "That's completely appropriate," he said, as we walked out. When I arrived back at my office, feeling guilty that I hadn't brought Jeffrey into my inner circle, I decided to call and invite him to dinner that evening at our usual location, Locanda Veneta. He readily agreed.

"I've canceled all my appointments," he told me. "I'm available to do anything I can to help." I spent the rest of the afternoon returning calls, conferring with Jody Dreyer, my assistant—who was working with the Wells family to coordinate funeral arrangements—and starting to think about what sort of memorial service was appropriate for Frank.

Dinner with Jeffrey was surprisingly uneventful. I didn't mention the presidency and neither did he. I did bring along a memo that Frank had finished writing the previous Friday. It described the responsibilities that we'd agreed to add to Jeffrey's job in the wake of our Aspen talk. These included overseeing the theater division; Hollywood Records; our new video game business; and our prospective partnership with several telephone companies to develop a new interactive programming service. Before I began to discuss the memo, Jeffrey interrupted me. "Let's discuss all this after the dust settles," he said.

Apparently, that didn't take long. When I checked in with Jeffrey the next morning, I immediately sensed tension in his voice. "I'd like to talk with you as soon as possible," he said. I asked Lucille to arrange a lunch for us in one of the private rooms off the main executive dining room. The fireworks began the moment we sat down. In contrast to the previous evening, he now took a hard line. "I'm hurt," he began. "I can't believe that you didn't offer me the job as president as soon as you found out about Frank's death on Sunday. I assumed that you decided to take his title as a short-term corporate thing, but I was amazed that you didn't bring it up at dinner last night. After eighteen years together, I've earned the right to be your partner."

"I'd rather not discuss this now," I said. "Let's concentrate on Frank." But Jeffrey wouldn't drop it.

"You can trust me to be as good as Frank," he blurted out.

At that point I jumped in. I hated having to be blunt, but I felt compelled to explain my position. "The issue is whether I consider you to be the right person for the job," I told Jeffrey. "I don't trust you in the same way I did Frank and it's impossible for me to consider a partnership without that level of trust. I've talked to you many times about your being so secretive and shutting me out, and pursuing your own agenda."

"The situation has changed," Jeffrey responded calmly. "The way things are now, I would be the perfect partner."

But that was precisely my concern. It was one thing to run the movie division, where Jeffrey's skills were proven and his business was largely limited to Hollywood. As president, he would be representing the company every day around the world. In my view, which was shared by members of our board, he hadn't yet demonstrated the stature, maturity, and judgment needed to be the president of a company that served as many constituencies as Disney did.

"Despite all the problems we've had, I would still consider the possibility down the road," I said. "We'll have to see how it goes."

Jeffrey grew more outraged. "I'm not going to audition for you after eighteen years," he said. "You ought to know me by now."

"It's not just about me," I responded. "You also have a serious problem with Roy Disney and other board members." Just the previous evening, Stanley Gold had told me that Roy was prepared to resign from the board of directors if Jeffrey was named to Frank's job. "Roy doesn't think you're ready to be president," I explained, "and neither do other members of the board. Why is it that you wine and dine the press and agents and actors and people like Steven Spielberg, but you can't reach out to Roy, who is the soul of this company and the person responsible for bringing us all here?"

"I can and I will," Jeffrey replied. "During the next sixty to ninety days, it will be done."

"You're being naive," I responded.

The conversation jockeyed back and forth, but it ended on a tense, negative note. As we finished, I put a question to him point-blank: "Are you saying to me that if I don't commit to make you president of The Walt Disney Company within the next sixty to ninety days, you will leave?"

"That's correct," Jeffrey replied.

When I returned to my office, I called and asked Sandy Litvack to come in. From the moment I had shared the news of Frank's death with him, Sandy had offered sound, thoughtful advice. Already, I found myself beginning to reach out to him as I had with Frank. Because Sandy was less emotionally involved with Jeffrey than I was, I asked that he try to serve as a mediator.

But Jeffrey's anger only seemed to grow. By the time Sandy returned from their meeting, he was outraged by what he felt was Jeffrey's inappropriate timing and his aggressiveness. He also feared that Jeffrey wouldn't be satisfied by any role but president. "We should try to see if we can satisfy him short of making him president," Sandy said, "but if we can't, there is probably no choice but to let him run out his contract and leave."

Plainly, passions were running high. For Jeffrey to quit immediately after Frank's death would only prompt more media attention, compound the company's trauma, and exacerbate the sense of anxiety that our employees were already feeling. On a practical level, we were just two weeks from opening *Beauty and the Beast* on Broadway and eight weeks from releasing *The Lion King* in movie theaters. I was especially loath to lose Jeffrey before those projects were launched. As I had done so often before, I found myself operating on two separate tracks. On one level, I was fed up, angry, and absolutely convinced that the only solution was to let Jeffrey quit. On another level, I still valued his strengths running our movie division and continued to believe that somehow things would all work out in the end.

On Wednesday morning, I called Jeffrey again, this time to calm the waters. I could tell he had cooled down overnight and perhaps had second thoughts about his approach. "I wish the subject of Frank's job had never come up," I told him. "This is no time to try to resolve our situation, and I'm not going to address the issue again for weeks."

To my surprise, Jeffrey was conciliatory. "That's fine," he said, "even if it takes several months." I felt relieved. My hope was that Jeffrey's aggressive behavior the previous day had been prompted by his own emotional reaction to Frank's death.

With that crisis on hold, I was free to devote all of my attention to Frank and his family. The funeral was held on Friday, April 8. It was limited to approximately one hundred friends and family members, and his son Kevin gave a moving eulogy. In all likelihood, Frank would have resisted a more public memorial on his behalf, but even Luanne agreed that it was important to offer his vast circle of friends and colleagues the opportunity to gather and mourn his death together. We set the memorial service for three days later—April 11—and decided to close the studio for the day and hold the service on the lot.

One of the first ideas for how to commemorate Frank arose during a call I received the day after his death from the Reverend Cecil Murray, the minister of the First African Methodist Episcopal (AME) Church, in south-central Los Angeles. In the aftermath of the riots that followed the Rodney King, Jr., verdict in 1992, Frank had typically jumped into the fray, looking for ways that Disney could make a difference to community residents who'd been hit the hardest. We made an immediate financial contribution and scores of volunteers from Disney went to work on the cleanup. We also set up a Disneyland jobs program, donated funds for a childcare facility, and opened a Disney Store in South-Central to be staffed with members of the local community. Perhaps our most significant idea was to start our Microloan Program, which eventually provided funding to sixty-eight start-up businesses in South-Central. In the process, we sought out Reverend Murray, whose church ran a number of outreach programs in the neighborhood. He ended up inviting Frank and me down for church services one Sunday. I still smile at the memory of standing on the pulpit alongside Frank and the members of the First AME choir. I felt a bit awkward and out of place, but Frank shared none of my inhibitions. When I looked over, he was swaying from side to side, clapping his hands, totally immersed in the music.

Now, two years later, Reverend Murray was calling to offer his condolences. I told him about our plans to hold a memorial and invited him to attend. "Would you like our choir to perform?" he asked. I told him that would be fantastic.

By early afternoon Monday, nearly five thousand people had gathered on our lot. Some had flown halfway around the world to be there. When I stood up to open the memorial, the loss hit me full force for the first time. I felt choked up and found it difficult to get my words out. "I am an expert on Frank," I began. "I spoke more often with him than any single person over the last ten years. Luanne and Briant and Kevin and Frank's mother, Betty, and his sisters and brothers and in-laws and nephews and nieces lived and played with Frank. But I talked and met and thought with Frank from sunrise to sundown—no, from sunrise to sunrise—almost every day of the year."

I spoke about our first days at Disney back in 1984, our last afternoon together, and the amazing ten-year adventure in between. "More than anyone I have ever met, Frank was willing to embrace the most creative and theatrical ideas. He was a man unfettered by jealousy, competition, or personal ambition. His personal agenda was the company's agenda. Every minute of every business day Frank was out for the interests of The Walt Disney Company. He was a man who held a moral compass that was always true." Finally, I talked about his energy and commitment. "Sleep was Frank's enemy," I said. "Frank thought that it kept him from performing flat out 100 percent of the time. There was always one more meeting he wanted to have. Sleep, he thought, kept him from getting things done. He fought it constantly. But sleep . . . Frank's enemy . . . finally won."

The range of speakers who followed were a testament to Frank's wide interests: Clint Eastwood, his former client and fellow adventurer; Bob Daly, the head of Warner Bros., who compared Frank to Clark Kent—"a tall, unassuming man with glasses but Superman underneath"; Warren Miller, a longtime skiing buddy who described him as "a man who lived and created life every day at 8,000 miles an hour"; and Robert Redford, with whom Frank shared a passion for the environment. Finally, Frank's younger son, Briant, made the simplest and most moving comment of all. "Dad," he said, closing the tributes, "I wish we had more time. You are my hero."

It was nearly a month before I found myself resuming a routine at work. The first possibility of a replacement for Frank arose unexpectedly when I attended a fund-raising dinner chaired by Stanley Gold, our board member, on May 2. The honoree and dinner speaker was Senator George Mitchell of Maine, then the Senate majority leader. Mitchell had recently announced his intention to leave the Senate by year's end after a long, distinguished career. As he spoke, I was impressed by his quiet passion, his common sense, and his obvious decency. I especially liked the fact that he communicated such passion about the importance of ethics in public life. Somewhere at midspeech, it occurred to me that he might make a strong president of The Walt Disney Company.

Mitchell had no experience running a company and knew little about the entertainment business, but he had other attractive assets—stature, class, judgment, and the practiced skills of a mediator. If we brought Mitchell in, I could continue to run the company creatively, Sandy could operate as my chief of staff, and Mitchell would effectively become our secretary of state—a critical role in any increasingly global company. Over the next two months, I had several long conversations with him. Ultimately, we decided not to proceed, in part because he still felt the desire to stay involved with public policy, and in part because he preferred to continue to live on the East Coast. Mitchell did finally agree to serve on our board of directors, but my search for a president continued.

During this period, I launched into a travel schedule that was frenetic even by my standards. On Saturday, June 11, en route to New York for the Tony Awards, Jane and I stopped over in Sioux City, Iowa, to watch Anders play in a hockey tournament. Over the next thirty days, I flew cross-country four separate times, traveled to fifteen different cities, and never spent more than forty-eight hours in Los Angeles at one stretch. I began to pursue other candidates to replace Frank, most notably Michael Ovitz. I attended premieres of *The Lion King* in New York and in Washington, D.C. I traveled to Orlando and to Chicago to promote the opening of our newest attraction at Epcot, *Innoventions*, which was designed to showcase the products of the near future. We also negotiated a deal with Saudi prince Al-Waleed in which he agreed to pay 1 billion francs for 20 percent of our new stock offering in Disneyland Paris. The deal not only reduced our exposure but had a broader impact on the park. "The prince's action," wrote *The Wall Street Journal*, "sends a message that an outside investor—and one who has shown considerable sophistication—has a belief in the ultimate success of the resort." Finally, we began preliminary discussions with General Electric about acquiring NBC.

When I returned at last to the office on July 5, one of my first calls was from Joe Roth. Two years earlier, in late 1992, Jeffrey and I had recruited Joe from Twentieth Century Fox, where he'd been chairman of the motion picture division. We agreed to finance his own small studio, which he named Caravan Pictures. In his mid-forties, Joe retained his youthful, Kennedyesque good looks, with longish hair, a toothy smile, and a perpetual squint. Even as an executive, he continued to dress casually in jeans and sport shirts, looking slightly uncomfortable on the rare occasions that he had to wear a suit. His background as both a producer and a director had helped to make Joe much more popular in the creative community than most studio executives. But while his style was relaxed and low-key, Joe was very disciplined, and highly competitive.

Funding Caravan was a way for Disney to produce more films without adding to the burden of the team at our existing labels. Jeffrey also saw Joe as someone who could eventually take over his job, freeing him to move up at the company. On this occasion, Joe was calling to remind me that the premiere for Caravan's next movie, *Angels in the Outfield*, was scheduled for the following Sunday at Three Rivers Stadium in Pittsburgh. "We're expecting thirty thousand people," he told me. "Would you consider attending and introducing the film to the crowd?" I wasn't eager to travel cross-country again, least of all for a movie premiere. However, with Jeffrey's future uncertain, Joe now struck me as the best candidate to take over as head of our movie division. Attending his premiere was an opportunity to show my support and to get to know him better.

"Jane and I are planning to spend the weekend at our house in Aspen," I said. "Why don't you and Donna and your kids join us, and then we can all fly to Pittsburgh together on Sunday." Joe seemed a little surprised by the invitation but promised to check with his wife. As soon as I hung up the phone, I called Jane to make sure that she had no other plans. Fortunately, she didn't. Minutes later, Joe called back. "We'd love to come," he said.

Joe and Donna were easy, gracious houseguests and our time together was relaxed and enjoyable. Their kids were five and ten, and I appreciated Joe's obvious closeness to his family. He brought the same passion and tenacity to coaching his kids' soccer teams that he did to his work. In the course of the weekend, we all went horseback riding, fishing, and hiking together. At one point, I experienced some shortness of breath while hiking, but I attributed it to the altitude. Mostly, I enjoyed the chance to spend time with Joe and Donna. Donna's father, I discovered, is the producer Samuel Z. Arkoff, who founded American International Pictures, a quirky independent movie company, and Donna had become an independent producer herself. Her latest film, *Benny and Joon*, with Johnny Depp, had opened a few months earlier.

Joe was raised in Roslyn Heights on Long Island. His father made a modest living running a plastics manufacturing business, but his passion was social activism. In 1958, when New York State began requiring children to recite the Regent's Prayer at school each day, Joe's father viewed it as a violation of the separation of church and state and recruited an ACLU lawyer to file a lawsuit. Joe, then ten, and his thirteen-year-old brother became two of the plaintiffs in the case. In 1962, the Supreme Court finally ruled that enforced prayer in schools was unconstitutional. Joe and his brother became pariahs at school. The family's house was picketed by the American Nazi Party and a cross made of kerosene-soaked rags was set on fire in their driveway. By his own description, the experience fueled his self-image as an outsider.

After college, Joe's first job was as a production assistant and gofer on a film at Zoetrope, Francis Coppola's company. Over the next decade, Joe made his living producing small independent movies and running a comedy club. His breakthrough came in 1986, when he hooked up with a wealthy Baltimore car dealer named Jim Robinson. Together, they launched a company called Morgan Creek and had a run of hit movies—among them *Robin Hood*, *Major League*, *Young Guns*, and *Dead Ringers* —that was rare for an independent. Most of the films were distributed by Fox. In 1989, Barry Diller and Rupert Murdoch recruited Joe to revive Fox's faltering movie division.

Once again, he oversaw a number of successful films, including *Home Alone*, *Sleeping With the Enemy*, *White Men Can't Jump*, *My Cousin Vinny*, and *Mrs. Doubtfire*. But by early 1992, Barry had left. When Murdoch declined to reward Joe with a better contract, he began looking for a new job. Several studios were interested, but he was drawn to Disney by an offer that blended the financing to make movies and the independence that he coveted. Caravan struggled with its first several films, but *Angels in the Outfield* looked as if it might become the label's first hit. In the course of our weekend together in Aspen we never talked directly about Jeffrey's job, but I asked Joe dozens of questions about his Caravan projects, his interests, his ambitions, and his views about our motion picture division in general. By the time we flew to Pittsburgh late Sunday afternoon, I was confident that he could do a very effective job running the studio.

The screening of *Angels in the Outfield* at Three Rivers Stadium was orchestrated by Dick Cook, who had grown up in the parks before moving to movie distribution and marketing. He had a great instinct for creating theatrical extravaganzas. This was a good example. By tying it to the baseball All-Star game, the movie was assured national media attention less than a week before it opened. A sweet, unabashedly sentimental fantasy, *Angels* seemed certain to find a large audience among kids.

Having reassured myself about Joe, I felt free to turn my attention to the other key piece in our personnel puzzle: a president to replace Frank. On the flight back to Los Angeles with Jane, I spent much of the time thinking out loud about the pluses and minuses of pursuing Michael Ovitz. Three days later, we had agreed to discuss the job when we flew together to Sun Valley for Herb Allen's annual conference.

"Ovitz has the potential to take a lot off my back," I told Jane. "I also think the business community would applaud our getting him. My biggest question is whether he could tolerate being number two, and whether he would be a team player. You have to understand, I don't want to feel as if I'm in competition with anybody. There's enough pressure in my job without having to worry about reaching an impasse on an important issue. My fear with Michael is that he would always need to be in the driver's seat. I don't know if I want to fight for the steering wheel for the next ten years."

"My interest is simple," Jane said. "I want your life to be easier. Don't you think this could help?"

"I'm just not sure how to say any of this to Michael," I replied. "If he starts having the idea that I'm someone who won't let him change a menu item in the commissary, that will scare him away. The truth is that I'm very happy to have all the divisions report to him, so long as he lets me know what he's doing. If we can agree on that, it could be a fantastic partnership."

During our flight together to Sun Valley, Ovitz made it clear he had little interest in becoming number two. Two days later, before we had a chance to finish our discussion, the issue became moot. The shortness of breath I'd felt hiking in Aspen the week before with the Roths turned out to have been an early warning signal. After returning to Los Angeles from Sun Valley late Friday, I found myself undergoing emergency quadruple bypass surgery. Within hours of waking up the next morning, Ovitz was standing by my bedside, having cut short a planned family vacation and returned to the role of my longtime friend. In his characteristic way, Ovitz took charge, to the point of posting guards outside the door and suggesting that we bring in a doctor from nearby UCLA for a second opinion.

My plan, before the surgery, had been to spend most of the month of August in Aspen. I was looking forward to the chance to relax in the wake of the three frenetic months that followed Frank's death. Now my doctors told me that Aspen's altitude made it a less than optimal place to recover from bypass surgery. Instead, I faced an enforced rest at home in Los Angeles. My main activity for the next several weeks was likely to be sleeping. "Don't think about returning to the office for at least a month," the doctors told me. "It will be at least two months before you have the strength or the stamina to resume anything close to a full-time schedule."

Despite these limitations, an unwelcome and final act in the drama with Jeffrey began to unfold soon after I awoke from surgery. In retrospect, I see that we were in the last stages of an unraveling professional marriage. After years of tension and attempts at reconciliation, the atmosphere between us had deteriorated into one of accelerating distrust. We were each now capable of being set off by the other in ways that we might once have simply let go by. By the time Jeffrey came to see me at the hospital on Sunday, there was a subtext of tension and awkwardness between us. Rather than being supportive and offering to do what he could to help, he seemed distant and uncomfortable.

Business at Disney continued in my absence, including the talks about acquiring NBC, under the code name "Project Brazil." A strategy meeting had been scheduled for the Monday morning after my planned return from Sun Valley, but obviously I couldn't attend. Instead, Stanley Gold, who had helped initiate the talks with NBC, came in to meet with Richard Nanula, Larry Murphy, and their teams. Both Richard and Larry had for years been strong voices opposing the acquisition of a television network. None of the major networks, they argued, was growing at anywhere near the 20 percent rate we set as our benchmark at Disney and had achieved for all but one of the past ten years. Larry was especially concerned that the job of assimilating and running a network would divert the energies of our top management from our own ongoing businesses and building the Disney brand. In the case of NBC, however, Richard was now at least mildly enthusiastic, and Larry was wavering—particularly if the price was right.

At least one external factor motivated this change of heart. The FCC was on the verge of granting the networks the right to produce and own programs without restriction, which would open up a significant new potential source of income. It was also likely to further restrict the access of outside producers such as Disney to produce shows for the network. Imagine, for a moment, that your livelihood depends on commuting to work on a major freeway. At first the cost of the tolls is within reason. Then the price starts going up, making it more expensive to reach work. Finally one day, the guy in the tollbooth won't raise the gate no matter how much you offer to pay. Things hadn't quite reached that point in gaining access for our shows on the major television networks, but they were clearly heading in that direction.

NBC had its own special appeal as a potential acquisition. Because it was just a division of General Electric—unlike CBS and Capital Cities/ABC, which were public companies—we could purchase the network directly, rather than making the sort of public tender offer that had the potential to prompt a bidding war. There was also the possibility of making a reasonable deal, given NBC's current struggles. After a long run at the top, the network was now running third in prime time, and suffering as well in daytime, Saturday mornings, and late night, in the wake of David Letterman's recent defection to CBS. That meant GE was less likely to be able to command a premium price for NBC, but also that the network had a considerable upside. Finally, there were indications that GE chairman Jack Welch was interested in holding on to some percentage of the network—which suggested that we might be able to gain creative control of NBC without paying full price to buy it all. The purpose of this Monday strategy meeting was to consider alternative structures for a deal and to begin discussing what price we would be willing to pay. Several options were bandied about. By the time it was necessary to make any sort of final decision, I expected to be back at the office.

It was during my hospital stay that a very public campaign was launched to win Jeffrey the president's job. On Wednesday, July 20, five days after my operation, both the *New York Times* and *The Wall Street Journal* ran prominent articles about the alleged impact of my illness. The *Times* article was written by its show business reporter, and it was headlined: "Hollywood Sees Tension at Disney." I knew that Jeffrey spoke frequently to the press, and the article left little doubt where the reporter's sympathies lay. "Mr. Eisner is secretive and has few close friends," Bernard Weinraub wrote. "Mr. Katzenberg is vocal, and has a range of acquaintances and relationships." It went on to quote "friends of Mr. Katzenberg" as saying that "he was somewhat disturbed to be treated as less a friend than an employee even while Mr. Eisner was in the hospital recovering from heart surgery." Most striking of all, the article quoted one of Jeffrey's "closest friends" delivering a stark ultimatum: "The question is, does Michael want to share power with Jeffrey? If he doesn't, Jeffrey will leave the company by the end of the year." My first reaction to the *Times* article was anger that Jeffrey or anyone connected with him would once again use a moment when I was highly vulnerable to force a showdown about his future. My second reaction was astonishment that he or his advisers might believe that taking his case public made sense. Under no circumstances was I interested in negotiating with Jeffrey through the media.

I returned home on Thursday, July 21, less than a week after the operation. As the doctors had predicted, I felt bone-tired. I had never before lacked for energy, but suddenly walking up a flight of stairs or making my way across the yard was utterly exhausting. I understood mine was a typical reaction to the extreme anemia that follows bypass surgery, but it was still frustrating. I wasn't used to limits of any kind and certainly not to the need for midday naps. Now I found myself falling asleep in the middle of conversations. To my relief, I was spared the other common side effect of bypass surgery, depression. Cardiologists aren't entirely sure why recovering patients get depressed, but there are powerful psychological triggers, including the sudden recognition of one's mortality, the increased sense of vulnerability, and the natural worries about not being able to resume a normal life.

All of these issues came up for me, but they didn't prompt depression. When Thomas Watson had bypass surgery shortly after turning fifty, he decided to retire as chairman of IBM and to change his life dramatically. Watson lived into his eighties, happy and mostly healthy. For better or for worse, it never once occurred to me that I wouldn't return to work at Disney. I wasn't ready to retire, or even to cut back. I still felt challenged and excited by what I did, and optimistic about the future, in spite of my setback. I couldn't imagine doing anything other than continuing to build Disney. Tired as I was in the weeks after my operation, I believed that I would ultimately feel stronger and healthier than I had been before it. My arteries, after all, were no longer clogged.

I was also aware that a bypass commonly holds for ten to fifteen years before a new one is needed. The only way to keep my arteries clear was to make at least two immediate and fundamental changes in my life—and ideally a third. The first was to shift to a strict no-fat diet in order to lower my cholesterol. One of the doctors I consulted was William Castelli, who launched and supervised a study of risk factors for heart disease in the adult population of Framingham, Massachusetts. Not a single person in the study with a cholesterol level under 150 has ever developed heart disease. Unfortunately, I've always hated diets. I also hate red lights and speed limits and I'm not overly fond of stop signs. But there are some things it makes sense to do, whether you want to or not. Thirty years earlier, I reluctantly quit smoking and no achievement since that day on July 4, 1967, is comparable. (Jane quit on July 5.) Given the research about the causes of heart disease, it probably also makes sense for everyone to eat a lower-fat diet. For those of us with genetically high cholesterol and a high degree of stress, a low-fat diet is absolutely essential.

That doesn't mean it's easy. In a world that still celebrates hamburgers and fries, cheeses and oils, ice cream and cakes, eating nonfat not only requires discipline, it sets you apart. To be the center of attention when you hit a home run in the ninth inning at the World Series or win the Nobel Prize in physics is almost surely fun. It's not so much fun to attract attention at a restaurant when you bring your own salad dressing, or press the waiter about whether the vegetable soup is really cooked without chicken broth. It's not fun when you're invited to someone's house for dinner and you have to explain that you don't eat meat, or cheese, or oil, or nearly anything else they might be planning to serve, but that a little nonfat pasta with tomato sauce would be just terrific.

I grew up thinking vegetarians were weird — people who shopped in health-food stores and named their children "Wind" and "Stream" and "Sunshine." I also grew up believing that special diets were for old people like my aunt Mamie and cousin Ida. In their cases, they were each nearing one hundred when they began their diets, and all they did was eliminate salt. I began my special, nonfat vegetarian diet at half their age. Now I wish my kids would follow suit—just say no to drugs, unsafe friends, and unprotected saturated fat. The leading cause of death in the Western world is heart disease. If most people went on a low-fat diet, those that didn't would become the center of attention—and the spotlight would drop off me and my fellow vegetarians. Longevity would also increase dramatically.

The second change I made was to begin a daily exercise program. Overwhelming evidence suggests that fitness is a strong protection against heart disease, so off I went to cardiac rehab—a medical euphemism to describe a gym for the aged. Suddenly I found myself on a treadmill for forty-five minutes three times a week, sandwiched between an eighty-three-year-old man who'd undergone a heart transplant and a seventy-nine-year-old woman with a quadruple bypass who never stopped talking. At fifty-two, I felt like the kindergarten kid who mistakenly gets dropped off in an eighth-grade classroom. In between workouts, we were shown films about diet, films about depression, and films about our rejiggered anatomy. This wasn't sex education, it was survival education, and I would have much preferred the former.

The third change my doctors recommended was to reduce the level of stress and anxiety in my life—a concept I'd never before considered. I sort of liked stress. In any case, reducing it wasn't going to be easy. Between the possible purchase of NBC, the ongoing business of the company, and the resolution of Jeffrey's future, my life wasn't about to get easier any time soon. Nonetheless, I was being pressured to relax, both by Jane and by my doctors. Resisting only created more anxiety.

Offered a choice of stress reduction techniques, I decided to give yoga a try. I can't remember where we found Yoga Lady, but she arrived at my house at the agreed-upon hour one afternoon. She was pleasant and gentle and warm. Awkward and nervous, I lay down on the floor. Yoga Lady put on mellow music and gave me instructions in unfamiliar poses, abdominal breathing, and chanting (a true leap of faith, the New Age having passed me by). Although I felt certain that the pressure of performing at something so completely alien was taxing my surgically repaired heart, I soldiered on. After returning to my office, I dutifully tried to keep up my yoga, but making it home in time for sessions took its toll. Doing yoga mostly became a way to offset the stress of making it to appointments in the first place. After several weeks I quit, rationalizing that my life would be far less stressful when I stopped trying so hard to relax.

In the weeks following my operation I mostly avoided speaking with Jeffrey, in part out of Jane's reluctance for me to be involved in anything that might impede my recovery. Our brief conversations on the phone invariably left me feeling angry. Once again, I asked Sandy to serve as a go-between. Jeffrey took the opportunity to turn up the heat still further.

"I'm no longer satisfied to have it be 'Eisner & Son,'" he told Sandy. "In the future, it will have to be 'Eisner & Eisner.' Frank was never Michael's equal partner. I intend to be." Finally, on August 7, I asked Jeffrey to come over to my house. It was a strange meeting—alternately tense and matter-of-fact, conversational and confrontational. After a half hour or so, he delivered the punch line. "It's time for me to move on," he said. I was slightly taken aback and I asked Jeffrey if he had accepted a new job.

"No," he said. "Not yet."

"Is it something that we can discuss?"

"We can," he said, "but I suspect that the decision has been carved in stone by other people." Jeffrey told me that he felt especially isolated from the board. "I know that Roy and Stanley are hostile to me. It would only be possible to make me president if you forced the decision on them," he said. "If that's the case, getting the job isn't worth it." I asked Jeffrey to be a little more patient. The presidency wasn't an option, but I still hadn't given up on finding some way to keep him at Disney. Whatever happened, I was eager to gain more strength before dealing with his situation. "Why don't you go home and put down on paper a description of the role that you envision for yourself?" I said. "Tell me how you would reorganize the company, which executives you would replace, what acquisitions you would pursue." He agreed.

The most pressing creative issue during this period was our progress on *Pocahontas*, the animated movie scheduled for release in the summer of 1995 but already well into production. Along with Roy Disney, I'd seen a rough cut of the film shortly before my trip to Sun Valley, and both of us had significant concerns. I was especially worried about the second act, which was confusing and lacked narrative momentum. I also had a problem with one of the songs and with the issue of language. The question was whether Pocahontas should speak in her native language in the early scenes or simply use English all the way through. The latter option had the disadvantage of being less realistic, but it would make the storytelling far easier. On Wednesday, August 10, two days after my meeting with Jeffrey, I spoke with him on the phone to discuss my concerns about *Pocahontas* in more detail.

"They're insignificant," he insisted. I reminded him that I'd given him comparable notes on each of our previous animated movies, which he always made sure were incorporated, and that our process seemed to work well. Grudgingly, he promised to see that my notes were addressed.

Jeffrey was clearly more reluctant than ever to keep me informed. He was even vague about when the next screening was going to be held, and he objected when he discovered that I had spoken with Peter Schneider late Thursday. The next morning, I received a handwritten note. "Your feeling the need to be calling Peter and checking up on me, and inquiring whether or not your notes are being addressed on *Pocahontas*, doesn't work for me at all," Jeffrey wrote. "But what may even be worse is what this says about your lack of confidence and trust in me to do what I said I would do. If this is how you see us dealing with one another in the future . . . it's not me."

I called Jeffrey. "I think your letter was wrong and inappropriate," I told him.

It was finally clear that we had reached an impasse. I wasn't going to give Jeffrey the job he wanted and he wasn't going to settle for anything less. The other issues were all secondary. Reluctantly, I turned my attention to creating a new management team for the studio. It was absolutely necessary to prepare the company for the future. My first priority was to negotiate with Joe Roth to take over as head of motion pictures. I also hoped that I could convince Jeffrey's number two, Rich Frank, to assume a broad new role as chairman of worldwide television. Finally, Peter Schneider and Roy Disney would take charge of animation. On Friday, August 19—nine days after my confrontation with Jeffrey over *Pocahontas*—I called Joe Roth.

"I'm going to be talking to Jeffrey during the next week," I explained, "and I want to know, regardless of how it turns out, whether you're interested in running the movie division, either under Jeffrey or directly for me." Joe said that he was, and I told him that I'd have Sandy call to negotiate a deal. I also asked that he keep our discussions completely confidential.

On Monday evening, I met with Rich Frank at my home. I told him that I was going to be meeting with Jeffrey in the next two days and that I wasn't going to be offering him the job he wanted. Given that, I wanted Rich to become chairman of television and telecommunications, and also to assume responsibility for home video and the Disney Channel. As difficult as it would be to lose Jeffrey, I was determined that it provide an opportunity for other executives to spread their wings. Giving Rich, Peter, and Joe broader responsibilities had the potential to reenergize their divisions. It also represented a means of renewing the company, a process which had unfolded much less smoothly and seamlessly than I'd hoped. But I knew that it's not always possible to orchestrate the process of change. Sometimes the best outcomes emerge from dealing with the most difficult crises.

On Tuesday, I asked John Dreyer to begin preparing a press release detailing the changes that were likely to occur. Mindful of the shock that followed Frank's sudden death, our goal was to make this transition as orderly as possible. On Wednesday morning, shortly before 9:00 a.m., I called Joe at home. I told him that I had a meeting with Jeffrey that morning. I still didn't say that Jeffrey would be leaving, but Joe surely sensed what was coming.

At 11:00 a.m., Jeffrey sat down across from my desk. He produced the four-page memo he'd written outlining how he envisioned his future and Disney's. Before he could hand it to me, I stopped him. It no longer made sense to discuss his recommendations. Having anticipated this moment for nearly a year, there was no good way to deliver the news.

"This is a day I've dreaded for a long time," I said. "I wish it hadn't come to this and that we could have made it work. But I'm not going to be able to give you the job you want, and you're not satisfied with the one you have." We talked briefly about the events of the past several weeks. Then I handed him the press announcement that we'd prepared. He absorbed the news calmly. The tension seemed to seep out of the room and our conversation turned to earlier years and better times together. It was bittersweet, laced with an undercurrent of loss and residual anger on both sides. But all that remained unspoken. On the surface, the meeting was surprisingly friendly and free of fireworks. Jeffrey later described it as the most relaxed talk we'd had in a year.

When he finally stood up to return to his own office, the primary emotion I felt was an enormous sense of relief. I called Jane and then began filling in the rest of our executives. I also called Joe Roth to tell him the news. "We need to get your deal finalized," I explained. "As a public company, we have to be sensitive to the impact these changes may have on our stock. We can't make our announcement until you have a signed deal memo." A press release went out at 2:00 p.m., and within minutes the calls from the media began to pour in. I spent most of the rest of the afternoon on the phone, talking with reporters and with our own top executives.

It was my first full day back at the office and by 7:00 p.m., I felt exhausted, physically and emotionally. My body told me that it was time to go home and crawl upstairs to bed, but my mind reminded me that I had a social obligation. For the past month, Carole Bayer Sager, songwriter, longtime friend, and the future wife of Warner Bros. chairman Bob Daly, had been extolling the virtues of meditation. She believed that Deepak Chopra, the New Age physician and best-selling author, was exactly what I needed and she showered me with e-mails about all the people whose lives Chopra had changed. I pointed out that most of these same people had gone through transformations before, from Esalen to EST, from diet to diet, and from spouse to spouse. But Carole was relentless. I finally left it up to Jane to make a dinner date that included Chopra. Jane went ahead, eager to help me cope with my new-found arteries in any way she could. Chopra flew in from North Carolina just for the dinner.

Carole met us at the door. As we walked in, candles were burning—or they might as well have been. Chopra was teaching Bob to meditate in the living room. Never, I'd wager, has Bob been happier to see another uptight studio executive enter a room. Sensing a graceful way to escape his transcendence, he jumped up to greet us.

We all sat down together—Bob and I like campers facing our first day in the wilderness, Jane simply curious, and Carole elegant and rapt. Bob made a sympathetic comment about the day I'd just been through, and a pregnant silence fell over the room. Finally Chopra spoke up. "We sold a million cassettes at Blockbuster," he said, "but I'm not sure they're carried deep enough." Or maybe it was a half million books at Barnes & Noble he was talking about. In any case, it wasn't transcendence. We went on to talk about his deals and his books and the people he knew in Hollywood, and eventually we discussed his ideas about meditation and the mind-body connection. Chopra was smooth, articulate, and charming. He was also soft and enticing, but home and my bed seemed even softer and more enticing. Between Chopra's lilting voice and my exhaustion, I found the door. Settling Jeffrey Katzenberg's future earlier that day had provided enough stress reduction for the next several months.

The immediate press reaction to Jeffrey's departure was muted, although there were outraged reactions from his close friends. My main concern had been that reporters would use the fact of Jeffrey's leaving, coupled with Frank's death, to build a case for instability at the company. Instead, while the stories rightly praised Jeffrey's successful tenure, they also lauded Joe Roth, Rich Frank, and Peter Schneider as strong and capable. Jeffrey himself was restrained and gracious in his public comments. Several weeks later, he announced plans to launch his own studio, DreamWorks, with his friends David Geffen and Steven Spielberg.

The other pressing issue was our accelerating talks about acquiring NBC from General Electric. On September 14, Stanley Gold, Richard Nanula, and I flew in to New York together, my first trip since my operation. We met with Welch and two of his top executives over dinner in a private dining room next to Welch's office in the GE Building. He'd arranged a nonfat dinner for me, unaware that he would face bypass surgery and similar lifestyle changes himself a year later. When we sat down, he made a proposal for a deal that we'd never discussed before.

"We want to sell you 49 percent of NBC and retain 51 percent ourselves," Welch began. "You would take charge of programming." Over time, he said, Disney would have certain options to buy majority control of the network. As for the CEO at NBC, Welch suggested that he wasn't open to making a change until Bob Wright, the current CEO, had been given a minimum of two years to try to turn the network around. Everyone else was calling for Wright's head, in the face of NBC's troubles. I respected Welch for standing by a struggling executive who had served the company well for many years.

Welch was highly persuasive about the deal he had in mind. There was something very attractive about taking creative control of a network for half the price of owning one outright. Welch even volunteered that he might consider sponsoring a GE pavilion at Epcot as a further incentive. By the time Richard, Stanley, and I got into the elevator shortly after ten, we were enthusiastic about the proposal. I no longer remember if any of us voiced doubts during the elevator ride down. They certainly began to arise in the car, on the way to a previously arranged postmortem at Sid Bass's apartment. When we ran Sid through Welch's proposal, I could sense everyone's excitement was rapidly fading. It had dawned on us that Welch was suggesting a very full price for a minority stake in a third-place network. His proposal gave us responsibility for turning NBC around but only half the potential reward if we succeeded and all the blame if we didn't.

Sid's reaction was simple: "I don't think it's favorable."

Suddenly, the whole evening seemed amusing. I was used to trying to sell others on deals favorable to Disney. In this instance, I'd been seduced by a consummate salesman into considering a deal that wasn't good for us at all. The next morning, I called Welch. "You did a great job selling us," I told him, "but with the benefit of a good night's sleep, the answer to the proposal is an unequivocal no."

Welch laughed, and so did I. It was as if he'd put his house on the market for more than it was worth, prepared to sell it only if someone paid the full asking price. We had made the right decision, but after two months of negotiation, we all felt an inevitable sense of letdown and disappointment. Buying NBC at the right price, which had seemed possible just twenty-four hours earlier, would have been a shot in the arm for Disney at a moment when we needed one. As it turned out, Welch had the right instincts. Bob Wright's leadership turned NBC around completely during the next two years.

Although news of our aborted deal never leaked, the media did begin writing stories about Disney as a company adrift. The most dramatic was a *Newsweek* cover picturing a bewildered-looking Mickey Mouse and the cover line, "Can the Kingdom Keep Its Magic?" There were also critical articles in *Vanity Fair, The New Yorker,* the *New York Times,* and several other publications, which dissected the company and the traumatic events of the past six months. At least one story suggested that Disney was now "paralyzed." In fact, Joe Roth quickly took charge of live action and Rich Frank of television, while Peter Schneider and Tom Schumacher did a superb job of keeping animation on track. Still, this spate of critical articles only served to feed the inevitable anxiety and uncertainty that follows major changes at the top levels of a company.

I was philosophical. Reporters are forever looking for a fresh, dramatic angle on a story. At Disney, I'd learned, the whole world always seemed to be watching. Everything we did was magnified in ways that would have rated little notice at other companies. For nearly a decade, the media had unabashedly celebrated our growing success and I'd been praised more than I deserved. Now, the story line had us struggling, and suddenly I was the chief villain. Neither of these extremes was true. We'd made our share of mistakes and suffered our failures during the best periods over the past ten years. Now we were facing a more difficult time, but not nearly as bad or as threatening as the press reports implied. Despite a year of extraordinary adversity and tumult, we were on the verge of reporting record 1994 earnings, including a 25 percent increase in net income over the previous year. Few of our competitors were creating any value for their shareholders, and we continued to do so.

My inclination was to take none of the outside attention too seriously. For better or worse, I wasn't inclined to spend time courting the media or the financial analysts. The best use of my time was to jump back into the creative work of the company, something which I had felt compelled to put on the back burner in the months following Frank's death and my bypass. My primary responsibility was to ensure that Disney continue to perform at the highest possible level, while retaining its commitment to excellence. Like the stock market, which has its ups and downs but accurately gauges values over time, I believed that the media would accurately reflect Disney's good performance in the long run.

Unhappy as I was that our employees and board members had suffered through a period of discomfort and uncertainty during the past six months, I also knew that change can be an engine of growth and a source of creativity. By definition, it drives us out of our comfort zones and forces us to rearrange our thought patterns. My own brush with mortality had sharpened my sensitivity to the inevitability and inexorability of change. So had the events within our company. Perhaps none was as painful — or as enlightening — as our experience with Disney's America.

CHAPTER

12

Disney's America

THERE WAS NO PROJECT DURING MY FIRST DECADE AT DISNEY ABOUT which I felt more passionate than Disney's America—and none that ran up against fiercer resistance. Building a Disney theme park based on American history seemed like a natural extension of the company's life-long focus on children and education, a perfect way of marrying our self-interest with a broader public interest.

The seeds of the idea were first planted in the summer of 1991. Chastened by the rising costs of Euro Disney, we began to look for ways to develop smaller-scale theme parks. Dick Nunis, then head of the parks, persuaded Frank and me to visit Colonial Williamsburg, the restored colonial town in Tidewater Virginia. Dick envisioned it as a potential site for a park with related themes. I had American history on my mind anyway. The next executive retreat we planned was to be devoted to the subject of democracy. The idea for an animated film based on the story of *Pocahontas* had been suggested at one of our recent Gong Shows, and I was in the midst of reading several books about John Smith and Pocahontas.

The visit to Williamsburg was intriguing, but when our strategic planning group took a hard look at the site, they concluded that it was the wrong location for a Disney theme park, which depends on several million annual guests. The business in Williamsburg was mostly seasonal, in the summers, and the drive from Washington, D.C., took nearly two hours—too far for most one-day visitors. Our visit did convince me that a park based on historical and patriotic themes could succeed, if we found the right place for it.

When we returned to Los Angeles, Frank and I authorized Peter Rummell and his Disney Development team to begin scouting for a site. Within a few weeks, they settled on the Washington, D.C., area. "It's no contest," Peter explained. "It has a huge tourist population, and they're just the kind of people who would be interested in a historical theme park." More than 19 million people visit the nation's capital each year and the vast majority are drawn by the city's historical sites, government buildings, and museums. When I was a teenager, my parents had taken me and my older sister there several times. I still remember racing my sister up the Washington Monument, fighting with her along the Potomac, and visiting the White House and the Smithsonian. We even walked past Vice President Nixon standing all by himself in the halls of Congress. It was impossible to replace these kinds of experiences, but the Disney park we had in mind had the potential to engage young people in American history in novel ways. Drawing on our natural strengths as storytellers, we could use these skills to be substantive without being dull, to bring historical events alive and to make the story of America more vivid and three-dimensional.

Our first important misstep was the decision to call the park "Disney's America." "Disney" and "America" just seemed to slide off the tongue together easily and naturally. Frank and I both liked associating Disney with America and America with Disney. But the name would prove to be a disaster. "Disney's America" implied ownership of the country's history, which only antagonized our critics. That was unfortunate because we were never interested in a park that merely reflected a Disneyesque view of American history.

While Peter's group looked for a site through the fall of 1992, we began putting together a team from Imagineering to design the park. It was led by Bob Weis, who had played the same role at the Disney-MGM Studios. I first met with Bob's group on a Sunday in January 1993 and we set out to generate as many ideas and points of view about the park as possible.

"Whatever we ultimately do, it should be built around a small number of emotionally stirring, heart-wrenching stories based on important themes in American history," I told our group. "We ought to have elements that are fun and frivolous and carefree alongside ones that are serious and challenging and sobering. We need the same sort of dramatic highs and lows that you find in any great film. If we're truly going to celebrate America, we need to capture the country in all its complexity." One suggestion was to find dramatic ways to tell the story of immigration. Other arenas that came up included the Native American experience; the writing of the Constitution and the birth of democracy; the story of slavery and the Civil War; the role of the military; the birth and death of the family farm; and the launch of the industrial revolution.

In the spring of 1993, Peter's team found what sounded like an ideal location, just outside the town of Haymarket, Virginia, only twenty miles from downtown Washington, D.C. More than 2,300 of the 3,000 acres we wanted to buy were controlled by a single entity—Exxon. The company's real estate division had purchased the undeveloped farmland at the height of the real estate boom in the late 1980s. They managed to win zoning approval for a large mixed-use development of homes and office buildings, only to abandon the project when the real estate market fell apart in the early 1990s.

With few prospective buyers for such a large parcel, Exxon was willing to sell an option to buy the land rather than insisting on an outright purchase. That enabled us to hold the land for a modest cost while we continued to design the park and began the zoning and approvals process with state and local authorities. Peter's team also set out to purchase or take options on a dozen other smaller adjacent parcels surrounding the main site. In none of the transactions, including with Exxon, did we let on that Disney was the buyer.

Early in August, Jane and I flew to Washington to tour the site for the first time. We landed at Dulles Airport around 9:30 a.m., rented a car, and drove to the site, where we met Peter and several of his executives. The drive took us less than half an hour, which I found encouraging. While the Disney's America site was just off Interstate 66, a main highway leading to Washington, it was still almost pure rural countryside. Hills and farmland extended as far as we could see. Jane and I spent several hours exploring the property. At one point, walking through a long-abandoned house, I went down into the cellar and discovered a pair of andirons that had to be at least a hundred years old.

The setting was so beautiful that I began to wonder how local residents would feel about our building a theme park there, no matter how much of the land around it we protected. But Peter and his group were reassuring that since the site had already been zoned once for a large residential and commercial development, we wouldn't have a problem—and indeed that local residents would welcome thousands of jobs in an area that was struggling economically. Our hope was to announce the plans for Disney's America sometime before the end of the year, but it was clear that we had a lot of preparatory work ahead. One focus would be to persuade the Virginia legislature to help underwrite infrastructure improvements such as the widening of Interstate 66. As with the renovation of the New Amsterdam Theatre, Disney's America wasn't economically viable without government subsidies. In this instance, the state was likely to be drawn to the project by its potential to create new jobs, generate additional tax revenues, and attract tourists.

As we moved forward, there were two key issues that we badly underestimated—and that would haunt us over the next year. First, we failed to recognize how deeply people often feel about maintaining their communities just as they are. This was especially true of the land to the west of us—the very heart of Virginia hunt country—where our neighbors included some of the most powerful families in America, among them the Mellons, the DuPonts, the Harrimans, and the Grahams. Many of these prominent families had maintained large homes in this pristine Virginia countryside for generations—huge farms with vast pastures and split-rail fences and barns filled with Thoroughbred horses.

For more than two decades, we would soon discover, these families had also generously funded the Piedmont Environmental Council, a local rural preservation group. There may have been no collection of people in America better equipped to lobby a cause, whether with Congress or government agencies or through the media. They had the financial resources to do battle, the expertise, and the political connections. Many of them did this sort of work for a living in Washington, and with Disney's America, they had a highly personal stake in the outcome.

The other issue that blindsided us was the Civil War battlefield in the town of Manassas, approximately five miles from our site. We knew that there had been a large controversy five years earlier, when a developer announced plans to build a shopping center close to the battlefield. Fierce opposition arose, led by historians and Civil War buffs, including Jody Powell, former press secretary to Jimmy Carter. Ultimately, the opponents prevailed, and plans to build the shopping center were withdrawn. But we believed—and so did Jody Powell, whom we consulted—that our location was far enough away from Manassas that it wouldn't be an issue. We couldn't have been more wrong. Our opponents did eventually make an issue of Manassas—and ultimately were successful at conveying the impression that our site literally sat on a Civil War battlefield rather than five miles from one. But all this was ahead of us. At the end of the day that Jane and I spent walking the site and talking with Peter and his team, I was more confident and enthusiastic about Disney's America than ever.

Our next mistake was assuming that we could announce the project on our own timetable. Our focus on secrecy in land acquisition had prevented us from even briefing, much less lobbying, the leading politicians in the state about our plans as they evolved. The consequence was that we lost the opportunity to develop crucial allies and nurture goodwill. The secrecy also precluded seeking out prominent historians, whose ideas and criticisms could have helped us shape our plans, alerted us to areas of potential controversy, and given the project more legitimacy from the start. Finally, the commitment to secrecy kept me or any of our top executives from meeting with top Washington politicians and opinion makers in advance of our announcement, to describe our plans in detail. By doing so we could have shared our genuine passion for the project and the seriousness of our intentions.

Without the freedom to thoroughly test the political waters, we weren't in a position to assess intelligently where opposition might arise, as it does in virtually every large-scale development. We chose an aggressive young executive named Mark Pacala to oversee the park, but by the time he came aboard in the fall of 1993, the key mistakes had already been made and events were moving fast. News of our plans began to leak in late October, and we found ourselves scrambling defensively to cover our bases. We never fully recovered.

With reporters hot on the trail of our plans, I called George F. Allen early in November. He'd just been elected governor of Virginia.

Completely coincidentally, it turned out that Allen was at Walt Disney World, vacationing with his family in the aftermath of his landslide victory. ("Mr. Allen, now that you've been elected Governor of Virginia, what are you going to do next?") Allen called me back from the Magic Kingdom, and I described our plans to him. "It sounds great," he said. "It's just the kind of project I want to bring to Virginia. I look forward to working with you." I also placed a call to Douglas Wilder, the outgoing governor, and he, too, expressed support. As Governor-elect Allen had, Gov. Wilder promised to show up for our public announcement, which we had now scheduled for Thursday, November 11.

On Monday, November 8, *The Wall Street Journal* ran a small item saying that Disney was planning a new park somewhere in Virginia, but provided no details. On Wednesday, as we continued racing to brief local Virginia politicians about the project, the *Washington Post* broke the story in more detail. Right away, we had a taste of what we were going to be facing. The front page of the *Post*'s Metropolitan section had two huge stories about the proposed park, one under the headline: "In Disney's Grand Plan, Some See a Smoggy, Cloggy Transportation Mess." Alongside were several pictures of the site along with the caption: "A Cinderella Story—Or a Bad Dream?" It was a strong dose of what the *Post* would deliver in its news pages and editorial columns over the next ten months. The following morning, more than 150 reporters, politicians, and local residents showed up for our official announcement in Haymarket.

Our hope was to demonstrate that considerable planning had already gone into the project and that our intentions were serious. Bob Weis and his team presented artists' renderings and scale models of our preliminary plans. They depicted seven themed areas, which included a Presidents Square; recreations of a Native American village; a Civil War fort; Ellis Island, the immigrant port in New York; a turn-of-the-century factory town; a state fair; and a midwestern family farm. In fact, we revealed far too much too soon. As with all our major projects, we knew that this one would go through many versions in the course of our planning. But by publicly revealing a project that looked relatively complete, we opened ourselves up to every critic with different ideas about what a park based on American history should and should not include. We also left ourselves vulnerable to the claim that any changes we subsequently made were a response to outside pressures rather than a natural part of our own creative process and our commitment to excellence.

At the news conference, reporters focused on the issue of authenticity, and the degree to which Disney might be expected to whitewash or trivialize the country's history. Contrary to these expectations, we had no interest in telling a sanitized or sugarcoated story, not least because doing so would make the park less interesting and emotionally compelling for visitors. But our attempts to address these questions backfired. When Bob Weis was asked a question about the kind of park we had in mind, he offered a simple example. "We want to make you a Civil War soldier," he said. "We want to make you feel what it was like to be a slave, or what it was like to escape through the Underground Railroad." Within days, critics had seized on this statement as the height of presumption. "How could Disney possibly evoke the experience of slavery in a theme park?" one editorial writer demanded. I wished that Bob had phrased his answer more felicitously, but his point seemed to me a reasonable one. We had no intention of trying to *replicate* the experience of slavery for anyone. How could we? But we were committed to bringing history alive by telling emotionally compelling stories in dramatic ways. Somehow, we never successfully communicated that distinction. The more we tried, the more we stepped on our own toes.

A second line of questioning at the news conference focused on traditional concerns raised by any large-scale development, namely, its likely effect on such issues as local traffic, air pollution, and population density. Both Bob and Peter Rummell made it clear that we took these issues seriously. We fully intended to work with local officials to assure that we addressed local concerns and more than met environmental standards, as we'd done very successfully at Walt Disney World. But none of these questions seemed likely to abate soon. Instead, local opposition coalesced swiftly. Within five days of our announcement, more than a dozen of the wealthy owners of Virginia estates to the west of our site had met to organize their opposition to our project. The Piedmont Environmental Council and several local environmental groups also began speaking out against the project, vowing to fight to the end.

Despite these critics, much of the initial response was more encouraging. Governors Wilder and Allen strongly endorsed Disney's America at the press conference. Key state legislators and local officials, including the powerful chairwoman of the Prince William County Board of Supervisors, also expressed support. And despite the toughness and skepticism of the *Washington Post*'s coverage, most of the media treated the announcement of Disney's America as an interesting, original, and ambitious undertaking. The initial *New York Times* article described the "utter exuberance" local residents felt about the project and made scant mention of potential opposition.

Bob Weis and his team were now finally free to solicit input from outside experts. In mid-December 1993, he and several other Imagineers flew to Washington to talk to leaders of several groups, including the Washington Indian Leadership Forum, the Congressional Black Caucus, the Virginia Historical Society, and the Smithsonian Institution. They received a uniformly warm reception, including offers of help. We also began seeking out historians as advisers. We saw ourselves as storytellers first and foremost. We needed experts to help us understand, interpret, and shape the dramas we hoped to portray. Although some prominent historians immediately took the position that an entertainment company like Disney shouldn't be dealing with history at all, others were more open-minded. If Disney intended to build a theme park devoted to American history, they told us, they were eager to try to ensure that we did so knowledgeably and responsibly.

Eric Foner, a professor of history at Columbia University and a scholar of nineteenth-century American History, had first contacted us in 1991 to raise concerns about an exhibit called *Great Moments with Mr. Lincoln* at Disneyland. Opened in the 1960s, the exhibit featured an Audio-Animatronics robot of Abe Lincoln giving a medley of several of his speeches. Foner's concern, having visited the exhibit, was that Lincoln's speech never mentioned slavery and that it failed to deal at all with the issue of race. We responded by inviting Foner to help us craft a more inclusive message for the narrator and for Lincoln—to be used at the Magic Kingdom's expanded Audio-Animatronics exhibit, the *Hall of Presidents*. He agreed. Where the original narrator had talked about "freedom and democracy" as the central ideals of the founding fathers, Foner worked with us to add the concept that such ideals represent "an unfinished agenda which challenges each generation of Americans, including our own." The poet Maya Angelou agreed to narrate the new show. We also added Bill Clinton to the exhibit as our forty-third president, and he agreed to record a short speech of his own, which the White House helped us to write. (I wrote four drafts myself. None sounded like the Gettysburg Address.) In the end, Foner's input made for a far more textured and powerful exhibit. Now he agreed to play a similar role in advising us on Disney's America.

Bob Weis and his deputy, Rick Rothschild, also met with James Horton, a prominent specialist in African American history at George Washington University who had initially expressed opposition to our project. After Horton heard firsthand about our intentions, he agreed to help craft the exhibit at Disney's America devoted to race. Properly designed, he later told a *Washington Post* reporter, "I am convinced that the Disney project can complement historical Washington and prove that serious history can be every bit as fascinating as fantasy and even more compelling."

On Saturday, January 15, 1994, we gathered the Disney's America team for an all-day meeting at one of the Imagineering buildings in Glendale. "The most difficult job," I told our group, "won't be to tell important stories about our history, or to deliver an enjoyable experience for our guests, but to achieve both these goals without having either one dilute the other." In our original plan, for example, we'd envisioned recreating a classic twentieth-century steel mill and then putting a rollercoaster through it. To do that, we began to understand, could trivialize and even demean the attempt to portray the steel mill realistically.

If we tried to mix theme park excitement directly with history, we weren't going to do either one justice. It was fine to create a Lewis and Clark raft ride, for example, but not to try to explain Manifest Destiny as part of the same experience. It was also important to tell stories like that of American soldiers—their role in defending and protecting our country—and to use our three-dimensional and multimedia tools to bring historical events alive. "What we need most of all is more edge and more depth," I said, toward the end of our meeting. "We need to keep working to create a day-long experience that makes our guests laugh and cry, feel proud of their country's strengths and angry about its shortcomings."

At the political and the grassroots level, support for our project grew. In February, a series of independently conducted polls showed that Virginians supported Disney's America by margins averaging 3 to 1. Under Mark Pacala's leadership, we also won over a growing percentage of community officials and local residents, who were attracted by the promise of twelve thousand new jobs and the substantial tax revenues the park would ultimately pay. Our critics from the Piedmont Environmental Council tried to minimize these figures, but even their own study concluded that Disney's America would generate at least $10 million a year in new state tax revenues and more than six thousand new jobs. These numbers had an effect at the state level as well. On March 14, 1994, with Governor Allen's strong support, the Virginia legislature approved a $140 million bond offering for highway improvements adjacent to the site and another $20 million to support a marketing campaign for Virginia historical tourist destinations, including our park.

None of this seemed to dampen the resolve of our opponents. Most important, several historians began raising the specter that our park threatened historical sites in the surrounding area, notably Manassas. The leader of these efforts was Richard Moe, president of the National Trust for Historic Preservation. In February, the *New York Times* came out editorially in opposition to Disney's America, arguing the same case that Moe was making. "Haymarket is not 42nd Street or Florida's piney woods," the *Times* wrote. "Putting a theme park there degrades a scenic and historic resource for a project that can be built elsewhere. As for parents who want to give their children history, let them—like generations before them—make the trip to Prince William County. Let them sit still at Manassas and listen for the presence of the dead."

In May, a group calling itself Protect Historic America was launched. Led by Moe, it included a prestigious group of historians, writers, and well-known public figures. On May 11, funded in part by supporters of the Piedmont Environmental Council, they held a press conference that featured several of their most prominent members. David McCullough, the best-selling author of *Truman* and host for Ken Burns's PBS series on the Civil War, described Disney's America as "a commercial blitzkrieg by the Panzer division of developers." He went on to liken the proposed building of our historical park to the Nazi takeover of Western Europe.

"We have so little that's authentic and real," McCullough said. "It's irrational, illogical, and enormously detrimental to attempt to create synthetic history by destroying real history." Moe warned that if Disney did manage to get the park built, the surrounding countryside would be "overrun, cheapened, and trivialized." The retired Yale historian C. Vann Woodward suggested that "it [is] pretty much taken for granted that Disney [will] misinterpret the past." And Roger Wilkins, a journalist and history professor, described our proposed park as nothing less than "a national calamity."

By any reasonable measure, this attack on Disney's America was dramatically overstated. But for our critics, the press conference served its purpose. Much like negative advertising in a political campaign, these incendiary claims were very effective in influencing public opinion and putting us further on the defensive. I was suddenly the captain of Exxon's *Valdez*. It no longer mattered that the park didn't really sit on a historic battlefield; or that by widening the highway that ran by our site we would be improving what had long been a nightmarish bottleneck for commuters; or that the road leading to Manassas already contained a dense, tacky strip mall development far more intrusive than the park we envisioned building. By the summer of 1994, opposing Disney's America had become a fashionable cause célèbre in the media centers of New York City and Washington, D.C. If people such as Arthur Schlesinger, John Kenneth Galbraith, and Bill Moyers opposed our plans, that was reason enough for others to join the fight.

Nonetheless, we kept pushing on, convinced that the best answer to our critics was to build a great park. Around the same time that the Protect Historic America group held its press conference, Bob Weis and his team were able to gather together a different, but equally impressive group of experts to meet with us at Walt Disney World, listen to our current plans for Disney's America, and offer their criticisms and their ideas. In addition to several academic historians, the attendees included James Billington, the Librarian of Congress; the Reverend Leo O'Donovan, the president of Georgetown University; Robert Wilburn, the president of Colonial Williamsburg; Sylvia Williams, director of the National Museum of African Art at the Smithsonian; and Rex Scouten, the chief curator at the White House.

We began by taking them on a tour of several Epcot exhibits with historical themes, ranging from *The Making of Me,* a film sponsored by Metropolitan Life that tells the story of human development from birth, to *American Adventure*, a twenty-five-minute Audio-Animatronics presentation that recounts the story of the founding of the country. After the tours, we sought their reactions. The gathered group turned out to be highly critical of *American Adventure*, which hadn't been significantly updated since it opened in 1982.

"My general impression is that it's not the America I know, neither from the scholarship nor from my own perspective," said George Sanchez, a history professor at the University of Michigan. "There's way too much that's ignored about American history. . . . So for me, my experience was very disjunctive." Others echoed his comments, several of them complaining that the exhibit seemed dated. More broadly, they voiced a criticism that we'd heard frequently in recent months. Disney, they argued, couldn't be trusted to depict American history in ways that were sufficiently complex, subtle, and inclusive. I was surprised by the intensity of their reaction, but not upset by it. Disney's America remained very much in the early planning stages, and the whole purpose of this meeting was to solicit more input and make it better.

"Entertainment doesn't have to be pablum, and it doesn't have to make you feel good," I said, when my turn came to respond. "Entertainment has to create an emotional response. It can make you laugh, it can make you cry, it can make you angry, it can make you sad. I don't disagree with 98 percent of what has been said here, but I do want to point out that Disney's America won't be a 25-minute experience like the *American Adventure*. The story we're going to try to tell at the park will take eight hours to deliver. It's going to be made up of fifteen or twenty different components. Each one will deal with a different aspect of the American experience. Disney's America has the potential to redefine The Walt Disney Company more than anything we've done. Our goal, when you finish an eight-hour day there, is that you'll have experienced an intelligent, entertaining, challenging view of America."

The next morning, a Sunday, we took our group of experts to see the *Hall of Presidents*. When we all reconvened at 11:00 a.m., I was prepared for another tough day. To my surprise, nearly every member of the group seemed to have been impressed and even moved by the *Hall of Presidents*. Plainly, the decision to enlist the help of a tough critic in Eric Foner a year earlier had made a difference. "Once you know what's wrong, it isn't difficult to make it right," I told the group. "We have the technology. We have the ability. We have the contacts. And we also have the commitment."

Midway into our second day, our participants began to believe that we were genuinely interested in their responses. They could see how personally involved we all were in the project, and that while Disney is obviously a profit-making entertainment company, that didn't preclude a sense of social responsibility or a willingness to engage intellectually with our critics. When we turned to the question of how to tell the story of immigration, I now felt comfortable saying that we were considering using the Muppets. Unusual as that might seem for such a complex subject, we were determined to make the exhibit accessible to children—in part by injecting some humor. If we had brought up this idea the day before, it might well have been dismissed out of hand. Now it sparked a rich, open discussion. Whereas the meeting had begun in a wary, adversarial spirit, it had slowly turned more collaborative. Suddenly, we had the benefit of highly knowledgeable partners in thinking about how to depict historical themes ranging from slavery to immigration in lively, novel ways without sacrificing depth or authenticity.

At the end of the day, Eric Foner captured what seemed to be a widely held sentiment among his colleagues. "Whatever you do is going to get criticism," he told our team, "but I'm convinced after this weekend that it is possible for Disney to do a job that will be entertaining, intellectually defensible, and satisfying not only to the company but to the rather critical-minded people who are in this room, and also to the vast public that you will be bringing in. I'm pretty persuaded that this park can be salutary for the country and that people leaving it will be stimulated to learn more and think more and read more about American history and visit more places."

I, too, felt reinvigorated about the project. "I hope that this is the beginning of our dialogue," I concluded. "We spent five years making *The Lion King* and still didn't have it completely right. But we got a lot closer. This park will change and evolve over the next several years, and we want it critiqued. It's much easier to change something in the planning stages than it is once it's built. So we like to hear it early, and directly. We're not experts and we're thick-skinned. This has been very valuable. It has stimulated a lot of ideas. It has refocused me, as I'm sure it has all of our people."

Two weeks later, over a weekend in late May, Jane and I took a two-day trip to Washington to visit a series of historical sites, including

Mount Vernon, Monticello, and Montpelier — all landmarks of the American presidency. We walked the same grounds at Mount Vernon where Washington himself had pondered the future of the new nation. We saw the office at Monticello in which Thomas Jefferson wrote the Statute of Virginia for Religious Freedom and the bedroom in which he breathed his last breath—on Independence Day, 1826. We were reminded, walking through Montpelier, of the role that James Madison played in ratifying the Constitution. Our tour was full of beauty and inspiration, but there weren't crowds of fellow tourists. "You have to understand," James Rees, the director of Mount Vernon told us ruefully, "that presidents like Washington have become politically incorrect."

The sad truth is that the level of knowledge about American history among young people is nothing short of appalling. In a 1993 poll of 16,000 high school seniors, 80 percent could not explain the Emancipation Proclamation and nearly 60 percent had never heard of Teddy Roosevelt. In a second poll conducted among seventeen-year-olds, 60 percent could not identify the *Dred Scott* decision and 50 percent couldn't name the era in which Thomas Jefferson was president. Obviously, it is important to preserve authentic historic landmarks ranging from presidential homes to Civil War battlegrounds. But it is also critical to find ways to reinspire interest in these sites and the events they commemorate. The multimedia approach we envisioned for Disney's America was scarcely the whole answer, but we believed it had the potential to help.

When Jane and I returned to Washington, after our tour of presidential homes, we spent much of the next day at the U.S. Holocaust Memorial Museum. In contrast to the static exhibits at so many museums—including the three presidents' homes we had visited—this was a truly multimedia approach to history. The experience was at once horrifying and deeply affecting: a vivid, three-dimensional evocation of the genocide of more than 6 million people, among them many of my own European relatives. Especially moving was the room containing thousands of pairs of shoes that had been confiscated from Jews as they were about to be gassed to death. The powerful smell of leather made the experience even more immediate. Jane and I were affected as well by the museum's meticulous recreation of the process by which one town was transformed from a thriving, happy community to a barren one in which nearly all the residents were killed by the Nazis. The museum's creators used many of the dramatic tools and techniques that Walt Disney had pioneered—film, animation, music, voice-over narrative—in this case to recreate and evoke the horror of the Holocaust. These were the same tools that we intended to draw on for Disney's America.

In mid-June, I made another trip to Washington, this one an effort to respond directly to some of our critics, and to undertake some of the lobbying that I should have begun a year earlier. It wasn't going to be easy. At the prompting of the Virginia preservationists and the historians opposed to Disney's America, Senator Dale Bumpers was about to have his government subcommittee on public lands look into whether our project genuinely threatened any historical sites. Any public hearing was sure to create more negative media attention. In addition, Secretary of the Interior Bruce Babbitt was considering conducting his own investigation. I flew east feeling both defensive and righteously indignant at the campaign that had been launched against our project. The intensity of my emotions was a double-edged sword. On the one hand, it made me a more passionate advocate for Disney's America. On the other hand, in the heat of the battle, it also prompted me to say some things I would later wish I hadn't.

On the afternoon of June 13, I had a meeting with reporters and editors at the *Washington Post*. The paper's coverage, I believed, had been unduly one-sided and harsh, and I arrived with a chip on my shoulder—never a good idea. Instead of trying to present our case calmly and logically, I was flip and defiant, in part because I mistakenly assumed I was speaking on background and wouldn't be quoted directly. The next morning, the *Post* ran a front-page piece that recounted my comments at length.

Two of them especially made me cringe. The first was my response to the widespread criticism of our plans to build Disney's America. "I'm shocked," I was quoted as saying, "because I thought we were doing good. I expected to be taken around on people's shoulders." The second was my reaction to the historians who'd attacked the project so vitriolically. "I sat through many history classes where I read some of their stuff," my quote read, "and I didn't learn anything. It was pretty boring."

My comments made me sound not just smug and arrogant but like something of a Philistine. The quote about being carried around on people's shoulders was an unfortunate shorthand I used to describe my surprise and disappointment that Disney's effort to undertake something serious and substantive hadn't been more widely encouraged and embraced. The glib reference to historians was an irritated response to a group of people who I believed had attacked us unfairly, without making any real effort to understand what we were trying to do. It didn't matter that I was also inspired by my share of teachers, or that Disney sponsors the American Teacher Awards precisely to honor great teaching. That didn't qualify as news. Looking back, I realize how much my brief moment of intemperance undermined our cause.

Later in the week, I spent two days paying calls to senators, congressmen, and government officials, including Bruce Babbitt and Dale Bumpers, whose committee was set to begin hearings. I also met with Virginia senator John Warner, a Republican who, like his Democratic counterpart, Charles Robb, and most of the state's politicians, supported Disney's America. The following day I met with Tom Foley, then Speaker of the House, who brought together a dozen congressmen for a lunch. In the process, I discovered that the overwhelming majority of legislators were intrigued by Disney's America and opposed to involving the federal government in what was obviously a local dispute. Nonetheless, a week later Senator Bumpers held what was almost surely the first Senate Energy and National Resources subcommittee meeting in history to attract dozens of journalists and TV cameras, and some five hundred curious onlookers. It was beside the point that the majority of senators, Democrat and Republican, took our side. The event once again focused attention on the controversy over our project rather than on its substance.

For me, the saving grace that day was the blunt testimony by George Allen, the Virginia governor, who remained a staunch supporter of Disney's America. "I think I'm on solid ground in suggesting that Senator Bumpers' committee wouldn't have held a hearing if opposition to this park had not become a crusade among well-connected folks who don't want it located within 30 miles of their neighborhood," Allen began. "With all other arguments faltering, [these] opponents turned to historians who don't like the idea of history-based theme parks. . . . They have the same right as other Americans to express their points of view. But in arguing that this project ought to be blocked because they fear that The Walt Disney Company will not interpret history to their satisfaction, these folks are practicing censorship."

A week after my visit to Washington, Protect Historic America took out an ad in the *New York Times* which reprinted the *Post's* version of my quote about boring historians. The ad was headlined: "The Man Who Would Destroy American History." This time I could only laugh. (All right, I probably didn't laugh, but I didn't get as upset as Jane did.) Fairness seemed to have given way to polemics. As William Safire put it, succinctly addressing our critics: "Historians don't own history." I tried to take a conciliatory approach. "The concerns of thoughtful critics have helped us to refine our vision of what this park can be," I wrote in an op-ed piece for the *Washington Post*, a week after my visit there. "We will now go forward with our dream and hope our detractors can hold their fire and wait to judge us and our work on its merits."

Jane and I spent the Fourth of July at her parents' home in Jamestown, New York, for a large family reunion. Jane's grandmother, who lived with the family as Jane grew up, was herself the oldest of nine children. All of them were born in Sweden and six had emigrated to America in the early 1900s. This was a reunion of their children and grandchildren—Jane's cousins, nieces, and nephews—and it reminded me of *The New Land*, Jan Troell's powerful film about Swedish emigration to America. The second-generation Americans who made up Jane's family now lived all across the country. They had laid down roots and built successful careers, from teacher to airline pilot. Now, in the backyard of Jane's childhood home over Independence Day weekend, we were experiencing firsthand a version of the immigrant experience. For two days, I spent hours listening to the stories of Jane's relatives, many of whom I'd never met before. I was reminded once again of what had sparked my interest in building Disney's America.

The first event that seriously undermined my resolve was the bypass operation I underwent in mid-July. Before surgery, my plan had been to spend most of August in Aspen, but I was also excited about undertaking a series of short one- and two-day trips aimed at seeking further ideas for Disney's America. These included visits to Santa Fe, New Mexico, for the annual Pueblo Indian Dance Ritual; and to San Antonio, Texas, to see its widely touted Fiesta, Texas, regional theme park. I was also scheduled to visit Winston-Salem, North Carolina, for a meeting that Bob Weis's team had put together with Maya Angelou and a series of prominent black leaders and historians. In this case, the plan was to discuss how we intended to portray the African American experience at Disney's America. Obviously, I had to cancel all of these trips. Equally important, the operation left me with less strength to deal with the continuous opposition to the park. Even so, I remained determined to move forward.

On Friday, August 5—exactly three weeks after surgery—I made my first visit to the office specifically to attend a lunch meeting about our progress on Disney's America. Jane came along as my chauffeur and traveling nurse. I listened to a report on each of the aspects of the park, and we spent some time discussing a possible name change to "Disney's American Celebration." Several members of our group felt that it was softer and less presumptuous. We also talked some more about a new round of protests that we knew our opponents had set for September, in Washington, and how we intended to respond. After ninety minutes, I was exhausted, but very happy to be back at work.

Much of my attention over the next few weeks was focused on resolving Jeffrey Katzenberg's situation. On August 29, six days after we announced Jeffrey's departure, I turned my attention back to Disney's America to attend a meeting reviewing updated financial projections for the park. Larry Murphy and Richard Nanula had been taking a hard new look at our numbers, in consultation with Mark Pacala and Peter Rummell. It was Peter who delivered their stunning conclusion. The new figures, he explained, showed that rather than the profit we'd previously projected for Disney's America, we were now facing the prospect of substantial losses. There were several explanations. First, the concerted efforts of our critics—which included raising a legal challenge to nearly every environmental approval we received—had forced us to spend far more than we anticipated on attorneys, land-use experts, and lobbyists. Largely as a result, our projected opening was going to be delayed by at least two years, which meant far higher carrying costs in the interim, and more spending to combat our opponents. Also, as we continued to refine and strengthen our vision of the park, adding attractions and exhibits, its projected cost had increased by nearly 40 percent.

These numbers were discouraging, but particularly so when Peter explained that projections for the park's revenues had been scaled back. "With the softness in attendance at our domestic parks and at Disneyland Paris, it looks like we might ultimately have to drop the price point for tickets at Disney's America," he explained. Finally, there was the issue of the length of the park's season. In our original model, the assumption had been that Disney's America would be closed for three months in the winter. Now that a dozen members of our team had spent a year living in the towns adjacent to our site, they had a different view. An eight-month season for the park seemed more realistic.

Unanticipated costs and obstacles are a part of any project. In this case, we simply had more than our share. Under ordinary circumstances, I would have sent our team back to conceive a scaled-down version of the park that made more economic sense. There was, after all, still reason for optimism. Mark Pacala's group won several more key zoning and environmental approvals in the summer and fall of 1994. On September 8, nearly ten thousand local supporters of Disney's America turned out for a country fair that we held in Prince William County Stadium to rally the troops and counter the critics.

I still believed that it was possible to get Disney's America built, but the question now was at what cost—not just financially but psychically. Frank's death, my bypass surgery, and Jeffrey's departure had resulted in a harrowing five months for the company. I still hadn't recovered my full strength. On September 15, after two weeks of soul-searching, we finally agreed that it wasn't fair to subject the company to more trauma. The issue was no longer who was right or wrong. We had lost the perception game. Largely through our own missteps, the Walt Disney Company had been effectively portrayed as an enemy of American history and a plunderer of sacred ground. The revised economic projections took the last bit of wind out of our sails. The cost of moving forward on Disney's America, we reluctantly concluded, finally outweighed the potential gain.

Having decided to give up the ship, we turned our attention to withdrawing in a way that avoided creating more ill will and left the door open to eventually building the park elsewhere. The key was to make peace with the historians who had so vocally opposed the project. I asked John Cooke, who was head of the Disney Channel but had consulted on the park from the start, to handle this mission. In addition to his passion for history, John was well connected in Washington. Among other relationships, he sat on the board of a Democratic policy group with Dick Moe, one of the earliest and most influential critics of Disney's America. John agreed to set up a meeting with Moe, and on September 19, they met for dinner in Washington, D.C.

"If we were to leave the site in Virginia," John began, "do you think that some of the historians would agree to attend a joint news conference and endorse our right to build the park in another location?" Moe responded encouragingly. John then asked whether some of the historians might agree to serve on a future advisory panel, helping Disney to further refine the content of a historical park. Again, Moe was positive. He also agreed to arrange a dinner in New York the following evening that would include David McCullough. That, too, went well. The following morning, John drove out to Princeton and had a successfull lunch with the historian James McPherson, yet a third prominent critic.

My plan was to confirm the decision to withdraw from Virginia to the board of directors at our regular meeting scheduled at the end of September. After that, we would share the decision with Governor Allen, our staunchest and most effective supporter, and with other local Virginia officials. Once again, however, our plans began to leak in the press. For Gov. Allen to read about our decision before we could share it with him directly was simply unacceptable. Instead, we decided to charter a plane and rush two of our Disney's America team—Mark Pacala and Bob Shinn, Peter Rummell's deputy—to see the governor in person.

Governor Allen was understandably dismayed by the news, but absorbed it calmly. At mid-meeting, an aide interrupted to say that reporters were gathering outside his door. The governor arranged for Pacala and Shinn to leave by a back door and then met with the reporters himself. To this day, I feel sorry that we couldn't give Gov. Allen more reasonable advance warning. By the next morning, September 28, the story was on the front page of the *Washington Post*. The war was over, but in the course of the battle we'd learned important lessons. A good idea never dies and I had no intention of giving up on a historical park permanently. In the meantime, there were plenty of other pressing challenges to occupy our immediate attention.

13

Renewal

BY EARLY OCTOBER 1994, OUR STOCK HAD DROPPED TO ITS LOW FOR
the year—a shade under $38 a share, down from a high of $48 back in
February. We believed that the market was reacting emotionally to recent events rather than rationally. Analysts and reporters continued to
focus on my health, Jeffrey's departure, and our setback at Disney's
America. In fact, our management remained very strong and so did our
core businesses, and we were on the verge of reporting record revenues
and earnings. Indeed, one issue we faced was how to invest our excess
cash flow. There were three options. One was to pay it out in a special,
large dividend. The problem is that our shareholders rightly expect that
Disney, with the leverage of its name, ought to be able to earn more with
its cash than an individual would by investing the dividends. The second
option was to make an acquisition, and we continued to look for the
right one, at the right price. The final option was to buy back our stock.
That was the one we chose at this stage. Companies such as Coca-Cola
and General Electric have done the same thing very successfully. Our ra-
tionale was simple: By buying back stock when others were selling it, we
were focusing on the intrinsic value of the company, which we judged
to be far greater than its current market price. Further, by reducing the

number of our outstanding shares, earnings per share would be increased for the remaining shareholders.

The key is being able to reliably assess your intrinsic value. This is done by taking each business you're in, predicting its cash flows into the future, and then discounting those numbers back to the present. Only companies that have strong five- and ten-year planning can do this with any semblance of accuracy. As long as the intrinsic value of a company substantially exceeds the market value, it makes sense to buy back stock, because over the long haul, markets value companies fairly and accurately. By the time we finished, we'd purchased nearly $1 billion of our own shares. I felt confident that we'd made a terrific investment.

There were already positive signs about the future. Bringing Joe Roth aboard provided an almost immediate lift to live action. Joe's first idea was to give more priority to producing Disney label, family live-action movies. Especially in the burgeoning home video marketplace, he pointed out, the Disney brand name conferred a unique advantage. Between our library of classic films and our enormous recent success in animation, many video stores had created special sections and displays exclusively for Disney products. To parents looking for movies for their young children, Disney was the equivalent of the Good Housekeeping Seal of Approval. At most studios, for example, a movie like *Angels in the Outfield* would do fine as a rental, but wouldn't generate significant sales. Marketed under the Disney label as a family movie, Joe estimated that *Angels* would sell 5 million copies. Right away, he set as a goal producing one or two Disney label, high-profile live-action movies a year that had the potential to be promoted as major company-wide events, much the way we had so successfully marketed our animated movies.

Within weeks, Joe had a chance to test his theory. *The Santa Clause*, starring Tim Allen, the star of *Home Improvement*, in his first movie role, was developed by our Hollywood Pictures label. Prior to Joe's arrival, it hadn't been viewed as a likely major hit. But after screening *The Santa Clause* in a rough cut, Joe decided it had great potential as a Disney holiday release. First, he decided to cut fifteen minutes and add an array of special effects. Then he chose to market the movie exclusively as a comedy. Rather than release *The Santa Clause* as a Hollywood Pictures film, he switched it to the Disney label, in part to make it more appealing to parents and young children and eventually on home video.

Finally, he chose to open the movie in advance of the holiday season, on November 11, in an effort to have a jump on other family movies, including Fox's *Miracle on 34th Street*.

It all worked. *The Santa Clause* received warm reviews, earned nearly $20 million in its first weekend at the box office, established itself as the big family hit for the Christmas season, and eventually became our second biggest live-action movie, after *Pretty Woman*. It was a classic example of the multiplier effect from true synergy. *Home Improvement*, which we produced for ABC, was already the number one show on television. Having Tim Allen as the star of *The Santa Clause* became a means to cross-promote both the movie and the TV series. Bob Miller, the resourceful young founder and publisher of Hyperion, our trade book publishing division, was able to time publication of Allen's autobiography, *Don't Stand Too Close to a Naked Man*, with the release of *The Santa Clause*. Buoyed by the wave of publicity from the movie and the TV show, the book became an immediate bestseller. By the middle of December, Disney had the top grossing movie in America, the highest-rated network television show, and the number one nonfiction book on the *New York Times* bestseller list. We also had the best-selling home video. In early November, *Snow White* was released on video for the first time, and it sold 10 million copies in its first week. By Christmas, our stock price was up substantially. Perhaps never before had Disney entertained so many people, so successfully, on so many fronts.

I was encouraged, too, by our progress in animation. *The Lion King*, which opened in June 1994, would ultimately earn nearly $1 billion worldwide, making it by far our most popular animated film and probably the most profitable film ever made, including *Titanic* (lions and meerkats don't demand a percentage of the gross). *The Lion King* was far from an obvious hit. In the early stages, there was great skepticism that a modern audience would embrace a movie that didn't include any human characters, much less one built around singing animals. But through countless drafts over five years, *The Lion King* evolved into one of those magical films in which everything comes together. It was visually stunning. The story of a son trying to live up to his father's legacy had a powerful archetypal resonance, and so did the simple themes of betrayal and retribution, responsibility and honor. Scar, voiced by Jeremy Irons, was a rakish villain, while Zazu, Pumbaa, and Nathan Lane's

Timon provided great comic relief. Elton John and Tim Rice collaborated on an extraordinary group of songs, including "Circle of Life," "Can You Feel the Love Tonight?," and "I Just Can't Wait to Be King." Above all, *The Lion King* was a film that played equally well to every kind of audience.

It was also a daunting standard to match. I began driving over to Glendale every Friday morning to spend two hours to discuss our current projects with Peter Schneider and Tom Schumacher, as well as to consider new ones. Both Peter and Tom moved seamlessly into their new roles in the wake of Jeffrey's departure. The boldest decision that Peter made during the fall was to halt work on *Toy Story*, our first fully computer-generated movie, to be directed by John Lasseter and produced in partnership with the studio PIXAR. *Toy Story* was scheduled for release in November 1995, less than a year away. But Peter felt strongly that the relationship between the movie's two main characters, Woody and Buzz Lightyear, didn't yet resonate emotionally.

Late as it was in the game, this decision would prove to be a critical intervention that helped Lasseter and his group transform *Toy Story* from an interesting but flawed film into a giant critical and commercial hit. *Toy Story, The Hunchback of Notre Dame,* and *Pocahontas*, our next animated movie, due to be released in the summer of 1995, all represented significant departures from previous efforts. *Pocahontas* was the first attempt to deal with real historical figures; *Toy Story* was a dramatic technological breakthrough; and *Hunchback* was an unusually complex story. Whether or not any of these movies would prove to have the massive appeal of *Beauty and the Beast, Aladdin,* and *The Lion King*, we felt satisfied that we weren't settling creatively. We were also confident that our next half-dozen animated projects—*Hercules, Mulan, Tarzan, A Bug's Life, Dinosaur,* and *Fantasia* 2000 (supervised by Roy Disney)—represented an ambitious mix of movies that would take us into the millennium.

In addition to Joe and Peter, there were a series of other young team members whose experience we were determined to broaden. Even the most talented executives are a blend of strengths and weaknesses, light and dark. One of the most difficult jobs in running a company is to keep people's energies focused by giving them new challenges. As we looked for the next generation of leaders at Disney, only those who could handle highly varied responsibilities were going to be candidates.

The company had become too interdependent to rely on highly specialized managers with narrow sets of skills. I was less drawn to people with perfect credentials for a given job than to those who had strong underlying qualities such as common sense, character, creativity, and passion. With those traits—and the right training and support—people tend to succeed at whatever jobs they're given.

During this period, Sandy Litvack increasingly assumed a devil's advocate role, and we spent hours tossing reorganization scenarios back and forth. Over time, a particular conclusion either began to seem worse for the wear and my enthusiasm for it faded, or it kept growing on me until it simply felt right. Barring unusual time pressures, I try to wait until one of these two instincts kicks in before I make any important decision. The first one, in this case, was to put Paul Pressler in charge of Disneyland. Just thirty-eight, Paul had done a brilliant job running the Disney Stores for the past three years, raising the quality of our merchandise dramatically. Only two months earlier, we'd opened our three hundredth store worldwide. The prototype for a completely redesigned and expanded version of the Disney Store, successful first at the Del Amo shopping center in Torrance, California, was now being used in all of our new stores.

On November 4, I joined Paul for the opening of our first Walt Disney Gallery, at the Santa Ana Mall: a 3,000-square-foot store devoted to more expensive collectors' items, including animation cels and Disney art. Paul had managed to find another, smaller niche in the retail marketplace. Athough he'd never run a theme park, he was clearly a galvanizing leader. What Disneyland needed was someone not only capable of generating new excitement for the park but also of developing the concept for an economically viable second theme park in Anaheim. Taking Paul out of the stores at the top of his game to do something completely different was a risk for him and for us. He jumped at the opportunity, which reassured me that we'd made the right decision.

To take Paul's place at the stores, we had another unlikely idea: Richard Nanula, our CFO. Like Paul, Richard was one of the most talented members of our team and moving him into a new job carried risks. First, given the void created by Frank's death, the need for Richard's financial acumen at the corporate level was higher than ever. I also enjoyed having him around, which was no small factor in the quality of life day to day. Richard didn't have any previous operating experience, but that was exactly why the idea seemed appealing. If he was going to continue to rise in the company, it was important that he broaden and deepen his credentials. At first, Richard resisted the new offer. He'd grown accustomed to having broad responsibility across the company and it was understandably hard for him to contemplate moving to a divisional job. "I love what I'm doing," he told me. "But I'll do whatever you think is right for the company and me."

"This will help you in the future, not hold you back," I assured him. Richard's move also created an opening at the CFO level, and we felt that a more transaction-oriented financial expert from outside the company would add a new dimension to our team.

The third key move was to put Al Weiss in charge of Walt Disney World. Both he and Paul would report to Judson Green. Here, I was following a different instinct. Al had spent his entire twenty-year career at Walt Disney World, having grown up and attended college in the Orlando area. At the age of forty, he was a strong manager—gracious but tough-minded, aggressive but well liked. Al had been especially effective overseeing the massive hotel development at Walt Disney World during the past three years. Ordinarily, I would have been tempted to move someone with his skills to an entirely new role in the company, as I was doing with Richard and Paul. But at Walt Disney World, the culture is so specialized and the operation so complex that it made more sense to promote from within.

Al took over at an opportune moment. After three years of flat attendance, there were already signs of a turnaround at the resort. Over Thanksgiving we had our biggest attendance ever for that period, and we continued to run ahead of projections in the weeks that followed. In part, we were helped by external factors. The economy had finally begun a strong turnaround. The wave of crime against tourists in South Florida had ended as inexplicably as it began, and so, too, the negative publicity that frightened off so many foreign visitors. In addition, many travelers had now sampled other highly touted resort destinations such as Las Vegas and Branson, Missouri, only to discover that they had less to offer families than Walt Disney World did.

We were also providing more reasons than ever to visit us in Orlando. A new marketing campaign had been targeted not just at our core audience of families but at other groups, such as younger singles and older couples. The goal was to bring attention to the broader range of options Walt Disney World now offered. At the Disney-MGM Studios, for example, the *Tower of Terror* had opened in July, along with Sunset Boulevard, a street filled with shops and restaurants, and attendance jumped nearly 15 percent during the next four months. At Epcot, we debuted two new attractions. One was *Honey, I Shrunk the Audience*, a dazzling three-dimensional special effects film that makes the audience feels as if it's shrinking. Even before its official opening, *Honey* was drawing lines longer than many of our most popular attractions. It had also been created at a fraction of their cost. The other lure was *Innoventions*, our own consumer electronics show, offering a window on the near future. Its interactive exhibits were popular with kids, especially Sega's state-of-the-art video games. At the Magic Kingdom, we opened an entirely new Tomorrowland, adapting several of the attractions that we'd designed for Discoveryland at Disneyland Paris.

On Sunday, November 27, after observing our traditional family Thanksgiving in Vermont, I flew down to Walt Disney World for the first time since my bypass. Most of my time in Orlando was spent touring our new attractions, but I also sat down on Monday afternoon with about 200 of the park's top managers for an employee forum. Mostly, I answered questions, but with an eye toward reassuring our team that I intended to put the difficult times of the past year behind us and to move forward aggressively. The most provocative question I received was whether we anticipated making any large acquisition in the near future.

"During the next several years, we should make a major acquisition," I replied. "The trick is not to make the wrong one. You have to be patient. You want to buy something for what it's worth—not what others tell you it's worth or what it might be worth if you turned it around. You want to make a choice that complements the Disney brand —where the sum of the two companies is greater than the parts. That's the deal we are still looking for."

The other area where we saw enormous opportunity was internationally. In the wake of the restructuring, Disneyland Paris was now on a far more secure financial footing, and there were signs that a turnaround was underway, much as our domestic parks were picking up. In addition, no fewer than four major television deals were in the pipeline to provide Disney programming overseas. One was in Germany; a second in India; and the third was a satellite-delivered service in Taiwan, which we hoped would reach much of Asia. But no deal was more complex or potentially more valuable than our negotiation with Rupert Murdoch's News Corp. to place the Disney Channel exclusively on his British Sky Broadcasting satellite-delivered programming service in England.

Murdoch operated from a philosophy that could scarcely have been more different than ours. He believed in owning the means of distribution wherever possible, and he was more than willing to pay a premium price for properties and exclusive programming that he believed served his strategic vision. We were far more conservative than News Corp. when it came to acquisitions. But if our appetites were very different, there were instances in which they could be complementary. In 1988, when Murdoch was first launching what would become BSkyB in England, we entered a joint venture to provide both the Disney Channel and a movie channel that we would program. Several weeks before the launch, BSkyB began running advertisements in Murdoch's British tabloid, *The Sun*, in which the topless "page 3" girl was shown with a satellite dish covered with the logos of the services that would be available on the new service—among them the Disney Channel. Obviously, this wasn't the sort of environment in which we felt comfortable. We ended up pulling out of the venture.

In the fall of 1994, Rich Frank and his European deputy, Etienne de Villiers, began negotiating to add the Disney Channel as a pay service on the cable systems that two American companies, Southwestern Bell and TCI, were building jointly in England. In mid-December, Murdoch heard about our negotiations, just as he was preparing to float a large public stock offering for BSkyB, the principal competitor to cable in England. For Murdoch, providing the Disney Channel exclusively on BSkyB was potentially a powerful lure for new subscribers: a prestigious, high-profile addition to his stock offering, and a blow to his cable competitors. He authorized his executives to make a substantial, preemptive offer for the Disney Channel. It included a guaranteed advance of $30 million to be put against the monthly fee paid by each subscriber who signed up for our service. In addition, the Disney Channel would be offered free to any BSkyB subscriber who bought at least two other pay movie or sports services—and we would still earn our monthly fee.

Both Rich and Etienne were eager to close the Murdoch deal quickly. "It's a home run for us," Rich told me. I shared his enthusiasm, but I had a conflicting interest: protecting the Disney brand. We had learned on the last go-round with Murdoch that it was critical to maintain exceptionally strict controls over the use of the Disney name and franchise. "There is no way that we can let them advertise the Disney Channel in any publications with salacious material, or offer the channel in combination with any R-rated movie service," I told Rich. "No deal, no matter what the size, is worth undermining the value of the Disney name."

In mid-December, Peter Murphy, a senior executive in strategic planning, flew to England both to help out in the financial aspects of the deal and to play the role of corporate protector—"brand cop"—on my behalf. Putting Peter in this role prompted a certain amount of tension with Rich and Etienne. "You're unnecessarily complicating a very favorable deal," Rich complained. I continued to believe that this sort of tension — between entrepreneurial initiative and a more conservative corporate perspective—ultimately served our company well. Had Murdoch held firm in the face of our demands, we would have walked away, as we had on other occasions in similar instances. At the same time, we needed executives like Rich and Etienne to seek out new businesses and to push the boundaries. In this case, Murdoch was under great time pressure, and his team finally agreed to every one of our key terms. By hanging tough, we were able to make the deal we wanted without jeopardizing the Disney brand.

As the holidays approached, I felt encouraged by the events of the past several months. At the previous Christmas, we had faced a highly uncertain future for Disneyland Paris, a continuing downturn at our domestic theme parks, terrible results in live action, and a burgeoning controversy over Disney's America. All this was now behind us. The losses and setbacks during the past year had been real, but the worst seemed to be behind us. I felt the same way about my own life and the life-threatening crisis I'd survived.

Shortly after the new year began, I received a letter from the novelist Larry McMurtry (*Terms of Endearment, Lonesome Dove*). It was a ten-page epistle in which he described his reaction to the heart surgery he had undergone three years earlier. McMurtry was fifty-five at the time, just a few years older than I was when I had my bypass.

"This is not stuff you will hear from cardiologists, because they don't know it," he began. "They know that something happens that's not good [following bypass] but they don't know what. . . . I imagine at some point you will have felt some of these feelings, if not all. I ceased to read, write, travel, run bookshops, lecture, write scripts, etc. I felt that I had become an outline; then I felt that someone was erasing the outline and that I was simply vanishing—evaporating. . . . I have felt largely posthumous since the operation. My old psyche, or old self, was shattered—now it whirls around me in fragments. I can generally gather enough of the fragments to make a fair showing, professionally, and I hope emotionally. But I am always conscious of working with fragments of a self, never the whole." He went on to describe some of his symptoms, including depression, insomnia, difficulty concentrating, an end to his type A ambition, and an enormous sense of frustration at not being able to remember the details of the surgery itself.

McMurtry ascribed much of this unsettling experience to the fact that during a bypass operation, one is kept alive by a machine. "The heart-lung machine allows for biologic survival," he wrote. "For a certain period of time one is technically alive, but in another and a powerful sense, dead. Then one is jump-started back into life, but the Faustian bargain has been made. You're there, but not as yourself. . . . I'm stronger and healthier in body, weaker and needier emotionally and in spirit. I'm younger in body, but very much older in spirit. . . . The basic difficulty is a feeling of having been severed permanently from the self I thought of as me for 55 ½ years. I am not that person now; I am another. I feel I'm mourning that self, and that mourning is not likely to end, however long I live."

I found McMurtry's essay haunting and unnerving. On the evening of the day that I received it, I sat down in front of the computer in my office and began trying to compose a response. "I just read your letter," I finally began.

I read it once and then again, and I feel honored to have received it.

When I read it for the third time, my heart (is it really mine?) finally stopped pounding and I was able to think about what I had read. . . . Why am I writing this letter now on a Friday at the office at 7:30 p.m.? . . . . I should go home and have dinner with my wife and four friends and watch *The Madness of King George*, but I don't really want to. I have seen this wonderful film already and I am not up to dinner conversation, especially after reading your letter.

A lot of what you write I understand and to some extent I have had similar feelings. But I do not have the problem to the extent you describe; only the vague shadows of the problem. Where I am most similar is my frustration in absolutely retrieving the "details" of what happened [during surgery]. I want absolute knowledge, absolute definition of the facts, the stitches, the talking, the machines, the silences, the near death, the re-birth, and mostly what the doctors said, thought, joked and yawned about during my operation. Was the World Cup or The Three Tenors (both occurred the weekend of my bypass) more interesting to them than my heart?

Next, I described for McMurtry the events leading up to my own bypass:

My tests showed a little blockage, but nothing to worry about. I started taking cholesterol-lowering drugs, Mevacor (Lovastatin), which seemed to work. This was my surface life: Great success at the office . . . Three great kids . . . Great wife . . . Type A life . . . Conflict . . . and Mevacor . . . And finally Euro Disney. . . . Then I stopped sleeping two years before my bypass . . . and like you, I hated that.

I have had worse problems than Euro Disney. I had had the long arm of parental conflict but I could deal with it. I forgot about the pain under exercise and just accepted it as part of my emotional life. The pain, I believed, was psychologically induced. I was capturing the attention of my father or some other parent. I did not have *real* pain. I had migraine pain, stomach pain, gas pain, airplane-fright pain, marketplace pain . . . all located in my arms. And then I went to Sun Valley to be part of a group of industry leaders talking about industry leaders. And I had such arm pain that I was sure I was the most nervous I had ever been. . . . It was bad enough that I came home a day early. I went to Cedars-Sinai Medical Center for a test to prove that it was all emotional and ended up with a stopped heart, as you did, and new veins, and a mammary artery to bypass all the anxiety. I was an emergency bypass patient who, I am told, would have been dead within two days.

At last, I got to the real point of my letter, which had dawned on me only in the course of writing::

Something has happened to me that is a big deal. I am no longer immortal. I am no longer even young. . . . I still go to the office and still am basically the same person, but there is this giant hole which I guess is called middle age. Or actually it is old age. . . . 52 is half of 104 and therefore 52 is not middle age. 52 for me is old age. That's the rub. . . . I went from kid to old guy in four hours. . . .

I do not like what has happened, but I guess it's better than many I know. I don't have cancer or any other horrible illness that I know about. But I am different. My life has a finite sense to it, and there is certainly a hollowness that comes with such realizations. I try not to think about it, but I think about it all the time. I didn't want to read your letter, but I read it three times, like one reads *Fanny Hill* in grade school. I work as I worked before, but I know it isn't as important as it was before. I used to put up with betrayal as a reality in life and now I won't let it in the door even if there is a blockbuster motion picture associated with it. . . .

When all is said and done, I do feel in the hollow of this new life one strange thing that you do not mention. I feel one positive. I feel one rush that offsets all the feelings you related. I feel one enormous explosion which I haven't felt since my first son was born. I died. And I know what that is. Although I feel the ceiling of death, at the same time I accept death for the first time and even look at it without fear. Death has always been for me the feeling of air turbulence, hitting the shoulder of the highway. . . . Not now. It simply is. I have been there and it was okay.

Someday I hope I can forget I have a physical heart, as I never knew I had one before. It was so much better having only a poetic heart. A physical heart is such a necessity. What a bummer!!!! Thank you for sending your thoughts on to me. Happy New Year.

Life, of course, went on. On January 26, 1995, we had our first meeting in four years with the Wall Street analysts who follow our company—and the first one in twenty-five years to be held on the Disney lot. My purpose was less to bring the analysts up-to-date on our strong results than to give each of our top division executives the opportunity to speak in some detail about their own businesses. Nothing else, I believed, would demonstrate more persuasively the depth and range of our newly configured management team. We held the event on one of our sound stages, and it attracted more than 130 very curious analysts. The presentations went on for more than four hours, but I never saw anyone walk out. One member of our team after another made impressive and persuasive cases—not just for their current businesses but for their visions of the future. Nearly every analyst who issued a report after the meeting included a buy recommendation for our stock, which jumped 6 points in nine days. This result was not by any means a forgone conclusion. The previous fall, after the top executives at one of our competitors met with the same group of analysts, that company's stock actually dropped in price.

The other key management change we made, in the spring of 1995, was a new chief financial officer to replace Richard Nanula when he took over the Disney Stores. We interviewed more than a half-dozen candidates, but from the first time I met Stephen Bollenbach, I sensed he was the right one. Two years earlier, Steve had engineered an innovative restructuring of the Marriott Corporation into two separate companies, one of which he now ran. Previously, as CFO for the Trump organization, he had worked out the deal with the banks that permitted Donald Trump to survive a near bankruptcy and eventually prosper again. Like Gary Wilson, Steve had a reputation as a superb financial mind and a creative dealmaker.

From the start, I knew it was unlikely that Steve would spend the rest of his career at Disney unless he became my clearly designated successor. Given his lack of experience in entertainment and his limited interest in the creative side of our business, I doubted that would happen. But even if Steve eventually moved on, there was great value in attracting a top financial mind and a highly sophisticated strategic thinker as we considered the next phase of Disney's growth. On April 4, we announced his hiring. As a measure of Steve's perceived value at his previous job, Marriott's stock dropped more than 5 percent.

It was never a secret where Steve wanted to put his energies at Disney. Richard Nanula had focused primarily on overseeing the financial aspects of operations and strengthening the Disney brand. Steve argued that between the strength of Disney's cash position, our relative absence of debt, and the tax advantages of borrowing money, a major outside acquisition ought to be a top priority. "Interest rates are low and the capital markets are as friendly as we're likely to see in our lifetime," he told me. "We can borrow cheaply and easily, and we ought to take advantage of that." A television network was the obvious acquisition, and we began to discuss the two remaining possibilities, ABC and CBS.

In the meantime, no single creative endeavor was more important to the company than our animated movies. As summer approached, much of the company's attention turned to our next release: *Pocahontas*. When it came to creating big events, Dick Cook and his marketing team had outdone themselves. On Saturday evening, June 10, more than a hundred thousand people were expected to attend the *Pocahontas* premiere in New York's Central Park. By coincidence, my son Eric's graduation from Dartmouth College was scheduled to take place during the same weekend.

On Saturday, after spending the day in Hanover, New Hampshire, for the first round of graduation events, Jane, Breck, Anders, Eric, and I boarded a plane for the one-hour flight to New York and the *Pocahontas* premiere. By the time we arrived at Central Park, it was threatening to rain, which instantly evoked childhood memories. More than four decades earlier, I had often played baseball on these same Central Park fields. I always hated worrying about the weather on the day of games. Bad weather had the potential to ruin the best-laid plans, and there was absolutely nothing you could do about it. If it started to rain with one hundred thousand people watching *Pocahontas*, we had no contingency plans. It hadn't been logistically possible to set a rain date. We were just going to have to make do.

Perhaps it was divine intervention, but the only time it rained that night was for two minutes during the one scene in the movie where it rains! Instead, I spent the evening worrying about the quality of the sound, the difficulty seeing the screen from certain vantage points, and the potential for disaster when such a huge crowd is huddled together so tightly. What I underestimated is the generosity of spirit that New Yorkers invariably summon up under challenging circumstances. Most people seemed to delight in the excitement of joining in a unique spectacle.

The event was hugely successful in generating publicity for *Pocahontas* and goodwill for Disney. It seemed a fitting symbol that our company had weathered the storms of the previous year and that the skies ahead were clearing.

Shortly after midnight, I gathered Jane, our three kids, my mother, my sister, her husband, and their two children in order to head back to Hanover for Eric's graduation ceremony. The rain finally caught up with us in New Hampshire. When we awoke the next morning, it was obvious that we were in for a downpour. Because the graduation speaker was President Clinton, security precautions were high. We were asked to take our seats in the Dartmouth football stadium a full hour before commencement began, and not bring any umbrellas—a precaution against their being misconstrued by the Secret Service as guns. Obediently, I insisted that we all abide by these requests. Virtually no one else took them seriously. When the torrential rains began, a sea of umbrellas instantly arose all around us. We spent the next three hours getting thoroughly drenched.

It hardly mattered. The moment that the senior procession began and I heard the band play the first chords of "Pomp and Circumstance," I felt just as choked up as I had at my own graduation from Denison, my sister's from Smith, Breck's from Georgetown, and Anders's from junior high school. It was after hearing "Pomp and Circumstance" at Eric's graduation from high school four years earlier that I went to Roy Disney and set out to convince him that few musical pieces are more powerful reminders of emotional moments in people's lives. I suggested we use it in our new *Fantasia*. Eventually, "Pomp and Circumstance" would become the music that accompanied a wonderful Noah's Ark segment during which Donald Duck helps to bring all of the world's animals onto the Ark and then rushes off to find Daisy at the last moment.

After President Clinton's commencement speech, there was a reception in his honor. It was bedlam, with hundreds of mothers, fathers, and grandparents clamoring to shake the President's hand. I could tell that my own mother wanted to meet the President, but after twenty minutes of waiting, it was also obvious that Eric was feeling restless. We all understood that this was his day, and so we headed back to his room. Jane and I helped him pack up the last of his dirty clothes and we stood around while he said his good-byes to his friends. At 3:00 p.m., Jane, Breck, Anders, and I boarded a plane headed to Los Angeles. My mother returned to New York. Before heading back to L.A., Eric planned to stop in Jamestown, New York, where Jane's parents lived. They hadn't been well enough to attend the graduation, and Eric decided that he wanted to see them before crossing the country to begin the rest of his life.

I felt very proud of him, and more hopeful than ever about the future.

14

Landing ABC

My memories of Herb Allen's annual conference in Sun Valley were scarcely sunny, but I was absolutely determined to return in June 1995. Practically, it was an opportunity to present the story of Disney's rejuvenation to a group of industry leaders. More important, it was akin to climbing back up on a horse after a bad fall. At the conference a year earlier, I had experienced the pain in my arms that led to quadruple bypass surgery three days later.

I was scheduled to leave my office at 2:15 p.m. on Thursday, July 27. My last meeting was a lunch with our strategic planning team. The purpose was to discuss the relative merits of potential acquisitions that we had been considering—most notably CBS and ABC, but also the record company EMI and several other longer shots. Larry Murphy's group had prepared a short summary of each of the potential deals, which incorporated the likely acquisition price, the value we put on the companies, and the prospective impact of each purchase on our earnings per share. The meeting included Larry and his two deputies, Peter Murphy and Tom Staggs, as well as Sandy Litvack and Steve Bollenbach, who was attending one of these periodic lunches for the first time.

Even before Steve's arrival, we had spent considerable time looking at the possibilities for acquiring a television network. Our first discussions with Capital Cities/ABC took place in the fall of 1993 and actually preceded our negotiations for NBC a year later. At the time, Tom Murphy was chairman, but Dan Burke—Steve Burke's father and Tom's longtime partner—had essentially taken over. Dan and I had several discussions about a possible merger, but nothing conclusive came of them. Early in 1994, Dan decided to retire, and Tom chose to return as CEO. We spoke intermittently and a year later—March 1995—I was in New York for a series of meetings and arranged with Tom to have dinner. Our conversation focused first on Disney's role as a program supplier to ABC, but it wasn't long before we began to discuss a merger. Over the next few weeks, we had several further conversations, but couldn't come to terms, largely because Murphy was only interested in a deal where we paid for Cap Cities with our stock. We continued to believe our shares were undervalued.

Early in May, Barry Diller called to suggest yet another approach to our investing in a network—in this case CBS. One year earlier, Barry had been stymied at the last moment in his attempt to buy CBS from Larry Tisch. They, too, had continued to talk. Now, Barry had in mind a deal in which Disney would agree to invest $750 million toward the acquisition of CBS in return for a stake in the network. Barry would borrow most of the rest of the $5–$6 billion purchase price from banks, and he would become chairman and chief executive. Essentially we would serve as passive investors. For us, the real value of the deal was the potential to gain guaranteed access for our programs — ideally a weekly Disney franchise show in prime time, the ability to program CBS's Saturday morning schedule, and the guarantee of two or three Disney-produced prime-time series. We had never before invested in someone else's deal, but Barry brought unique talents to the equation, financially and creatively. Agreeing on issues such as independence and our degree of involvement was certain to be difficult, but we felt confident they could be resolved. The problem was that Barry himself was unable to settle on a purchase price with Tisch that made economic sense to him, or to us. For a second time, his negotiations ended unsuccessfully.

Within our group, the interest in a large acquisition — and specifically in buying a network—only seemed to grow in the wake of these aborted negotiations. Adding Steve Bollenbach to the equation helped to tip the scales. Larry Murphy and Richard Nanula had long been the strongest and most persuasive voices for sticking to our Disney-branded businesses and resisting the lure of any expensive acquisition. Now Steve had taken Richard's place at the table—literally and figuratively—and an aquisition was his highest priority from the day he arrived in April 1995. Peter Murphy and Tom Staggs, the two people who spent the most time analyzing potential acquisitions, had long been enthusiastic voices in favor of a network. We'd been through similar discussions at least a dozen times during the past decade, but as our team sat down together for lunch several hours before my departure for Sun Valley, I could sense a certain electricity in the air.

It was Peter who delivered the status report on our options and their implications. He focused first on ABC and CBS. Tisch was still eager to sell CBS after negotiations with Barry broke down. He was seeking $80 a share, meaning an acquisition cost of approximately $5.6 billion. Cap Cities was selling for $105 a share. Our best estimate on the price that Tom Murphy had in mind was somewhere between $120 and $130 a share, or approximately $20 billion for a much bigger group of assets.

"I've been pushing a network acquisition for seven years," Peter began, "and I continue to believe in the value of owning one. CBS is a sick asset that needs to be turned around. Cap Cities is a collection of mostly healthy assets with strong management. CBS is a turnaround play. Cap Cities is a strategic, synergy play. CBS costs less, has a bigger upside, but is very overpriced. ABC costs much more, but there is less to turn around, and the likely price is more reasonable."

Staggs now chimed in, making it even clearer where his and Peter's preference lay. "CBS is just broadcasting," he said. "With Cap Cities, we get the broadcasting and strong management that we've been after, but we also get ESPN, which makes us a much bigger player in cable."

I had been quiet, but now I couldn't resist playing devil's advocate. "I still like CBS," I said. "It doesn't cost as much, and I think we can fix it."

"I'm leaning toward ABC," Sandy said, "but I understand CBS. It's smaller and more bite-sized."

"My argument," said Peter, "is that we have a compulsive culture at Disney. We put the same time and energy into a small acquisition such as Miramax that we would into a $20 billion acquisition like Cap Cities. There is a dilution of effort with something small. I think it makes more sense to do one big thing that brings a larger return on the human capital expended."

Bollenbach had been biding his time. Now he finally jumped in. "There are two reasons I fundamentally like Cap Cities over CBS," he said. "First it's a much better deal. Second, it makes a much bigger stride toward solving the problem of what to do with our cash. With CBS, we have not leveraged up the company to nearly the point that I think we should. The debt markets are at nearly historic lows. The cash flows out of a Cap Cities–Disney combination would make it possible to very quickly pay down any debt we take on. To me, the issue is simple. Either we buy a relatively little house and overpay for it, or we go after this big mansion and get a bargain."

In Richard's absence, Larry was the sole dissenter, but his opposition was less strenuous than it had been in the past. "My first choice is still that we do nothing," he said. "The Disney strategy of sticking to our knitting and building our own brand has been very successful. But I also recognize the attraction of buying a network. Our competitors are starting up their own networks, and there's no question that the issues of access for our programming are looming larger. I also agree that ABC is the strategic move. The problem is that it may well be performing at its peak, which means that we have exposure on the downside. That's why I'm still intrigued by the idea of CBS. I see how we can turn it around."

"Larry, you're obviously right that ABC is heading south," I said. "But it can be turned around over time and in any case, it only represents a small percentage of the overall corporation."

"If we can get ABC at a reasonable price, then it's probably the right choice," Larry replied. "But I'm going to be the last person to say yes on either one. I'm worried about diverting attention from our Disney businesses and creating a huge new management challenge at a time when we have plenty to do in our own businesses."

The other related issue was whether ABC was likely to achieve the 20 percent annual rate of growth we had always set as our benchmark for Disney. Here the concept of "hurdle rate" was critical. Hurdle rate is not a track term, but rather refers to the return that a particular investment or acquisition must deliver in order reliably to create value for a company. For instance, a riskier investment such as launching an entirely new business, which has a wide range of potential outcomes, must have the potential to earn a higher rate of return than a proven investment such as a new theme park attraction, which has a narrower but more predictable upside. It was highly unlikely that ABC could achieve 20 percent a year growth, but in this case, there were other strategic reasons that the acquisition made sense.

Peter Murphy now jumped in to advance the case for ABC that I found most compelling. "The real issue isn't the next five to ten years," he insisted. "We can continue to grow at 20 percent a year by sticking to our knitting. It's what happens to Disney ten years from now, all the way through to 2050. The challenge of the future is going to be operating as a global entity and creating an entertainment engine around the world. The players that establish themselves internationally are going to be the ones that matter in the future. Cap Cities gives us a chance to do that, not only with ABC, but with ESPN and their other cable properties like Lifetime and the Arts & Entertainment Network and the History Channel."

Before lunch ended, Steve turned our attention to a potential acquisition that he had recently added to our list. Code-named "Elmer," it was certainly the longest shot of all, but that didn't deter him. "I think Time Warner is a great fit for our company," Steve explained. "It's big, it has great assets, and we could buy it cheaply, because the stock is undervalued. The problem, obviously, is that it would be a much more complicated deal to do. And, of course, our move would be contested." Here Steve was being euphemistic. Any attempt to buy Time Warner would almost certainly involve a bitterly hostile takeover battle. Gerald Levin, its chairman, had fought hard to retain his independence—and was certain to do so again if a bidder came after his company.

As Steve continued singing the praises of the deal, I could see Larry's eyes growing wider and his eyebrows arching higher. "You're talking about the single most complicated, aggressive, unpleasant transaction that we could conceivably undertake," he finally interjected. "Not to mention the huge culture clash between the two companies if we did succeed. I just don't think it's realistic."

Steve remained unfazed. "I trust that our management would be able to sort out these kinds of problems," he said. "In today's world, if you're willing to pay the right price, it's almost axiomatic that you will get the company you are after. A bidder gets to that price and the target company's board recommends the deal. This one would be complicated, but I'm pretty confident we could do it."

I sided with Larry—unequivocally. Going after Time Warner would mean launching a full-scale war, and winning it would require absorbing a company that represented a terrible cultural fit with ours. It made far more sense to me to pursue a friendly deal with CBS or Capital Cities. As our lunch ended, we agreed that if the opportunity arose in Sun Valley, I would talk with Tom Murphy or Larry Tisch, but that I wouldn't go out of my way to make something happen.

The other negotiation I had resumed actively pursuing was with Michael Ovitz, whom I also expected to see in Sun Valley. Although our talks had foundered a year earlier, I was still interested in attracting him to Disney. In mid-May, word surfaced in the media that Ovitz was negotiating with the chairman of the Seagram company, Edgar Bronfman, Jr., to head MCA/Universal, which Seagram had just purchased. I wasn't happy to hear the news. Ovitz knew the movie and television businesses as well as any executive in Hollywood, and I suspected that he might also be very good at running the Universal theme parks. I preferred not to have to compete with him. The problem was commanding Ovitz's attention. By the time I reached out to him again, he was deep in negotiations with Bronfman on a deal that would reportedly guarantee him as much as $250 million. On the last Wednesday of May, Ovitz finally agreed to a lunch at my house. I didn't know it yet, but his negotiations with Seagram had begun to hit rough seas. For the first time, he seemed willing to entertain the possibility of coming to Disney as a number two. Even so, when our lunch ended, I still assumed that Ovitz would end up at MCA.

I was soon proved wrong. On Monday, June 5—the same day that Ovitz was featured in a *Newsweek* cover story about his impending move—the MCA deal fell apart. The immediate result was that he became available again. We didn't have much opportunity to talk during the next few weeks but I assumed that we would in Sun Valley. Instead, Ovitz went up two days before I did. The next day, Edgar Bronfman,

Jr., announced that he'd hired Ron Meyer, one of Ovitz's partners at CAA, to head MCA, and that the two of them would be coming to Sun Valley together. Ovitz decided to leave.

"I just don't feel comfortable at someone else's coronation," he told me early Thursday morning. Any discussions about his coming to Disney would have to wait. At midafternoon Thursday, following the strategic planning lunch, I boarded a plane along with Bollenbach, Sandy Litvack, Wendy Webb, who handles our investor relations, and Joe Roth, with whom I was scheduled to make our Sun Valley presentation the next morning. Jane decided to stay home.

When we landed, shortly after 5:00 p.m., Herb Allen was waiting to pick me up. I wasn't certain why my stock had risen with him since the last conference, but a great deal had changed in my life and Disney's. Our company was moving aggressively forward. We had begun to build a new management team. I felt healthier than I had in a long time. I was even sleeping well again, having happily discovered that my earlier troubles weren't a function of unconscious anxiety or middle-aged angst, as I'd feared, but rather of Lovostatin, the cholesterol-lowering drug I'd been taking before my bypass. Recently, it had been found to cause insomnia in some patients. The moment I stopped taking it, I started sleeping soundly again.

When Allen dropped me off, the first person I saw was Barry Diller—the new, athletic Diller—riding toward me on a bicycle. We talked for a few minutes about CBS, and Barry reiterated that the deal we had discussed to buy the network together no longer made any sense to him. After checking into my condominium—also an upgrade from the outlying room I had the previous year—I walked over with Barry and Diane Von Furstenberg to the patio where dinner was being served. At 10:00 p.m. Joe Roth came to get me, so that we could go over to a conference room to look at the audiovisuals we would be using for our presentation the next morning.

I woke up in time to attend the 8:00 a.m. Time Warner presentation by Jerry Levin and Bob Daly. Next, I went to watch the entertainment panel, moderated by Jack Valenti. At one point, Jeffrey Katzenberg, now a head of DreamWorks, took out a water gun and began spraying his fellow panelists. A few minutes before the panel ended, I slipped out to prepare for my own presentation with Joe. The room filled up quickly—in part, I'm sure, with people curious about the state of my health.

"I come to you today not so much as a representative of The Walt Disney Company," I began, "but as a proxy for the late Frank Wells. He made Herb Allen a promise to update this group on Disney every other year, and from what I gather his last reports were pretty straightforward: Disney's business was either good or better. Well, let's see, this past year we've had Disney's America . . . Euro Disney's restructuring . . . tourist shootings and Hurricane Andrew in Florida . . . fire, floods, and a giant earthquake in California . . . not to mention certain executive changes. . . ." After a beat, I switched tacks. "Seriously, business was fantastic last year, and even better than good this year. We've just had our second-biggest opening in history with *Pocahontas*. . . . We're on track to meet our financial goals in 1995 and the years ahead. And actually I'm quite grateful for my heart surgery. For one thing, the doctors told me that they left in the artery that was marked 20 percent return on equity and 20 percent growth in net income. They just passed it through a channel that said, 'not at any cost.' . . . The fact is that Disney's knack for self-renewal has enabled the company to grow at a 28 percent annual rate."

When I turned the presentation over to Joe, he described his strategy for reinventing live action, built around making major events out of one or two Disney-label films each year. He also spoke about our continuing success in home video and animation, and capped his talk with a powerful five-minute clip that Peter Schneider had arranged from the upcoming *The Hunchback of Notre Dame*, before handing the podium back to me. I ended by reading a letter that Warren Buffett had sent me two years earlier. "In 1965," I quoted him, "I bought 5 percent of Disney for approximately 4 million dollars. That's the good news. The bad news is that I sold it a year or two later at about a $2 million profit." I explained that I hadn't been able to resist writing back to Warren, to tell him what his position in Disney would be worth had he chosen to keep it through 1993, when he wrote to me—namely, $552 million.

"Since Warren's here today," I added, "I just thought I'd bring him up to date. If he had held on to that original investment over *all* these years, today his $4 million would be worth $869 million. But don't feel too badly for him. If Disney had purchased $4 million worth of Warren's Berkshire Hathaway stock in 1965 . . . it would be worth in excess of $6 *billion* today."

Joe and I stayed around to answer a dozen questions, but by 12:30 p.m., I was on my way back to my room to pack. Discussions about a network acquisition hadn't materialized, but there would be other opportunities. We could afford to be patient. My plan was to have a quick lunch, say a few good-byes, and then head to the airport, where Jane was meeting me so that we could fly together to Aspen for the weekend. I was walking down the path to my condominium to pick up my bags when I ran into Larry Tisch and his wife, Billie. They'd attended our Disney presentation and stopped to say something complimentary about it. The previous evening, Barry had told me that Westinghouse was on the verge of making an offer for CBS.

"I've heard the rumors that you're about to make a deal," I said.

"Yes," Tisch responded bluntly. "They're true."

"Will the deal close?" I asked, fishing for details. "Is Westinghouse going to be able to get the financing?"

"What makes you think it's Westinghouse?" Tisch said, but he kept up this charade only for a moment. "The deal will close," he added seconds later. "It's already been before their board, and they have a financing commitment from Chemical Bank."

At that moment, the wife of a top executive at Chemical Bank walked by and Tisch stopped her. "Isn't it true that Chemical has committed to financing our Westinghouse deal?" he asked her, point-blank. To my amazement, she confirmed that her husband had indeed made such a commitment.

"Wouldn't you rather make the deal with us?" I asked Tisch, after the woman had moved on.

At this point, Billie jumped in. "Yes, absolutely," she said. Tisch concurred. "I'm going to be in Los Angeles over the weekend," he said. "Call me at the Bel Air on Sunday night or Monday morning and we'll talk about it some more." I promised I would. We parted ways and I walked on toward my room.

I was still digesting the conversation when I looked up and saw Warren Buffett coming toward me. He, too, stopped to tell me how impressed he had been by our presentation.

"The funniest thing just happened," I told him. "I ran into Larry Tisch and we ended up talking about our buying CBS. Unless, of course, you want to sell us Cap Cities for cash." I was hoping that the possibility of Disney's buying CBS might make Buffett, the largest shareholder in Cap Cities, more eager to sell us the company.

"Sounds good to me," he said without hesitation. "Why don't we go talk to Tom about it?" He was referring to Tom Murphy.

"I don't know where he is," I said.

"I'm just going to meet him," Buffett told me. "We have a date to play golf with Bill Gates. Why don't you walk over with me?"

When we caught up with Murphy, Buffett made the pitch for me. "Michael wants to pay cash for Cap Cities," he said. "I think he's right. Any time we ever bought anything at Berkshire that worked out, it was in cash. What do you think, Tom?"

Murphy seemed slightly taken aback. Just three months had passed since our last negotiation ended unsuccessfully. "I'd have to think about it," he said. We talked some more about the deal and I slipped in, as casually as possible, the story about what had just occurred with Tisch. Murphy knew that we were seriously interested in a network, and that CBS was in play. Whatever doubts he still had about selling Cap Cities, Disney remained one of the few potential buyers with whom he felt comfortable.

There was something extraordinary about the whole scene. I had run into Tisch, Buffett, and now Murphy literally as I prepared to leave Sun Valley. Murphy himself was about to head off with Buffett and Bill Gates, two of the wealthiest businessmen in America, to play golf. In the meantime, here we were, standing together in a parking lot in the middle of Idaho, talking about a $20 billion transaction. After a few minutes, Bob Daly, the head of Warner Bros., walked by, pointed to me, and yelled out to Murphy jokingly, "Don't sell your company to that guy!" Daly had no way of knowing that he had guessed exactly what we were discussing.

Murphy told me that he would give the question of cash versus stock some thought. "I promise to get back to you early next week," he said. There was no discussion of price.

We said our good-byes, and after picking up my bags and dropping them in my car, I headed for the dining room to try to track down Steve Bollenbach. Sandy had already left, on his way to meetings in Europe, but I found Steve in the buffet line out on the patio. I pulled him away to a nearby grassy area and briefly described my extraordinary set of encounters.

"It feels to me like one of these deals is going to happen," I said, and we talked briefly about cash versus stock. Next, I found Diller and filled him in. I wanted to make it clear that we were considering pursuing CBS without him. He raised no objection. I also told Diller about my conversation with Buffett and Murphy, and asked if he might be interested in running ABC. I had no idea where such a discussion might lead, but at this stage I was free to test the waters. He looked at me with a smile and told me pleasantly that he doubted he would.

I arrived in Aspen about 6:00 p.m. on Sunday, and immediately called Peter Murphy and Tom Staggs back in Los Angeles. They picked up separate extensions. "Well, guys," I said, "you sent me out on a fishing expedition and I've come back with two bites. Now we have to figure out what to do about them."

The following day was the anniversary of my bypass surgery. I spent most of it with Breck, cutting down trees and brush to create a new horse trail near our house. In the afternoon, I spoke with Sid Bass, who had just arrived for a vacation in Aspen. I filled him in briefly, and then faxed some forty pages of documents about CBS and Cap Cities over to his house. Several minutes later, Sid called to say that nothing had arrived. For a moment, I panicked that I'd sent the whole package to the wrong fax machine. Two minutes later, Sid phoned again to say that the pages had begun to arrive. He promised to call back as soon as he'd read the material.

In twenty minutes, the phone rang for a third time. "This Cap Cities deal looks pretty good," Sid told me. "Unless the price Tom has in mind is way out of line, we should probably go ahead and make the deal." Sid is nothing if not understated, and this was about as exuberant as I'd ever heard him get about a deal. For anyone else, it was the equivalent of dancing on a table. I felt encouraged. That evening, Jane, Breck, and I flew back to Los Angeles so that Breck could be home in time for an editing session he had scheduled on the student film he was directing for his USC film school thesis. I phoned Larry Tisch at the Bel Air Hotel at 9:00 p.m., but he was out to dinner. The next morning he called me back and we spoke briefly.

"Don't you have a new guy who does this sort of thing?" Tisch asked, obviously referring to Bollenbach. I told him that we did.

"Why don't I just talk to him?" Tisch asked.

That was fine with me. "I'll have him call you right away," I said.

On Tuesday morning, I heard from Tom Murphy. He told me that he had thought about it, and that if we were going to make a deal, it had to be in Disney stock, not in cash. "I want my shareholders to have a ticket on the horse race, a chance to ride on the future of the new company," he explained. "Also I don't want them to have to pay capital gains, which they would have to do if we made the deal in cash."

"Tom, we can't make that kind of deal," I replied. "Our stock is too undervalued. It's not fair to our shareholders. But maybe there's a way to do something. Would it make sense for me to come and see you in person?"

"I'm happy to meet any time," he told me.

I had to be in Vermont that Saturday for my nephew's wedding, and I told Murphy that I could stop off in New York on Friday. He said he would invite Dan Burke to join us. I said I would bring Bollenbach. I knew that Steve had already made plans to see Larry Tisch at 9:00 a.m. that same day, so I set my meeting with Murphy for 11:00 a.m.

I flew into New York on Thursday evening along with Steve and Peter Murphy. Steve believed that if the Cap Cities negotiation didn't work out, a CBS deal could still be made. He was convinced that Westinghouse would prove unable to close its deal, and that Tisch would feel compelled to drop his price to a more reasonable figure. After years of dealing with Tisch, I was skeptical, but I knew that it wouldn't hurt to keep our options open. When we went to see Tom Murphy on Friday morning, I liked the idea of being able to mention that we had just met with Tisch.

I arranged to meet up with Steve and Peter just after their CBS meeting on Friday morning. The price that Tisch had told them he was seeking had climbed yet again—to $80 a share, plus what Steve estimated would be another $5 a share in interest payments by closing. Steve and

Peter simply promised to get back to him. The three of us met outside the Cap Cities/ABC headquarters on West 66th Street. Rather than talk last-minute strategy in front of the building, we decided to stroll around the block. The walk took less than ten minutes, but we were able to discuss price one last time. We agreed to make an offer of $115 a share.

The meeting with Murphy and Burke went on for more than two hours, much of it taken up with reminiscing about the old days at ABC, both mine and theirs. When the discussion finally turned to the deal, I reiterated that we didn't want to pay with our stock, both because we believed that it was undervalued and because Disney was growing at a faster rate than Cap Cities. Dan Burke responded with a very personal, emotional speech. We would be ill-advised, he argued, to make a deal for Cap Cities entirely in cash.

"I'm a Disney stockholder myself and a very happy one," Dan said, negotiating for ABC, "but if you put close to $20 billion of debt on your company to buy ours, I would sell my Disney stock, because I think you would owe too much money. You'd just be leveraging the company over the moon." Murphy agreed with Burke, and he went on to talk about the risks to Disney of having to service a large debt during an economic downturn. I had my own concerns about taking on too much debt, not least because of our sobering experience at Euro Disney. But I was also aware that Bollenbach and the rest of our team believed we could more than easily handle the interest on $20 billion from the combined cash flows of Disney and Cap Cities.

We finally set the cash-stock discussion aside and turned to price. Cap Cities stock was selling at $106 a share. "We're prepared to pay $115 a share," I told Murphy. This offer represented a relatively small 10 percent premium above the market's average price over the last ninety days. Neither Tom nor Dan jumped up to shake my hand, but neither one rolled his eyes or shook his head in disbelief, either. I immediately took this as a positive sign. It was perfectly possible, we believed, that they might have had in mind a price as high as $130 a share, in which case they would have instantly rejected my $115 offer. I found myself wishing that I'd offered $110 instead, but I also sensed that we were very close to settling on a price. The tougher issue now was whether we could agree on a currency in which to make the deal. Even after discussing several more options, we still seemed to be at an impasse. Tom promised to call me after the weekend, but I left believing that another opportunity had probably passed.

At 2:00 p.m., I flew to Vermont to attend my nephew Doug's rehearsal dinner and his wedding the next evening. Doug is my sister Margot's son, and he'd met his future wife, Lauri London, four years earlier, when they both worked in New York City. Their marriage turned out to be a terrific event. Our entire extended family—cousins, aunts, uncles, as well as friends I hadn't seen since childhood—all gathered. The wedding was held just after sundown on Saturday, under the apple trees on our family orchard. It was followed by a big party, and then a brunch on Sunday afternoon. We stayed in the area visiting friends and family, including Jane's in Jamestown, until Tuesday afternoon. Then we flew up to Toronto for the initial theater preview of *Beauty and the Beast* by our first road company.

I received no call from Tom Murphy on Monday, which I took as confirmation that the negotiations had failed. However, when I arrived in Toronto on Tuesday and checked in with my office for messages shortly after 6:00 p.m., I learned that Murphy had called a couple of hours earlier. It was too late to reach him back. I spent the evening happily watching *Beauty and the Beast* for perhaps the twelfth time. Afterwards, Jane and I went out to dinner with Rob Roth, the director, Matt West, the choreographer, and several members of their team. We spent two hours discussing the show.

The following morning I left my hotel too early to call Murphy. When I arrived at the Toronto airport, I had no Canadian money for the pay phone, wasn't permitted to use my American credit card, and had to hold off calling again. We stopped in Buffalo to go through customs, and I finally reached Tom from a pay phone there.

"I've thought about your offer," he said. "We don't want to do any of the deals we discussed. What we are prepared to accept is one share of Disney, plus $65 in cash." In short, he was talking about a deal half in stock and half in cash. Our stock had closed at $55 the previous day, which meant that he had in mind a purchase price for Cap Cities of $120 a share—just $5 above what we'd offered the previous Friday.

"That sounds like a pretty good idea," I responded, "but I have to think about it and talk with our people." I still wasn't thrilled by the idea of giving up so much stock, but the price seemed reasonable.

"Sid will like this deal," Tom said, tweaking me.

"It sounds like we're getting someplace, Tom," I answered, trying to find a balance between matter-of-factness and enthusiasm. "I'll be back to you."

Our company plane stopped next in Jamestown, in order to drop off Jane so that she could spend a few days with her parents. Once again, I walked over to a pay phone, this time to call Bollenbach in Burbank. I explained the deal that Murphy had offered, and Steve was immediately intrigued. I told him that I was due back by 4:00 p.m. He agreed to pull together our strategic planning group for a meeting as soon as I landed. Next, I made quick calls to Sid Bass and to Sandy Litvack, who had just returned from Europe, filling both of them in. Murphy was right about Sid—he liked the sound of the deal.

When I arrived at the office, our group was already gathered in a conference room. The opinions broke down along predictable lines. Peter Murphy and Tom Staggs thought that we should immediately accept Murphy's offer. So did Steve and Sandy. Larry Murphy felt that it was still a bit pricey. We talked about a series of potential counteroffers and finally decided that I should go back and see if Tom Murphy might consider a little less stock and more cash. The other issue was that by coincidence we had released record quarterly earnings earlier that same day. The market responded by driving up our stock two points, to $57. This suggested another opening to me. Because Tom was seeking $120 a share—$65 in cash and $55 from our stock—he ought now to agree to $63 in cash, since that would now give him his $120. For Disney, the $2 difference would mean paying nearly $500 million less for Cap Cities. We all agreed that this would be our main counteroffer.

On the morning of Thursday, July 27, I called Murphy at 7:00 a.m. from the treadmill in my basement. I wanted to reach him as early as possible—it was already 10:00 a.m. in New York—because I'd heard from Barry Diller that the CBS-Westinghouse deal was on the verge of closing, after all. Once that occurred, I would lose the leverage of having CBS as an alternative to Cap Cities. When I reached Murphy, I began by suggesting the notion of less stock and more cash. He immediately rejected it, as I'd suspected he would. Then I went to my fallback.

"You and I agreed on a price of $120," I said. "With our stock now at $57, we really ought to pay $63 in cash."

Tom would have none of it. "Michael," he said, "I told you when we spoke yesterday the deal that we were willing to make. I didn't know that you were just about to release your earnings. I want $65 in cash and one share of stock. That's the deal. The only question now is whether you want to make it or not." It doesn't pay to negotiate from a treadmill. I've never gotten anywhere at five miles an hour.

I promised to call Tom back later in the morning with my final answer. The first call that I made when I arrived at the office was to Bob Iger, the president of Cap Cities, who was widely assumed to be Murphy's heir apparent. I didn't know him very well, but I felt sure that Tom had filled him in on our negotiations. Iger had presided over a very successful period at ABC, and I knew that he was likely to feel disappointed and displaced by his company's sale, since it meant that he would no longer be Murphy's immediate successor. I also knew that for the sake of continuity, it was critical that he stay on as president of ABC for at least a reasonable period. Before we finally agreed to a deal for Cap Cities, I wanted to be sure that we were going to be able to make one with Iger.

"I want to talk about your staying on," I explained, when I reached him.

"It's difficult to enter into a negotiation with you before a deal is made," Iger replied, quite correctly. "I'm the president and COO of Cap Cities, and I'm on the executive committee. Ethically, I'm not even sure what my position should be. I need to think about it. I'd like to call you back." I said that I understood, but in a sense I'd already heard the answer I was after. If Iger had overwhelming objections to the merger, I was fairly certain that I would have been able to sense them in his response.

Shortly before noon L.A. time, I called Murphy again in New York. Steve and Sandy were sitting on the other side of my desk. We had agreed that I would take one last shot at negotiating better terms on the deal, but it was more out of my own competitiveness than anything else. "I need to get *something*," I told Tom, knowing that the deal was already fair.

"Michael," he said, "I've told you what we're prepared to do."
I paused for a moment. "Okay," I said. "You've got a deal."

The words sounded stark, and a bit startling. Until that moment, I'm not sure that either of us ever quite believed a deal would finally happen. We were talking, after all, about the second largest acquisition in corporate history. Could it really all come down to a phone call? I felt like the actor who becomes an overnight star after quietly working at his craft for years. We had considered buying ABC since 1984, when Sid Bass and I first met with Leonard Goldenson, ABC's founder, about the possibility. He sold the company instead to Tom Murphy and Cap Cities the following year. Now a decade and dozens of conversations later, Tom and I had made an "instant" deal.

There wasn't a lot of time for celebration, or for second-guessing. It was critical, we all agreed, to keep the deal from leaking publicly before it was signed. Even rumors that we were negotiating would immediately drive up the Cap Cities stock price. Once the company was in play, there was also a possibility that other bidders might appear on the horizon. Our best hope was to close the deal as quickly as possible, while keeping the circle of people involved in it as small as possible. With a transaction of this size, involving two such visible companies, maintaining confidentiality wasn't going to be easy.

Sandy suggested that he pull together a group to fly to New York right away to begin work on the closing. Within an hour, he had hired Dewey Ballantine, his old firm, to represent us. Early in the afternoon, Murphy called again to say that Cap Cities would be represented by Cravath, Swaine & Moore. By then, I'd already spoken to Roy Disney, Stanley Gold, and Sid Bass; and with Warren Buffett and Dan Burke, from the Cap Cities side. By four o'clock, Sandy, Steve, and a small team they'd gathered were on the Disney plane headed for New York. For a $19 billion transaction, our circle was so far barely more than a dozen people. To my delight, we had managed to go this far without the help of any investment bankers, agents, or middlemen. I spent most of the rest of the afternoon calling other members of our board to describe the deal and to make sure that they had time to adequately digest it.

On Friday morning, I drove over to the Animation building in Glendale to screen the third act of *The Hunchback of Notre Dame*, which still didn't work completely. Later, Peter Schneider told me that he was surprised that I'd been able to concentrate on the screening in the midst of such a huge negotiation. I was reminded of a story I once heard about Babe Ruth playing in the World Series. He'd already hit several home runs. The seventh game was approaching, and a reporter asked Ruth how he managed to bear the pressure with fifty thousand fans in the stadium screaming every time he came to bat, and his whole team counting on him. "Well," Ruth replied coolly, "I just keep my eye on the ball." The pressure I felt was hardly comparable to Babe Ruth's, but over the years, I have learned to screen out everything but the task at hand. Divided attention is the surest route to mediocrity. Whatever happened with ABC, *Hunchback* was going forward, and it was important to Disney's future.

After the screening, I returned to my office and resumed trying to reach the rest of our board members. I was especially interested in talking to Stanley Gold, who had broadcast experience and to whom I had often turned for counsel on key issues during the past ten years. I also had a further conversation with Bob Iger. To my relief, he seemed enthusiastic about the deal. "I want you to know that I totally support it," he told me. "I think it makes sense from a business standpoint. On a personal level, I'm losing the opportunity to be CEO, but I'm only forty-four years old, and this is a chance to be part of a historic merger. I'd love to be involved." I couldn't have hoped for a better response. The only remaining issue was to work out a new deal with Bob.

I also talked to Sid Bass at his office in Fort Worth on Friday. "I hear Warren Buffett is on his way to New York to join Tom Murphy," I told him. "If possible, I'd really like to have you at my side. How about if I pick you up on my way there tomorrow?" Sid told me that he'd be happy to come along, but he was reluctant to have me fly out of the way to pick him up. I assured him it was no inconvenience.

I didn't sleep well that night. The deal numbers began swirling through my mind, and in my half-sleep at 3:00 a.m. I somehow managed to convince myself that we didn't have the cash flow to cover the debt we would be taking on. I awoke at dawn wanting out of the marriage even as we prepared to go to the altar. At 7:30, I picked up the phone and called Steve Bollenbach in New York. "We can't do this," I told him, and then described what had occurred to me about cash flow. Steve walked me back through the deal, reassuring me that it was indeed sound and reasonable. "It's a big step," he concluded, "but it's a prudent one."

Shortly after 10:00 a.m., I boarded the plane with Jody Dreyer, my assistant, feeling more relaxed in the full light of day. When we arrived in Fort Worth, Sid was waiting for us in his car on the tarmac. Once we were airborne again, he took out his laptop computer and showed me that we had only gone 138 nautical miles out of our way to pick him up. I laughed. We were about to make a $19 billion transaction. If having Sid by my side required a 2,000-mile detour, it hardly seemed an undue burden.

We landed in New York at 7:00 p.m., and by the time we arrived at the Dewey Ballantine offices at 52nd Street and Avenue of the Americas, it was after nine. A war room had been set up on the twenty-second floor, and there were people gathered in a series of adjacent conference rooms—the strategic planning team in one; a corporate public relations group in another; lawyers in the other rooms doing due diligence and preparing contracts. Our goal was to close the merger in time to announce it before the stock market opened on Monday morning. Sandy brought Sid and me up-to-date on the outstanding deal points. The biggest remaining issue was what Cap Cities would agree to do for Disney in the event that another buyer came in after we announced the deal and topped our bid. A breakup fee is a standard component in any major acquisition. The issue was not so much the fee itself, which we ended up negotiating at $400 million, or a fairly average 2 percent of the purchase price. The sticking point was what guarantees of access for our programming we would receive in the event that the acquisition didn't go through.

Basically, we asked for the same guarantees that we sought from Barry Diller in the CBS deal: a weekly prime-time Disney movie, several specials, the right to program Saturday mornings, and guaranteed slots for prime-time series that we produced. So far, Cap Cities had agreed to the Disney movie—and nothing else. Sandy had dropped our demand for guaranteed prime-time series, but I was reluctant to make any other concessions. It was late, but at my insistence, we called Tom Murphy and Warren Buffett, who were having dinner together at a nearby restaurant. They agreed to come back to talk through these issues.

"The issue of access is critical," I explained. "We want a commitment to Saturday mornings, a weekly Disney movie, and three Disney specials a year. Without that, we may have a problem." Tom was noncommittal, and the issue was left unresolved. By the next day, they had agreed to these points.

I stayed at my mother's apartment that night and returned to Dewey Ballantine late Sunday morning. Sandy brought me up to speed on our negotiations, including the outstanding points on Bob Iger's contract. The biggest remaining event was a telephone meeting of our board of directors scheduled for 3:00 p.m., seeking their approval of the merger. The Cap Cities board was scheduled to convene at 5:00 p.m. with the same mission in mind. Our board call lasted nearly three hours, as we took our board members through the deal point by point, and answered their questions. At the end, the vote to approve the acquisition was unanimous. Just about the time that our call ended, the Cap Cities board meeting began over at ABC headquarters.

At 7:00 p.m., I went back to my hotel to meet my mother for dinner. I had told her about the proposed merger earlier in the week. Now it was about to close. "Pretty exciting, isn't it?" I said, as we sat down together.

"Yes," she said. "I can't believe that Amy's getting married." Her granddaughter, my sister's other child, had just announced her engagement.

"You're right," I said, smiling. "That's the much more exciting merger."

When I returned to Dewey Ballantine at 9:00 p.m., I learned that the Cap Cities board had met for three and a half hours and then decided to hold off their vote until the following morning, in order to allow themselves a little more time to reflect. Murphy assured me that he expected no problem. The merger now had an inexorable momentum.

At 7:30 on Monday morning, Jody Dreyer called to say that the Cap Cities board had approved the sale. Ten minutes later, the news was out on the wires and Tom and I were on *Good Morning America* being questioned by a slightly stunned Charlie Gibson. At 9:00 a.m., the key players on both sides, including Warren and Sid, the largest stockholders in the two companies, gathered in a Cap Cities boardroom to hold a conference call for Wall Street analysts. By the time the call was underway, there were 465 people on the line.

"Everyone I've talked to in either company believes that one plus one here equals four," I began and went on to talk for a couple of minutes about the merger's strategic value. Next, Steve took the analysts through the financial aspects of the deal. Perhaps nothing was more significant than the seal of approval from Warren Buffett. "I've been a critic of many deals that have taken place over the years," he told the analysts. "I think this is the most sensible deal I've ever seen from both a financial and an operational standpoint and I'm delighted as a Cap Cities shareholder."

The rest of the morning was consumed by phone calls. I spoke not just to our own key people at Disney, but to other CEOs, including Jerry Levin at Time Warner; Sumner Redstone at Viacom; Jack Welch at GE; and the founders of DreamWorks, with whom ABC still had a major prime-time production deal. My conversation with Jeffrey Katzenberg, our first in more than a year, was surprisingly tension-free, and he wished us well. I also spoke with people important to Disney and in my own life, ranging from Luanne Wells to Alan Menken to Bill Bradley, as well as with a number of journalists. At midafternoon, Tom Murphy and I participated in a live satellite hookup, moderated by Peter Jennings, to ABC employees around the world. Around 5:00 p.m., we boarded a plane for Washington, D.C., where we ended our day by appearing on *Larry King Live* and then on ABC's *Nightline* with Cokie Roberts. After sixteen hours of almost continuous talking and running, I was operating mostly on adrenaline. I felt exhilarated, but surprisingly calm. I believed that we were doing the right thing.

The world mostly seemed to agree. Praise for the deal—from Wall Street, the press, and even from our competitors—was almost unanimous. The next morning, Tom and I did a whirlwind round of courtesy calls to key members of Congress and to the FCC commissioners, who would ultimately have to approve the merger. At 4:30 p.m., I boarded the plane again, this time to fly back to Aspen. For months, I had been planning to spend August there, holding a few creative brainstorming sessions but mostly vacationing and thinking about the future. Now it was clear that I wasn't going to have much time to relax.

The most pressing issue was what to do about Michael Ovitz. As we prepared to close the ABC acquisition I had filled him in, but we hadn't seriously discussed his coming to Disney in more than a year. Suddenly, our company had more than doubled in size. Clearly, the job I had to discuss with Ovitz was bigger than ever—and so was the importance of my enlisting help. Jane especially continued to press the latter point. I decided to seek out Sandy Litvack as a sounding board. Bringing in Ovitz would necessarily change Sandy's role, but to a remarkable degree I'd found that he was capable of setting aside his own agenda in favor of what he objectively believed was best for the company.

Sandy and his wife, Judy, arrived in Aspen late Saturday. We spent the next day relaxing and taking a hike together with our wives. That evening, Sandy and I sat down together alone. "I want you to think of yourself as if you were an outside adviser rather than an executive in the company," I told him. Then I took out a yellow pad, drew a line down the middle, and wrote "Pro" on one side and "Con" on the other. Certain facts spoke for themselves. From a standing start, Ovitz had built CAA into a Hollywood powerhouse with a talented, loyal group of employees. "He is obviously hardworking, energetic, and entrepreneurial," Sandy agreed. "In all likelihood, he would take some of the burden of running the company off of you."

"He also has unmatched stature in the entertainment industry and he knows all the players personally," I added. We both agreed that bringing Ovitz to Disney was likely to be widely perceived as a coup in Hollywood and on Wall Street.

The cons were subtler, but no less significant. "The biggest question to me is whether Ovitz can be comfortable as a number two," Sandy said, echoing my own long-term concern, but one I hadn't shared with him before. Sandy also wondered whether Ovitz could comfortably make the transition from a privately held company to a public corporation, with far more people looking over his shoulder, including a board of directors, analysts, shareholders, and regulatory agencies. We both agreed that Ovitz would face a difficult transition from the role of agent and dealmaker at CAA to that of operator and buyer at Disney.

One final issue could be viewed as a pro or a con, Sandy suggested. Michael had been my good friend for two decades. Bringing him aboard would give me a partner with whom I felt unusually comfortable and familiar. But, as Sandy pointed out, this carried risks. "The difficulty of entering into a business partnership with Ovitz," he said, "is that if things go wrong, you not only lose a colleague, you lose a friend. It could be very messy." For more than two hours, we talked these issues back and forth without any clear resolution. When we finally turned to Sandy's situation, I wasn't surprised that he had misgivings about my bringing in someone over him.

"One of the things I've valued most about the past year is that I've been your closest counselor," Sandy said. "If you hire Ovitz, that's obviously going to change."

"The only way this is going to succeed is if we're a team, working together," I said. "You and Ovitz have different skills, but I believe they can be complementary. I don't think your role will be diminished." Even then, Sandy made no attempt to hide his skepticism. By the time he and Judy left, it seemed possible to me that he might leave the company if I decided to make Ovitz president. Early the next morning we spoke again, this time by telephone. "I've talked about it with Judy," Sandy said, "and I want you to know that I'm prepared to do everything possible to make it work."

Ovitz himself had arranged to come to Aspen at the end of the week to continue our talks. The key issue was whether he felt more comfortable than he had a year ago about coming to Disney as second in command. If the answer was a sufficiently enthusiastic yes, and we thoroughly discussed all of the issues, then I was strongly inclined to go with him.

Bob Iger was scheduled to arrive in Aspen on Thursday, a day before Ovitz, to brief me about ABC. It would be our first opportunity to spend some time together. I picked him up at the airport at noon, and we went back to my house and had a long lunch together. I was immediately impressed. He had brought along several detailed briefing books and he gave me a thorough, insightful rundown on each division of Cap Cities. He also took me through every piece of important business the company was currently involved in, described all of the key executives, and listed what he considered to be the company's potential trouble spots. One was prime time, where ABC had dominated for years. The combination of cable's continuing inroads and an NBC resurgence led by *ER*—the show that I'd watched on the plane back from Sun Valley a year earlier—suddenly threatened ABC's prime-time dominance.

"We've got real problems, and fixing them is going to have to be a priority," Bob told me. The good news, he said, was that ESPN's results were running far ahead of projections, and that its immense profits would likely soon outstrip ABC's. I found Bob intelligent, thoughtful, and also unusually open. I felt relieved. Having a strong leader at the top of ABC was critical to a successful merger of our two companies.

Early the next morning—Friday, August 11—I received a call from Barry Diller, who mentioned that rumors were circulating in Hollywood that I was talking to Ovitz about coming to Disney. I tried as casually as I could to switch the subject, but I was immediately concerned. If Diller was already hearing these stories, it was likely that the others would too, before long. My plan had been to discuss the job with Ovitz at a leisurely pace over the next several weeks. If news of our talks were to leak before we came to a resolution, it would be embarrassing and uncomfortable both for Disney and for Ovitz.

I spent most of Friday morning taking a long walk with Iger in the mountains surrounding our home, and continuing to talk. Around noon, I dropped him off at the airport. In the afternoon, Jane and I had arranged to take a family Jeep trip with the Ovitzes and their three children up Independence Pass. We stopped by a lake, had a picnic lunch, and all the kids went swimming. It was a beautiful day, and we didn't talk much about the job. At 5:00 p.m., the two families parted. Michael and I agreed that we would meet again over the weekend. He was intending to return to Los Angeles on Monday morning to sit down with the top agents at CAA, who had hired a lawyer to represent their interests in the wake of Ovitz's aborted deal with MCA. His most immediate priority was to hold together the agency that he had spent more than two decades building.

Minutes after I walked in the door of our house, Michael called. "I just got off the phone," he said. "It's all over L.A. that you and I have been talking. My associates are going to ask me about it when I meet them on Monday morning. I have a real problem." Whoever was responsible for the leak, it had the effect of accelerating our talks. Michael immediately drove over, and we spent the next seven hours discussing the job from every angle. Once again, I was clear that I intended to remain chairman and CEO, but I also said that each of our operating divisions, including ABC, would report to him as president. The sole exception, I said, would be animation, where I felt most personally and creatively involved. While Michael made it clear that he would still prefer to be equals, he now seemed willing to accept the notion of being number two.

Finally, we spent considerable time talking about compensation. I was determined to make a deal that was consistent with the precedents in our company, including my own contract, and Frank's. Unlike Ovitz's previous job offers, including the recent one from Seagram, we weren't prepared to offer him any guaranteed bonuses, or restricted stock, nor were we willing to buy out his share of CAA. The salary we offered was $1 million a year—considerably less than the average earned by the presidents of most Fortune 500 companies. What we did offer were stock options. Most of Michael's compensation would be contingent, as mine was, on Disney's performance. If the company did well over time, he would be rewarded, along with our shareholders. If we chose to let him go, Michael would hold on to a percentage of his stock options. This protection seemed reasonable in light of his having to give up earnings of nearly $20 million a year at CAA as well as his ownership stake in the agency, valued at more than $100 million. As a result, much of our discussion focused on how many options Ovitz should receive and when they should vest. By 1:00 a.m., when we finally agreed to quit for the evening, we were both exhausted.

Shortly before 6:00 a.m. on Saturday, I woke up and put on shorts, a T-shirt, and sneakers, hoping to have a chance for a bike ride before what I knew would be a very long day. One of my goals was to achieve a consensus on Michael before he and I came to any final agreement. I reached Tom Murphy on the East Coast first. He was totally supportive. "I can't imagine your finding someone with a stronger reputation," Tom told me. "Go for it." Our board members all echoed Tom's sentiments.

Over the next several hours, I spoke with Ovitz a dozen times from his house. As late as 1:30 p.m., there were still a few final deal points outstanding and I joined a conference call with Ovitz, Irwin Russell, who was handling Disney's negotiation, and Bob Goldman, Ovitz's representative. The call lasted ten minutes. Ovitz asked for a few moments to himself before making a final decision. At almost exactly 2:00 p.m., the phone rang again.

"Judy and I have talked it through," Ovitz said. "I'm putting myself in your hands. Let's go forward."

By the end of Sunday, Steve Bollenbach, Sandy Litvack, and Joe Roth had each independently raised issues about their degree of independence and authority once Ovitz arrived, and about how my relationship with each of them might be affected. I took these concerns seriously, but I also recognized that they were an inevitable and understandable response to my bringing in a high-profile new president from outside the company. In time, I trusted, the dust would settle and the tensions would dissipate. I never did get my bike ride.

On Monday morning, August 14, we announced Ovitz's hiring, and the response was uniformly enthusiastic in the entertainment industry, on Wall Street, and in the media. "Ovitz Ideal Pick for Global Giant," ran the headline in the *Los Angeles Times*. Disney shares led a rise in the Dow Jones Industrial Average, jumping 2.5 points, to 59. Even our competitors agreed that the addition of Ovitz made us more formidable. With the purchase of ABC, Disney had grown overnight to nearly twice its previous size. Our job now was to lead our newly configured company into the brave new media world.

CHAPTER

15

Making It Work

THE STATISTICS ARE HUMBLING.

As many as 60 percent of all acquisitions destroy rather than enhance shareholder value. More than half of the deals since the 1980s produced shareholder returns below industry averages. A majority were eventually divested. In short, most fail over time. As Warren Buffett once put it, acquisitions are typically born of "an abundance of animal spirits and ego." They reflect the drive among CEOs to be the biggest kids on the block, to command the front page of *The Wall Street Journal* and the *New York Times*, to treat dealmaking as a grown-up version of Monopoly.

Even when acquisitions make strategic sense, the first and most common mistake is overpaying. Companies pay a premium to the market for control—typically 25 to 50 percent more than the stock price on the day of the offer. Often, the acquired company is overpriced relative to its *real* value. Synergies and cost-efficiencies, if they materialize at all, are frequently insufficient to offset overpaying in the first place. Finally, disparate cultures are rarely melded smoothly, and ongoing frictions undermine operations. At Disney, we had spent more than a decade resisting major acquisitions for precisely these reasons. ABC was the first one that made sense to us. In our view, we paid a fair price for a great company that represented an ideal strategic fit. Having finally found the right match, we were determined to beat the odds and make the marriage work.

The strengths of the two companies seemed remarkably complementary. By melding Disney's skills at creating and marketing content with ABC's in distribution, we had the potential to be a far stronger competitor on an increasingly global stage. Our competitors were no longer just Hollywood movie studios and television networks. The bigger challenge now came from international entertainment and information giants such as Microsoft, Time Warner, News Corp., Bertelsmann, Viacom, and Pearson. For years, it was enough for Disney to produce great products—movies and television shows, books and records, attractions in our theme parks and merchandise in our stores. That remained our primary mandate and always will. But at a time when consumers are inundated with information and offered more choices than ever, reaching them requires highly visible distribution platforms, powerful brand names, and the sheer leverage to cut through the clutter.

The acquisition of ABC gave us two additional brand names that were powerhouses in their own right—ABC itself (which includes ABC News and ABC Sports) and ESPN, the leading network for sports. Our task was to use these brands, much as we had the individual divisions at Disney over the years, to make our new company greater than the sum of its parts. ABC provided a primary vehicle through which to distribute Disney programming into every American television home, which represented an extraordinary value at a time when access for our programs had become an increasing concern. Disney had the power to enhance ABC by making available to the network all of our creative content, including our strongest feature and animated films, television movies, and children's programs. Putting the two companies together also gave us the opportunity to use Disney's synergistic skills to aggressively expand ESPN's reach; to cross-promote among the three brands, Disney, ABC, and ESPN; and to use their combined leverage in the marketplace.

ABC's assets included major stakes in three other cable services with growing brand identity—the Arts & Entertainment Network (A&E), Lifetime, and the History Channel. Each of them filled a distinctive programming niche and broadened the palette of choices we now had to offer the audience. Not least, the acquisition of ABC provided an opportunity to broaden and deepen our management, both by moving talented young executives from Disney to ABC and vice versa, and by attracting new talent to the combined company.

There were undeniable risks ahead. Some related specifically to the Disney brand. With the purchase of ABC we were transformed into a broader-based media conglomerate. Suddenly our new divisions were being referred to as Disney's ABC, Disney's ESPN, and even Disney's Miramax. The strategic issue became how to permit artists in our non-Disney-branded businesses creative freedom without allowing their choices to tarnish the Disney brand. We quickly discovered that there are no formulas. For our non-Disney businesses, it was possible to be too safe and restrictive, which leads to bland products and drives away artists, or to be too loose and laissez-faire, which ultimately threatens the trust of Disney's core family audience. As problems arose about how to handle a given situation, we struggled to make the right strategic decision, but we also focused on our responsibilities as corporate citizens. The First Amendment confers the precious right of free speech and protection from interference by the government. But because no outside authority dictates our choices, we carry an obligation to set our own standards and boundaries.

Our strategic and our ethical priorities have turned out to be surprisingly compatible. The same lines that we won't cross out of concern for potentially negative impact on the Disney brand have turned out to be the lines we wouldn't cross even if we didn't have a Disney brand to protect. Societal standards have undeniably evolved. We live in an age that is generally more tolerant and open than the one in which I grew up. Nonetheless, there are boundaries of taste, civility, and appropriateness that we apply in turning down opportunities, no matter how much profit we might be sacrificing as a result. Conversely, there are artistic choices we support knowing that they're sure to generate controversy and protest. It is possible, we have found, to make a distinction between entertainment that is artistically daring and provocative as opposed to that which is simply exploitative and degrading. More than ever, with the purchase of ABC, these are choices we must make every day.

The merger also raised financial risks. All three major networks continued to lose audience to a growing cast of competitors, and ABC, in particular, was on the verge of losing its dominance in prime time. Our two companies were headquartered on opposite coasts, posing many of the same difficulties that it would to nurture a new marriage across a distance of three thousand miles. Both companies also boasted proud and distinctive cultures. For all of Disney's historic success with synergy, it remained to be seen whether we could extend the same co-operative spirit throughout ABC, and what tensions and resentments might arise in the process. The trick was to help ABC and ESPN strengthen the identities that made them stand out in the first place, while also enlisting them as players on a bigger team with broader interests. The advantage was that our companies knew each other very well —both from my own ten years working at ABC, and from our many business dealings during the past decade.

All three network founders—NBC's Sarnoff, CBS's Paley, and ABC's Goldenson—ran businesses subject to strict government regulation and constant scrutiny. Their actions were shaped partly by a desire to avoid any actions that might threaten their incredibly valuable franchises. They were also highly ethical men. When Goldenson sold ABC to Tom Murphy and Dan Burke at Cap Cities, he chose two people with a similar sensibility. At Disney, it was Walt and Roy who set our company's ethical tone. Their decisions were also influenced by the need to earn and maintain the trust of parents with young children. While there were plenty of differences between Disney and ABC, our two companies shared a set of core values that I first learned at Camp Keewaydin: Work hard. Help the other fellow. Tell the truth. When you make a commitment, stand by it. Be tough, but fair.

The first crisis we faced grew out of a decision that was intended to make the merger easier, namely the hiring of Michael Ovitz as president. My hope was that Michael would play a primary role both in bringing Disney and ABC together and in managing our next phase of growth. Hiring an outside executive represented a significant risk, but I believed that Michael brought a unique set of skills to the job. To my dismay, he proved to be a dissonant fit. Rather than relieving me of operating responsibilities, Michael became a source of added stress in my life. Worst of all, he prompted accelerating unrest and unease among other executives at the company at a time when melding a new team was one of our most critical tasks.

In hindsight, I see that I was drawn to Michael partly out of an idealized vision of what he had created at CAA. What I underestimated was how big a leap it would be for him to move from running a relatively small private company to serving as president of a large public corporation. Agents are measured by the size and scope of their deals, and they're rewarded for negotiating the biggest possible fees for their clients. They aren't primarily responsible for the quality of the products that result from their efforts, nor for the long-term financial consequences of the transactions they orchestrate—the two most important priorities at Disney. Adapting to this new and very different corporate culture proved far more difficult for Michael than either of us ever anticipated.

There were times during Ovitz's first several months when I believed that hiring him had been the right decision. He brought to Disney his boundless energy and tenacity. On matters of taste—whether it was the design of a new hotel, the entrance to a new theme park, the marketing campaign for a new attraction, or the rough cut of a movie—he often had the best judgment in the room. When Andreas Deja, one of our top animators, was considering other offers, Michael's persuasiveness and charm played a key role in convincing him to stay. When we set out to recruit executives, Michael's involvement in several negotiations helped to win them over. When we visited divisions of the company together—whether it was animation or consumer products or Walt Disney World—his contributions were intelligent and thoughtful. The same was true of the synergy meetings that he ran in Europe and Japan.

But over time, a very different pattern emerged. I encouraged Michael to devote himself to building and strengthening our current businesses. As we structured it, every division in our newly configured company but animation reported to him. He also had responsibility for integrating and expanding our international businesses. Instead, I sensed he was more interested in making new deals and acquisitions. During his first several months on the job, he suggested a litany of possibilities, ranging from buying an NFL franchise and an NBA team to acquiring a record company to making large overall deals with talent. I was loath to dampen Michael's enthusiasm and aggressiveness, but in nearly every case, when our strategic planning group ran the numbers, they concluded that the deals couldn't be justified economically. Faced with these facts, Michael would eventually accept the conclusion, but only after a host of people had invested considerable time and effort investigating and evaluating his suggestions.

My initial vision was that by turning over more responsibility to Michael for running Disney day to day, I could free myself to become more deeply involved in our creative endeavors. Unfortunately, it didn't work out the way that I had anticipated. Instead, the more relentlessly he pursued deals without support from the executives whose divisions would be affected by his actions, the more I felt prompted to create checks and balances on his authority, and to remain involved myself. It was a negative cycle that fed on itself. Frustrated by his feelings of ineffectiveness, Michael became hungrier to prove himself, and less and less willing to take the time to absorb the information necessary to do his job effectively.

From the start, Michael kept himself so busy it was nearly impossible to find any time to speak with him face to face. Sometime in midfall, I decided to sit down for an extended talk to see if I could prod him gently in certain directions and away from others. The core of my message can be summarized in a few sentences. "The 'deal' is not the essence of Disney, although we are a big transaction-oriented company," I said. "Operations are the thing. The deal is a means to an end, to get television series made, movies produced, theme parks built, consumer licenses awarded, talent connected. But the deal cannot take the lead." To this day, I'm not sure that Michael understood, much less accepted, my point.

During this same period, Steve Bollenbach made a similar offer to sit down with Michael, hoping to familiarize him with the company's financial operations. Michael's initial response was enthusiastic. He promised to set up a meeting, but never did, even though Steve made the overture on several subsequent occasions. The result was that Michael not only sacrificed an opportunity to learn how the company ran financially but also antagonized Steve. Over time, people running divisions across the company related similar experiences to me, saying that they were finding it nearly impossible to command Michael's sustained attention even on key issues that they were facing.

Michael's relationship with the Hollywood community and with the media also began to change. In the early years of CAA, he assiduously avoided publicity. Secretive by nature, he also believed that the limelight belonged with his clients. In part because his agency became extraordinarily successful and in part precisely because he avoided attention, the media grew more and more interested in Michael. Eventually, he decided to do a few interviews. Although even a single negative sentence in an article could be very upsetting to him, most of the articles were glowing, and he took great pleasure in them. The laudatory notices led to more business, which prompted more press attention, which added to his mystique. All of that helped him to broaden his role from agent to Hollywood power broker to investment banker, eventually advising huge companies such as Sony and Matsushita on potential acquisitions in Hollywood. Along the way, Michael learned to love the attention, and he became a moth to the media flame.

It was a Faustian pact. As a powerful agent, representing high-profile celebrity clients, Michael enjoyed an almost entirely favorable press. But his role changed when he became a Disney executive. Without his CAA client list, the media no longer feared the consequences of his wrath and felt emboldened to report on his perceived missteps, perhaps in part to exact revenge for the limits that journalists felt he had long imposed on them.

Michael also had growing troubles within Disney. At the end of January 1996, Steve Bollenbach asked to see me urgently. He explained that he'd decided to resign in order to accept a position as the chairman and CEO of Hilton Hotels. It was an attractive offer, but Steve made it clear that a decisive factor in his decision was his unwillingness to work with Michael any longer. "I just don't think he understands or is interested in enhancing shareholder value," Steve told me.

While I respected Steve highly, I believed that his comments reflected impatience and overreaction. Several months later, his comments to a reporter would reveal that his enmity for Ovitz ran much deeper than I realized initially. When he first told me about his plans, my most immediate concern had been to replace him without undue disruption. I decided to bring Richard Nanula back from running the Disney Stores to take over as CFO.

As for Michael, he seemed increasingly frustrated and at sea, unsure where to put his attention. As a result, his efforts weren't serving the company well. In the aftermath of Steve's departure, most of the top executives of the company found a way to communicate to me the difficulty of trying to work with Michael. Several told me flatly that if he stayed on, they would ultimately have no choice but to leave, as Steve had. Disney wasn't mired in the usual corporate politics. This was a full-blown crisis, and it was tearing the company apart. I had recovered from one major crisis—eighteen months after my bypass I felt healthier and stronger than I had in years—only to have created a new one.

For the first time, I began actively looking for a way to end the business relationship with Michael. My goal was to minimize the damage. In the course of several painful meetings, I encouraged him to look for a new job and promised to help in the search. If he was offered an opportunity to be a CEO elsewhere—a very reasonable possibility—that would provide a way for him to leave gracefully. In the meantime, however, the media had begun to circle the story of Michael's struggles at Disney. A rash of negative articles appeared in quick succession—first in *The New Yorker*, but then in *Newsweek*, the *Los Angeles Times*, the *New York Times*, and *Vanity Fair*. The more reporters sought me out for comment, the more untenable Michael's and my positions became.

I had no desire to make the situation worse than it already was, and I hardly relished the inevitable speculation, once Michael left, that I was incapable of working with a partner. Nonetheless, it had become painfully obvious to both of us that the time had come to part ways. On Thursday evening, December 12, 1996—sixteen months after his arrival—Michael and I met in my mother's New York apartment and talked mostly about what to say in the press release announcing his departure. There was no overt hostility in our meeting, but it was clear that one of the casualties of our professional split was going to be our friendship—precisely the bad ending that Sandy Litvack had warned me about back in Aspen. When Michael left the apartment shortly after 1:00 a.m., I was relieved to have a terrible burden lifted, but saddened for both of us that I had convinced him to come to Disney in the first place.

Personnel is the most important responsibility for any chief executive and bringing in Michael was obviously a mistake. In this instance, we were fortunate. As difficult and costly as his brief tenure turned out to be, the company continued to prosper during his year as president. That was largely a testament to Disney's underlying strength, and to the efforts of our key operating executives. Under a new reorganization of the company, Judson Green remained in charge of the theme parks and Bo Boyd continued to oversee our consumer products. Joe Roth assumed primary responsibility for producing Disney's creative content (with the exception of animation, which Peter Schneider ran), and Bob Iger took charge of all of our distribution outlets—not just ABC itself, but our syndicated television division and all of our cable operations, including ESPN and the Disney Channel.

Among all of our key people, I knew Bob Iger least well at the time of the merger. He quickly emerged as a significant force in the company. In addition to running ABC, he became the point person in the efforts to bring the two companies together. To a very complex job he brought a range of skills—not least that he woke up very early in the morning and worked very late in the evenings. Bob left his apartment each morning in time to begin his workout at 5:30 a.m. at the Reebok Club, adjacent to ABC headquarters. At 6:30, he was behind his desk, reading the morning newspapers and responding to his e-mail, including whatever I sent him the previous night. Our schedules were oddly complementary. By virtue of the time difference, I was often finishing my memos to him at 2:00 or 3:00 a.m. in Los Angeles just as he was getting out of bed in New York.

During a difficult transition, Bob brought to his job a sense of unflappability that made people around him comfortable and secure. In his twenty-four years at ABC, he had succeeded in every job he'd been given. His career at the network began in 1974 when he joined ABC Sports, then run by Roone Arledge. Over the next nine years, he held eight jobs—a trajectory similar to my own. His big break came at the 1988 Calgary Winter Olympics, where he oversaw the scheduling. When snow melted in the warm weather, causing a crisis for the network and a high degree of anxiety for everyone, Bob's coolness under pressure won the admiring attention of Dan Burke, president of Cap Cities, which had purchased ABC just two years earlier. Anyone who could stop snow from melting before an Olympics broadcast had a big future at the network!

A year later, in 1989, Burke and Tom Murphy decided to send Bob to California as president of ABC Entertainment, overseeing the prime-time schedule, which was then in third place. Bob had literally never read a script, but once again he proved to be a quick study. One of his first big hits, *Home Improvement*, was produced by Disney. Other hit shows during his tenure included *America's Funniest Home Videos, Grace Under Fire, Coach*, and Steven Bochco's *NYPD Blue*. He also had his share of interesting failures, including *Cop Rock,* Bochco's gritty show featuring singing cops and criminals, and *Twin Peaks*, David Lynch's dark, stylized serial drama set in the Pacific Northwest. During Bob's five-year tenure, ABC improved steadily in the ratings and became by far the most profitable network. In 1993, he was named president of ABC Television. The following year, he moved back to New York as heir apparent to Tom Murphy.

While Bob had more reason than anyone to feel disappointed when we bought ABC, he never complained. Instead, he jumped into his expanded role. No opportunity seemed as clear-cut or as important as enlisting ABC to help renew Disney's core commitment to children and families. One of our first moves, much as it had been when we got to Disney in 1984, was to relaunch *The Disney Sunday Night Movie* on ABC. For the past several years, it had run on the Disney Channel. Moving it to ABC provided an opportunity to reach a larger audience and also to build a strong series for the network in a time slot in which it had been struggling. Beginning in the fall of 1997, we ran a mix of animated classics, live-action versions of *Oliver & Company* and *Cinderella* (the latter starring Brandy and Whitney Houston), and a series of original movies under the *Wonderful World of Disney* umbrella. The architect of this success was Charles Hirschhorn, whom we brought over from the motion picture division to reinvent the Sunday movie. Ratings for the time period increased dramatically, particularly among younger children and their parents.

The ABC Saturday morning schedule was an equally compelling opportunity. Though the potential number of viewers was far smaller than on Sunday evenings, the Saturday shows could be targeted specifically to our core constituency of young children. As early as October 1996, just months after the merger with ABC had been approved, I wrote a long memo about children's programming to our teams at both Disney and ABC. "The growth of The Walt Disney Company in many ways hinges on the amount and quality of children's programs produced for broadcast television in the United States, and was an important reason for the merger," I began. Then I listed all of the markets around the world in which our Disney programming was already being aired, including more than one hundred hours a week just in Western Europe. I also noted that we were responsible for programming Disney Channels in several countries. Within three years, that number would reach at least ten. It was almost impossible to overstate the importance of creating original programming in television animation that could play around the world. Without a primary domestic outlet like ABC on Saturday morning, it would have been impossible to justify the costs of original production. Having a home base for our children's programming was the equivalent of a rocket launching pad.

By the time we acquired ABC, Dean Valentine and Barry Blumberg, the two people in charge of TV animation, were already moving in a new direction. For example, they made long-term deals with two of the best creative teams at Nickelodeon: Paul Germain and Joe Ansolabehere, who were the key creators of *Rugrats*, an animated series about the world from a baby's point of view; and Jim Jinkins and David Campbell, creators of *Doug*, the animated adventures of a resourceful eleven-year-old who survives by his wits. We also recruited Geraldine Laybourne, the key executive responsible for building Nickelodeon into the highest-rated children's network, to oversee Disney/ABC Cable. The issue we faced at ABC was how to create a group of Saturday morning shows that drew kids in once a week and kept them watching.

Peter Hastings, the writer-producer who was part of the team that created *Animaniacs* and *Pinky and the Brain,* designed *One Saturday Morning* as an environment that included a home base with its own distinctive look. It included short, clever animated and live-action bits that ran between shows, effectively transforming our Saturday morning schedule into a weekly event. We also worked hard to raise the quality level of our shows. For the new version of *101 Dalmatians,* for example, Jinkins and Campbell came up with story lines that reflected problem-solving and strategic thinking, but not in an explicitly educational way that might turn kids off. In our first full season beginning in the fall of 1997, the mix of original Disney and non-Disney programs proved enormously successful, even as it eschewed the violence typical of children's cartoons. ABC's ratings for the *One Saturday Morning* time slot jumped more than 30 percent. Ratings for Fox, long the leader, dropped by nearly 30 percent.

The merger also became a means to reinvent the Disney Channel. To run it, Gerry Laybourne hired Anne Sweeney, who had been one of her key deputies at Nickelodeon and turned out to be a terrific choice. John Cooke had begun the transformation of the channel from a subscriber-driven pay service into a basic cable network with no separate monthly fee, and was now in charge of our government relations and our relationships with corporate sponsors. Anne set out to widen the Disney Channel's audience still further. In just two years, it doubled in size, reaching nearly 42 million homes—even as it continued to add 1 million homes a month. Rather than one-shot event-driven programming that we relied on to lure viewers to renew their monthly subscriptions, Anne's team developed a new slate of regularly scheduled programs, designed to attract viewers back every week.

One of Anne's conclusions was that families were desperate for ways to spend more time together. *The Magical World of Disney* became an aggressively promoted nightly 7:00 p.m. movie that included animated classics, Disney-label live-action movies, and a blend of other family-oriented movies that parents could watch together with their children. The audience of nine- to eleven-year-olds for the Disney Channel nearly tripled within a year. In the early mornings, when most viewers are likely to be preschool children with their parents, programming was built around live action and animated shows. In the later evenings, the approach was to resurrect classic Disney television, including such shows as *Zorro, The Mickey Mouse Club,* and Disney cartoons collected under the name *Ink & Paint Club.*

The response to these vintage Disney programs was so enthusiastic that it inspired us to move forward on an idea we'd long been considering. In April 1998, Anne oversaw the launch of a complementary new network, Toon Disney, devoted exclusively to Disney-owned shows. Once again, we recognized an area of unmet demand. Our notion was to give parents with very young children an alternative at any time of the day to the more sophisticated and sometimes violent fare offered by other networks. To our surprise, in a cable universe with severely limited remaining channel capacity, we were able to reach 6 million homes with the Toon Disney launch. Each of these initiatives—the reinvention of the Disney Channel, the advent of *One Satur-*

day Morning, and the launch of Toon Disney—was facilitated by the ABC merger.

ESPN was the other huge asset that we inherited by merging with ABC. It had become by far the leading brand in sports programming and scarcely needed our help. Immensely profitable, in 1997 it earned more even than NBC, the number one rated network. Launched in 1979 as a network covering high school and college sports in Connecticut, ESPN's distinctive personality—comprehensive in its coverage, cheeky in its attitude—was shaped by a group of sports fanatics. Steve Bornstein joined ESPN a year after its launch, at the age of twenty-eight. Like Bob Iger at ABC, Steve rapidly worked his way up the ladder. By the time he was named president of the network in 1990, ESPN had become the highest rated of all cable networks.

Over the years, ESPN acquired rights to a growing list of high-profile events: major league baseball, NCAA basketball, NHL hockey, the Tour de France bicycle race. The two turning points for the network were deals that Steve orchestrated in 1987. The first was for rights to air NFL football on Sunday nights, which gave ESPN a toehold in the most popular of all sports programming, previously available only on the major networks. The other move was hiring John Walsh, a former print journalist, as managing editor of *SportsCenter*, ESPN's news and highlights show, which airs three times a day. John recognized that it was possible to lure viewers to ESPN with strong reporting about sports, even in instances where the network didn't have broadcast rights to a big event. Steve supported John's notion of hiring reporters and setting up bureaus to cover sports just as seriously as the major networks covered news.

Steve also oversaw the expansion of the ESPN brand into other arenas. In 1992, the ESPN Radio network debuted, providing sports coverage to over four hundred affiliates. The following year, he launched ESPN2, a second network aimed at a younger audience. Focusing on less mainstream sports such as arena football, lacrosse, and roller hockey, the new network also created its own counterculture Olympics: the Extreme Games, featuring such events as bungee jumping, in-line skating, mountain biking, skateboarding, and windsurfing.

In 1994, ESPN hired a Seattle-based start-up company called

Starwave to create a sports information Web site on the Internet, which was still in its most nascent stages. With more than fifteen thousand pages of constantly updated sports information, ESPN SportsZone quickly emerged as the most popular content site on the Web. I myself became a late night devotee of SportsZone's fantasy basketball league, which allows fans to create teams using players from NBA teams and compete in games based on how their players perform in real games. Our league is called the Duck Pond, and I do most of my playing around 3:00 a.m., when everyone else I know has gone to sleep.

ESPNews was launched in 1996 as a third network devoted exclusively to sports news and highlights. Steve and his group also aggressively took ESPN international, both by selling programming in some 120 countries and by investing in 20 sports networks around the world. In 1997, ESPN rounded out its offerings by buying Classic Sports, a sports cable channel that focuses on historic sporting events and draws on the extensive libraries kept by each of the major sports leagues. ESPN's strength has also served Disney in at least one other way. By offering ESPN and the Disney Channel together in several countries internationally, we are now able to make better deals for both networks.

What Disney brought to ESPN was our long experience in broadening and promoting a strong brand. Before the merger, ESPN signed a deal to create a modest-size sports theme restaurant at Walt Disney World, which opened in 1996. Once the merger went through, we were able to add to the fledgling concept our own strengths both in launching restaurants and in creating themed entertainment. By this point, we had lured Art Levitt back from running the Hard Rock Cafés to help us develop regionally based entertainment ventures. Art went to work on the ESPN project immediately. In the fall of 1997, we announced plans to open our first two ESPN Zones, in Baltimore and Chicago. The expanded concept is close to 40,000 square feet—three times the size of the Orlando venture—with features ranging from some two hundred overhead monitors carrying live sports events to an entertainment arena in which guests can play sports in a virtual reality.

The second expansion of ESPN grew out of our experience in retailing. We decided to test our first ESPN Store in the same Glendale mall where we launched the first Disney Store. Here the idea was to offer a unique line of gifts for people who are fanatical about ESPN and sports generally. Our goal was to attract ESPN fans themselves, but also friends and relatives, girlfriends and boyfriends, wives and husbands looking to buy the perfect sports gift. As with the Disney Store, we designed the ESPN Store as a stage set—in this case inspired by *SportsCenter.* During its first nine months, our first ESPN Store outperformed the average Disney Store. By the end of 1997, we'd moved forward on plans to open two more, with the goal of reaching ten by early 1999.

The third and most natural brand extension was *ESPN: The Magazine,* an idea initiated by John Skipper, who became senior vice president, general manager, of this new venture. *Sports Illustrated* had completely dominated the field for more than four decades. ESPN now represented a highly recognizable brand name for a sports magazine. Our competitive fires were further stoked when *Sports Illustrated* and CNN joined forces in the fall of 1996 to launch a cable sports network intended to compete directly with ESPN. For the magazine, our key job was to differentiate ourselves from *Sports Illustrated.* One way was with an oversized format and a less glossy paper stock. We didn't rule out someday going weekly, but beginning biweekly was economically prudent. It also encouraged an editorial focus that was more feature-oriented and forward-looking. As editor, we hired John Papanek, who had once been the managing editor of *Sports Illustrated* and was drawn to the possibility of creating something younger and hipper.

Perhaps no new venture since our merger has used the assets of both companies to better effect than Radio Disney. ABC Radio owns and operates thirty stations, and syndicates programming to nearly seven thousand affiliates. Back in 1992, ABC had come to us suggesting a Disney radio network aimed at kids. We turned them down partly because we were unwilling to use the Disney name in a joint venture in which we lacked creative control, but also because we knew nothing about radio. Bob Callahan, head of ABC Radio, suggested the idea again shortly after the merger.

The opportunity was unmistakable. More than 75 percent of children ages six to eleven listened to radio every day, but not a single network or format had been targeted to their interests, or their musical tastes. Instead, these kids tune in to stations aimed primarily at teenagers and young adults, featuring songs with lyrics and deejays with patter that are often age inappropriate and to which their parents might reasonably object. Radio Disney was our solution. We launched in four test markets in November 1996, with music ranging from oldies to pop to soundtracks (including Disney's), as well as quizzes, features, contests, news from ABC, and sports news from ESPN, all aimed at kids. By mid-1998, we had expanded to thirty stations, including five that we owned outright.

I tune in to Radio Disney myself when I'm in the car. I don't listen out of corporate loyalty (okay, maybe a little; I doubt I'd listen as much if it was called Radio Kodak). But the primary reason is I like it. I can understand what the deejays are talking about and I recognize most of the songs they're playing, every one of which has a melody and a beat. Our largest advertiser is General Motors. They know that millions of kids listen to the radio in cars, but they've also deduced that it's not the eleven-year-olds who are doing the driving. My favorite times are the weekends, when the thirty most requested songs are played—a range from "My Heart Will Go On" to "Do the Bartman" to "Reflections." How could anyone not like a station that plays Celine Dion, Bart Simpson, and music from *Mulan*, all in one cycle?

Ironically, the one aspect of the ABC merger that isn't yet working is the network itself. There are bright spots on parts of the schedule. In addition to Saturday morning, ABC continues to dominate in daytime. Our news division still boasts an unmatchable team led by Sam Donaldson, Peter Jennings, Ted Koppel, Cokie Roberts, Diane Sawyer, and Barbara Walters. In four of our top five markets, ABC-owned stations lead the competition—in large part because they have the strongest local news operations. Unfortunately, there is no comparably upbeat story about prime time. Although it only represents 10 percent of our broadcasting profits, prime time remains ABC's most visible face to the world, and it attracts disproportionate attention. We knew that many of ABC's strongest shows had peaked when we bought the company. What we failed to foresee was how precipitously long-running hits like *Roseanne, Grace Under Fire,* and *Coach* would decline, and how weak our own new series development would turn out to be. We also underestimated how powerfully NBC would emerge. But the unavoidable bottom line is that ABC has yet to turn around.

Even so, it's hard for me to dwell in a dark cloud very long before I start seeing silver linings. In a company the size of Walt Disney, it's probably inevitable that at least one business will be struggling at any given moment. The bad news for all of the major television networks is that the audience has discovered other options. The good news is that many of them are turning to networks we own in whole or in part, including ESPN, the Disney Channel, Lifetime, A&E, the History Channel, Toon Disney, and E! Entertainment Television, our most recent purchase. As viewers demand more specialized programming, we continue to look for ways to provide it. As part of our ongoing effort to strengthen our programming efforts all around the world, we promoted Bob Iger to chairman of the ABC group and president of Walt Disney International in early 1999, and brought Steve Bornstein over from ESPN to become president of ABC.

Even before ABC turns around in prime time, we seem to have beaten the odds. The acquisition has been a success—above all, for our shareholders. The intrinsic value of ABC's assets has increased, meaning that they're worth more today than we paid for them. The key strategic goals of the merger—to guarantee access and distribution for Disney programs, and to enhance our ability to compete in an increasingly global marketplace—have been achieved beyond our expectations. Through ABC we've increased the reach of the Disney brand around the world, even as we've used our own strengths to help build and enhance our new brands, most notably ESPN.

The melding of two companies' cultures is a drama not unlike bringing together two families. Both inevitably require time and patience. ABC and Disney are now deeply interwoven. Whether it's Radio Disney, ESPN Zone, *One Saturday Morning* or any of a dozen other projects in the pipeline, the sum of our combined efforts has begun to exceed what either company could do alone. In the end, that's what a good acquisition is all about.

CHAPTER

16

Reinventing Disney
(Again)

WHILE MUCH OF OUR ATTENTION AFTER BUYING ABC TURNED
to making the merger work, running the overall company remained our
top priority. Even with the addition of ABC and ESPN, 70 percent of
our profits still came from Disney-branded products. The biggest change
was the intensity of the competition we now faced. Our success in areas
ranging from animated films to theme parks had prompted other powerful players to aggressively seek a larger share of businesses that we'd
long had mostly to ourselves. Our mandate was to stay a step or two
ahead of the pack. As competitors sought to follow our lead, and often
to imitate our past success, we turned our efforts to rethinking and reinventing our businesses, each of which had faced its own series of challenges during the early 1990s.

Nowhere did we move more vigorously than in our theme
parks. At Disneyland Paris, the highest priority was to put the park on
sound financial footing. Between dramatically cutting back overhead,
dropping prices, and vastly improving marketing, we began to orchestrate a turnaround. Perhaps the most important symbolic event revolved
around François Mitterrand. In the spring of 1994, weeks before *Beauty
and the Beast* arrived on Broadway, Jane and I and Breck, our oldest son,
attended a preview performance of the show in Houston with former

president George Bush. The conversation turned at one point to Disneyland Paris, where our struggles were making news. I mentioned that Mitterrand had still refused to visit the park, and Bush immediately offered to help.

"I have a great relationship with the president of France," Bush said. "I've known him ever since I was vice president." He went on to explain that he had plans to take his children and grandchildren to the Mediterranean that summer and was also hoping to visit Disneyland Paris with them. "Why don't I invite President Mitterrand to dinner in the park?" Convincing the president of France to embrace such a visible symbol of America seemed to intrigue Bush. He was certain that Mitterrand wouldn't turn him down. In any case, it was an amazingly generous offer on his part.

Bush was as good as his word. On July 29, he and his family dined with Mitterrand at L'Auberge de Cendrillon in the middle of Disneyland Paris. The press camped outside waiting for them. When they emerged in front of the castle of Sleeping Beauty—La Belle Au Bois Dormant—Bush turned to Mitterrand and actually said, "Smile. Come on, François, *smile!*" Flashbulbs popped. The next morning, the photo of Mitterrand and Bush waving from the head of Main Street appeared on the front page of nearly every newspaper across France. At the height of the summer, in a country in which the president helps to set the cultural agenda, this image served as a powerful symbolic endorsement for the park.

While the economy in much of Europe had yet to fully turn around (unemployment in France currently runs at 12 percent and 20 percent for those under twenty-five), our successful financial restructuring brought an end to the negative stories about the park. In turn, attendance jumped from a low of 8.8 million in 1994 to more than 10.6 million in 1995. By the end of 1998, it will reach nearly 13 million—an increase of over 60 percent in just four years. As the park finally became profitable we began to add new attractions, including a multiplex theater, convention facilities, and a Planet Hollywood. The next key challenge will be to build a second park—the project we'd felt compelled to put on hold back in 1994. As we move onto sound financial footing, this is the surest way to extend guests' length of stay.

At Disneyland, we faced a similar issue. The negative impact of the riots and the earthquake in Los Angeles in the early 1990s receded with time, and attendance picked up, increasing to a record 15.5 million in 1995. Paul Pressler brought new energy to Disneyland, and we launched attractions ranging from an Indiana Jones thrill ride to the entirely new Tomorrowland, both overseen by Tony Baxter. The bigger issue was how to transform Disneyland from a one- or two-day experience into more of a resort destination. For years, our efforts had focused on developing a second park to be called Westcot and patterned after Epcot. Enthusiastic as we were about the concept for Westcot, the projected cost of building it simply grew too high. (We'd already gone that route in Europe. One such mistake in a decade is more than enough!) As we continued to look for a viable alternative, we remained on the lookout for ways to make Anaheim itself a more desirable destination. City officials agreed to change much of the streetscape around Disneyland as well as to eliminate all the unsightly signs and above-ground wires. But they also needed our help.

The Mighty Ducks became one part of the answer, unlikely as that may seem. My obsession with hockey went back a long way. Both Eric and Anders are hockey players, and Jane and I have spent countless hours accompanying them to practices, games, and tournaments. For years, Jane urged us to do a movie about the culture of youth hockey, until finally in 1991, with Eric and Anders playing nearly every week, I suggested to Jeffrey Katzenberg that we commission a script. Like *The Bad News Bears* back at Paramount, *The Mighty Ducks* was a heartwarming story about an unlikely team that prevails against the odds. It became one of Disney's very few hits in 1993. Several months before it opened, I received a call from Bruce McNall, then owner of the Los Angeles Kings hockey team, asking if we might be interested in owning a second franchise in the L.A. area.

Professional sports is rarely a good business. In our case, buying a hockey team became compelling for other reasons. Anaheim had already constructed a beautiful new $110 million sports arena in the belief that "if you build it they will come"—only to discover that no professional sports team was interested. As a result, we were able to make a very reasonable deal to play there, and to solve Anaheim's problem in the process.

We decided to name our new team the Mighty Ducks, which

gave us instant national awareness, and an opportunity to cross-promote with our *Mighty Ducks* movie franchise. Our merchandise, for example, immediately outsold all NHL teams combined. With the guidance of an extraordinary young man named Dave Wilk, we also launched Disney Goals, based on a program that he had pioneered in New York City called Ice Hockey in Harlem. In addition to teaching several hundred inner-city kids in Anaheim each year to play hockey—using the Frank Gehry–designed practice facility we built for the Ducks—Disney Goals offers boys and girls regular tutoring and engages them in community service. Having a professional hockey team and programs related to it was good for Anaheim, and therefore also good for Disneyland. A similar motivation drove our subsequent decision to purchase the California Angels and to work with the city to completely refurbish the team's stadium. Anaheim didn't want to lose the team to another city, and once again, we stepped in. Big profits from the two franchises were never our primary goal—fortunately!

At Disneyland, the idea for a second park grew out of a three-day brainstorming retreat in Aspen in August 1995. Three dozen people attended. By the end of the second day, there were passionate advocates for no less than a half-dozen approaches—among them a combination aquarium and water park; a park devoted to Hollywood and entertainment; and a new version of Disney's America transplanted to Anaheim. As our meeting came to an end, it dawned on me that each of these ideas represented potential components of a much bigger umbrella theme—namely, California—which embodied a certain magic all its own.

Over the next few days, this concept grew on all of us, and eventually we settled on the name Disney's California Adventure. Under the direction of Paul Pressler and an Imagineering team led by Barry Braverman, planning on the new park began almost immediately. The opening date is now projected for the spring of 2001. In addition to a new park, the expanded Disneyland will also include a 350,000-square-foot retail, dining, and nighttime entertainment complex, as well as our first hotel inside a park designed by Peter Dominick, the architect responsible for our Wilderness Lodge at Walt Disney World.

Disney's California Adventure evolved into a celebration of the California dream, with areas devoted to the entertainment and culture of Hollywood; the lifestyle of the beach and boardwalk at the Pacific

Ocean; and a district called the Golden State, celebrating California's multifaceted history and cultural richness—everything from the Gold Rush to the aerospace industry to Silicon Valley to its national parks. This area will also incorporate an idea called The Workplace, which we had first considered a decade earlier. It was never built, but the idea refused to die. In its new and compact form, the attraction will showcase how the products we use in our lives are made—from sourdough bread to chocolate, to wine, to the silicon chip. Watching as razor blades were being manufactured in my grandfather's factory during my youth mesmerized me, and so did the tours that our family took of the Hershey chocolate factory in Pennsylvania and the Corning Glass Works in upstate New York. Now, those experiences were paying off in my adult life. For some reason I've always found drama in assembly lines—the excitement of watching products taking shape like a succession of photographs coming to life in a darkroom.

If our aim in Anaheim was to transform Disneyland into a full-fledged resort, the goal at Walt Disney World was to enrich and diversify its range of offerings. The biggest and symbolically most important decision we made was to give the Animal Kingdom a go-ahead in the summer of 1995. Judson Green brought a special passion to the project. He and his team learned a key lesson from our experience at Disney's America, where we had failed to consult experts in advance. Even before we announced our plans for the Animal Kingdom, we recruited an advisory committee of leading zoological and conservation experts, ranging from Roger Caras, president of the American Society for the Prevention of Cruelty to Animals, to Jane Goodall, the renowned primate researcher. From the start, our advisers helped shape everything from facility designs to conservation information programs, to animal management policies.

The idea for the Animal Kingdom was inspired in part by Walt Disney's lifelong love for animals and by the *True-Life Adventures* nature film series, which his nephew Roy had helped to produce. Disney films such as *The Living Desert* and the Academy Award–winning *Seal Island* focused on animals in their natural habitats. Re-creating that experience was one of the central goals of Animal Kingdom. Above all, the park was a leap into unknown territory. The centerpiece would be more than fifteen hundred real animals, often with agendas of their own. Rather than guiding and directing experiences, as we did in our other parks, we would encourage visitors to come to the Animal Kingdom to explore and discover for themselves.

The design and planning of the park reflected the eclectic, adventurous spirit of the Imagineer in charge, Joe Rohde, a striking character with a dramatic handlebar moustache and a dozen exotic earrings dangling from one overstretched earlobe. Under Joe's direction, we set out to create something more magical and multifaceted than an ordinary zoo—a blend of live animals, models of extinct species, and fantasy animals, including the classic Disney characters.

The park's central icon reflects its ambition and attention to detail: a 145-foot-high "Tree of Life," with more than 100,000 man-made leaves, each attached by hand, and more than 300 different meticulously hand-carved animals. Inside the "Tree," the Imagineers have produced one of the most unusual shows in any of our parks: "It's Tough to Be a Bug," based on the characters from *A Bug's Life*, John Lasseter's next computer-animated film. The bug show features a cast of hundreds of thousands of little creepy creatures, not just on the screen, but somehow eerily making their way into the audience. This theatrical experience is the most advanced use of film and in-theater special effects that we've ever attempted. It's also one of the first times we have been able to use odor to powerful effect. You can imagine the meetings and tests we conducted to determine just how disgusting and long-lasting the smell should be for our stinkbug.

We also took advantage of Disney's film heritage with animals by building shows around *The Jungle Book* and *The Lion King*. Woven into the experience are thrill rides such as "Countdown to Extinction," loosely based on our upcoming movie *Dinosaur* (synergy never sets on The Walt Disney Company!). We also built Conservation Station, an educational center devoted to research and the preservation of endangered species. Of course, the Animal Kingdom's ultimate magic derives from the real animals. By far the largest number of them are gathered on the 120-acre savanna of our African Safari: lions, zebras, gorillas, giraffes, ostriches, gazelles, and hippos, all grazing in a natural habitat. Within a short time, a second Asian Safari will open. Whatever doubts we may once have had about the Animal Kingdom's viability were answered on April 22, 1998, the day the park opened. The crowds were so large that we were forced to close our gates to further guests by 9:00 a.m. Over the next few months, attendance has exceeded every expectation, and the ratings from guests are the highest we've received for any park in our history. In a way, the Animal Kingdom takes us full circle. Thirty years ago, all you could find on our Orlando property were vast herds of grazing animals and some rather intimidating reptiles. Today, after billions of dollars of investment, we have unveiled our most original theme park concept yet: vast herds of grazing animals and some rather intimidating reptiles.

The opening of the Animal Kingdom capped a dramatic turnaround at Walt Disney World, marked by record earnings and attendance during each of the past three years. It was fueled in part by several other new initiatives, including the multifaceted Downtown Disney. The Marketplace is devoted mostly to shops featuring Disney merchandise, including our 50,000-square-foot World of Disney Store, which had sales of over $100 million in its first year. Pleasure Island is our nighttime entertainment complex, where the two newest additions are a Black Entertainment Television SoundStage Club, featuring R&B, soul, and hip-hop, and a Wildhorse Saloon, built around Nashville country music. The most recent addition to Downtown Disney is the West Side, which includes a Wolfgang Puck Café; a House of Blues; Gloria and Emilio Estefan's Bongos Cuban Café; a Virgin Megastore; a twenty-four-screen AMC theater complex; and a year-round Cirque du Soleil, the French-Canadian circus. The goal is to offer guests an even more diverse set of choices when they visit Walt Disney World. To help continue this process, we named Paul Pressler president of Walt Disney Attractions in the fall of 1998, overseeing all of our theme parks, while Judson Green became chairman, with a special focus on our efforts to expand internationally.

Two other ventures grew out of a similar impulse, each targeting a different audience. Wide World of Sports was designed both for competitive athletes and for sports fans. As we discovered with the Mighty Ducks, the California Angels, and most of all through ESPN, spectator sports are themselves high drama and entertainment. Under the direction of former Cincinnati Bengals linebacker Reggie Williams, we built a 200-acre state-of-the-art sports facility designed by David Schwartz, including a baseball stadium, an indoor fieldhouse, a track-

and-field stadium, a dozen tennis courts, and fifteen playing fields. In turn, we were able to make deals to become home to the Atlanta Braves for spring training and exhibition games (we even managed to lure Braves owner Ted Turner and his wife Jane Fonda to our property); for the Harlem Globetrotters for training and several games each year; and for events ranging from the U.S. Men's Clay Court Championships to the Women's National Basketball Association predraft camp.

Perhaps most important, we entered a long-term arrangement to host more than one hundred Amateur Athletic Union (AAU) championships each year. The AAU events have a value on at least two levels. First, it's exciting to have the country's best young athletes in any given sport competing in some part of our facility nearly every day. In addition, they generate another important source of business. Athletes and coaches, along with their families and hometown fans, travel to Walt Disney World from all across America to stay with us, often for several days at a time. We're in a position to offer not just great sports facilities, but also first-rate hotels and restaurants, a half-dozen theme parks, and nighttime entertainment. For athletes and their families, the competitions also became vacations.

As with the sports complex, the cruise business represented both a market opportunity and a way to build and enhance Walt Disney World. Cruises are the world's fastest-growing vacation alternative, and young families remain the least served segment of the market. By packaging three- and four-day cruises in combination with several days of vacation at Walt Disney World, we had the potential to nearly double the average guest's length of stay with us. For several years, we had tried such an arrangement in partnership with Premiere Cruise Lines, licensing our name for one of their ships. It was very popular, but it made all of us increasingly uneasy not to have control over the product. Finally, I decided that I'd better find out just what sort of cruise experience our guests were having.

In 1992, Jane and I made plans to fly to Florida with our youngest son, Anders, and a friend (both then thirteen years old), to experience the three-day cruise for ourselves. Just as we were preparing to leave, I learned that the weather report for the Caribbean called for heavy rain. Jane convinced me that we couldn't cancel because we'd committed to Anders, but I wasn't much interested in a trip that meant not only floating on water but being pelted by it. Instead, just before our departure, I woke up Breck and begged him to come along and replace Jane and me on the cruise—in the role of baby-sitter. With his usual enthusiasm, he said, "Sure," before he was half-awake, and off we went to Florida.

Anders and his friend couldn't have been more excited. We all boarded together, but Jane and I sneaked off just before the ship departed and returned to our hotel at Walt Disney World. That night, Breck called from the ship. "Dad, this is the best fun we've ever had," he said. "Lightning is everywhere and the waves are coming over the bow." I gulped. He assured me that the ship's employees had assured him there was no danger. The only waves I felt were ones of relief. The next morning, Jane and I flew to Nassau and sneaked back onboard the ship. During the day, we experienced everything—meals, games, gambling, entertainment—and then we sneaked back off again. The guests seemed happy enough. The problem was that it just wasn't Disney.

Early in 1993, spurred largely by Larry Murphy and his strategic planning group, we decided to build two cruise ships of our own. We also contracted to build a port terminal designed by Arquitectonica on the east coast of Florida, just an hour or so from Walt Disney World. We knew very little about big boats, so we did what we always do when we consider a new venture. We undertook a crash course in the business, and then tried to figure out how to leverage Disney's strengths to create something unique. We began by recruiting Art Rodney, president of Crystal Cruises, a company widely considered one of the best in the business. As with a new hotel or office building, we focused first on design. Several leading Scandinavian ship designers collaborated on a look that combined the classic elements of 1930s and '40s ships such as the *Normandie*, with Disneyesque whimsical touches such as a bronze statue of helmsman Mickey and a fifteen-foot Goofy hanging upside down from a boatswain's chair. We named the first ship the *Disney Magic* and the second the *Disney Wonder*. Both have a capacity of just over 2,500 passengers. Next we focused on ways to make the experience special for families. Virtually an entire deck was set aside for children's activities instead of gambling activities. To accommodate parents and their children, staterooms were built 25 percent larger than the industry standard. Rather than a single place to eat, we built four themed restaurants. In

"Animator's Palate," for example, guests enter a dining room that is totally black and white when they sit down, and then watch as the room comes to life with each new course, until it's fully color-animated by the end of the meal.

By the time that we launched our first ship on July 30, 1998, we were almost fully booked for months ahead. Years of attention to detail in design paid off in ways that surprised even me. When I visited the *Disney Magic* in Venice during the final week of construction to go through rehearsals for the ship's three original shows, I found myself exploring every nook and cranny of the ship from the engine rooms to the staterooms, the health club to the dinner club. I especially liked the foghorn on the smokestack playing the opening bars of "When You Wish Upon a Star." Anders even convinced me to visit the brig—although I'm confident that it won't get much use among our Disney guests.

The most ambitious of our new initiatives at Walt Disney World —building a new town from scratch—was born of practical land-use considerations, and nurtured by a blend of idealism, the chance to make good on Walt's unrealized dream for a city of the future, and the sheer fun of undertaking a project so grand in scope. Soon after Frank and I arrived at the company, we initiated a master planning process for Walt Disney World. Even after setting aside land for three new theme parks and 60,000 hotel rooms, and 9,000 acres for a permanent nature preserve and wildlife conservancy, there remained some 9,000 available acres south of U.S. 192.

The most appealing idea was to develop the property ourselves. We had no interest in building a bland tract-housing development, or another gated, insular, upper-middle-class vacation community focused on golf. What seemed most exciting was to design a new town from the ground up—one with purpose and diversity which incorporated the best new ideas in planning. This would also be an opportunity to pull together in a collaborative venture the extraordinary architects with whom we'd begun to work. As initial sources of inspiration, we drew on the grace and livability of places like Savannah, Georgia, where it so happened my grandmother grew up; Charleston, South Carolina; and the resort town of East Hampton, on Long Island. In each of these communities, careful initial planning and attention to architecture and design had promoted not just beauty but comfort, convenience, and a sense of intimacy. Houses, churches and synagogues, shops and parks, had been systematically and thoughtfully intermingled in the design process.

For our own town, we eventually settled on the name Celebration. Disney's role, as we envisioned it, was to oversee the master planning and to encourage a high level of quality in every aspect of the undertaking. Education seemed like one natural focus. Disney's primary constituency is children, and good schools are the single most important factor cited by young families in choosing a community. We agreed to work with local county officials to plan and help fund an innovative public school at Celebration — a deliberate alternative to other public schools in central Florida. Our notion was to incorporate the latest ideas in educational thinking, including multiage classrooms, coursework adapted to individual student needs, and a highly interdisciplinary curriculum.

We knew that an experimental approach would be controversial. My children attended a similar school, the Center for Early Education in Los Angeles. When Breck was eight years old, my parents asked what grade he was in. "Continuum purple," Breck blithely replied. A simple "second grade" would have been far easier to explain to my mother. Jane and I were relieved when the school adopted a more standard language. In the meantime, the Center's curriculum was superb, the excitement about learning in the open classroom was palpable, and all three of our sons had exceptional elementary school educations there. Despite some early complaints about the Celebration school, applications soon far exceeded openings, and standardized test scores for students at all levels significantly exceeded state averages.

A second focus at Celebration was on health. Here the goal was to shift from the traditional hospital focus on treating chronic illness to one aimed at prevention, diagnosis, health, and wellness. We recruited the highly regarded Florida Hospital to operate an outpatient medical facility and health care campus on fifty acres just outside the center of town.

The third focus was the design of Celebration. Bob Stern and Jaque Robertson oversaw the collaborative development of a master plan that eventually called for a population of 20,000. Each of the architects we recruited was assigned a building in the town center. Bob Venturi designed Celebration's bank; Philip Johnson the town hall; Cesar Pelli the movie house; William Rawn the school and teaching facility; and Michael Graves the post office. A lake was created just off the town center. Bike paths and nature walks were interspersed all through Celebration.

"Ours is a town, not a subdivision," Bob Stern would explain later. "We wanted to provide ways for people to know each other through walking, porch sitting, and biking. There's nothing new about that. It's just that in America, we've forgotten how to make those towns in the last fifty years."

For the homes themselves, we decided to set strict architectural guidelines. Far from an attempt to ensure the bland conformity of most modern housing developments, this was a way of ensuring diversity of design and attention to detail. We settled on six mid-Atlantic architectural styles — Colonial Revival, Classical, French Country, Coastal, Mediterranean, and Victorian. No home was permitted to be identical to its neighbors, and each one had to include at least one special element —a bay window or a balcony, a cornice or a columned porch.

We also set out to use certain design principles to encourage community. We laid out modest-sized lots and built narrow streets. Each home was required to include an open front porch facing the street. Because garages in front of houses typically create both a visual eyesore and a further barrier between people, each home at Celebration has its garage in back, along an alley. In Walt's early vision for Epcot, he hoped to have garbage removed by pneumatic tubes from inside people's homes. We couldn't make that economically viable, but we did insist that trash pickup take place in the alleys behind homes. We also intermingled houses and rental apartments at different price levels as a way to ensure an economically diverse population. Finally, nearly every home in Celebration is within walking distance of the town center, and so is the school, encouraging people to walk, but also giving children unusual freedom of movement. "Celebration is the most important thing happening in architecture," the architectural historian Vincent Scully told the New York Times. "It marks a return of community."

After nearly six years of planning, Celebration's town center began to take shape in mid-1994. In August, our Preview Center opened —the last building designed by Charles Moore before his death. So many people expressed interest that we decided to hold a lottery for Celebration's first 120 apartments and 350 home sites. Several thousand people showed up. A year later, hundreds of residents began to move into their homes.

Some critics have complained that Celebration is, as the writer Michael Pollan wrote in the *New York Times Magazine*, "a little too perfect, a little too considered." This is hardly the worst criticism that can be leveled against a town, and it isn't one shared by the vast majority of its residents. More than three years since the first of them moved in, only a small percentage have chosen to sell. Celebration is the fastest-selling residential development in Central Florida in its price range. You need only stroll through town on a weekday evening or a Saturday morning to understand why. What you'll see are people sitting on their porches, talking to the neighbors, or walking around town, while their kids are out bike-riding and Rollerblading—a far cry from the deserted streets of so many commuter suburbs.

I'd be happy to live in Celebration myself. I like its friendliness and cleanliness, the high standards of design, the unmistakable community spirit and pride. I like the fact that it harkens back to idealized 1950s television family comedies where houses had picket fences and Donna Reed and Jane Wyatt stood on their porches and waved good-bye to their kids as they walked safely off to school. The new town we've built may not solve inherent problems in America, but it does serve as one potential model with obvious appeal. Celebration has become the most written-about town in America, and its visitor center alone still draws more than fifteen thousand visitors a month.

Much as rethinking our theme parks spawned multiple initiatives, including Celebration, Joe Roth responded to the competitive challenges in the (non-Disney) live-action movie business by making a fundamental strategic shift. Several factors influenced his thinking. One was the growth of the international market, which now accounts for more than half of all movie revenues, and an even higher percentage of profits. Overseas audiences are especially drawn to action films and to a small number of proven stars such as Harrison Ford, Bruce Willis, Arnold Schwarzenegger, and Mel Gibson. A second consideration was the intensely crowded and competitive marketplace—not just the fact that more movies than ever are being produced, but that demands on people's leisure time are more intense and more varied than ever.

Taking these factors together, Joe decided to focus special attention on big, star-driven movies that had the potential to break through the clutter. The risk was that producing these kinds of films is very expensive. Joe's strategy ran directly counter to the one we'd employed at Paramount and in our early years with Touchstone, and I can't deny that even today it makes me nervous. But I also recognize that the world has changed. Ultimately the key in making big-event movies is to be highly selective—to choose only great ideas and to give each film the close attention it requires.

The first two successful projects that grew out of Joe's philosophy were *Phenomenon*, starring John Travolta, and *The Rock*, with Nicolas Cage and Sean Connery. Both were released in the summer of 1996. *Phenomenon* was a contemporary *Charly*, in which a likable hero is temporarily transformed from an ordinary man into a genius. *The Rock* was a hip prison escape drama which turned out to be the last producing collaboration between Jerry Bruckheimer and Don Simpson, who died of a drug overdose in 1996. (When I received word of his death, I realized it was a call I'd been dreading for twenty years.) Both films earned more than $100 million at the domestic box office.

As head of our Disney label, David Vogel enjoyed consistent success until his departure from Disney in 1999. Joe's other strategic initiative was to target one or two Disney-label live-action movies a year that could be promoted as events. The first attempt was the live-action remake of the animated classic *101 Dalmatians*. The film opened in the fall of 1996, and it attracted kids and adults in equal measure, spawned a run on Dalmatians as pets, and ultimately became our most profitable live-action film ever. Its strong performance bore out Joe's thesis that the entire company—from parks to publishing to consumer products—could be mobilized to help cross-promote and market the right Disney live-action film.

In 1997, our two biggest Touchstone bets paid off again and became worldwide hits: *Ransom*, a thriller directed by Ron Howard and starring Mel Gibson; and *Con Air*, another prison break movie, this one set aboard a plane, with Nicolas Cage and John Malkovich, produced by Jerry Bruckheimer. In addition, *George of the Jungle* emerged as a Disney-label live-action hit. Joe also purchased the foreign rights to two of the summer's biggest action hits produced by other studios: *Face/Off* and *Air Force One*. The result—supplemented by continuing revenues from *101 Dalmatians*—was our most profitable year ever in live action. In the summer of 1998, we scored with two other big films, *Armageddon*, once again from producer Jerry Bruckheimer, and Disney's remake of *The Parent Trap*. *Armageddon* is the most expensive movie Touchstone has ever made, and it will also be one of our most successful, earning box office revenues between $400 and $500 million around the world. In a clear generational divide, older film critics were dismissive of the film, while the MTV-bred young audience completely embraced it.

If much of the rest of our 1998 slate performed weakly, it was largely due to the failure of what might be termed "mid-range" movies. These included a half-dozen films based on modest ideas that probably should have cost $20-25 million each, in which case they would have broken even or earned a modest profit. Instead, by paying first-tier prices to newer directors and actors who have yet to establish themselves as box office stars, many of these films ended up costing between $30 and $60 million each. Controlling production and marketing costs—most especially for films with limited potential to reach the widest possible audience—is more critical than ever. Joe has consolidated all of our labels under David Vogel, and we are intensifying our continuing effort to cut back on overhead, development and talent deals, and above all, perhaps, on the number of films we produce. We also decided to move Peter Schneider over to become president of Walt Disney Studios, under Joe Roth, with special responsibility for all Disney-label movies in both television and film.

Meanwhile, Harvey and Bob Weinstein have continued to move successfully against the movie grain, focusing on lower-cost, less-star-driven films. Miramax's results, both critically and commercially, demonstrate that it's possible to make more than one approach work. In 1996, Miramax films, including *Emma*, *Sling Blade*, and *Chasing Amy*, earned wide praise and respectable profits. *The English Patient*—a haunting, complex film produced at a relatively modest cost—won nine Academy Awards, including Best Picture, and went on to earn more than $200 million at the box office. Under its Dimension banner, Miramax also released *Scream* in 1996, completely reinventing the horror movie genre. *Scream* built a cultlike following and remained in theaters for nearly eight months. *Scream 2* did equally well when it opened in 1998.

Perhaps no film more vividly embodies the Miramax approach than *Good Will Hunting*. Ben Affleck and Matt Damon—then both little-known actors—wrote the screenplay, their first. The Weinsteins used the script to attract a quirky but talented director in Gus Van Sant, as well as Robin Williams, who agreed to play the role of Matt Damon's therapist. The movie was produced for $21 million, less than half the average cost of a film today.

In an era of 4,000-theater openings, Miramax launched *Good Will Hunting* in just seven big-city theaters—an effort to slowly build word of mouth. The movie earned deservedly rapturous reviews and Miramax added more theaters each week—particularly after the film earned nine Academy Award nominations, including Best Screenplay, and Best Supporting Actor for Robin Williams. By the time Damon, Affleck, and Williams won their Academy Awards, *Good Will Hunting* was playing in 2,200 theaters. Ultimately, it earned nearly $140 million at the domestic box office, the highest-grossing independent film ever. Miramax also managed to hire Tina Brown from *The New Yorker* to start a new magazine in 1999, as well as to help develop movies and TV shows that grow out of the magazine's content.

In contrast to live action, the competitive pressures we faced in animation were a direct outgrowth of our enormous long-term success. One result was to prompt the launch of an entirely new business in made-for-video animated films. Produced far less expensively, these "video premiere" films have nonetheless drawn critical praise and proved immensely profitable. The first two, *Return of Jafar* and *Aladdin and the King of Thieves*, were sequels to *Aladdin*, while *Belle's Enchanted Christmas* followed *Beauty and the Beast*, and *Simba's Pride* was the sequel to *The Lion King*. The overall video business is staggering in its size and growth. During the past three years, led by our classic animated titles, Disney has sold more than 440 million videos—two for every man, woman, and child in America. Among the twenty-five top-selling videos of all time, Disney has seventeen.

The success of our animated films and video premieres also helped to convince other studios that they, too, should be in the business. Because it takes three to four years to produce an animated film, the immediate issue we faced wasn't competition in the theaters, but rather for talent. Both Warner Bros. and Twentieth Century Fox announced new major commitments to animation, but no one spent more lavishly than DreamWorks.

From the start, the three DreamWorks founders—Steven Spielberg, Jeffrey Katzenberg, and David Geffen—made it clear that they expected animation to be a key driver of their company's future profits. Armed with a bundle of cash from investors, Jeffrey set out to build a studio from scratch, and to recruit the several hundred artists necessary to produce an animated movie. Not surprisingly, he focused his primary sights on Disney, offering dozens of members of our animation team salaries two and three times what they had been earning. Some of them accepted the offers, but it's a testament to the leadership of Peter Schneider and Tom Schumacher that we've lost very few of our top animators to any of our prospective competitors. The more immediate effect of the new competition was to drive up everyone's costs of production dramatically. In a labor-intensive business, the issue became supply and demand. In order to make new long-term deals with the artists that we valued most, we were compelled to pay them at the new market rates.

A second impact of *The Lion King*'s phenomenal performance was to set a benchmark for success in animation that prompted unrealistic expectations. While *Pocahontas* was artistically successful and earned more than $400 million in worldwide box office revenues the following summer, it was still compared unfavorably to *The Lion King*. In the fall of 1995, the computer-animated *Toy Story* represented another dramatic creative leap. It was also immensely profitable by any standard except *The Lion King*'s.

Our two subsequent animated movies, *The Hunchback of Notre Dame* in the summer of 1996 and *Hercules* in 1997, were hits by most ordinary movie measures. *Hunchback* is one of my favorites among all of our animated films—a multilayered retelling of Victor Hugo's classic story about a man grappling with the tragedy of being trapped in a tortured body. Our version certainly wasn't as dark as Hugo's novel (hardly appropriate for our audience), but it had richness and depth. If anything, the film went a bit over the heads of young children. As for *Hercules*, it couldn't have been more different. Lighthearted and larger than life, it harkened back to earlier Disney cartoons—but in this instance with a very modern sensibility, sophisticated style, and hip sense of humor.

The reason that these two movies attracted smaller audiences than our previous efforts may well have been that the marketplace itself had changed. During our first decade at the company, audiences treated each of our animated movies as special events. After a long run of mega-hits and with more animated movies being released than ever before, it grew increasingly difficult to turn each one into a major event. It's even possible that marketing our animated films so ubiquitously backfired to some extent. Audiences may have felt saturated and perhaps a little over-whelmed by all the promotion that took place before they ever saw the movies. Finally, there is more competition for audience, and not just from other animated films. Young boys in particular have been drawn away during the past couple of years to cartoon-like live-action films such as *Jurassic Park* and *Men in Black*. Our best hope is not to worry much about the competition and to focus instead on retaining our own commitment to excellence and innovation. *Mulan*, our summer movie for 1998, achieved that goal, drawing not just enthusiastic notices but the largest audience of any animated film since *The Lion King*. We have high hopes, too, for *A Bug's Life*, due for release in November 1998; *Tarzan* in the summer of 1999; and *Fantasia 2000*—our animated movie for the mil-lennium.

By far our greatest opportunity for expanding the Disney brand lies overseas. Intellectual property—led by movies—has now become America's leading export, exceeding even the aerospace industry, the longtime leader. Large, single-product-driven companies such as Coca-Cola and Gillette already earn two-thirds of their revenues internation-ally. Disney derives just 20 percent abroad, even though these revenues have increased more than twenty-five-fold since 1984. In the United States, the average person spends $65 a year on Disney products. In countries such as Japan and France, where we have our biggest foreign presence, spending on Disney products is approximately $45 per capita. In the next tier of countries, such as Italy, Germany, and Spain, that fig-ure drops to $15, while in the third and lowest tier—Latin America, East-ern Europe, China, and India—it drops to between 10 and 15 cents. By increasing spending in these latter two tiers to even a fraction of the first tier, the profit impact would be huge—as much as 50 percent over Disney's current operating income. In addition to more aggressively exporting our movies and our consumer products, we are actively looking at several countries around the world—most notably China—as venues for our next full-scale theme park.

Whatever we do, the willingness to take creative risks remains critical to our success around the world. During our first decade at Disney, for example, we struggled to establish ourselves in the music business with Hollywood Records, the new label we launched in the early 1990s. Rather than throw in the towel when we fell short of expectations, we have dramatically expanded our presence. Walt Disney Records is now by a wide margin the most successful children's record label. In 1997, under Joe Roth's overall leadership, we acquired Mammoth Records, one of the top independent labels, and also launched Lyric Street Records in Nashville to handle country music artists, run by Randy Goodman. More recently, we named Bob Cavallo as chairman of our expanded Walt Disney Music Group. Cavallo has an exceptional track record, having developed and managed artists ranging from Earth Wind and Fire, Prince and Little Feat, to Alanis Morrisette, Seal, Green Day and Savage Garden. I'm more confident than ever that our music division will become a substantial profit center for the company.

There is no more satisfying example of the rewards of prudent risk-taking than our experience in adapting *The Lion King* for the stage. Soon after *Beauty and the Beast* became a hit on Broadway, Peter Schneider and Tom Schumacher took over our theater division. We began developing several new theatrical projects, including a musical concert based on *King David*, which opened at the New Amsterdam Theatre in the spring of 1997; and an Elton John–Tim Rice version of *Aïda*, which we eventually renamed *Elaborate Lives, The Legend of Aïda* and which premieres in Atlanta in the fall of 1998. Our stage adaptation of *The Hunchback of Notre Dame* will open in Berlin in June 1999. The impetus to produce *The Lion King* for the theater was prompted by a brief conversation I had with Joe Roth in the fall of 1995 as we walked back from a staff lunch.

"How come we aren't doing *The Lion King* as a stage show?" he asked.

"None of us has figured out a way to do it yet," I told him. "It doesn't make sense to try and do Bert Lahr dressed up like the lion from *The Wizard of Oz*, and it won't work to go and imitate *Cats*."

"You've got to find a way," Joe replied. "It's the most successful film ever made, and it has a huge built-in audience. If you don't, you're nuts." He was right. Peter and Tom were also right in arguing that it was critical to do something completely different from *Beauty and the Beast*. The show's success had established Disney on Broadway. Now we could afford to try something more daring and experimental.

Tom came up with the idea of approaching Julie Taymor, a multitalented artist who had worked in avant-garde theater and large-scale opera as a director and a writer, but also designed costumes, puppets and masks. Putting a strong, conventional story in the hands of a highly experimental director can be very successful, as it had been with David Lynch on *The Elephant Man* back at Paramount. Julie's most recent work was a visually and musically spectacular version of *Juan Darien*, which played at Lincoln Center and earned five Tony nominations. The only creative stipulation we made was that whatever liberties she ultimately took with the staging, style, and visual presentation of *The Lion King*, she remained faithful to the music, and to the story itself, which lay at the heart of the film's enormous appeal.

Julie first presented her ideas to us in January 1996. In August, we met again in New York City, for a read-through of the script. At that point, she showed us in detail the puppet and mask concepts she'd developed, based on the novel idea that actors in their animal costumes would wear masks above their heads or hold animal puppets aloft in front of them. It was a completely original visual experience. In effect, the audience would be watching two versions of the same character—the actor and the mask, or the actor and a puppet. The final workshop took place in January 1997, on the stage of the nearly completed New Amsterdam. Even in unfinished form at an unfinished theater, there was the thrilling sense that we were watching something magical and unique. For the first time, we could sense the scope of Julie's production, from the majestic sets to the film's classic songs intermingled with evocative African-inspired songs from our record album, *Rhythm of the Pridelands*, to the use of a hidden turntable to create the effect of the wildebeest stampede.

Peter and Tom spent much of the summer in Minneapolis,

where *The Lion King* had its tryout. I flew back and forth a half-dozen times, both to give my notes and because I loved watching the play evolve. On November 13, *The Lion King* premiered as the first full-scale production at the fully restored New Amsterdam, which itself received rave reviews. The response to the show exceeded our best hopes. "It's a gorgeous, gasp-inducing spectacle. The show appeals to our primal childlike excitement in the power of theater to make us see things afresh," said *Time* magazine. "A marvel, a theatrical achievement unrivaled in its beauty, brains and ingenuity," was *Variety*'s assessment. In the *New York Times*, Vincent Canby described *The Lion King* as "one of the most memorable, moving and original theatrical extravaganzas in years." Within weeks, the show was all but sold out for the next year.

The *New York Times* editorial that ran soon after the play's opening was especially satisfying. "The choices [in *The Lion King*] demonstrate the agility and imagination of Ms. Taymor and her colleagues. But they also demonstrate something even more striking—the Disney Corporation's willingness . . . to reinvent a known and fabulously profitable product not by dumbing it down . . . but by allowing Ms. Taymor to test the limits of representation and theatricality. . . . There is a useful formula in Disney's decision to use its profits to restore the New Amsterdam Theatre and to unleash Ms. Taymor. Commercial prosperity licenses—even obliges—cultural risk." In June 1998, the show won the Tony Award as Best Musical, while Julie Taymor won as Best Director.

The artistic triumph of *The Lion King* has already enhanced Disney's reputation around the world. Equally important, the show serves as a powerful statement to Disney's own cast members about the importance of forever reinventing ourselves. No millennium message could possibly serve us better.

CHAPTER

17

Cocooning and Connecting

As I look ahead at Disney's prospects and my own, the future seems both exhilarating and daunting. Companies are designed to be immortal. Our job is to keep Disney young by forever looking ahead and anticipating what's next, without sacrificing the wisdom and stability of our past. Engaging these issues every day (and eating a nonfat diet) is what keeps me feeling young as time marches on.

Technology is evolving at such a furious pace that predicting the future is a sure route to humility. Just three years ago, no less an authority than Bill Gates warned that expectations for the Internet shouldn't be "cranked too high." Gates recognized the potential of the Internet, but underestimated the immediacy of its impact. The moment he caught on, of course, he shifted his company's strategy virtually overnight. Microsoft may be our most daunting competitor. Nonetheless, the experience suggests at least two lessons. One is that the next big wave can take even the most accomplished swimmers by surprise. The other is that a key to survival in an unpredictable sea is to be nimble and resilient.

Fortunately, Disney operates on a basic premise that hasn't changed. People want to be entertained and informed. At Disney, we do that through storytelling. For all the dire forecasts, no new medium of entertainment has rendered another obsolete. Radio survived television and is a more profitable business than ever. Network television has survived cable and a hundred channels of choice. Movie theaters have prospered alongside videocassettes. And live theater has survived in successive incarnations from the first cave-dwelling storytellers, to the traveling showcarts of the Middle Ages, to modern forms ranging from the National Storytelling Festival in Jonesboro, Tennessee, to the yearly performances at the arts festival in Edinburgh, Scotland, to the extravagant musicals of Broadway.

In the mid-1980s, a market researcher named Faith Popcorn predicted a phenomenon she labeled "cocooning." By that she meant "the impulse to go inside when it just gets too tough and scary outside. To pull a shell of safety around yourself . . . so you're not at the mercy of a mean, unpredictable world." In the future, she and other experts argued, people would increasingly entertain themselves in their homes. Certainly, there are more indoor options than ever before. Cable television and other satellite services offer more programming choices, including theatrical movies virtually on demand. The rapid emergence of the Internet has spawned a vast range of new alternatives that includes information on every imaginable subject, along with e-mail, instant messaging, chat rooms, products to purchase, discussion groups, and the sheer fun of surfing the Net.

The digital age will soon usher in perfect, high-definition pictures and five-channel surround sound on big-screen televisions—making it more attractive than ever to settle back for an evening in the family video room. In the slightly more distant future, the convergence of the television and computer will prompt a whole new level of interactive television. And amid all this dazzling new technology, people will continue to do what they've long done at home: read books and magazines.

But for every action there is an opposite and equal reaction—not just in Newtonian physics, but also in popular entertainment. What some future forecasters have overlooked is a basic truth about human behavior. People will always go out—and they do so more willingly than they did a decade or two ago, not just because the economy is booming, but in response to the dramatic decrease in urban crime. There may be more indoor entertainment options, but the average person who spent twenty-five hours a week watching television in the mid-1950s spends only marginally more than that on home entertainment today, even with the addition of the Internet, video games, and all the new channels and cable networks. Kids want to go outside and play; teenagers don't want to date with their parents in the other room; and even parents aren't content to be cooped up. (We're human, too!) All people crave contact and connection and communion. No matter how exciting it is to stay home, we need to go out, meet and greet, touch and talk with other people.

I see it vividly in my own experience. By Friday night, after a long week, I only want one thing: to drive home and settle in—to tune into a sports event on television, watch a movie, read a book, answer e-mail, or play Fantasy Basketball on ESPN. But by Saturday evening, if I've spent the previous twenty-four hours inside, I start to feel some of the caged animal energy that I associate with my father when I was growing up. I'll do anything to get out of the house—see a movie at the multiplex; have dinner at a restaurant; attend a hockey game at the Pond; go to a concert or the theater (and listen to Radio Disney on the way); or even take a trip to a mall, so long as there's a Disney Store to visit. Only the prospect of shopping for clothes with my wife could keep me indoors.

At Disney, we're operating on two tracks. It's yin and yang, the paradoxical pull of the opposites. We're convinced that people will seek more diverse entertainment in their homes, but also that they'll take advantage of familiar outdoor gathering spots and seek out new ones. Nowhere have we made this bet against bigger initial odds than on New York's 42nd Street, where we invested in the New Amsterdam Theatre three years ago. At the time, it would have been hard to conjure a seedier, scarier place to open a theater and a Disney Store. But once we made our commitment, other businesses followed. Times Square grew cleaner and safer, and tourists began to flood back.

Within the next two decades, tourism will likely become the largest worldwide business. Partly this is attributable to the growth of free-market democracies around the world, and partly it's because the Internet is helping to make the world a smaller and seemingly more accessible place. Disney's multibillion-dollar commitment to luring people from their homes includes not just new theme parks and sports teams and the Broadway theater, but also smaller, "location-based" entertainment ventures in cities across the country. Our ESPN Zone sports restaurants are just one example. Club Disney is a second—a state-of-the-art play center where parents can bring young kids for indoor interactive activities outside the home, and for birthday parties.

Our most ambitious and futuristic location-based venture is DisneyQuest—a two-to-three-hour interactive theme park experience contained in a 100,000-square-foot building. Where Club Disney is aimed at children under ten, DisneyQuest's target audience is older kids, teenagers, and young adults. Our first one opened in the summer of 1998 on the West Side at Walt Disney World, and a second opened in Chicago in June 1999. Conceived by Imagineering, DisneyQuest represents a collaboration with leading software developers who have designed new forms of entertainment using cutting-edge technologies such as virtual reality. In one area, for example, guests can literally design the roller coaster of their dreams on a computer—and then climb into an adapted F-14 pitch-and-roll simulator, and experience the ride they've just created and programmed. We also remain committed to luring people out of their homes the old-fashioned way—by making live-action and animated films. There is still nothing so magical as sitting in a darkened theater with a group of strangers and sharing the powerful experience of a great movie. It remains the least expensive, most enduring popular entertainment available outside the home.

Still, the Internet and the coming digital age have raised the competitive stakes inside the home. One of the unanticipated bonuses of the ABC merger was the relationship it gave us with Starwave, the Seattle-based Internet company that joined ESPN in 1994 to design and run the Web site, SportsZone, and then ABCNews.com. Most significant of all are the people behind Starwave, including Patrick Naughton. Patrick was the chief technologist for Sun Microsystems, supervising development of the Java language that transformed the creation of interactive content on the Internet. In 1997, Disney bought a substantial stake in Starwave from its owner, Paul Allen, co-founder of Microsoft. In the spring of 1998, we bought Starwave outright.

The Disney executive who recognized the potential of the Internet early on was Jake Winebaum. An entrepreneur and a fount of ideas, Jake began his career in magazine publishing at Time Inc. In 1991, he came to Disney with a concept for a magazine aimed at families called

FamilyFun, which we bought. It was an overnight success. The strong reader response to a section of the magazine devoted to computers, along with his daughter's own interest in them, inspired Jake to suggest a second idea, *Family PC,* which we also launched and eventually sold. Next, he proposed a family on-line service, which became our first Web site.

Disney.com debuted in February 1996, largely as a promotional site for the company's products, but also as a way to test the Internet waters. Jake and his group focused their early efforts on expanding and constantly redesigning Disney.com, as well as a sister site, Family.com. They also began developing a third service specifically for kids. Early in 1997, we debuted Disney's Blast Online. A pay subscription service, it offers games, interactive stories, kids' news, and "D-mail."

By early 1998, several members of our on-line group recognized a broader opportunity to bring our brands together in a single service that we have tentatively named Go Network. Our ambition was to establish an entity capable of competing with the other leading Internet networks. America Online established its current dominance by launching early and marketing itself aggressively, but also by offering subscribers a broad range of services, as well as diverse content, mostly licensed from others. Companies such as Yahoo!, Netscape, Excite, and Infoseek have staked out territory originally as search engines—gateways through which to navigate the Internet's ever-expanding but often bewildering array of offerings. All of these networks derive their primary value from having large numbers of people treat them as a home base—the first window that they access when they sign on to the Web. The more visits that a site receives, the more attractive it becomes to advertisers. Internet users have demonstrated that they like to visit many sites, but also that they tend to return to the ones they know best.

In an effort to make ourselves more competitive in this new world, Disney purchased a 43 percent share of Infoseek, the fourth-largest Internet gateway, in June 1998. By including our immensely valuable Starwave asset as part of the purchase price, we were able to invest just $75 million in cash for a share of Infoseek whose market value at the time was approximately $900 million. We also negotiated for warrants that give us the option to acquire a controlling interest in the company after three years. The result of the Disney-Infoseek alliance is a unique and unprecedented collection of brands, advanced technology, and marketing experience. In January 1999, the Go Network was launched, incorporating Infoseek's search engine capacities and the best of Disney's content.

Disney's strongest suit is the excellence of our brands and the exclusive content that we're in a position to provide. Disney's Club Blast has already established itself as the best children's Web site, ESPN SportsZone as the premiere sports site, ABCNews.com as one of the leading sources of twenty-four-hour news. We also have powerful brand names in entertainment (ABC, as well as E! Entertainment Television, our most recent purchase), women's programming (Lifetime), and science and technology (Discover). Go Network will gather all of these offerings, along with services such as e-mail and instant messaging, under one umbrella. Our strongest on-line competitors have a head start, but most of them still rely on aggregating content from others, rather than producing their own. Eventually, the most successful players in every entertainment and information medium have proved to be those who produce the best original programming.

As we envision it, Go Network will enrich people's lives in many ways. Call up Go Talk, for example, and you'll be able to communicate in new ways—not just by sending messages, but by actually talking with as many as half a dozen other people who are on-line at the same time; or by attaching video clips and sending them on-line. A Go Network site devoted to money will keep track of finances, follow investments, provide on-line banking, and even serve as an overall portfolio manager. Go Shop will be designed to search out the best products and the best deals on the Internet in any given category, and also to hook you up with a professional Web shopper who will find precisely what you're looking for on the Internet.

Go Network will also serve as a central hub through which people can gain access to every business and every form of information and entertainment that Disney offers. Already on Disney.com, for example, users can click on to our Disney Store site, choose a sweatshirt and a character of their choice, personalize a message, and then order the design they've created. Or they can select the Walt Disney World site, and then choose among our hotels, look over floor plans, book their rooms, and purchase tickets to the parks. Rather than replacing Disney outdoor entertainment, Go Network will reinforce and supplement our parks, stores, restaurants, and movies. When the number of homes with access to the Internet reaches the critical mass that cable television finally did during the 1990s, Go Network has the potential to be one of our most important new businesses.

At ABC, the coming digital age will likely revolutionize the network television business during the next decade. The digital spectrum represents the most significant technological breakthrough in television since the invention of color. When the government recently allocated additional digital spectrum space to each of the major networks, the purpose was to make it possible to provide high definition television (HDTV). This technology represents a giant leap in picture and sound quality. Because HDTV requires viewers to buy new equipment, which will only be available for the first time late in 1998 for a high price, few consumers will be able to afford it in the near future. But we believe it's a technology that will eventually take hold. Just as Walt Disney was a pioneer in introducing color to television, so we'll begin one of the first network experiments with HDTV this fall by test broadcasting *The Wonderful World of Disney* in the new digital format.

It's a second use of the new digital spectrum that will ultimately make digital TV a commercial success. Through compression technology, we will be able to use some of the new digital space to deliver additional programming—a phenomenon that's being called multiplexing. So long as there are only a small number of viewers with access to HDTV, it won't make sense to spend substantial sums to produce new programming. What will be possible is to inexpensively "repurpose" existing programming. For example, ABC owns each of its daytime serials, and right now each one is aired just a single time in the middle of the day. Potential viewers who are busy at work (and don't record with VCRs) lose the chance to see the shows. Using the digital spectrum, we'll be able to redeliver the soaps early in the morning, or during prime time, or both. The same could be true of *World News Tonight* or *Nightline* or other news programming. For viewers, it will be a source of great convenience. In pure economic terms, it's a way of generating more income for programs that we've already paid to license or create. Ultimately, this will help ABC to survive economically in a television and cable marketplace with more competitors than ever.

Perhaps the most exciting effect of the digital age will be to revolutionize the transmission of data and other forms of information. One result will be to hasten a marriage between television, the computer, and the Internet that is being called "convergence." On a single screen, it will soon be possible to simultaneously view entertainment, access information, and communicate interactively. Go to the ESPN SportsZone site, for example, and you'll be able to watch a baseball game on the screen and also to track it statistically in real time. When a batter comes to the plate, you'll have the tools to call up on the screen the batter's previous record against the pitcher, where he's statistically most likely to hit the ball, how the fielders have played the batter in the past, and whatever other statistical information might seem relevant. At a football game, it will be possible to choose between multiple feeds—the announcer for the home team, or the visiting team, or a microphone attached to the referees themselves, or simply live audio from the field, as if you're there. (Athletes may even be forced, for the first time, to clean up their language!) If you watch a news magazine show, the options will include watching one segment but not another, or stopping midway to call up further information on an aspect of a particular report.

One of the benefits of Disney's success is that we can afford to invest not just in businesses for the immediate future, but also in longer-term research and development, as well as in projects that marry our self-interest with a broader public interest. These range from the American Teacher Awards, to the Disney Young Musicians Symphony Orchestra, to bringing thousands of children from disadvantaged backgrounds to our theme parks around the world for special events, to establishing the Disney Wilderness Preserve and purchasing 8,500 acres near Walt Disney World, in addition to those we've already set aside on our property. In each instance, we have chosen to support good works that have a direct impact on our core constituency of children and families, and that relate to the businesses we're in. Beyond that, our own Disney cast members—responding to the President's Summit for America's Future—committed last year to one million hours of volunteer service through the year 2000, in areas ranging from mentoring high school students, to supporting safe houses for battered women, to working in children's hospitals.

When it comes to creating the entertainment and information of the future, and the technology to support it, we now have more than 2,000 Disney cast members across six divisions on the case. We also recently added to our board of directors Judith Estrin, chief technology officer and senior vice president of Cisco Systems, an advanced technology company. Co-founder with her husband Bill Carrico of three successful start-up companies during the past sixteen years, Judith gives us another level of expertise as we move into the future.

No group at our company takes a longer view than the R&D team run by Bran Ferren as part of Imagineering. In 1993, we bought Bran's small design, entertainment, and technology company, Associates & Ferren, which worked on projects for the U.S. Navy while also designing special effects for Broadway shows, films, and rock concerts. Bran cut a distinctive figure from the first day he joined Imagineering, with his bright red beard and perpetual uniform of safari jacket, wrinkled khakis, and New Balance sneakers. Armed with a wide-ranging mind and a broad base of knowledge, he effectively became our chief technologist.

Bran's most practical mandate was to help us address technological and design problems in our ongoing businesses. Members of his 150-person team have since been involved in projects ranging from solving the problem of soft ice at the Pond, home of the Mighty Ducks, to designing a three-dimensional sound system for our *Alien Encounter* ride at Walt Disney World, to helping to create the virtual reality attractions at DisneyQuest. Bran's broader charter is to dream about the future. Two years ago he hired an extraordinary group of fellow dreamers we now call the Disney Fellows. They include Danny Hillis, the pioneer of massively parallel supercomputing; Marvin Minsky, father of artificial intelligence at M.I.T.; Alan Kay, who helped to invent the concept of the personal computer at Xerox; and Seymour Papert, a leader in devising ways to help children learn using computer technology.

Our hope was that a few of the Fellows's projects would turn out to be not just imaginative and promising, but also practical and usable in the near term. Already, Alan Kay has helped to develop a new programming language for our on-line initiative that takes a leap beyond Java, as well as a new form of on-line entertainment for kids called E-toys, which can be downloaded directly from the Internet. Danny Hillis is working on a free-ranging robotic dinosaur that carries its own controls and can run by itself. Bran himself has spearheaded the development of a high-quality digital projection system that will allow movies to be delivered instantly to theaters, rather than using film, which is expensive to print and to distribute. A dozen members of Bran's group are collaborating on Disneyspace, a new technology concept which will allow people to experience a theme park in a virtual world on-line at home, and then continue the experience at an actual park. Off in the bluer sky, our futurists and technologists are working on self-optimizing systems, neural nets, and object-oriented operating systems. Those notions don't mean much to me or most people I know, but Bran assures me they will in a few years, or perhaps by next month, or maybe even by the day after tomorrow.

But for the first time in my life, thinking about the future can also be bittersweet. As much as I still enjoy interacting with our exceptionally creative executives, I'm also aware that many of the faces have changed in recent years—and will continue to do so. It's inevitable in a company with so many talented and competitive people that not everyone's ambitions can be satisfied. Some people hit midlife crises, or long for more independence, or feel compelled to take a break from the corporate world altogether. Others reach the highest level that seems appropriate to their skills and are better off seeking new challenges elsewhere. Still others, with great strengths and the potential to move up, receive attractive offers from different companies before we can accommodate their desires.

It's an enormous compliment to Disney that our executives are in such high demand. More than a half-dozen have left to become CEOs of other corporations in the past few years. I'm certainly sad to see valued members of the Disney family move on, but change at the higher levels also gives us the opportunity to draw on our enormous bench strength, promoting younger, talented executives like Tom Staggs, thirty-seven, who has taken over as chief financial officer, and Peter Murphy, thirty-five, whom we recently named head of strategic planning. Meanwhile, at ABC we've recently been able to promote a trio of exceptionally talented women—Anne Sweeney, to become president of Disney/ABC Cable Network while continuing to run the Disney Channel; Pat Fili-Krushel to move from head of daytime to president of the ABC Television Network; and Laurie Younger, to become senior vice president and CFO, ABC, Inc.

Hearing a great idea still prompts the same sharp rush I feel when I hear a piece of good news about one of my sons. At the same time, I'm aware that many of the most exciting ideas—building a new theme park, or starting a new business, for example—can take a decade to launch. That makes my mind skip a beat, hoping that my heart won't follow. I feel healthier and more fit than ever, but I'm simultaneously more aware of time's inexorable passage.

Life is a race that I began when I was born, but didn't truly appreciate until I nearly died. The race is about getting it all in. At a more personal level, imagining the future can be exhilarating, especially when it comes to my children. I enjoy daydreaming about attending the Academy Awards and watching Breck head to the stage to accept a Best Director award. He has yet to direct a full-length feature film, but he has established himself as a "hot" director of commercials. I like projecting Eric being named president of a company, or launching a new business of his own. Of course, he's just graduated from business school. And I get a kick out of imagining my youngest son, Anders, as he skates around the rink at the Stanley Cup finals, having just helped his team win the seventh game by recording a shutout in the goal. Of course, he's only a sophomore on his Division One college hockey team, playing back-up. I also want to be around for the flowering of the digital age—and for whatever age comes after that. For years, I listened to one of my parents or my grandparents say about some future event, "Oh well, that's for the next generation." Now I occasionally find myself saying the same thing. I don't really mean it, just as I suspect my parents and grandparents didn't, either. I'm eager to see what's ahead for my kids, and I'm even ready for grandchildren. But I also want to experience whatever comes next myself.

As I look around in meetings now, I'm no longer the youngest person in the room. Instead, I've become the one who's looked at for wisdom, maturity, vision. I do my best to fill the role, but deep down, I don't think of myself that way at all. I feel like a kid, just the way I always have, and I'm relieved that I do. When I was growing up, everything in the future seemed unimaginably far off. "1984" referred to George Orwell's distant science-fiction vision. The year 2000 was eons away. If the word "millennium" had shown up on my SATs, I wouldn't have known what it meant. But the future has shrunk. Time now passes in a blur. Nineteen hundred eighty-four—the year that Frank Wells and I arrived at Disney—has long since come and gone. I've finally learned the meaning of the word "millennium," and now it's around the corner.

In 1996, I attended Mahler's Symphony of a Thousand at Carnegie Hall. At one point—probably during a slow section—I began reading the program and discovered that the symphony had been commissioned in the 1890s to mark the coming turn of the century. It occurred to me that we could do something similar at Disney to honor the millennium. After a nationwide search, we hired two American composers—Aaron Jay Kernis (who has since won the Pulitzer prize) and Michael Torke—to write two symphonies. One is about the past fifty years and the other is about the hopes and fears for the one hundred years ahead. The Disney Symphonies for the Third Millennium, featuring a choir of two thousand children, will premiere in New York in the summer of 1999. Epcot, a park long devoted to the future, will serve as the ongoing home for our millennium celebration.

I know that I am exceptionally fortunate. I'm healthy, I'm married to a woman I love, I have three great sons, and most days when I wake up in the morning, I look forward to going to work. I know in my heart (especially in my heart) that life can be complicated and difficult and uncertain, but that isn't my everyday experience. I'm as Panglossian as ever. If I go to a Mighty Ducks game and they fall behind by three goals with a minute and a half to go in the last period, I still believe that they'll pull it out. When they come up short, I don't dwell on it. I spend far less time looking back in regret than I do looking forward with anticipation. There is so much to be done.

Acknowledgments

I DON'T PRAISE PEOPLE ENOUGH, PERHAPS PARTLY BECAUSE RECEIVING praise so embarrasses me. Except when it comes to my children, I am too stingy with compliments and too slow to express my appreciation, even though I know how much people need it and how often they deserve it.

As with nearly everything I've done in my career, this book is the result of a collaborative effort. As coordinator in my office, Virginia Hough has been unflappable, good-natured, and so meticulously organized that she frequently recovered even the most obscure anecdote from the earliest draft on a moment's notice. Virginia, Lucille Martin, Beth Huffman, Dee Case, and Mindy Wallace have patiently and perseveringly nurtured this manuscript (and me) through its many incarnations. Kase Waddell isn't simply the world's fastest and most accurate typist, but the only one I know who also corrects grammar, syntax, and facts about film history. Virginia Heffernan brought her training at *The New Yorker* to fact-checking this manuscript—on break from writing her own Harvard dissertation on finance in turn-of-the-century fiction. Virginia's thoroughness, conscientiousness, and attention to nuance awed everyone who spent time answering her many questions.

John Dreyer initially approached the project with some reluctance but, realizing the depth of my determination to complete the book, dutifully subjected every word and detail of the manuscript to close scrutiny and offered many helpful suggestions.

I'm also deeply grateful to Bob Miller and his group at Hyperion, the Disney book division, who have been involved in this project from the start and are publishing this paperback edition. Over the past five years, I've sought out Bob for publishing advice on countless occasions and at all hours, and his instincts have nearly always proved right. Bob tells me I owe special thanks for all her efforts on this edition to Jennifer Lang of the Hyperion editorial department.

The team at Random House, who published the original hardcover edition, were equally enthusiastic and supportive in pushing the book past the finish line—most notably Harry Evans, who acquired the book originally; Ann Godoff, his successor, who made it all happen; Daniel Menaker, who edited and embraced the manuscript; Wanda Chappell, associate publisher; and Cathy Hemming, Random House's publisher. Ann Adelman did a meticulous job copy editing the manuscript. Rick Kot, now at Little, Brown, also provided important early editorial vision. Lesley Krauss demonstrated special grace under pressure in getting the manuscript to the printer on time.

Several other people have generously read portions of the manuscript and offered sometimes painful, often insightful, but always useful comments and criticisms. They include Sandy Litvack, my trusted adviser and chief of corporate operations at Disney these past several years; Sid Bass, Bill Bradley, Val Cohen, Barry Diller, Roy Disney, Michael Kaye, Kathy Robbins, Dave Smith, and Dan Wolf. Irwin Russell, my longtime lawyer, not only read the manuscript in several drafts, but also handled all negotiations with his usual blend of diplomacy and acumen.

Frank Wells helped to conceive this book, and I miss his contributions more than I can say. Dozens of members of the extended Disney family, past and present, made themselves available for interviews—and in many cases for multiple interviews. A special appreciation to those who gave so freely of their time: Tony Baxter, Philippe Bourguignon, Bo Boyd, Steve Burke, Wing Chao, Ron Clements, John Cooke, Jim Cora, Roy Disney, Jody Dreyer, Bran Ferren, Rich Frank, Stanley Gold, Judson Green, Bob Iger, Art Levitt, Susan Lyne, Michael Lynton, Bill Mechanic, Ricardo Mestres, Larry Murphy, Peter Murphy, John Musker,

Richard Nanula, Anne Osberg, Marc Pacala, Paul Pressler, Joe Roth, Peter Rummell, Irwin Russell, Peter Schneider, Tom Schumacher, Marty Sklar, Tom Staggs, Mickey Steinberg, Dean Valentine, Ray Watson, Bob Weis, Al Weiss, Gary Wilson, Jake Winebaum, and Ken Wong. Thanks, also, to those who contributed to helping re-create my pre-Disney days, among them, Leonard Goldberg, Larry Gordon, Fred Pierce, Fred Silverman, and Marty Starger. And finally my appreciation to two people who have been an important part of my life longer than almost anyone else: John Angelo and my sister, Margot Freedman.

The Walt Disney Company now employs more than 115,000 cast members around the world. While I can't thank each of them individually, they are truly extraordinary. I have worked at three companies in my career, and interacted with employees at dozens more. None compares to the Disney cast. Most CEOs receive letters from customers every week complaining about how they've been treated by careless employees. I have the opposite experience. The largest part of my mail each day comes from people expressing appreciation for one of the cast members in our parks, or in our stores. They are Disney's front line and our goodwill ambassadors. Thousands of others work behind the scenes to make the Disney magic that shows up in our movies, television shows, theatrical productions, and consumer products. I salute our cast on stage and off. Their character, commitment, and passion are the true secret to our success. They make the Disney brand what it is.

"Acknowledgment" is the wrong word to use to express the depth of my appreciation to Tony Schwartz, the catalyst, researcher, and co-author of this book. Tony first talked to me about doing a book in 1984. And then again in 1985, 1986, 1987, 1988, and 1989. He began presenting ideas about how to write the book in 1990. He started outlining a structure in 1993. He launched into full-time interviewing and writing in 1994. Tony has been tireless yet patient; aggressive yet polite; enthusiastic yet focused for all these years. He knows more about The Walt Disney Company than anyone, probably including me. He also has a wonderful wife, Deborah, and two great daughters, Kate and Emily. Along with his creative talents, he makes good life choices. An unexpected bonus happened in our decade-long trip to the printers. Tony also became my good friend.

As in so many parts of my life, the person who deserves the

most appreciation of all is Jane. Our relationship is built on give and take, discuss and rehash and discuss some more. I am a risk-taker by nature. Jane is more careful and circumspect. I can be extreme and un-restrained. Jane is calm and refined. For thirty years, she has counseled caution but never stood in the way of action. For thirty years, she has embodied reason but never forced me to be totally reasonable. For thirty years, she has provided stability but never made me feel limited or confined.

Wherever possible, Jane travels with me on business, especially now that our sons are grown. I like to share the events of the day with her, and I value her input. We have discussed this project on every air-plane trip we've taken for the last five years—sometimes in words, but mostly in the looks we exchanged each time I opened my laptop to work on the manuscript. To the very end, Jane objected to my writing, and especially to my publishing, this book. She argued that people who write books in the middle of their careers are being unduly vain; that the task is better left until one becomes sentimentally reflective or retires, whichever comes first; and above all, that one's privacy is something to be cherished and protected. Everything that Jane said was reasonable and almost impossible to refute, but my passion to go forward finally won the day. As with so many issues during the past three decades, though, Jane made me proceed more thoughtfully, and her apprehensions and admo-nitions improved the final product.

This is my chance to say so publicly. Jane is remarkably selfless, but I too frequently fail to tell her how much I value her concern, her caring and her unconditional support. She's a dedicated mother to our three terrific sons, but I rarely let her know how much I appreciate the role that she's played in their lives. Most important, I don't tell her nearly often enough that she's beautiful and sweet, strong and funny and loving, and that she makes everything in my life better.

Index